THE

LANDS and PEOPLES

of the

LIVING BIBLE

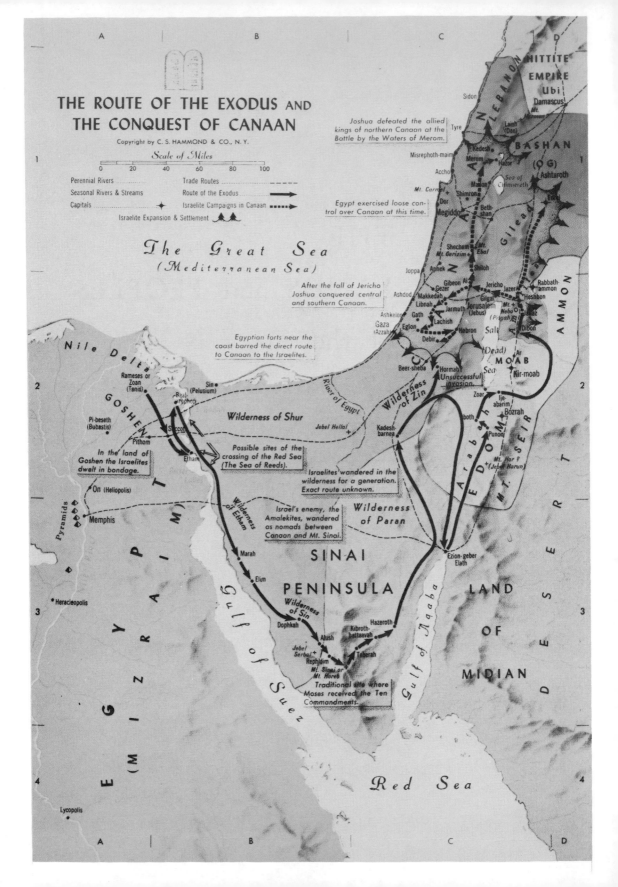

THE ROUTE OF THE EXODUS AND THE CONQUEST OF CANAAN

Copyright by C. S. HAMMOND & CO., N.Y.

Scale of Miles

0   20   40   60   80   100

Perennial Rivers
Seasonal Rivers & Streams
Capitals
Israelite Expansion & Settlement

Trade Routes
Route of the Exodus
Israelite Campaigns in Canaan

Joshua defeated the allied kings of northern Canaan at the Battle by the Waters of Merom.

Egypt exercised loose control over Canaan at this time.

The Great Sea
(Mediterranean Sea)

After the fall of Jericho Joshua conquered central and southern Canaan.

Egyptian forts near the coast barred the direct route to Canaan to the Israelites.

Nile Delta

Rameses or Zoan (Tanis)
Sin (Pelusium)
Baal-rephon
GOSHEN
Pi-beseth (Bubastis)
Pithom
Succoth
Etham

In the land of Goshen the Israelites dwelt in bondage.

On (Heliopolis)

Pyramids

Memphis

Wilderness of Shur

Jebel Helal

River of Egypt

Wilderness of Zin

Kadesh-barnea

Possible sites of the crossing of the Red Sea (The Sea of Reeds).

Israelites wandered in the wilderness for a generation. Exact route unknown.

Israel's enemy, the Amalekites, wandered as nomads between Canaan and Mt. Sinai.

Wilderness of Etham

Wilderness of Paran

Beer-sheba

Hormah
Unsuccessful invasion.

Heracleopolis

Marah

Elim

SINAI PENINSULA

Wilderness of Sin

Dophkah

Alush

Kibroth-hattaavah

Hazeroth

Taberah

Rephidim

Jebel Serbal

Mt. Sinai or Mt. Horeb

Traditional site where Moses received the Ten Commandments.

Gulf of Suez

Gulf of Aqaba

LAND OF MIDIAN

DESERT

Ezion-geber Elath

Sidon
Tyre
Leshem (Dan)
Kedesh
Merom
Misrephoth-maim
Hazor
Sea of Chinnereth
Accho
Madon
Ashtaroth
Mt. Carmel
Shimron
Dor
Bethshan
Megiddo
Shechem
Mt. Ebal
Mt. Gerizim
Shiloh
Joppa
Aphek
Gibeon
Ai
Jericho
Jazer
Rabbath-ammon
Ashdod
Gezer
Gilgal
Jerusalem (Jebus)
Mt. Nebo (Pisgah)
Heshbon
Makkedah
Libnah
Jarmuth
Ashkelon
Gath
Lachish
Hebron
Debir
Egion
Gaza (Azzah)
Salt (Dead) Sea
Ar
Dibon
MOAB
Kir-moab
Zoar
Ije-abarim
Bozrah
both
Punon
Mt. Hor? (Jebel Harun)
Arabah
EDOM
MT. SEIR
AMMON

LEBANON
BASHAN (OG)
GILEAD
HITTITE EMPIRE
Ubi
Damascus
Mt.

E G Y P T
(M I Z R A I M)

Lycopolis

Red Sea

THE

LANDS and PEOPLES

of the

LIVING BIBLE

A Narrative History of the Old and New Testaments

By BERNARD R. YOUNGMAN·
Edited by WALTER RUSSELL BOWIE

BELL PUBLISHING COMPANY
NEW YORK

ACKNOWLEDGMENTS

Grateful acknowledgments are made to the following for the use of copyright photographs: Picture Post Library, Ewing Galloway, Paul Popper, The British Museum, Black Star, Shell Photographic Unit, The Rev. R. Clements, J. Allan Cash, J. C. Rogerson, John Markham, Mirrorpic, Donald McLeish, Pictorial Press, E.N.A., The Hague Museum, Camera Press Ltd., The Mansell Collection, Aerofilms Ltd., Mirror Features, Kosmos, Eric Deuchars, A. F. Kersting, Exclusive News Agency Ltd., Central Press Photos Ltd., Charles E. Brown, G. H. Pritchard, The Greek Information Office, Keystone Press Agency, T. W. Dickenson, Fox Photos, Ltd.

The drawings were prepared by Y. M. Poulton, P. Savoie, T. A. Steele and Michael Ford to whom thanks are also due.

Acknowledgments are also made to The Student Christian Movement Press for permission to use the illustration of a model of the Hebrew Universe.

This book is based on a four volume work, *Background to the Bible*, originally published by Hulton Educational Publications, London.

This 1982 edition is published by Bell Publishing Company, distributed by Crown Publishers, Inc., by arrangement with Hawthorn Properties (E. P. Dutton, Inc.)

Manufactured in the United States of America

Library of Congress Cataloging in Publication Data

Youngman, Bernard R.
The lands and peoples of the living Bible.

1. Bible—History of Biblical events. 2. Bible—History of contemporary events. I. Bowie, Walter Russell, 1882-1969. II. Title.
BS635.2.Y68   1982   220.9′5   82-9618

ISBN: 0-517-38582-1

h g f e d c

Contents

Introduction

A brilliant and beloved university teacher of this century, William Lyon Phelps, once wrote: "Everyone who has a thorough knowledge of the Bible may truly be called educated; and no other learning or culture, no matter how extensive or elegant, can, among Europeans and Americans, form a proper substitute. Western civilization is founded upon the Bible; our ideas, our wisdom, our philosophy, our art, our ideals, come more from the Bible than from all other books put together."

That last sentence is a tremendous assertion, but it is true. We cannot understand and appropriate our great inheritance for mind and spirit unless we know the Bible.

But how shall we know it? "By reading it, of course," may seem to be the answer. And that is the primary answer. We can be thankful for the fact that through the many centuries innumerable men and women, the unlearned as well as the learned, have turned directly to the pages of the Bible and found there a light for their thinking and an inspiration for their souls.

It is also true that for the richest understanding of the Bible we need perceptions which not all of us immediately have. The Bible touches a vast field of both time and space. It is related to particular events, particular places, and particular peoples. Its message of God is a message that was given in history. The patriarchs and kings and prophets of whom it tells were men whose actions and whose words have their full meaning for us only when we realize the conditions they faced and the kind of world in which they lived. And that is true even of the supreme figure of all. The climax of the Bible is the life of Jesus; and

that life belonged not to some legendary place and not to some dim and unknown time, but to a specific country and to a period that the Gospel of Luke takes pains to date as "In the fifteenth year of the reign of Tiberius Caesar, Pontius Pilate being governor of Judea."

Thus for the Old Testament and for the New Testament there is great importance in realizing the backgrounds of the Bible. The history of Israel was intersected by the parallel histories of Egypt, of Babylon, of Assyria, of Persia and of Greece; the events that led, humanly speaking, to the crucifixion of Jesus were linked with the relationship between Jewry and Rome; and the spread of the early Christian Church can be fully understood only in the light of conditions in the Roman empire.

In the last century there has been a flood of archaeological discoveries that open up a whole new range of exciting knowledge concerning the ancient world: excavations at Ur of the Chaldees from which Abraham came, at Nineveh and Babylon, at Jericho and other towns of Canaan; the investigation of the Dead Sea scrolls; the finding of monuments and the deciphering of inscriptions that bring to life whole eras of history that had been a sealed book before. We can know now what the splendid but cruel civilization of Egypt was like when Moses led the people of Israel in their exodus to freedom; know—and in the recovered sculptures almost see again—the terrible power of the Assyrian armies before which Israel trembled; appreciate from the excavations at Megiddo and at Elath the short-lived glories of the kingdom of Solomon; and among the uncovered ruins of Babylon feel again the reality of the Jews' captivity where they wept as they remembered Zion. Prophecies such as those in the Book of Isaiah, cryptic symbols such as those in the Book of Revelation, flash into clearer meaning when we grasp the realities in history which called them forth. Places and persons that without the new knowledge might have been only names grow vivid, and events of the Bible that might have been only words on a printed page are seen in their full dimensions.

All of which gives the reason for Mr. Youngman's stirring book, first published in England and now—with a few brief additional paragraphs and minor editorial changes which he has permitted—republished in new form for what should be a wide circle of American readers. Here, by text and by illustrations, he has set the Bible in new perspectives.

It will be seen also from his frequent use of such phrases as "scholars tell us," that Mr. Youngman has the modesty to make plain that his interpretations of the Biblical content allow for judgments in some cases varying from his own.

But as we follow the wide sweep of what he has written, we can perceive more vividly than before the great panorama of God's movements in human history, from his choice of the people of the Covenant, through the long period of patriarchs and prophets to their fulfilment in the life and crucifixion and rising-again of Christ, and on into the beginning of the Church that is the new Covenant of his Spirit.

Walter Russell Bowie

Part I

PATRIARCHS, JUDGES and KINGS

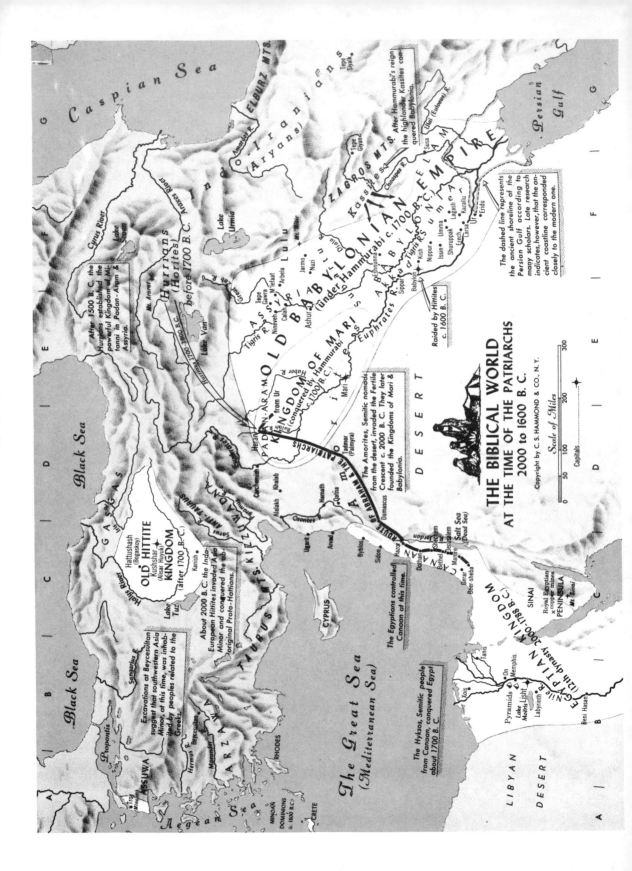

THE BIBLICAL WORLD
AT THE TIME OF THE PATRIARCHS
2000 to 1600 B. C.

Copyright by C. S. HAMMOND & CO., N.Y.

Scale of Miles

50   100   200   300

Capitals.............

After 1500 B.C. the Hurrians established the powerful Kingdom of Mitanni in Padan-Aram & Assyria.

Excavations at Beycesultan suggest that southwestern Asia Minor, at this time, was inhabited by peoples related to the Greeks.

About 2000 B.C. the Indo-European Hittites invaded Asia Minor and conquered the aboriginal Proto-Hatians.

The Egyptians controlled Canaan at this time.

The Hyksos, Semitic people from Canaan, conquered Egypt about 1700 B.C.

The Amorites, Semitic nomads from the desert, invaded the Fertile Crescent c. 2000 B.C. They later founded the Kingdoms of Mari & Babylonia.

After Hammurabi's reign the highlander Kassites conquered Babylonia.

The dashed line represents the ancient shoreline of the Persian Gulf according to many scholars. Late research indicates, however, that the ancient coastline corresponded closely to the modern one.

Raided by Hittites c. 1600 B.C.

Caspian Sea

ELBURZ MTS.

Persian Gulf

ZAGROS MTS.

Kassites

Black Sea

The Great Sea (Mediterranean Sea)

Aegean Sea

DESERT

LIBYAN DESERT

SINAI PENINSULA

Royal Egyptian x copper mines

Mt. Sinai

OLD HITTITE KINGDOM (after 1700 B.C.)

Hattushash (Bogaskoy)

Kushshar (Alishar Huyuk)

OLD BABYLONIAN KINGDOM (under Hammurabi) c. 1700 B.C.

KINGDOM OF MARI conquered by Hammurabi c. 1700 B.C.

PADAN-ARAM

Hurrians (Horites) before 1700 B.C.

Iranians (Aryans)

Babylon

Ur

Erech

Larsa

Eridu

Nippur

Isin

Umma

Shuruppak

Lagash

Kazallu

Kish

Sippar

Susa

ELAM

AKKAD

SUMER

Damascus

Tadmor (Palmyra)

Carchemish

Khaleb

Alalakh

Ugarit

Arvad

Byblos

Sidon

Hamath

Qatna

Orontes

CANAAN

Hazor

Shechem

Bethel

Jerusalem

Mamre

Dothan

Gerar

Beer-sheba

Salt Sea (Dead Sea)

ROUTE OF ABRAHAM

Haran

from Ur

Balikh R.

Habor R.

Euphrates R.

Tigris R.

Diala R.

Choapes R.

Ulai (Eulaeus) R.

Mari

Ashur

Nineveh

Calah

Arbela

Nuzi

Jarmo

Tepe Gawra

M'letaat

Mt. Ararat

Lake Van

Lake Urmia

Lake Sevan

Cyrus River

Araxes River

Tepe Giyan

Tepe Siyalk

EGYPTIAN KINGDOM 2000-1788 B.C. (12th dynasty)

Pyramids

Memphis

On

Xois

Tanis

Beni Hasan

Lake Moeris

Labyrinth

Nile

CRETE

RHODES

CYPRUS

Troy

Minoan Dominions (c. 1600 B.C.)

Propontis

Halys River

Sangarius R.

Hermus R.

Maeander R.

Sarus R.

TAURUS MTS.

CAUCASUS

Mt. Argaeus

Kanish

ARZAWA

ASSUWA

KIZZWADNA

GASGAS

Light

I

Abraham

(GEN. 11:31, 32; 12:1-9; 13:3-18; 17:1-8; 18)

To know the background for the long and crowded story of the Bible, one needs to look first at the map of that part of the continent of Asia which is called the Near East. There are tracts of desert or of semidesert; but conspicuous also is the great curve of developed land which the Patriarchs knew as the Fertile Crescent. From the valleys of the two great rivers, the Tigris and the Euphrates, it stretches northwestward and then southward along the narrow plain between the Mediterranean Sea and the desert, to the mouth of the river Nile. Through that Crescent ran the caravan routes that carried the commerce of wide regions and rich cities.

Palestine itself is a very small country, barely one hundred and fifty miles long and only fifty-five miles at its widest point. However, it is a land bridge between Egypt and Mesopotamia, and it is easy to see why possession of it was always coveted by neighboring nations for trade and power. Palestine has been the battleground of these nations. Note, too, the great trade routes on the map, and picture the winding camel caravans along the line of the Crescent, extending from Egypt and Africa northward to meet those from the Persian Gulf, and intersecting others from the north at the big cities of Haran in Syria and Nineveh in Assyria. A glance at the map will also show why little movement ever went eastward—across the vast Arabian Desert —with its miles and miles of sand, and the home, even today, of restless nomads and dangerous brigands. This desert is not to be confused with one of the same name to the east of the Nile valley.

Near the mouth of the "great rivers" was Sumer, later called Chaldea. Here there was an alluvial plain, built up of

The kind of house in which Abraham lived; the rooms are built around an open courtyard.

Examples of Sumerian drinking cups, discovered at Ur.

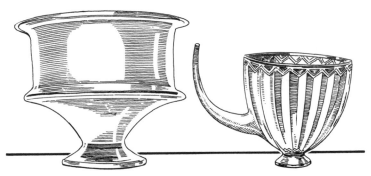

soil brought down by the rivers. Even today the network of canals which used to irrigate the plain can be followed; without their water it could only become like the desert, so near it is to its edge.

UR OF THE CHALDEES

It appears from Genesis 11:31 that Abraham, the great figure from whom the inheritance of Israel began, was a Sumerian, born at Ur. Scholars are uncertain about the date of his birth. Some say 1700 B.C., others say about 2100 B.C. Ur of the Chaldees is well known as an ancient city of almost legendary origin. In its Babylonian days it was nearer the river mouth, which during the centuries silted up so that Ur is now some 120 miles from the Persian Gulf. Excavations have revealed that countless days before Abraham, primitive men lived there in mud villages until conquered by the Sumerians, who rebuilt the city and brought to it new crafts, arts, and civilization. Examples of these crafts have been unearthed, and many idols, temples, and sites of bazaars have been brought to light, to show how the people worshiped, lived, and traded. Abraham was a citizen of a great city and inherited the traditions of an ancient and fine civilization.

the Great Light," the people gathered. Human sacrifice—usually of the first-born male—was practiced, and a ghastly ritual was followed on some occasions. When a reigning king was buried, there was human sacrifice on a large scale, and he

What the Ziggurat probably looked like in the days of Abraham.

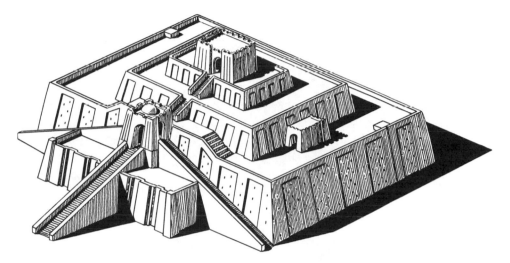

Abraham's father, Terah, may have been a rich sheikh or chieftain, possessing large flocks of sheep and herds of cattle, camels, and slaves. Why, then, did he decide to leave Ur and journey northward to Haran?

WORSHIP AND IDOLS

The answer is probably connected with the form of worship then common in Babylonia. Ur was the center of worship of the moon-god, Sin. (This is only a name and has nothing to do with sin or wrong-doing as we use the word.) The moon-god's temple was placed high on top of an enormous mount called a ziggurat, ascended by hundreds of stone stairs. The one at Ur has been excavated, and one can see from the pictures and drawings what a huge mount it really was. In the temple, called the "House of

went to his rest surrounded by his soldiers, his courtiers, women, and attendants, all victims of a wholesale slaughter.

It may be that Terah was a moon worshiper, but that when Hammurabi (probably the Amraphel of Shinar in Gen. 14:1) conquered Ur and set up Sun-worship, even saying that the sun-god gave him his laws, Terah refused the change and migrated to Haran, where the moon-god ziggurat was called "House of Joys." He, with his possessions, traveled up the valley of the Euphrates, journeying by day and camping by night.

ABRAHAM'S GOD

We have already heard about two gods —the Sun and the Moon. There were many others connected with food and crops and the weather. Typical examples are two Hittite gods of thunder that prob-

An oasis where a natural spring enables palm trees to grow. Some oases are many square miles in extent and tribes are able to grow crops. This one is in Sinai, the traditional "Well of Moses."

ably found their way into Palestine when the Hittites entered the country (later in our story). But some people began to think that there must be one who was finer and stronger than any of them; in fact, he might have made the sun and the moon and he might have controlled the winds and lightning and thunder! It was a daring thought, for this unknown god was difficult to picture; he couldn't be seen in any shape or form, as could the other gods, but he was real enough to those who thought of him at all. Abraham was one of these, and the more he thought of it, the more he felt sure he ought to give this god special sacrifices and worship to him alone. Our Bibles refer to him as Jehovah, but a more exact rendering would be Yahweh. That is

what Abraham's descendants called Him, and through the centuries they learned to regard Him as the Creator who loved them. This was a very slow process, but it prepared the way for the wonderful message of Jesus, that Yahweh was not only Almighty, He was a Father, too— "the Father Almighty."

It was after Terah had died that Abraham felt more strongly than ever what seemed to his heart and conscience to be a heavenly call to leave Haran and to travel southward into Canaan. He, with his wife Sarah and Lot, his nephew, and their flocks, herds, precious possessions and arms for protection against marauding tribes and wild animals, trekked southward and became known as Hebrews—"they who crossed the river." His was a peaceful journey, probably because the people he met were descendants of the tribes who had migrated from Babylonia to Canaan even before Terah had.

THE LONG JOURNEY

The great caravan edged along the desert, stopping at oases for watering sheep and cattle and for their own rest.

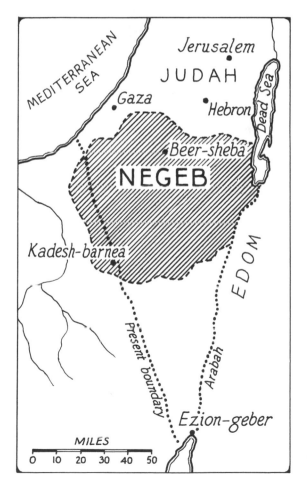

Sometimes the wadis were muddy and dry, giving little hope of water. Abraham, probably looking much like a fine old sheikh, may have worn a long white cotton shirt, tied at the waist with a broad colored sash; a brown camel's or black goat's hair cloak with perpendicular stripes, and on his head a large flowing scarf of silk bound round with a two-inch-wide rope of camel or goat hair. On his feet were sandals, stout soles of leather under the feet, a thong or string of hide passing round between the ankle and the heel, brought over the top of the foot and between the great toe and the second toe, and fastened to the sole by a leather button. (At night, sleeping in his day clothes, he would merely unloose his girdle and remove his sandals.) In his hand he carried a staff—a rough bough of a tree but as powerful in meaning as a king's scepter.

Sarah, too, may have worn a robe of cotton—dyed blue with the rind of pomegranates—and a similar headdress. The sleeves were quite three yards long; in these were carried her personal belongings. When Sarah worked she tied the sleeves behind her neck and tucked her trailing robe into her girdle so that she could move easily.

Southward, at length, they traveled down the narrow Phoenician plain, the Mediterranean on their right and on the left the desolate Lebanon mountains and the hills of Galilee. Cutting inland to avoid the Mount Carmel range, they crossed the fertile Plain of Esdraelon— the battlefield of later wars between the tribes and their enemies—and then the hills of Samaria rose before them. Far over to the east the Jordan writhed tortuously like an enormous snake between its ravine-like banks of limestone. A few miles farther south, at one thousand three hundred feet below sea level, it widened into the Dead Sea—aptly named, for in it is no life, no fish or plant, and

The Negeb or South, an area of desert and scrubland.

15

the sea is so salt that one cannot sink in it.

Abraham pitched his tent at Shechem, under the oaks of Moreh. This was a sanctuary to one of the Canaanite gods; the oaks were terebinth or turpentine trees, yielding a resinous sap; they gave a pleasant shade from the hot sun. Later he moved to Bethel and then journeyed southward through the Negeb, which

Wells. Water is a vital need even today; well water is usually spring or "living water."

means "the dry" or "the South"—probably semidesert lying between Hebron and the wider desert (see map). It is important to note that the rainfall decreases gradually in this district, and desert and semidesert areas are still common. These made the Wilderness. Failure of water between the months of May and October—the dry season—drove Abraham into Egypt.

On their return, with their flocks and herds greater in size, the herdsmen of Abraham and Lot quarreled over water supplies. Lot, in making his choice, looked to the west, where lay the barren rocks of Judaea; he gazed long to the east, to the green pastureland of the Jordan plains that promised an easier life

for him and his men. Lot went toward Sodom, and Abraham moved to Hebron, which lay in a fertile valley between high hills.

ABRAHAM'S ENCAMPMENT

Here he set up an encampment, no longer a nomad but a chieftain in his own right, deciding to settle in this new land. Life was patriarchal; that is, whole families of several generations were together, often in the same tent, all obeying the authority of the oldest male member of the family. They would all assist in the work entailed by their flocks and the simple growing of crops just sufficient for their own needs in the area immediately around their own tent. Abraham's tent, being the largest, possibly one hundred and twenty feet long, stood in the center, facing the way strangers or visitors and traders would approach. Small encampments were circular, but such an arrangement must have been extensive, so it was more than likely that the camp was a huge square of tents arranged in straight lines. Each tent, or "house of hair," was of black goat's hair woven by the women into coarse sackcloth, which was waterproof and heatproof as well. It was a parallelogram in shape, held up by three rows of three poles, the middle one the highest. The height was up to eight feet; tent pins or pegs were used to steady the tent (see Isa. 54:2). These were two to three feet long; they were driven in by a large mallet with a head three feet long and eighteen inches in circumference.

Inside the tent were two apartments, curtained off in such a way that the only entrance was the open side of the men's section, which was on the right-hand side of the tent. Another curtain was draped round the sides and parted open to make the doorway. In the men's apartment meals were served and visitors entertained; in the women's section meals were prepared. Sarah could easily overhear the Stranger say she would have a son (Gen. 18:9-10). In this part, too, were kept household goods—cooking pots, water jars, skins, lamps, stones for grinding corn, sleeping mats, spinning wheels, and so on. The usual food was of flour balls dipped in sour goat's milk, or a kind of lentil soup. The flour was ground from corn grown near the encampment, the earth being barely scraped with a shallow wooden plow (see Chapter 11).

Abraham would have to dig wells where natural springs seemed likely—"living water." Each was protected with

Eastern hospitality; the picture is modern, but the customs have been the same since earliest days in Palestine.

a ring of stones, and the drinking troughs near by were filled with water taken up in leather buckets or waterskins. Water is obtained in this manner to this day, except that the buckets of leather have given way to oil cans. The women did this work; normally, a man would not think of doing it, or even of helping.

BEDOUIN HOSPITALITY

The hospitality of the Bedouin is a sacred duty even in modern times. All guests are treated with courtesy and kindness. Today, a sheikh will give his best quarters to his guest and provide a whole goat roasted in its own gravy with rice and sour camel's milk! Abraham greeted his visitors probably in the same manner as the greeting of today, by keeping his head erect, inclining forward slightly, raising his right hand to touch his forehead, lips and heart. The first act was to offer water and towels to remove the dust of the journey and to refresh the sandaled, hot feet. Even at short notice, food was provided. Abraham's visitors came at the hottest time of the day, but immediately Sarah and the slaves were bidden to prepare a meal—calf, curds, and milk. Sharing was a sign of friendship and no names were asked until after the meal, lest the guest be a member of an enemy tribe and the rule of hospitality be broken. Although a chieftain, Abraham would wait on his guests, and the conversation throughout would be as slow and as leisurely as the meal.

2

Abraham and Isaac

(GEN. 21:1-21; 22:1-14; 23; 24)

When Isaac, whose name means "laughter," was born, Sarah, fearing for his inheritance, grew even more jealous of Hagar, Abraham's slave wife and Hagar's son Ishmael. She persuaded Abraham to send them away—after all, they were only slaves! Hagar and Ishmael wandered toward Beersheba through the wilderness —rough, rocky countryside, waterless, with low scrub, where wild animals roamed. Suffering from hunger and thirst, they gave up all hope, when suddenly, in her last despair, Hagar found a well. They were helped by a friendly people, and years later Ishmael became the leader of this nomadic tribe, whose weapons were bows and arrows—a desert-archer tribe in the Wilderness of Paran. His descendants are today the pure Arab stock—the Bedaween (Bedouin) desert dwellers, "wild-ass men" (Gen. 16:11, 12). The Jews are descended from Isaac, who was now growing up, the "apple of his Mother's eye." As Abraham saw around him the child sacrifice practiced by the Canaanites, he began to think that in order to be equal to the Canaanites in his own devotion, he, too, must offer his child to the Lord he worshiped. Among the more gruesome finds at Gezer is a small altar of rough limestone, on it the remains of an eight-day-old baby! As late as the sixth century B.C. Jeremiah was condemning this practice.

In Genesis 22 is the story—in its first part so poignant and so pitiful—of how Abraham prepared to offer his beloved son as the ultimate expression of his obedience. With Isaac and with some of his servants, he sets out on a three-day journey to "the land of Moriah," believed to be one of the mountains of Salem, later called Jerusalem. On the third day he had reached "the place of which God had told him," and there he left the servants and went on farther with Isaac, taking wood for the burnt offering, fire in his hand, and a knife. (It is not known

The wilderness and mountains; the two usually go together, frightening, forbidding and awe-inspiring. This is like the Wilderness of Paran into which Hagar and Ishmael went.

how the Hebrews kindled fire in those days, but probably by some method of rubbing sticks together.) He laid Isaac on the altar he had built, and prepared to slay him.

Then comes the saving climax: Abraham's hand is arrested just as he draws the sacrificial knife, and it is revealed to him that there is a truer way to worship than by human sacrifice.

Although a chieftain, Abraham merely camped in Beersheba, and did not "own" land; so when Sarah died, he had to buy a burial plot for her. He went to the "Gate of Hebron." Trading, bargaining, quarreling, settling complaints . . . all these were done here, in public, "at the gate." (The Judges of our later stories did their work "at the gate.") Abraham bargained with Ephron, a Hittite, and bought the Cave of Machpelah for four hundred shekels of silver. The weight value of a shekel varied with famine and plenty, so we cannot even guess at what this amount was in our money. Note the extreme courtesy in this public transaction, for Ephron's, "Take it, I give it thee," was only a polite introduction to a prolonged price bargaining. The traditional site of the cave is in the possession of the Mohammedans, who also remember Abraham as the "Father of the Faithful."

JEWS AND ARABS

The people of Ephron, the Hittite, came from Asia Minor (shown on the Bible Lands map), and for a long time were formidable rivals to Egypt. They were smelting iron between 1500 and 1300 B.C. Rameses II (of whom you will hear in connection with the Exodus) sent a letter to a Hittite king asking for a supply of smelted iron, and the king replied regretfully that he had none available at the nearest port for export. The physical features of the Hittites were like those we expect in the Jew—broad-shouldered, heavy of face, hooked nose; so different from the Arab stock with slender figure, straight nose and clear-cut face.

Growing old, Abraham realized that Yahweh's promise could come true only if Isaac were married and had children. He, therefore, instructed a trusty servant, Eliezer, in what he had to do. It is still a nomadic custom for parents to arrange a marriage, even without their children's knowledge. There was certainly nothing strange in Eliezer's journey to find a wife for Isaac amongst Abraham's own people. Abraham forbade him to choose a wife from the Canaanites. He did not want his son to marry a "foreigner," especially an idol worshiper; in any case, it was Isaac's duty to marry within the family, a cousin for preference. But a bride had to be paid for, so Eliezer took ten camels laden with gifts, and journeyed to Haran, the home of Nahor and other kinsmen who had stayed there when Abraham had left so many years before.

HOW ELIEZER FOUND REBEKAH

Eliezer probably forded the Jordan and moved eastward toward Damascus, his home town; though the story has such a sense of urgency it is not likely that he stayed there more than one night. Outside the walls of Haran he stopped at a well, for his camels needed water, and it was just the place to meet someone to help him. The well was outside a village or a city so as to allow of free movement in watering flocks. All water was fetched by women—except men water carriers, a despised occupation. It was sunset, and in the cool of the evening the women came with their pitchers, some from long distances, among them the young Rebekah. It was Eastern courtesy to give water to a stranger, and Eliezer made his request a natural beginning to his conversation. It was even more kind for Rebekah to draw water for his camels. Why he allowed her to do this without offering

A girl carrying her waterpot; she will learn to carry very heavy jars with ease and grace.

to help is probably because it did not occur to him, for this kind of work was definitely women's. As the other women moved away, carrying their heavy pitchers on their heads and shoulders with grace and ease, Eliezer took out his gifts—a ring and two bracelets of gold. The ring would be a nose ring, a much prized ornament; it is passed through a hole bored in the nostril so that the jewel in the ring lies against the cheek (see Ezek. 16:12). Rebekah recognized these as betrothal gifts, and ran indoors to tell her family of Eliezer's visit.

Once again we see an example of Eastern courtesy and hospitality. Eliezer was a stranger and needed food and lodging, which were given him without question as to who he was or where he was from. His camels were stabled for the night, too. They were fed with crushed straw and barley; crushed straw is still the usual food for animals and is obtained after the heap of straw produced in the winnowing has been trampled on by oxen or broken under threshing sledges (see Isa. 41:15, 16).

THE RETURN

Eliezer insisted on telling his errand before eating. He was equally insistent to get away next morning, and Laban was impressed with the gifts sent as dowry—jewels, silver, gold, ornaments, raiment; he saw in this visit the hand of Yahweh. Even if Rebekah had refused, she would have had to go. Marriage was binding and this was a good offer. So, despite the fact that she had to leave her people and journey many miles to marry a man much older than herself, she went willingly, with Deborah, her nurse.

Abraham had died by now, and Isaac was watching and waiting for his bride-to-be. He must have seen the dust of the caravan and watched the silhouettes of the camels on the skyline as he wandered into the countryside. He hastened to meet them. Rebekah, assured by Eliezer that the approaching figure was her future husband, drew her veil across her face—again the Eastern custom—not to withdraw it until after the wedding ceremony. This latter was a simple affair, for Isaac had merely to take Rebekah into his tent in the sight of witnesses, which he did. There was feasting and a great celebration for several days, but since Isaac still missed his mother and father it is possible that he did not continue the celebration for the usual length of time. Rebekah would live in Sarah's tent and take over the home duties that women in the East were expected to do.

3

Esau and Jacob

(GEN. 25:27-34; 27; 28:10-22; 29:1-30)

Esau and Jacob were of very different natures. Esau was strong, energetic, a skillful hunter; Jacob was reserved, thoughtful, a shepherd with time to think. They were twins, but Esau was the first-born, and one day would be receiving the blessing and birthright from his father— a very important event in Eastern life. Jacob thought about it craftily, and he waited for a chance to deceive both Esau and his old father.

His chance came one day when Esau went out hunting. Jacob knew that his brother would have a hard day, climbing and scrambling over the rocks and down to the drying wadis. He knew Esau would return famished. He hung a cooking pot over a "fire of thorns" (see Exod. 22:6; Ps. 58:9; Isa. 27:4). The "boiling" was a very delicious thick red soup of lentils, and the smell of it must have been wonderful to the exhausted Esau. The thought of that soup was more to him at that moment than any "birthright." Would

Esau let Jacob have the birthright in exchange for the soup? That was what Jacob asked. Perhaps Esau supposed that Jacob was not in earnest, but recklessly he said yes. It would be too late when he realized what he had done: that he had thrown away his spiritual headship of the family for a "mess of pottage." (In the Bible story this is given as the reason why the "elder" came to "serve the younger," that is, why Edom, Esau's country, became subservient to Israel, Jacob's country.)

Isaac probably did not know of all this when he told Esau to go and get him wild deer—venison, "savoury meat"— after which he would bestow the blessing on Esau. Rebekah knew, and planned for the deceitful move whereby Jacob put on pieces of kidskin for Isaac to feel and believe to be the hairy hands and arms of Esau. (Usually a kid was accounted much too valuable an animal to kill except on rare and important occasions; and to

24

Salutation in the East. This is how Laban greeted Jacob.

Rebekah and Jacob this was certainly an important occasion.)

(Note in the two blessings of Isaac in Genesis 27 the repeated reference to the "dew of heaven." It is not easy to see the point of this unless one realizes that this dew is really a mist that rolls in from the Mediterranean in the evenings of the hot season, when there is no rain at all. It is this fine night mist that makes it possible for crops and vegetation to grow, and sweetens the air for human beings [see Hosea 6:4]. It probably would not sweep so far inland as to reach Esau's kingdom, Edom. Even today nomads plant a tree and pile loose pebbles around the trunk in order to get water; the dew condenses and percolates through the pebbles to the soil to water the tree. This is called a "dew mound"; the photograph shows dew mounds in the Negeb some three thousand years old.)

JACOB'S JOURNEY

When Esau learned (as is told in Gen.

27) that he had really forfeited his father's blessing to Jacob, the supplanter, he was furious. In fear for his life, Jacob fled to Haran, to his uncle Laban, of whom his mother had told him.

ness. We are familiar with this idea when we remember Stonehenge, cromlechs, menhirs, and other upright stones or monoliths.

Jacob arrived at the well of Padan-

Dew mounds in the Negeb; 3,000 years ago these heaps of pebbles were piled around the stems of trees to preserve water. The trees are gone, but the mounds remain in this desert region.

On his way, at Bethel, he had the vision of the ladder reaching up to heaven which is told of in Genesis 28. One might wonder why such a vision should have come to Jacob, who had seemed so grasping and unscrupulous. And how could it be right that it should be Jacob who would play the greater role in Bible history? It may be that the answer lies in this: Esau was the kind of man who let the appetite of the moment blind him to any higher interest. But Jacob, in spite of all his unlovely early traits, had an appreciation for the long-term values that are more important than food or drink.

He called the place of his vision Bethel —house of God—and raised a huge stone pillar, a mazzebah, to mark its sacred-

aram and saw Rachel. She was probably only ten or eleven, for any girl older, like Rebekah, would have been in the company of other women, and she was alone. We have to remember that according to Eastern custom girls of this age were often betrothed. Jacob behaved courteously, and, unlike Eliezer, not only moved the heavy covering stone of the well but also watered Rachel's flocks. For one thing, Rachel was not strong enough to do it by herself; for another, Jacob already loved her; and, besides, he was himself a shepherd and knew what the sheep needed.

Laban greeted Jacob with a kiss—the usual greeting of equals. He put his right hand on Jacob's left shoulder, and kissed his right cheek; then reversing the action, kissed his left cheek. Jacob would return the salute; only men did this. Rachel had been tending the sheep, a difficult and dangerous task for one so young, but now Jacob was to prove a useful worker for Laban.

THE SHEPHERD'S LIFE

Daily he drove his flocks through the rough desert plains and hills, seeking pasturage, water, and shade in the stunted shrubs and scrub. Sometimes he made a reed pipe by binding together two hollow reeds and cutting holes in them; then he would play simple tunes, sad or gay. When sunset came he led his sheep back to the stone fold. This was merely a circular structure of rough stones laid in such a way as to hold firmly without mortar or clay. The wall is about three feet wide at the base and slopes up to about a foot wide at the top. The size of the fold is governed by the number of sheep it is to hold. There is no door, the narrow entrance being guarded by the shepherd himself. He is the door, Jesus said, using this illustration so familiar to His hearers: "I am the door; through me if anyone come in he shall be saved, and he shall come in and go out, and find pasture" (see John 10:9). Jacob may have carried a sling, indeed he was almost bound to have carried one, but he certainly had a club of oak. This was the "rod," two feet long, with a rounded head, often spiked with nails or hard flints; it is carried on the belt so that the shepherd's hand is free to carry the "staff," but he lies down with it in his hand, the cord at its end wound round his wrist for safety (Ps. 23). Thus able to protect his flock, he is indeed the "good shepherd," ready "to lay down his life for the sheep" (see John 10:11, 15, 17).

Having no possessions, Jacob wore the poorest of shepherd's clothes—a short goatskin jacket over his torn knee-length cotton shirt—and went barefoot (see Heb. 11:37). He drove his flock into the sheep runs, desert pastures full of danger from wild animals and lurking brigands, constantly on the alert for any signs of attack. This "driving" is somewhat different from the "leading" one usually has in mind when thinking of sheep and their shepherds in the richer pastures.

Jacob seems to have had some primitive understanding of breeding and kept to himself much knowledge of cattle and flocks. In this way he eventually developed his own to large numbers of strong and healthy animals. But this was not for some time, and, meanwhile, having no dowry to give for Rachel, he offered to work for Laban seven years without pay so that he might marry her.

A sheepfold, built of stones.

4

Jacob and Laban

(GEN. 31-33:1-17)

Jacob's seven years of devoted service for Rachel ended in an anticlimax. The wedding celebrations must have been bitter to him, for when he took the veil from his bride's face and put it on his shoulder to indicate his promise to care for her all his life, he found he had been tricked! It was Leah, not his beloved Rachel! According to Eastern custom, the first-born girl had to be married first, and Laban insisted that Jacob must accept the bargain. Jacob appears to have hated Leah, who was probably unprepossessing, anyway; she was "tender-eyed," which means that she lacked the brightness of eye so appealing in Eastern beauty, or she may even have had weak eyesight. Laban bargained for another seven years for Rachel; it says much for Jacob's character that he agreed because of his love for Rachel, but we also know that he continued to cheat Laban in his work

as a shepherd. This further seven years' service, when reckoned in wages, made his dowry several times the usual amount paid.

THE "TWELVE TRIBES"

Jacob had many children and it is through his family that the Hebrew people changed from the status of a family to that of a tribe—in fact, many tribes. The children of Jacob and Leah—Reuben, Levi, Simeon, Judah, Issachar, Zebulun—all became heads of tribes; so did Rachel's children—Joseph and Benjamin, although it was Joseph's sons, Ephraim and Manasseh, who appeared later as the heads of the tribes; and other children by slave wives—Gad, Asher, Dan, Naphtali—made the total twelve tribes in all. We shall meet these tribes later, when we

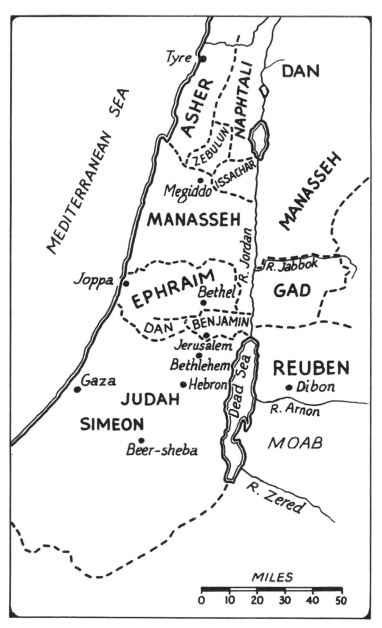

Map of the Twelve Tribes. Two of these bear the names of sons of Joseph.

JACOB DECEIVES LABAN

Jacob repaid himself well by keeping in his own flocks all the best animals. Then, while Laban was away for a long spell, he packed up all his possessions, shall find out how they "inherited" Canaan, the Land of Promise.

lieved to look after the crops and insure that they grew well. They may have been of only superstitious worth to him—lucky charms—but they were common among the Amorites and Canaanites, who really believed in them—even that ownership of them gave special rights. Rachel had inherited the superstition, for she had them hidden under the colored cushions of the

A drove of camels such as Jacob sent as a gift to Esau.

and with his wives set off southward; this time he went along the eastern edge of the Jordan, probably following the main route through Damascus and the eastern foothills of "the mountains beyond Jordan."

Laban pursued him and caught up with him at Mount Gilead, and reproved him for leaving so deceitfully and, further, for taking the household teraphim. These were the little terra cotta images of the goddess of fertility, Astarte, who was be-

camel furniture—the packsaddles on which she rode. These packsaddles were used as seats in the tents.

Jacob, in his turn, reproached Laban for his equally deceptive treatment for twenty years; they agreed to let bygones be bygones, and put up a cairn of friendship at Mizpah; such a heap of stones would easily be broken down by wind and weather through the years, so it is not surprising to find that its position is quite unknown in the highlands of Jordan.

Laban returned to Haran. Jacob continued toward his father's home in Beersheba, but now realized that his way led through Esau's country, Edom, to the south of the Dead Sea. Edom means "red," which may refer to Esau's hair or to the red pottage, but more likely to the reddish cliffs found there. Seir, where his descendants settled, certainly means "hair," which may again refer to Esau. Remembering Esau's threat, Jacob knew his danger only too well, and guessed that Esau might attack the unwieldy camel caravan and take his possessions. He divided the caravan into two, hoping one might draw the attack from the other, and in his anxiety sent them ahead over the brook Jabbok, a tributary of the Jordan—a mere brook in the dry season, a rushing torrent when the rains came.

JACOB ACCEPTS GOD'S GUIDANCE

Despite his plans to appease Esau, Jacob felt the need of Yahweh's help. Look at his prayer—the first to be recorded in the Old Testament—in Genesis 32:9–12, and see how he quite humbly gives thanks and asks for God's protection; but he does not regret what he has done in the

The Brook Jabbok and beyond, a field and frightening landscape. This is where Jacob is said to have "wrestled with the Angel."

Drawings of terra cotta household gods —teraphim. Rachel had some of these hidden under her pack saddle; they were supposed to ward off evil and served also as lucky charms.

past—at least, we are not told so. He is still the self-sufficient Jacob. His strange experience at Penuel is not absolutely clear to us. It is probably a Hebrew folk-lore story, retold with Jacob as the hero. The old story told how the river spirit tried to stop anyone trying to cross the ford, and fought until daybreak to do so. In our story, the river is Jabbok. Forcing a spirit to tell his name was important in magic because knowing his name gave Jacob a special power over him. Jacob became lame, and this made him remember that he could not get just what he wanted from God by force or by cheating. His whole life up to now had been spoiled by deceit, but at last he had learned to be true. His experience was, as we say, the "turning point" in his life. At Penuel

—which means "face of God"—he had wrestled with God for a blessing, and was no longer Jacob the Supplanter, but Israel the Perseverer with God.

The Bible story goes on to tell of Jacob's plans to ingratiate himself into Esau's favor with presents—droves of his animals. Esau was generous and forgave Jacob, who may have seemed to him to be a better man than the man he had known many years before. Their reunion was strengthened when some time later they met at Isaac's burial.

WHAT DO THE STORIES MEAN?

It is important to note that these stories of Jacob and Esau appear to have been made to explain tribal movements and migrations throughout the Bible lands in general and Canaan in particular. Esau represents Edom; the tribe quarreled with the tribe of Jacob, which migrated north-ward to Haran, where was formed a union of Aramaean tribes or clans. Later there was a separation and Jacob's tribes moved southward into Canaan; those he left behind became the Syrians, of whom we hear later as enemies of Israel. By this time Edom, a branch of the older Semitic settlers, had occupied much of the south. Consequently, there was armed opposition to the southward movements of Jacob's tribes, although some appease-ment was made through gifts, and Jacob's tribes moved away from Edom and after a stay east of the Jordan eventually crossed toward Bethel and Shechem.

What has happened may be that the writer of these accounts has taken the story of Jacob and legends of tribal movements and woven them together, with Jacob as the hero of them all.

5

Joseph

(GEN. 37—TWO STORIES—SEE TEXT)

Not many narratives anywhere can match in vividness the story that begins in Genesis 37—the story of Joseph, the lad who, beginning with great imagination and high hopes, was plunged into a succession of what seemed inexplicable evils, yet kept his faith in God and thereby maintained his own integrity, and, at last, won through to conspicuous victory.

In order to understand the background of the Joseph story we must look at Egypt, one of the great nations mentioned in Chapter 1. Observing on the map the river Nile and tracing it to its delta mouth, one sees how close this is to the south of Palestine. Egypt as a country obviously depends upon the Nile for its fertility; the flooding caused by the heavy spring rains at the river's source in Central Africa spreads throughout the valley, enabling men to grow crops, especially corn, in the silt and alluvial deposits brought down by the floods. Nowadays, dams and canals control careful irrigation for crops and water supplies; centuries before Christ, however, there were primitive but equally careful plans for irrigation canals in the otherwise waterless areas; some of these methods still exist.

We know a great deal about Egypt; when the Western world was wild and unknown, inhabited by savages, Egypt was a great nation, highly cultured and civilized, having cities, palaces, temples. Even the Pyramids were ancient in Joseph's time. We are always hearing fresh news of important discoveries in Egypt. One of these was the finding of the tomb of a Pharaoh of the Third Dynasty, about 2700 B.C. Joseph is believed to have lived about 1700–1600 B.C. Excavations of temples and tombs have revealed embalmed bodies (mummies), furniture, jewels, vases, jars, household articles, even food; and whole palaces (or, at least, their ruins) have been dug clear from the desert sands. Every-

The Pyramid and Sphinx, strange mysteries of the desert, centuries old even in the days of Joseph.

body knows about the Sphinxes, huge statues with bodies like crouching lions and heads like human heads, their faces strange and mysterious.

Of the Pyramids, three are at Giza (Gezer, Gizeh), one for each Pharaoh buried there. Pharaoh means Great House; this originates from the belief in those times that the great king was really a god—a "son of the Suns." Modern historians—in England, for example may speak of "houses" or "families" of Tudors or Windsors, but in Egypt they were called dynasties; these are numbered, for example, the Fourth Dynasty, under King Cheops. Not long ago two "solar" boats five thousand years old were discovered. They were made of coniferous wood, probably from Lebanon, and the bows were curved in papyrus; they were about ninety feet long and were steered with a thirty-foot oar. These boats were supposed to carry the soul of King Cheops from this world to eternity to keep company with the sun-god on his unending voyage around the world; one was for journeying by day westward, the other for the return at night, eastward.

EGYPTIAN HISTORY

The national events of the Egyptians, wars, conquests, etc., were recorded in their strange writing and pictures on the walls of towers and obelisks. Sometimes they were written on clay tablets, baked hard and stored on shelves rather like books in a library; scholars have deciphered these, too, and have given us much information about Egypt at war, work, and play. One important discovery was of a limestone slab or stele, seven and a half feet by three feet, under the base of an enormous statue of Rameses II outside the Temple of Ammon at Karnak; on it is the history of the wars against Asian overlords and Cushite or Nubian kings, and the creation of a new kingdom.

We learn that after many centuries a kind of civil war broke out; the people fought among themselves and, taking advantage of their weakness, powerful nomadic tribes swept into the Nile valley on their superb horses and chariots and conquered the country. These were the Hyksos, the shepherd kings—probably a mistranslation of the real name, but suf-ficient to make the Egyptians hate *all* shepherds for generations (see Genesis 46:34). It was one of these Hyksos kings who favored Joseph, possibly because he saw in him one of his own nomadic race. Joseph became his Chief Governor, or Food Controller, at the new capital these

The golden mummy mask of the head of a Pharaoh; his false beard is broken off, the ear pierced for an earring, the head-dress bears a cobra to ward off enemies, and the necklet is of chains.

The kind of chair and water jar used by the Egyptians at the time of Joseph.

Pharaohs had built at Tanis (also known as Zoan and Avaris).

WHAT HAPPENED TO JOSEPH?

There are two distinct stories of the selling of Joseph, each derived from an account written in one or other of the two divided kingdoms years later. The first, from the Southern Kingdom, and the second, from the Northern Kingdom (see Part II), were both vivid accounts, but each being a story of the Jews, the compiler, rather than omit either, decided to weave them together. (Compilers often did this, and sometimes it is difficult to separate one story from another.) We call these two stories J and E; you may meet these letters in other books about the early Bible stories. Here are the parts of this particular story to examine separately and read as different versions of the same events in Genesis 37:

J story: 2b–4, 12–17, 23–27, 28b, 31–35.

E story: 5–11, 18–22, 28a–29–30, 36. ("a" is the first half of a verse; "b" is the second.)

You will see that in the J story the characters and people are slightly different from those in the E story. Thus:

J story: Israel, Tale-bearer, Shechem, Judah, Ishmaelites.

E story: Jacob, Dreamer, Dothan, Reuben, Midianites.

In both stories we find that the brothers were very jealous of Joseph, and it was not merely because Jacob had given him a pretty coat. Look in your Authorized Version of the Bible at Genesis 37:3; you will see that in "coat of many colors" the word "many" is in italics, showing that it was put in by the translators. In the margin the word "colors" is suggested

Here is the boat used to carry the soul of the Pharaoh on his last journey. The Guardian slaves are aboard and the "eye" painted on the side is to enable the boat to see where it is going.

as "pieces." In the margin of the Revised Version, however, the coat is described as "a long garment with sleeves." You can see from these that some people think it was a brightly colored coat. But Bible scholars tell us that it was more likely a plain white shirt with extremely long pointed sleeves, that Joseph had worn. Now, in Joseph's days, only two persons wore such a garment—the sheikh and his heir or successor. It is now clear why the anger of the brothers was against Joseph—his father had made it obvious that he was not to do their kind of work; in fact, that he was to be the head of the tribe, although he was (next to Benjamin) the youngest of them all. The brothers were hurt and angry at this sign of favoritism; it is probable that Jacob loved Joseph the more because he was his beloved Rachel's first son. The anger of the brothers was made even greater when Joseph began to boast about his dreams. All ancient peoples believed that dreams were important, and the brothers had a fear that Joseph's had a special meaning.

Joseph went in search of his brothers. Shechem lay in a fertile valley between Mount Ebal and Mount Gerizim. The brothers, finding little pasturage in the summer heat, had moved on to Dothan, at the south end of the Plain of Esdraelon; it was walled and stood on a hill, the center of caravan routes crisscrossing the two plains. The pit into which Joseph was put was a cistern for storing rain water, but at that time it was dry. It was bottle-shaped, the "neck" being about three feet in diameter and as many deep, the lower part widening into a chamber some twenty feet in diameter and depth. Escape would be practically impossible without someone outside to aid with a rope.

The Ishmaelites (or Midianites) were Arab traders, probably carrying spices, frankincense and myrrh from Syria and Gilead; fording the Jordan near the Sea of Galilee, they would pass through Dothan on their way to the coastal plain, down to Egypt. The twenty pieces of silver would be twenty shekels' weight, not to be confused with the thirty received by Judas for betraying Jesus—the ancient piece of silver was worth about seventy cents.

The traders readily bought Joseph, for they knew it would be easy to sell at a considerable profit this fine, strong and handsome lad.

6

Joseph in Egypt

(GEN. 39-44)

Joseph was brought as a slave into the house of Potiphar, the Captain of the Guard; this title has a gruesome meaning—"chief of the butchers or slaughterers"—but he was certainly a Court official.

The accompanying pictures of Egypt will convey some idea of what Joseph must have seen on his arrival in this strange and fascinating land. Palaces, temples, pyramids, houses, people in different dress—rich and poor, gardens, furniture, processions, boats on the Nile. There is no doubt that his natural alertness (so disliked by his brothers, but an indication of great intelligence) found a new interest here, and excitedly he took in all the things happening around him. He may have seen the temple of Queen Hatshepsut, near the Valley of Kings, at Thebes, being built by slave labor, for this temple is believed by some scholars to be of the same period as that in which Joseph lived.

It was not long before he began learning the new language and strange customs of the land; he quickly attracted the attention of his master and mistress, who gave him every encouragement to learn. He certainly mastered the art of writing and counting, for he found this knowledge most useful in his eventual promotion as Governor under Pharaoh. He also learned of the making of paper from the papyrus reed that swayed in the Nile waters. The reed grew a stem six inches thick and twelve to fifteen feet high. The stem was sliced into strips laid together for the size needed, and another layer was put on top running across the first, with thin gum between. These were pressed under heavy stones or hammered, then dried, after which the surface was smoothed down. A "book" would be made by joining sheets to form a continuous roll; "roll" is, of course, the more correct description; one in the British Museum is 185 feet long! When the writ-

Drawings on Egyptian walls at Thebes.

ings were to last for a long time they were carved on walls and pillars; and the figures of birds and beasts, men and women, boats and so on, when painted in with beautiful colors, made the finished record brilliant and attractive. The pen was also cut from the stem; the ink was made from wood charcoal and gum. It was kept in a special palette, with shallow round holes for the colored inks and a long groove for the pens. Joseph most likely kept his records of transactions on papyrus rolls for easy carrying; they would not be as heavy and cumbersome as clay tablets!

One of the customs of the country was to shave both head and face, although, strangely enough, for important occasions men wore both a wig and a beard! If you look at the Pharaoh's head you can see where his false beard has been broken off; in other pictures the beard is clearly seen. The hair was cut straight across the brows and fell thickly in many curls at the back. The chief officials wore the usual kilt of white linen, over which was a white cloak stiffly starched so that it stood out in front, while a gold-thread girdle was around the waist, the tassels hanging knee-length.

UNEXPECTED PROMOTION

Pharaoh's wise men were probably priests of Ra; part of their duties was the interpretation of dreams. Joseph's explanation of Pharaoh's dream was so amazing that the king decided Joseph was the very man to organize the storing of food against the famine.

Pharaoh gave Joseph a signet ring bearing a seal to stamp on his decrees and orders. He also gave him fine linen—a coat or robe with long flowing sleeves, beautifully colored and embroidered,

An Egyptian wearing his special head-dress; probably Ra, the sun-god.

41

An Egyptian harvest scene. In May, the barley ripens, and is cut with sickles and gathered into sheaves. After harvesting, women go to the fields to glean.

probably of silk. Then came a gold chain of office bearing a scarab—a gem cut like a beetle. Although Joseph had given all the credit of his ability to interpret Pharaoh's dreams to his own God, Yahweh, Pharaoh arranged for him to marry a daughter of the priest of Ra, the sungod, whose temple was at On or Heliopolis, a few miles northeast of where Cairo now stands. Cleopatra's Needle in Central Park in New York City was one

An Egyptian peasant farmer. Patient, industrious and religious, he supports a family on ten acres of Nile land.

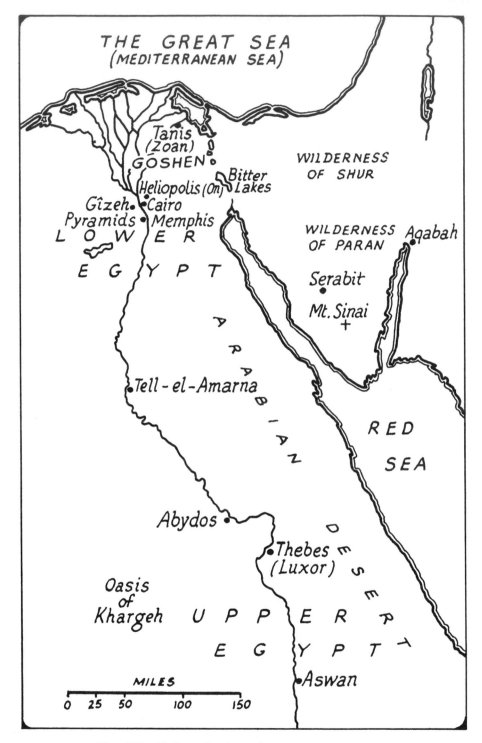

The Nile Valley showing places mentioned in this part of our story.

of the obelisks from the front of this temple.

Joseph built granaries and hoarded all the corn he could get. Ruins called the "Pits of Joseph" are still to be seen in Goshen. When famine came he sold the corn fairly and carefully, so that none went in want. News spread far and wide that there was "corn in Egypt," so that his brothers were sent by Jacob into Egypt for corn.

A STRANGER TO HIS BROTHERS

Joseph pretended that his brothers were bent on spying out the likeliest places for invasion on the northeast, where there were few natural fortifications. A vast entrenchment has been discovered in this region, showing that the danger was fully realized by the Egyptians. Joseph talked to his brothers through an interpreter and they did not know that he could understand their own Hebrew tongue. They left with their asses laden with corn; on their way they probably stayed overnight at an inn or caravanserai or campground, such as the one which has been excavated at Jerash, north of Jabbok.

On their second visit they brought as special gifts delicacies unobtainable even in Egypt—balm, honey, nuts, almonds.

Egyptian paintings show these gifts being presented to Pharaoh. Note that Joseph and his brothers had their meal at separate tables; Egyptians never ate with Hebrews (see Gen. 43:32). In any case, to have a meal for guests at noon was a rare occurrence, for the usual time for such a meal was at sunset. But Joseph was Grand Vizier, and could do such things; it probably made a great impression on his brothers, who rapidly felt some strange power in this man who seemed to know so much about them.

Benjamin was shown special favor— Eastern hospitality ordained that he should be given more than he could eat, especially bread. The loaf was made of unleavened wheat meal, toasted, and rather like a pancake of about eight inches across. No doubt Benjamin as a hungry youngster did full justice to the loaves, but even he would not have managed five times as much food as was given to his brothers. The cup put in his sack was Joseph's personal divining cup. This was used in divining by water. Pieces of gold or money or jewels were put in the goblet, and from the shapes produced or movements in the water it was believed that some people could foretell the future. (It was rather like reading tea leaves.) This was called hydromancy, and Joseph was supposed to possess these magic powers.

7

Joseph and Reconciliation

(GEN. 45; 46:1-7, 28-34; 47:1-6, 11-19, 27-31; 48:1-20; 50)

Having tested the brothers a number of times, Joseph at last revealed himself to them. They "rent their clothes," always a sign of dismay and sorrow. "Thou art even as Pharaoh"—did Joseph remember his dreams? They were certainly at last fulfilled.

Note how Joseph gives the credit to Yahweh; in all the years he had been in Egypt, associated with idol worship, even marrying a daughter of the priest of Ra, he had kept his father's faith in Yahweh. He had no doubt whatever that Yahweh was with him. "God sent me in advance of you to preserve you." "It was not you who sent me hither, but God." "God hath made me lord of all Egypt."

With another five years of famine to pass, Joseph sent for his father, Jacob, to come and settle, with all his people and flocks and herds. Pharaoh agreed, and offered to give them the "good of the land of Egypt"—Goshen (now Wadi Tumilat), lying to the northeast of the

Nile delta. Here they could be free from interference of any kind, especially as the Egyptians despised shepherds and herdsmen. Joseph, too, knew that it would be wiser to have his kinsmen well away from the center of the country, and so less likely to be absorbed into the Egyptian nation. Yet another good reason for their occupying Goshen was to act as a sort of buffer to invading nomadic tribes if this should become necessary.

Ox carts were sent to help in the transport. In spite of the fact that Jacob had traveled away from home before, he felt a little anxious about this proposal. He was a believer in Yahweh, who was his "local" god; he could not be absolutely sure that Yahweh would also travel with him to this new land. Joseph had taken a step further in his belief than his father. However, Jacob left Hebron, and at Beersheba seems to have been assured of Yahweh's company, and he continued happily from the "high place" toward

Egypt. (This doubt may seem strange to us, but we must remember that the realization of God's presence everywhere was slow and gradual in the minds of His people.)

Joseph went out to meet his father, riding in Pharaoh's second chariot. This appears natural enough, but it was Eastern courtesy—the farther the journey toward the guest to "bring him in," the greater the courtesy. Pharaoh also sent for Jacob and showed great kindness toward him; he seems to have realized that Jacob himself was a great Bedouin sheikh and a ruler. Joseph continued to live in Memphis but often visited his father.

Meanwhile, his plans developed, and through him Pharaoh became more and more powerful. For their food the people bartered everything they had—even their freedom when their property had gone—and in their thousands they were reduced to mere serfs and slaves.

Joseph had two sons, Ephraim and Manasseh. Jacob's blessing fell upon Ephraim, the younger, and indeed, in later years, the Manasseh tribe was overshadowed by his brother's. The two tribes were ranged alongside those of the sons of Jacob. We hear later of Ephraim as the Northern Kingdom.

HONOR TO THE CHIEFTAIN

After some years, Jacob died. Although he was of nomadic ways and a chieftain of his people, he was treated with Egyptian honors. But his burial place was in Canaan, and in the heat of Egypt's climate it was necessary to embalm his body to preserve it for the long journey. His body was steeped for some days in pitch and spices, then wrapped in yards and yards of linen, after which the "mummy" was put in a sarcophagus or shaped "shell." If it was buried in Pharaoh's tomb it was put into a rectangular coffin, probably of alabaster, which was shaped inside to take the form of the sarcophagus. Some of the king's servants might be killed, too, so that in the Egyptian heaven they could be ready to work for him there as they had done on earth. When the people realized that this was a cruel thing to do, they made little figures of workers in clay, and these "Answerers," as they were called, were put inside the coffin. It was believed that when the great king was called upon to do some kind of work in heaven—the "Field of Bulrushes"—the Answerers would do it for him. It is very possible that in the coffin of Jacob some of these little figures were also placed, so that in Yahweh's heaven he might have his servants to work for him, too.

The full seventy days of Court mourning were accorded him. A great funeral procession escorted him to his burial in the grave of Machpelah.

Before he died, Joseph was so certain that Yahweh would see His people to the Promised Land that he made his family promise to bury him in his beloved Shechem, in Canaan. This was not done until many years later (see Joshua 24: 32), when his sarcophagus was borne to its final resting place.

47

8

Moses in Egypt

(EXOD. 1-2:22; 3:1-18; 4:1-17; 5:1-18; 6:2-8; 7:14-25; 8; 9:1-12, 22-35; 10:12-29; 12:1-14, 21-36)

The Hebrews had multiplied in Goshen and the new Pharaoh feared their numbers and potential power. He reduced them to slavery, as brickmakers; and, according to Exodus 1:15-22, he also ordered that all Hebrew boy babies should be put to death.

BOYHOOD OF MOSES

But among those who were rescued from that fate which the Pharaoh had decreed was one who was to play a great part in history. A Hebrew mother named Jochebed took her baby and put him in a little ark made of bulrushes daubed with pitch, and hid him among the reeds at the bank of the Nile. The daughter of Pharaoh came to the river to bathe, saw the ark and the baby, and took him home and named him Moses. According to some scholars, the Princess may have been Hatshepsut, daughter of Rameses II, believed to be the Pharaoh of the

Oppression. As a Queen, years later, she sent out her ships on a wonderful voyage of discovery beyond that part of Africa we now know as Somaliland, and had the story told in pictures on the walls of a temple she built to the god Amen. One of the gigantic obelisks she had reared at Karnak still stands.

Moses was an Egyptian name, similar to that of the Pharaohs Ahmose and Thutmose. Growing up in the Court as an Egyptian prince, in luxury and splendor, he would play with movable toys— as of a baker rolling his pastry on a board —and animals and ninepins. When he was ill the doctor would say, "He isn't ill, he is bewitched. You must take a beetle, cut off its head and wings and boil the body in oil. Now cook the head and wings, put them in snake fat, boil, and see that he drinks this mixture." Probably Moses got better before he took his medicine!

C L E O P A T R A

This is a cartouche—a name in hieroglyphics, with its English equivalent. Discovery of the Rosetta Stone (Part II) helped scholars to decipher these names and the Egyptian writing.

HIS EDUCATION

We are told in Acts 7:22 that Moses was instructed in all the wisdom of the Egyptians. This meant that at four years of age he would go to school—a "writer in the house of books." He learned to read and write the wise sayings of the great men, and was flogged daily to encourage him to learn quickly! There was little arithmetic—mainly simple adding and subtracting—although Moses must have heard about Ahmes, an Egyptian priest who wrote on a papyrus roll enough to tell us that he could do algebra and geometry as well.

When Moses had to write he used pictures and signs done with his pen dipped in charcoal and gum. He drew an eagle for an "a" and an owl for an "m," and when one examines a page of Egyptian writing he will see that it is a long series of pictures of birds and animals and people. These are hieroglyphics. As learning progressed, only parts of the pictures were drawn to represent the letter or sound, to save time. When he wrote on clay, Moses used a sharp-pointed reed and jabbed it into the soft clay, which was left to bake hard in the sun. These tablets were often cushion-shaped, about three inches by four and a half inches; some were in the shape of a cone. Pharaohs often covered their palace walls, statues and temples and obelisks with picture stories of their deeds, which is how we have been able to find out so much about them.

When he was older, Moses was sent to another school, where he was taught more advanced mathematics and philosophy, all about the stars, and also about the arts which the magicians of Egypt practiced.

SOME THINGS HE SAW

He learned to be a courtier, of course, and to speak the language of the country and follow its customs. His mother told him all about his own people and their worship of Yahweh as the one true God, and he always had that at the back of his mind. He would watch the feluccas on the Nile and the slave-driven galleys as they pulled up river or down to the open sea. He must have gone to the temples of Ptah at Memphis, Amen at Thebes, Ra and Osiris, and even joined in the worship. He went hunting lions, fishing and fowling for wild duck on the marshes —with a cat (of all animals!) to retrieve the birds knocked down with throw-sticks not unlike boomerangs.

His Egyptian dress would be royal and splendid, and he would wear exquisite jewels and ornaments. Because of the great heat, his shoulders were usually brown and bare to the sun, perhaps protected by a colored silk cloak. On his journeys he saw miles and miles of crops —wheat, maize, vetch, irrigated by the life-giving Nile waters, tended by Hebrew and Egyptian slaves. Here and there were small groups of naked slaves toiling at the shaduf, a device for bringing up water

Oxen are turning a very large screw and the water runs into channels between the crops.

for the camels and for watering furrows not reached by the canals; the leather bucket swung to and fro glistening in the sun, balanced at the other end of the pole by a hard-baked clay weight.

MOSES GROWS UP

For part of his education Moses was sent to the priests, perhaps to Thebes or Heliopolis (the On of Joseph), only eighteen miles distant. The priests had shaven heads and often wore a panther skin across their shoulder over their white robe. There Moses studied the records of earlier Pharaohs in the libraries of clay tablets. Near Thebes was the Valley of Kings, in whose rock tombs were carvings

and paintings of each king's welcome from the gods, together with dreadful pictures of tortures, representing the king's long journey to the Abode of the Blessed. Other pictures showed scenes of his life, the work and play that he once enjoyed. Moses wondered at the Sphinx, as Joseph had done. What stories could it tell, as it reared seventy feet into the sky and stretched its lion's body to a length of two hundred feet? Who carved it from the desert rock? Who built it with solid blocks of stone? Why were there rows of these smaller ram- or jackal-headed sphinxes leading to the pyramids soaring five hundred feet into the hot skies? Then he would see away in the distance an enormous statue of Rameses being drawn by sheer slave force over the burning sand to be placed in some chosen spot in honor of the king. His heart would burn with anger as the cries of the slaves—his people—came through the clear air toward him and as he shaded his eyes against the glare of the sun he could make out their sufferings as they cracked under the strain.

Hittite soldier with helmet and weapons.

On his way back to the temple he would pass through the bazaars and watch traders from Palestine bartering spices and balm and goods of all kinds. Moses was probably a soldier too, a leader of some Egyptian campaign, for he was mighty in "words and deeds." He was familiar with the leather-clad spearmen and the lighter clad bowmen who accompanied his chariot; or he may have had a company of Sardinians as his own guard, wearing armor and carrying two-edged swords. His chariot was light and difficult to control as the two horses pulling it

strained in their fierce speed. He tied the reins around his waist to leave his hands free for fighting. Perhaps at Kadesh in north Syria, when later he fought against the Hittites, he gained fighting experience that served him in good stead when he became the leader of the Israelites.

Toward the end of his reign Rameses, with his favorite wife Queen Nefertari, moved to Tanis on the Nile delta, twenty miles from the sea. Here Moses saw merchant ships trading with East Africa and other countries; these ships were built in Syria. Tanis was then called Pi-Rameses, House of Rameses, and by the Egyptians themselves, Sekhet Tcha—"the place of foreigners," the foreigners being the Israelites. The Bible calls it the "field of Zoan." The Israelites, of course, built the city, and this is recorded on the stele of Rameses found at Bethshan; they built it on the site of the old Hyksos city of Avaris.

Bricks were made from clay mixed with chopped straw, which was put into molds and left to bake in the sun. Egyptian pictures show the slaves working under the lashes of their taskmasters, both making bricks and hauling their heavy burdens for the construction of temples, palaces, and pyramids.

MOSES LEAVES EGYPT

When Moses fled from Egypt in fear that his killing of the taskmaster would be discovered, he knew he would be stopped at the fortifications on the east leading to the Wilderness of Shur. So he skirted the coast of the Red Sea in the foothills of the range running parallel to it, possibly following the track of the miners working the turquoise mines at Serabit, where Queen Hatshepsut had built a temple for the miners to worship in their own way—with burnt offerings, stone altars, and monoliths. Part of the land, even if not Midian itself—and there is some doubt as to that—was inhabited by the Midianites. Jethro, a "shepherd-priest of Midian," was an educated man, and appreciated Moses as an equal; he was able to give much advice and guidance to Moses, whose trust in Yahweh he strengthened and encouraged.

It was while tending Jethro's flocks that Moses was given his orders by God during his strange adventure of the "burning bush." All sorts of explanations have been given for this experience. Perhaps the nearest is the one given by Louis Golding in his book, *In the Steps of Moses, the Law-Giver* (Rich & Cowan). He tells how, near Sinai, he saw a pillar of air and sand whirled into the sky over an acacia tree which "went up in flame" so that "every thorn was a spit of fire" as the sun suddenly came from a bank of cloud and lit it with its gleams. It really seemed that "the bush burned in the fire and was not consumed." Then the cyclone hurtled along one of the wadis and the tree was left lonely once more. This was indeed a wonderful sight, a miraculous sign of God and Moses turned aside to get a closer view of it. Then he heard the voice of God.

He was so awed that he even forgot the normal sign of respect in the East—to remove his sandals. Then he received his orders. God had a purpose—to bring His people to the Promised Land—and Moses felt he was called to carry it out; that is why, very much against his will, he returned to Egypt.

The actual Mount Horeb is unknown; some say it is Sinai, some Jebel Musa; others place it in the mountains north of the Gulf of Akabah. The pictures show the traditional bush—or at least a grafting from it—at the Greek monastery built there, and also the grim grandeur of Sinai.

MOSES RETURNS TO EGYPT

Moses found a new Pharaoh on the throne. This may have been Merenptah or Amenhotep II or even Rameses II—according to the dates accepted for this difficult period. Whoever he was, the ruling king made it clear to Moses that he was not prepared to let the Israelites go "three days' journey into the wilderness" which might have been understood as meaning to Serabit, on a kind of pilgrimage. His answer was to oppress the people even worse than before; they would now have to find their own crushed straw from the stubble and threshing-floor of the previous year's harvesting, and still make the same number of bricks as before. And the penalty for failure? Not merely lashings and whippings, but, it is believed, as many children as there were bricks lacking were taken from their parents and put into the walls. Excavations have revealed the skeletons of children, in long clay jars, each pathetically containing food for the last long journey.

A great black granite slab was discovered at Thebes in 1896. It is the stele of Merenptah, on which the hieroglyphics tell of the desolation and destruction of Israel.

9

The Exodus

(EXOD. 6:2-8; 7:14-25; 8; 9:1-12, 22-35; 10:12-29; 13:17-22; 14; 15:22-16:27; 17; 18; 19:1, 2; 20:1-17; 25:1-22; 32:1-4, 15-24; 33; 34. NUM. 11; 13:16-14:9; 20:1-21. DEUT. 34:1-9)

WHEN DID IT HAPPEN?

The account of the Exodus (going out) as we now have it may not have been written down until about 850 B.C., some five to six hundred years after it took place. This means that the stories are traditional, having been handed down by word of mouth for many generations, and as has happened with so many similar stories, they now vary in details, and have been expanded in the long telling. There are several differences of opinion among scholars over the date and route of the Exodus. Briefly, the alternative dates are three:

(a) At the time the Hyksos kings were being defeated and forced to leave Egypt, in 1580 B.C.; this would have given the Israelites a good chance to leave without interference.

(b) At the same time as the invasion of Canaan by the Habiru (Hebrews) about 1380 B.C., two hundred years later than (a).

(c) Shortly before the entry into Palestine of the Philistines, known to be about 1300 B.C., eighty years later still.

Of these, the third is the date most generally accepted. The full reasons are too difficult to go into in detail, but there are some good ones that we can understand:

1. Archaeological evidence—what men have found in their excavations.
2. In Exodus 13:17, the Philistines are mentioned (see [c]).
3. In the Joshua account iron is mentioned; we know that the Hittites brought iron into Egypt in the first half of the thirteenth century, if not before.

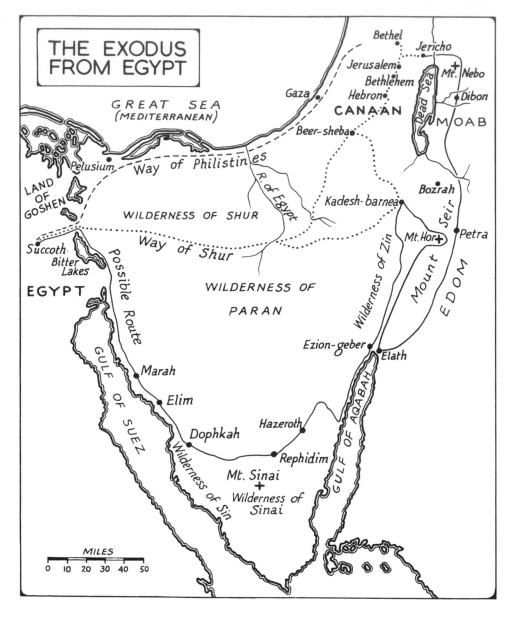

Three possible routes; the traditional Bible route is shown by the unbroken line.

4. A huge stone pillar has been found at Thebes, with written "proof." This is the stele of Merenptah. What seems to have happened is that not all the Israelites went into Egypt with Jacob, and those staying in Palestine near Hebron would have their own traditions and stories which would be interwoven with those of the Israelites of the Exodus. Merenptah was a Pharaoh who lived from 1225 to 1198 B.C., following Rameses II, who was called the "Pharaoh of the Oppression" and had died at the age of ninety, having lost nearly all his conquests. Merenptah invaded Palestine, and recorded on his stele some of his victories, including the words "Israel is desolate, her seed is not."

We have to admit, too, that other scholars prefer an "early" date for the Exodus, making Amenhotep II the Pharaoh of the Oppression; others, again, say that the Pharaoh of the Oppression was Seti and the Pharaoh of the Exodus was Rameses II. These arguments give rise to interesting books worth looking up in a library.

WHAT WAS THE ROUTE?

Here, too, there is much uncertainty. Refer to the map as you read the next few paragraphs. Moses probably led the people to Sinai or Kadesh in his anxiety to get away from the pursuing Egyptians and also to ensure food and water supplies. Probably he avoided Sinai itself (or Jebel Musa) for there were Egyptians working turquoise mines there; it would have been difficult, too, for many people to have lived in such bleak and unfriendly surroundings. But some scholars say that the number of Egyptians (and soldiers, for that matter) near the mines—worked for the most part by friendly Midianites —would be very small and the Pharaoh could ill spare more. Others say Sinai was a volcano; if so, it is more likely to have been, not where tradition places it, but among the mountains of Edom, perhaps near Petra.

By which route, then, did the Israelites travel? The most obvious way was due east, crossing the lakes at low water; this is a route followed by traders even today. Or, they could have gone by a way farther north, along the sea coast toward Gaza. Few of the places mentioned in the Bible story are known today, which adds to the difficulties. Again, many different traditions seem to have been interwoven, with the main one leading to the Covenant at Sinai—for the Covenant was the most important thing that ever happened to these people.

WHAT WAS THE COVENANT?

Let us try to get a clear idea of what the Covenant meant to them. Boys often make themselves "blood brothers" by rituals of their own which make them very special friends ready to stand up for one another in all sorts of trouble—they are united as "one." "Blood bonds" are not unknown in some native tribes, especially in parts of Africa.

Genesis 15 records one between Abraham and Yahweh. An animal was killed and its body laid on the ground with a gap between head and tail. Abraham then walked between them, Yahweh being represented by a fire. The two, having walked together in the body of the sacrifice, were in this way bound as "one." In the Exodus story the same idea is present. Yahweh is represented by the altars and the people by their leaders. The blood of the animals is collected; some of it is then thrown over the altars, and after their acceptance of Yahweh's laws, some of it is thrown over the leaders. Yahweh and Israel are in this way "made one" (see Lev. 19:2; Deut. 6:4 ff). In all these agreements, or covenants, the life-blood is the important part of the ritual.

The Laws of Moses have been studied closely and compared with the Laws of Hammurabi. Many of these early laws were quite well known in neighboring countries centuries before Moses, and indeed after, so it is not surprising to find that the laws Moses gave to his people were for the most part very much like those of Hammurabi. We know, too, from the Tell-el-Amarna and Ras Shamra Tablets, that the Hebrews knew the art of writing in their own script at this time.

HOW MANY WENT ON THE JOURNEY?

One other question in connection with the Exodus is often asked. Just how many people did travel from Egypt to the Promised Land? The Bible figures indicate about two million, which would have meant a caravan some six hundred miles long! This seems incredible. Some scholars say that the translation from the Hebrew is wrong, and that the six hundred thousands of men mentioned should read six hundred families—which would give about five or six thousand people. Goshen, where they lived, would have held about that number, even if they had all gone, and the number was apparently too small for Egypt to have bothered to mention in her records.

Whatever the details, known and unknown, it is the story of escape "from the house of bondage" under Moses that appeals to us; and this great deliverer brought to the Israelites such a close understanding of Yahweh through his trust and the great Covenant that they knew He was their God, and they were His chosen people through all the centuries that were to follow.

The Journey

LET MY PEOPLE GO!

Moses' pleas for his people's freedom to worship Yahweh fell upon deaf ears, and Pharaoh's heart was hardened more and more against them. He flatly refused, despite the succession of disasters (plagues) that befell the Egyptians, which the writer regarded as miraculous, and so described them.

But the sequence of the *plagues* may well have arisen from quite natural causes; in fact, as the waters of the Nile failed, such events were almost expected—which may have helped to strengthen the king's stubbornness. The writer certainly reveals a close knowledge of the Nile, with its dark-red, undrinkable and evil-smelling water, its thousands of frogs, and its armies of flies and mosquitoes that infected cattle and flocks with disease; children and animals suffered from boils covering their bodies from head to foot —a common occurrence; heavy hailstorms destroyed crops. Millions of locusts (grasshoppers) shut out the sun and deafened the ears with their rustling wings; they devoured every leaf and blade and lay ankle deep over the waste land, rotting. And we must imagine the result of the blinding khamsin or sandstorm which lasted often for two or three whole days in a darkness that could be felt. Lastly came some kind of dreadful epidemic—a kind of "Black Death," of which we read in earlier English history. It was the succession of disasters, crowned by this last, that eventually forced Pharaoh to change his mind, and let the people go.

THE PASSOVER

For nine months they had waited, and

to the Israelites their last night in slavery was forever memorable. Their *Passover* Feast celebrates it. The festival itself was, in fact, older than the Exodus. It was the Spring Festival of the nomads, when firstborn lambs were sacrificed to win the favor of their gods. The blood of the lamb was sprinkled on the entrance to the tent to prevent pestilence and evil spirits from entering. But this feast was transformed into something more real to the Israelites by their wonderful release from bondage. (Christ's Passover made it a Feast of Redemption for everybody.)

Passover was a meal of roast lamb, unleavened bread (yeast was supposed to putrefy the bread and was not therefore suitable for sacrifice) and herbs. Moses had ordered the people to be ready to leave, dressed for the journey. So they waited with their loins girded, their robes tucked into the waist to prevent hindrance of free movement, and ate their meal standing up! Usually, these Israelites sat cross-legged and dipped into a common bowl and ate with the fingers. But they were in such a hurry that, when the final order to leave came at midnight, they had to carry some of the uncooked bread in the kneading troughs. It is not surprising that for years afterward they would remember this, their last meal in Egypt, and talk about it to their children and children's children.

THE JOURNEY BEGINS

In this exciting atmosphere of tense waiting and hurried departure, then, the *Exodus* began. Moses led his people by the same route he had already traced. He would wish to avoid caravan routes such as that across the Shur and Way of the Philistines (see map). He walked ahead, as had Abraham years before, bearing his staff of leadership; this was most likely of almond wood (Num. 17:1–10).

Obviously, the Egyptians were glad to see them go, after such a succession of happenings so clearly linked with the demands of Moses; they loaded their slaves with jewels, ornaments and clothes. And true to their promise, the Israelites took with them the embalmed body of Joseph in its heavy coffin, for they had said they would bury his bones in the Land of Promise. So, the realization that they were free at last slowly dawned upon them, and the knowledge that the God of Moses was with them became clear.

CROSSING THE REED SEA

They reached one of the lakes connected by shallow rivers to the Red Sea, the head of which was probably farther north than it is today. The lake was the Reed Sea or Sea of Reeds, and should not be confused with the Red Sea marked on most maps. The actual crossing place is unknown; possibly it was the southern end of Bitter Lake, which lies to the north of the Gulf of Suez. The chain of lakes then existing is today followed by the Suez Canal. Note that the east wind in Exodus 14:21 is from the southeast, which would drive the waters northwest to provide a ford shallow enough to cross. The pursuing Egyptian chariots became stuck in the mud and the returning waters flooded them; but Pharaoh was not drowned, as is generally believed.

The excited joy at their deliverance was celebrated for the Israelites by Moses and Miriam his sister in a song of rejoicing (read Exod. 15:1–19). This is a fine example of Hebrew poetry, and though written down many centuries later contains fragments of the original song.

THE PEOPLE GRUMBLE

Once across the Reed Sea, however, with their pursuers destroyed, the Israelites—although they did not know it—were to experience great hardships: miles of desert, lack of water, shortage of food,

Tamarisk (tarfa) trees by the water's edge; these provided manna.

unfriendly tribes, exhausting heat, intense cold. In following their journeyings we must not forget the background and up-bringing of their deliverer. Moses was an intelligent, educated, experienced leader. It was well that he possessed qualities of understanding and command, for guiding and handling these people was no easy task. The Israelites, too, in their idol worship learned in Egypt, had lost touch with Yahweh, and Moses longed to bring them back to Him. Needless to say, when disaster and danger overtook them, they put all the blame on Moses. On one occasion, after leaving the oasis Elim and moving into the desert, their food ran out. Immediately they called upon Moses to attend to their needs, complaining bitterly that it was his fault. Patiently, he led them to supplies of manna and quails. Manna was a sticky, honey-like juice, which caked into a white-scaled sugary substance, from the secretions of insects on tarfa or tamarisk trees; boiled and strained, it was eaten with unleavened bread; the ration of one omer was about three quarts. Quails, somewhat like partridges, came on the prevailing winds in flocks and were easily caught as they fell exhausted. Even today, thousands migrate across Sinai, and Egyptians catch them in nets.

The Israelites trekked on to Rephidim, which is unknown today; it was here that their waterskins were empty. Once more they cried to Moses, and once more he gave them the necessary supplies. The rock he struck was porous limestone, which is capable of retaining water; when the rock is struck a hard blow the water gushes out.

The rock-strewn, burning sand of the wilderness must have seemed interminable; even when it was arrayed in brilliant short-lived spring wild flowers the Israelites found little joy; but oases and shaded wadis and taller trees brought them rest and shade and water. Near Sinai was a valley wide enough for an encampment, but the ranges of granite hills seem such an inhospitable district that some scholars think it unlikely that this was in the south of the plain. It might rather have been in Edom, volcanic and awesome to the Israelites. Kadesh is not accurately identified, either; it has been placed at Petra in Edom, "rose-red city, half as old as time." The fact that farther north there are many tarfa trees, which might have provided manna in abundance even in those days, suggests that it ought to be farther north of the point usually shown on the map. It was certainly an oasis of some size, probably between the Wilderness of Shur, Paran and Sin, lying to the north of these. It was already occupied by the Amalekites, and the only way to obtain possession of it was to fight. Joshua's victory established him as a military leader, although the people placed the greater faith in Moses, as is seen from the account of the fighting.

MOSES THE "JUDGE"

While he was here, Moses was able to put into practice the good advice given him by Jethro, that he should entrust some of the lesser duties and responsibilities to other men and look after the more important things himself. Note the acceptance by Moses of this idea, and how it points to his being a person possessing great humility and common sense.

This gave him time to organize men to spy out the Promised Land. Before he could lead his people much farther he must know how far he was from his goal and what kind of place it would be for them to enter. How promising was it? What dangers would they find? What kind of enemies lay in wait for them? Could they be overcome? The spies brought grapes from Eshcol, a wadi near Hebron. Their news that Canaan was a land "flowing with milk and honey" indicated that it was fertile, being well watered, with natural tree growth, a place ideal for habitation, a flourishing land in which it would be a joy to live after their many years of wandering.

But they were to wait years longer before they reached nearer than the borders of the Land of Promise. Many things were yet to happen.

THE LAWS

At some time in their wanderings, Moses left his people to climb into the mountain to talk with his God. There, the story tells us, he was inspired to

Jebel Musa, the traditional Mount Sinai —rugged, forbidding. There is a monastery there today, where the famous manuscript Codex Sinaiticus was found.

understand God's laws. They were probably on small tablets, certainly small enough to be carried. They bore laws reminiscent of those learned by Moses in his Egyptian schools; they are similar in content to the precepts found in the Book of the Dead, and are much like the Laws of Hammurabi, written many years even before Moses. The main difference—and a most important one—is that the laws which Moses brought down from the mountain were religious, linked with the worship of Yahweh and acknowledgment of His care—and even love—for His people.

Tired of waiting, and quick as ever to put the blame on Moses for his delay, the people went to the leaders and demanded

some kind of idol to represent the Yahweh they found so difficult to picture. Aaron was the priest, and he must do something about it; perhaps even he was afraid Moses had gone for all time; Joshua was

The Tabernacle, a portable sanctuary or tent of meeting during the wanderings in the wilderness.

with Moses. So it was that Aaron made the golden calf—the common form of a bull idol familiar to the Israelites. Moses, of course, was furious—and surely bitterly disappointed—that in his absence the people could so easily and so quickly forget his words. How his patience was tried! Note, too, Aaron's feeble excuse, that he had put the earrings into the furnace, and that then "there came out this calf!"—quite overlooking his own share in the whole affair.

WHAT WAS THE TABERNACLE?

But Moses had something else for the people. Now that he had them, Yahweh's laws must be housed, and there must be a place where God Himself might dwell, so that the Israelites could never say He had left them so long as they had His dwelling-place with them. So they built a Tent of Meeting, a tabernacle or holy place. It was not so elaborate in the wilderness as the writers have made it; the drawing given here will make clear what it probably was. Inside, it was adorned with gold and ornaments, jewels and fine linen, brought by the people from their stores. Others brought sweet-smelling incense and oils. Bezaleel and Aholiab were skilled craftsmen whose skill was attrib-

The view from the ruined Crusader chapel on Mount Nebo as it is today; from here Moses looked for the first and last time over the Jordan Valley to the Promised Land.

uted as gifts from Yahweh (see Exod. 36). Acacia wood was cut from the trees to make the Ark of the Covenant (see Special Note on Exodus at the beginning of this chapter).

The Ark contained the ephod enclosing the Urim and Thummim (yes and no) of the oracle (see Chapter 13) and, later, the Decalogue (Ten Commandments), and was placed in the Holy of Holies. On the altar were placed twelve loaves of bread and golden seven-branched candlesticks surmounted with shoe-shaped bowls of oil with rags for wicks. On their journeyings the people carried the Ark before them, at the head of the caravan; it was attended by priests chosen from the Levites. In this way Yahweh literally went before them, leading them through miles of mountainous country and pitiless desert. The Ark was to play an important part in their history (see I Sam. 4–7; I Kings 8:8).

THE END OF THE JOURNEY

Carrying the Ark before them, they passed through the Valley of Moses on the last stages of their wanderings. There

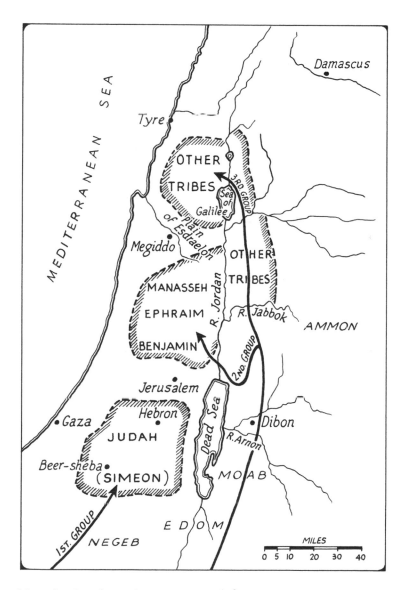

Map showing the main movements of the Israelites as they entered the Promised Land; the arrows show three main lines of advance.

63

is still such a valley of that name, and it is very possible that this is the traditional one of several rocky defiles leading down to the green valleys cultivated by the Bedouin camping there. The Israelites seem to have paused in this region, at Hor, probably some fifty miles north of the Gulf of Akabah on the Mount Seir range in Edom. There, their three great national festivals were probably established—Passover, Pentecost (fifty days after Passover—a week of weeks) celebrating the harvest of corn, and Tabernacles—the Jewish Harvest Festival or Ingathering, during which time they lived for a week in tents of tree branches (booths) on the mountain tops to commemorate their past wanderings. The feasts have all undergone various changes throughout Hebrew history, but their first importance remains.

With the Promised Land in sight, Moses said good-bye to his people from the plain of Moab and climbed Mount Nebo, from whence he could see the land he was not allowed to enter. To the southwest were the plains of the Dead Sea; due west lay Jericho; northward, the winding Jordan fed by its mountain streams. We do not know Moses' burial place, although, again, there is a traditional site. But Moses is known to us as one of the greatest men in history— reformer, founder of a nation, lawgiver, man of God.

1O

Joshua

(NUM. 13:17-33; 14:1-4; 21:21-26; 22; 23; 24. JUD. 1:17, 18, 27-36. JOS. 1:1-9; 2; 3:1, 14-17; 5:10a-6:27; 7:2-12, 19-26; 8:1-29; 24:2-25. PS. CIV. 10-35. SONG OF SOL. 2:8-17)

SETTLING IN CANAAN

After the death of Moses the people tended to break into groups. Some felt they would settle more easily apart from the main tribes, others were perhaps more selfish and anxious to grasp what land they could; some were attracted by the land they saw and felt they had traveled far and long enough. So we find the tribes of Simeon and Judah moving northwest through the Negeb in south Palestine, to settle near Hebron, a fortified city in the foothills. Others continued along the east of the Jordan and forded it at points north of the Dead Sea and north of Galilee. By this time, the occupants of the kingdom had begun to realize that the movements — infiltrations — of the Israelites were significant and dangerous, and began to prepare resistance. The Amorites in Moab, themselves an invading army, fought under King Sihon; the Israelites won, defeated the King of Bashan, too,

and continued their own invasion of Canaan, the Land of Promise.

Canaan differed greatly from what it had been in Abraham's time. Other nations and peoples in the intervening centuries had invaded and settled. Encampments had given place to villages and towns, and walled towns to fortified cities. War was frequent and fierce. Babylonia and Assyria were already aware of the need to possess Palestine as their land bridge to Egypt, who herself commanded much of the country. A powerful new race from Crete had settled along the seaboard in cities like Gaza and Askelon. These were the Pulasati or Philistines, sea rovers who had been driven by Rameses II from the Nile delta and allowed to settle along the Mediterranean. They wore armor and carried small round shields and heavy broadswords, while their feathered headdress was similar to that worn by the American Indians of another day. They were too powerful for

65

the Israelites for many years, and eventually gave their name to the country; in this way Canaan became Palestine—the land of the Philistines.

The Canaanites themselves were idol worshipers, and where the Israelites could not capture, but merely infiltrated, settled and even intermarried, they accepted the idol worship. The result was to undermine their allegiance to the one God, Yahweh.

WHO WERE THE CANAANITES?

What did they find, then, as their invasion continued? (see Ps. 104; Song of Sol. 2:8–17). This was indeed a land of milk and honey, to them. There was sufficient rainfall to guarantee water supplies for the year; pasturage for sheep and cattle was plentiful. This meant a new mode of life—staying in one place

Terraced hillsides, the same today as the Israelites saw when they entered Canaan; terracing makes cultivation easier and prevents the washing and blowing away of good top soil.

and growing their own food—agriculture. The Canaanites grew wheat, barley, fruits, and had vineyards on the hillsides; olive orchards produced the precious oil used in cooking, burning, and washing. There were all kinds of trees for building purposes, for making tools and simple plows. There were houses, too, mud huts with flat roofs, walled towns—each under the rule of a king (see Joshua 10:1–3). The Israelites found Baal worship—superstition and belief in corn gods; the Baalim were given special open-air altars and shrines or groves, usually on the tops of hills—the "high places." Human sacrifice was still practiced and there were cruel customs.

We must remember, however, that the Canaanites had much to teach their invaders, about trade as well as about agriculture. They were craftsmen, traders, and merchants; they traded in perfumes and spices to Egypt for gold and silver ornaments, pottery and scarabs. Their caravans are shown on Egyptian walls, the Canaanites in gay jackets, carrying metal weapons and musical instruments; asses carried their merchandise. They corresponded with Babylonia on sun-baked cuneiform-written tablets, nearly three hundred of which were found in 1887 at Tell-el-Amarna.

THE CLIMATE

The climate, too, had an important bearing on the life and occupations of the people as they settled to their new existence of farming and agricultural ways. In Genesis 8:22, we find there are six seasons—seedtime, harvest, cold, heat, summer fruits, bare season.

Seedtime is from mid-February to April, for spring and early summer sowing; at this time, what the Bible calls grass—all wild growth including brilliantly colored wild flowers—springs up everywhere.

Harvest lasts from May to June.

Philistines, with round shields, sword and headdress.

Summer fruits ripen during mid-June, July, and August.

Heat, during September and October, is due to the hot, fierce, and scorching sirocco, which brings drought as it blows from the Arabian Desert.

Bare season, November to the end of December, is the time that the crops are in and everywhere the land is bare of grass and leaf, and the ground is waiting for the plow.

Cold, intense and bitter, is experienced during the two months of January and February—which completes the cycle of the year.

Rain is most important in any country. In Canaan, from May to October, there was no rain at all, and the ground was baked hard. Then came the "former rains," after which plowing could be done in November and December. The "latter rains" fell in the "first month" of the Jewish year—in our March and April. The Israelites had to learn from bitter experience the hardships of this climate, with probably little help from their neighbors; and they had to do it while establishing themselves firmly in the land they were occupying, and defending what they had taken despite the onslaughts of the enemy from all sides.

BEGINNING THE CONQUEST

You may wonder how this was made possible. We have to remember that the ruling power at this time was Egypt, but when her armies were absent—as they were more and more frequently as her strength waned—the Canaanites fought among themselves for power, one king against another. This internal squabbling gave Joshua and the tribes their chance to gain control of certain chosen parts of the country. Nor was this control complete for many years, for it was difficult to dislodge the Canaanites from the fertile valleys, and the tribes themselves were separated from one another by Canaanite cities or mountain ranges.

Some tribes stayed in fertile Gilead, and those crossing the Jordan were separated by the Plain of Esdraelon. This made a three-pronged drive, and conquests were slow. The Book of Joshua gives the account of these victories as though they were due to an all-out united dramatic conquest; the Book of Judges, however, is the more likely account, as it tells of a gradual control, tribe by tribe; for they were a long time learning to unite into a conquering nation under one leader.

The famous Tell-el-Amarna letters just referred to tell of the movements of the invaders of Palestine at this time. They include letters between the Pharaohs of Egypt and Egyptian officials in Palestine, and contain complaints that the Habiri or Hebrews were occupying the king's cities; they reveal also the slower methods of conquest — treachery, nomadic settling, and the eventual withdrawing altogether of Egyptian armies. There was probably a line of strong towns to be overcome, too, and all these are mentioned in the account of the fighting. If these are marked on a map and joined, it can be seen what districts they protected: Gath, Lachish, Bethshemesh, Socoh, Azekah, Hebron; Gerar, Bethpelet, Beersheba; Dor, Taanach; Megiddo, Bethshan, Gezer, Jerusalem, Jericho. Some of these were not captured until many years later, for example, Jerusalem by David and Gezer by Egypt as a present for Solomon.

One of the strongholds captured by Joshua was Lachish; this was probably a chariot city or "posting station," and excavations even now going on there have revealed it as a city of much history, dating as far back as 5000 B.C. Ai was destroyed by Joshua in such a way that few traces of it are to be found; Joshua subjected it to what was known during the Second World War as the "scorched earth policy."

PLANNING THE CAPTURE OF JERICHO

Jericho is the city we usually associate with Joshua. It was the "city of palm trees" and a rich trading center commanding the plateau of Ephraim. Joshua knew that he had to bring about the fall of the city in order to control the center of Palestine. A look at the map will show why this was so necessary. Before he attacked the city Joshua sent ahead two spies, who hid under the stalks of drying flax on the flat roof top of a house belonging to a woman named Rahab. Flax is the plant from which linen is made, and we know that for thousands of years before Christ this was a cloth much prized in Bible lands. Rahab's father might, therefore, have been a weaver or a dyer; the cord which let down the spies from the housetop was colored red, however, which might indicate that he was a dyer rather than a weaver. He was hardly likely to have been both, since in those days people kept to their separate trades and passed on their skills from father to son. The red dye, which must have been used to color the cord, was probably made from a tiny insect that lived in oak trees.

"ON DRY LAND"

At the time Joshua marched down the

Jordan plain toward Jericho it was April, and the weather was hot and rainless. The river Jordan was a torrent since it had been fed by the melting snows of Mount Hermon; the name Jordan means "the descender" or "the rushing river." The problem facing the Israelites now was how to cross the river, for Jericho was on the other side. They had reached the bottom of the gorge, where it was unbearably hot and damp and infested with lions—in the Pride of the Jordan jungle. They looked for a shallow ford. If you examine the pictures of the Jordan you will get a better idea of what they faced and what they found, for parts of the Jordan are indeed calmer and shallower than some views of it might suggest. The twelve stones that were set up at Gilgal to signify that "Israel came over Jordan on dry land" are a sign that Yahweh in some miraculous way had helped the Israelites in their difficulty just as He had done so many years before when they had crossed

Sand and hills—desert wilderness.

69

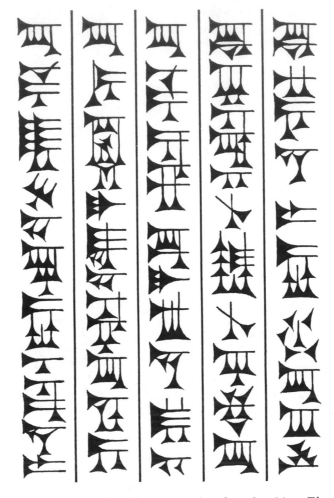

Cuneiform or wedge-shaped writing. The Tell-el-Amarna tablets were written in this form; this example is a copy of part of Sennacherib's record of the Siege of Jerusalem.

the Reed Sea at the beginning of their long, long journey. What may actually have happened is that some kind of landslide had dammed the river to the north of Joshua's men, since such an event is known to have happened in 1267 and again in 1927; at the same time the river had drained away to the Dead Sea in the south. The effect of such an event in both the years mentioned was to leave a shallow ford across the river over which an army might have marched.

JERICHO FALLS

With the Ark at their head, Joshua's men moved toward Jericho, carrying swords, shields, bows and arrows; the priests bore aloft their rams' horns, which they blew with great energy at the given signal to advance. We are told that "the walls fell down flat." Archaeological excavations have shown that the walls certainly fell down, some say because of an earthquake. The lower part collapsed under the upper sections as though the walls had, in fact, fallen under themselves. These massive walls were arranged so that an outer one of six-foot thickness circled an inner one of twelve-foot thickness; the outer one, being on the debris at the edge of the slope, was not sufficient to support the houses built on it. There is also some belief that branches and tree trunks were secretly placed between the walls and set alight at the signal; this would certainly have caused collapse of the walls and fire in the city.

Joshua "devoted" the city to Yahweh, that is, he offered his first conquest as he might have given his firstborn, to Yahweh, complete. The inhabitants were slaughtered, the golden vessels were taken for Yahweh, and the city was burned to the ground; all this was done in the belief that it would please Yahweh and be the first step in fulfilling the Covenant. The Israelites were slow to realize that God did not need sacrifices of that kind.

Joshua then marched toward Shechem, defeated the Gibeonites at Beth-horon, and secured a strong position in Mount Ephraim. In Shechem, Joseph's body, after its long journey, was at last laid. It says much for the Israelites that, through all their hardships, fears, and troubles, they kept their promise to Joseph. The modern city of Nablus stands today where Shechem once stood.

Note how Joshua repeated the words of Moses and reminded the Israelites of their duty to Yahweh; he urged them to "fear the Lord and worship him in sincerity and in truth . . ." This they promised to do, but, as we shall see in the next chapter, it was not long before they forgot, for the excitements of Canaanite idol worship took hold of them once more.

Gideon, Deborah and Ruth

(JUDGES 2:11-19; 3:5-11; 4; 5; 6:1-6, 11-40; 7; 8:1-27. RUTH)

There are two stories of Gideon, so closely interwoven that they cannot be separated; there are also two accounts of Deborah's exploits, one in verse, the other in prose.

ENEMIES EVERYWHERE

The background of these stories is of the time when the Hebrews were learning the simpler forms of agriculture, tilling the ground and growing their own crops. They had settled for the most part in tent villages in the Ephraim plateau; they produced wine and oil and gradually passed from being members of wandering tribes to becoming peasant farmers. There are three things still to bear in mind—danger from the guerilla tactics of desert tribes, continued united resistance from the Canaanites, and the menace of the Philistines. This last established the national unity of the tribes, under Saul, in an all-out effort to defeat their enemies;

this was finally done under David. Meanwhile, the tribes were controlled and guided and led by various "Judges"—warriors, deliverers, and counselors. Gideon and Deborah were two of these Judges.

For several years Israel had been harassed by the Midianites, descendants of Abraham and Keturah. They had intermarried with the Ishmaelites and spoke a language similar to theirs which was not unlike the tongue of the Israelites themselves. Living mostly on the desert fringes, they wandered wherever they liked and plundered whenever they had the chance. Just as the crops were ready for harvesting, the Midianites swooped down like locusts, even bringing their cattle and flocks and camels to feed on the Israelites' grazing grounds.

In their despair, the Israelites cried to Yahweh, whom they had forgotten so quickly when everything had gone well. An unknown prophet warned them that

A Bedouin, nomadic desert-dweller. Note his strong features and his hair.

they must return to Yahweh, who was displeased at their idol worship. Even Gideon's father worshiped Baal, the farm god, represented by a mazzebah and shrine; there was also the sacred pole Asherah, the goddess of fertility. (The word baal is common in place names; it means "lord of," as Baal-zephon, Lord of Darkness, Baal-hamon, Lord of Riches.)

Gideon was one of those who realized how right the unknown prophet was; he thought a great deal about it as he tried to thresh his grain in secret, away from the Midianites. He dared not go to a high place to let the wind get at the chaff, so he went behind the winepress in the vineyard. Threshing and winnowing were normally done on the threshing-floor, a special flat ground high enough for the work to be done without hindrance. The sheaves would be opened and spread out on the floor and be beaten with a flail or kind of heavy sledge, and the straw be gathered on one side; then the grain would be heaped and tossed into the breeze until all the chaff had been winnowed away. But Gideon had to get behind the oblong press, an excavation in which the grapes were trampled on to press out the juice; obviously, this was almost a useless place, but better there than in the open, where he might be attacked and robbed, perhaps killed.

CALLED TO LEAD

While occupied with his work—and his thoughts—Gideon noticed the angel sitting under a turpentine tree in the cool

A wooden plow made from the branch of a tree; such a plow would barely scratch the surface for sowing the corn, but it was sufficient.

74

shade. The answer to his anxieties came with a shock. *He,* Gideon, was to fight the Midianites! His first thoughts were to give food to his visitor and to offer sacrifice to Yahweh. Then he set about his first duty. He had to show the Israelites that Yahweh was on their side if they wanted Him. He took ten men and destroyed his father's gods and shrine and erected a new altar to Yahweh. That was a tremendously brave thing to do. But what a wise father Gideon had. "Let Baal plead for himself," he said—and in saying so he realized how useless his gods were and how right his own son was. The people were quick to see this and rallied to Gideon's call to war. He sounded the war trumpet—a long, narrow tube opening to a bell shape. The echo rang in and around the hills for all to hear. Even Gideon's enemies heard it and prepared for attack.

Gideon felt Yahweh was guiding him as he decided that many of his great army were at heart afraid; he sent them home —two-thirds of them. He still had ten thousand, but gave them yet another test, retaining only those who drank "with one eye on the bushes opposite"—seasoned campaigners. He knew that Yahweh was with him for he had seen the miracle of the fleece.

"FOR GOD AND GIDEON!"

The Midianites had joined forces with the Amalekites and nomads of the eastern districts; they had pitched camp in the Valley of Jezreel at the southern end of Esdraelon. The Israelites prepared themselves on the slopes of Mount Gilboa (not Gilead). The Bible account in Judges 7 is vivid and straightforward. Note that the northern tribes of Asher, Zebulun, Naphtali, and Manasseh united in this warfare—the first signs that the tribes are getting together for a common purpose. Ephraim's chiding is well-timed— they did not like being left out of the invitation to help.

The battle was a triumph of strategy. The effect of the silent approach in the darkness, the sudden blazing of torches as they were drawn from the pitchers, the lamps, the shouting, the trumpets, all these combined to terrify the enemy, whose only route of escape was over Jordan—right into the path of the Ephraimites, who by now had been warned to catch them as they fled. The cruelties at Succoth and Penuel remind us only too well of the brutality of the wilder Bedouin of those days; Gideon's threat seems to have been to drag naked bodies over the thorns and briers in the wilderness scrub.

The Israelites captured a great deal of booty, including moonlike crescent ornaments and trappings on the camels; these were worn to keep away "the evil eye." The earrings were also part of the spoil and weighed seventy pounds. We have been used to thinking of the ephod as a bag containing the oracle, and later we shall see it as the word for a little apron. In this story it is an idol. We find it strange that Gideon should make the Israelites an idol; he meant it to be in honor of Yahweh, of course, for neither he nor the people had become used to the idea of worshiping an invisible god. Israel did not need much encouragement to become idol worshipers once more, especially after a victory had been won in the name of Yahweh; so we are not surprised at the disasters that seemed to follow soon afterward.

A WARRIOR WOMAN

The Song of Deborah indicates some of the beginnings of unity, too, for under Deborah and Barak six or seven tribes fought successfully against the Canaanites under their king, Sisera. The story is given in Judges 4 and 5, in which there is bitter criticism of those tribes who, for all sorts of reasons, failed to join in this great united effort.

The battle was at Megiddo, in the

Plain of Esdraelon. Deborah lured Sisera across the Kishon to Megiddo, and Barak attacked from Mount Tabor, the two forces converging to drive the enemy into the river. A storm caused Kishon to overflow, and, like the Egyptians, the Canaanite chariots stuck in the mud and were helpless. Yahweh was hailed as a mighty god of war. Sisera fled.

The only place for Sisera to hide was in the women's apartment of the tent; for a stranger to enter this was a serious breach of Eastern courtesy and etiquette, and death was the accepted penalty. Jael's murder of Sisera was dictated to some extent by the code that demanded the life of the intruder. She gave him goat's milk made sour by the butter left in it—a potent drink at any time, but to the exhausted Sisera a veritable drug. Part of Jael's work as a woman was to drive in the tent pegs for her tent; it was a relatively small matter for her to drive one into Sisera's temples. This does not excuse her taking a life, but it does explain part of the reason for her killing an enemy. It is sad to contemplate the jibing references to Sisera's mother, but Deborah seems to enjoy her cruelty.

The Song of Deborah is probably the most ancient piece of Scripture we have in the Bible, for although it was made up at the time of the event it seems to have been handed down to the writers, who recorded it almost exactly as it was composed. From 1300 B.C. it was sung by camp fires and recounted over and over again for centuries in all its fierceness and exact detail. It must have been sung with gestures and miming, spitting and shouting, in triumph, scorn, rejoicing; the only plaintive notes in it were those of the lute or guitar of the time, as the player strummed the strings in accompaniment to the singing.

A GENTLE WOMAN

The story of Ruth serves as a great contrast to that of Deborah, and has a place here. At some time during the period of the Judges, probably because the Israelites had not become used to the climate and its effect upon their simple agriculture, there was a shortage of food. The famine was so serious that many people, including Elimelech, left Bethlehem in Judah, crossed the Jordan and settled in Moab among the descendants of Lot. While there, Elimelech and his two sons died, leaving his wife Naomi and her two daughters-in-law, Ruth and Orpah, both Moabitish women.

Some ten years later Naomi decided to return to her home village of Bethlehem and to her husband's property. Orpah stayed with her people, but Ruth wanted to go with Naomi. Read Ruth 1:16, 17, and see how beautiful was her pleading.

Ruth won Naomi by her love and they returned to Bethlehem, where Naomi lost no time in telling her neighbors about Ruth, who had even forsaken her god Chemosh to join the Israelites, accepting Yahweh as her new God. Boaz was a distant relative of Elimelech's, and must have heard about Ruth. Note his greeting, "The Lord be with you." Our "good-bye" means just that—"God be with you." When Ruth went gleaning (see Deut. 24:19) to gather the stalks of grain left by the reapers, he behaved courteously toward her, seeing to it that she had plenty of grain and water to drink, and allowing her to share in the common dish and to soak her food in wine—a special relish. Some of the food was parched grain, obtained from roasting it over a fire. Ruth carried home an ephah, about a bushel, of grain in her veil; this was not a thin face covering as we know it; it was a heavy covering of thick material over head and shoulders, quite two yards in length. She would cover her face with her sleeved arm as Eastern custom demanded.

Ruth gleaned through both barley and wheat harvests, the men working in "the threshing-floor at night" from late afternoon to sunset in the cool sea breeze. Ruth claimed protection from Boaz, who

"found a path
Through the sad heart of Ruth,
    when, sick for home,
She stood in tears amid the alien
    corn."

Naomi decided to sell her property. By Eastern custom the nearest relative had the first right to buy this and marry Ruth. Boaz went to "the gate of the city" to discuss the matter. Before public witnesses the nearer relative waived his claim. To make this transaction valid, he had to take off his sandal and hand it to Boaz, who held it up for all to see (Ruth 4:7). Boaz then bought the property and married Ruth, giving Naomi some fifty shekels of silver—about $25—as dowry.

Ruth had a son called Obed. His son was Jesse, the father of David, who became the greatest king of Israel (see Chapter 15).

The story of Ruth is called an idyll— a story of peaceful, gentle village life in war-ravaged Canaan. Its special message was that God cared so much for everybody, not merely for His own "chosen race," that even David could have a great-grandmother who was not herself an Israelite. The story may have been told many, many times before it was written down, for it may belong to about 1150 B.C., quite seven or eight hundred years before it was recorded in writing. How wise was the writer not to let such a gentle story pass into oblivion.

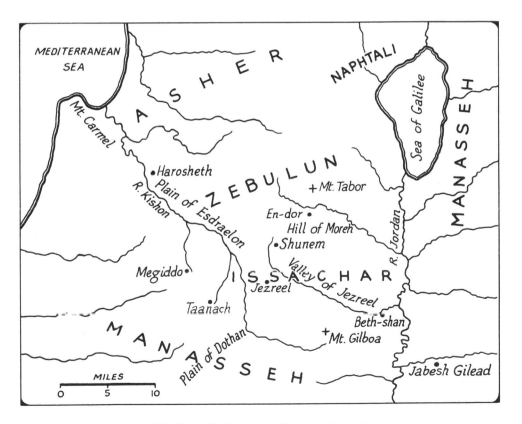

*The battlefields of the Plain of Esdraelon
in the times of the Judges.*

12

Jephthah and Samson

(JUDGES 10:17, 18; 11; 13-16)

Jephthah and Samson were two of Israel's "Judges," whose duty it was to settle disputes, lead battles, and generally serve their people. There were many of these judges, and the exploits of several of them may have been attached to those best known as the stories were told and retold over the camp fires.

A RASH PROMISE

The story of Jephthah usually centers on the rash vow he made and its sad consequences; but we must also consider his work as a leader. The Ammonites were descendants of Lot, and lived on the east of the Jordan between the river Arnon and the brook Jabbok. They now encamped in Gilead opposite the Israelites, whom they had beaten back after crossing the Jordan into Judah. Without a leader, the Israelites were in desperate straits; after some persuasion, Jephthah

agreed to challenge Ammon on their behalf.

Read carefully the vow he made. It seems almost like a bargain, as was Jacob's vow some years before. But vows were common—and binding. Jephthah's daughter, like Miriam, played her timbrel and danced to meet her father on his victorious return—and she danced, unwittingly, to her doom!

It is usually assumed that Jephthah's daughter was put to death. This may not have been true. Moses had forbidden human sacrifice, although it was still common in other tribes, especially among the Canaanites. Bear in mind that in the East a girl who never married was considered disgraced. This is difficult for us to understand, but such shame was very real in those days, and her friends would come to sympathize with her in her sadness and loneliness.

Whatever the ultimate fate of Jephthah's daughter, the story does point to the danger and futility of rash vows and promises. You will have noted, too, that the "local" god of the Ammonites was Chemosh—the god of Ruth before she left Moab to go home with Naomi.

THE "STRONG MAN"

Samson has been called an "Israelitish Robin Hood." He belonged to the tribe of Dan, and was dedicated as a Nazarite to deliver the tribes from the Philistines. A Nazarite abstained from wine and cer-

were in constant fear of them. Most of the stories of Samson are folklore and tell of his personal war against the Philistines, set in the valley of Sorek, where Zorah, Bethshemesh, and Timnah were situated (see map). Sorek was guarded by the fort of Gezer as it leads from the Shephelah district. At Timnah he fought and single-handed killed a lion; a swarm of bees made their nest in the skeleton, and he used this incident as a riddle— riddles were a very popular amusement in those days—"Out of the eater came forth meat. Out of the strong came forth

tain foods, and never used a razor on his face or head (see Num. 6:1–8). Samson's name probably means "sun's man."

The Philistines had established themselves along the Israelite frontier in the cities of Gath, Ekron, Ashdod, Gaza and Askelon; they thus controlled the trade routes and east–west passes; their weapons were of iron, and they obviously had great power over their neighbors, who

The brook Jabbok as it is today. It flows through the land of the Ammonites.

sweetness." For the right answer he wagered thirty linen shirts and thirty changes of raiment; changes of raiment were garments of fine material usually embroidered in brilliant colors.

His Philistine bride-to-be deceived him by giving away the answer, and Samson

All that is left of the ancient walls of Askelon, once a proud city of the Philistines.

killed thirty Philistines in order to provide the garments to settle his bet. Needless to say, the Philistines were furious. In revenge for further deception by his bride's father, Samson set fire to the crops of the district by letting loose pairs of foxes tied tail to tail and carrying brands of fire. Corn, vineyards and even olive orchards suffered. In their anger, the father's neighbors burned down his house, killing its occupants, then set out to capture Samson.

IN SEARCH OF SAMSON

He was even betrayed into their hands by his own people, who feared what might happen to them if Samson continued his exploits. But he escaped and camped in rocky Etam. Once he ventured

to the gates of Gaza and carried away the gates and posts to a hill near Hebron. Next, the Philistines tried to get him through the deceit of yet another of their women, Delilah. We know how well she succeeded; for her betrayal of Samson she received eleven hundred pieces of silver —about $500. Samson's strength really lay in his vow, of which his hair was only the outward sign. When he realized he had been deceived he felt he had betrayed Yahweh. He was carried away by the Philistines, who bored out his eyes—a common enough brutality in those days. At last Samson was in their hands.

Most pictures of Samson at the mill show him striving to move the heavy mill wheel as might an ox. These are probably wrong. The Philistines wanted to insult him as well as punish him, and how better could they do this than by giving such a strong man women's work to do! He had to grind corn at a hand-mill, usually the work of two women, grinding the corn between two heavy stones. In his blindness he was degraded, too.

It was only natural that the Philistines should celebrate their capture of Samson. They worshiped Dagon, a god half man, half fish—probably "dagan," a Hebrew word meaning grain, that is, a god of agriculture. A temple to Dagon has been found at Bethshan, and in such a temple the Philistines held their feast. Samson, whose hair was growing and with it his renewed faith in Yahweh, was made to perform feats of strength to amuse the onlookers. They did not guess that his power had completely returned. As they stood in the portico and on the flat roof, Samson pulled down the wooden pillars supporting the roof, and those inside and out perished in the collapse and confusion.

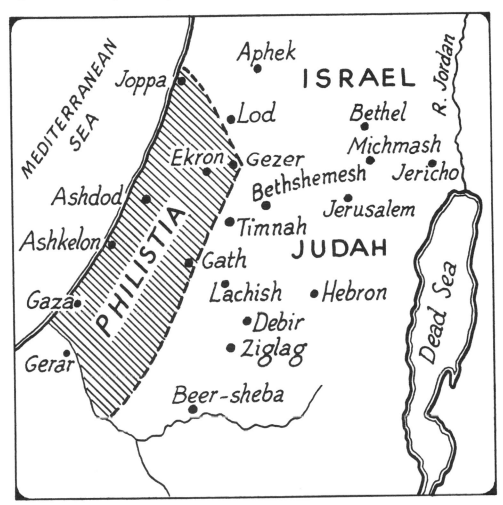

Home of the Philistines and their great cities; other place names occur in the story.

13

Samuel and Saul

(I SAM. 1; 2:11-21; 3; 4:1-18; 5; 6:1-18; 8; 9; 10:1-24; 11; 14:1-46; 15)

SAMUEL'S TASK

There are two stories of Samuel's work, one in which the real hero is Saul and the other in which Samuel is the hero; in one Samuel is only an insignificant prophet, in the other he is judge and ruler of Israel. We shall see that these confusions—for the stories are so interwoven that they cannot always be separated—continue into the stories of Saul and David.

Look again at the map of Palestine. Note once more its smallness—it certainly *seems* small enough to unite. But find the hills stretching from Carmel to Gilboa, the hill country of Jerusalem separating the low-lying Judah from Jordan, then, farther west, the fertile Philistine plains. Canaanites still occupied their strongholds, the Philistines were hostile on the very borders, and the mountains, too, helped divide the land. Much work was to be done by a strong leader before the tribes could really be brought together under a single ruler. Samuel's task was to find that someone.

THE ISRAELITES' HARVEST FESTIVAL

Before he was born, his parents, Elkanah and Hannah, came from their home in Ramah, nine miles north of Jerusalem, to make their annual offering at the Tabernacle in Shiloh. The "house of Yahweh" was probably of mud brick or quarried stone. Eli, a Levite, was High Priest at the sacrifices given during the Feast of the Tabernacles, or, as it was so often called, the Vintage Festival. The Feast of Ingathering is yet another name; it is held in October. The last harvest of the year was the olive harvest. The people depended upon the olive for food and countless other purposes—oil in their lamps, healing oil for animals, for wash-

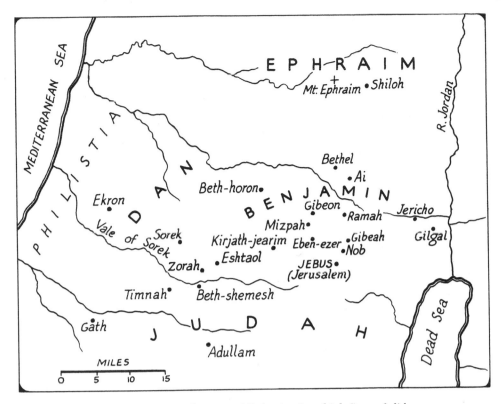

The part of Palestine in which Samuel did most of his work.

ing, and so on; and the cruse of oil was indispensable (see I Kings 17:12; 5:11; II Kings 4:2).

The olive tree has a gnarled trunk and bears silvery-sheened leaves; it grows wild, of course, as well as in the carefully watched orchards. The people wait for the agreed signal of the village elders and then all go out together with beating rods and collecting pots, for the fruit. Women and boys beat the tree and shake the branches, and a good yield is up to fifteen gallons of raw oil from a single tree. The olives are crushed in the press; sometimes the pulp is put into sacks of horsehair and again trodden by women; more often it is poured into reed or wicker baskets, piled up and forced into yet another press. The oil is collected in jars and stored for use during the year.

This festival served partly as a Harvest Festival, and also reminded the Israelites of their wanderings in the wilderness. For a week the people slept in little huts made of boughs and branches of trees, often placed on the flat roof tops—a sea of green huts around the Tabernacle. Even today, Samaritans in Nablus—the old Shechem—keep this feast; they close their houses and shops and live in the little dwellings and booths they have made on the mountain top.

During the feasting, an ox or a sheep would be killed with much ritual; the best went to the altar, some to the priests, the rest to the offerer of the sacrifice and his family. It was a time of music and great rejoicing, so it was natural that Eli should have thought Hannah had had too much wine. Note that I Sam. 1:5, is probably a mistranslation and should read "a single portion."

SAMUEL IS PROMISED TO GOD

Eli told Hannah she would have a son, and Hannah was so glad that she dedicated him there and then to serve Yahweh when he was old enough. Her Song of Thanksgiving should be compared with the *Magnificat* in Luke 1:46–53, and with Psalm 113:7, 8.

When Samuel was about six or seven Hannah kept her promise and brought him to live with Eli near the Temple. His work was to tend the lamp, which was probably of olive oil held in a shaped dish containing a rag wick; it would burn dimly until the morning.

The story of Samuel's call to serve Yahweh is a favorite and familiar one to us all. While helping Eli, he wore a white linen ephod, which was a short simple tunic or robe with a girdle; his mother brought him a new one every year. In later years the ephod was only waist length, fastened behind with bands of bright colors—scarlet, purple, blue and gold. On each shoulder was a precious stone bearing the names of the tribes— twelve in all, six on each. In a kind of breastplate was a pocket containing sacred parchments (see Exod. 28:16, 19). This the High Priest wore, and as time went on his ceremonial robes must have increased in splendor. One of his most valuable possessions was a kind of three-pronged fork "a flesh-hook of three teeth" (I Sam. 2:13); this he used for sticking into the roasting sacrifice; he might choose the best pieces for himself if he were like, for instance, the sons of Eli, who even selected special pieces *before* the sacrifice was begun! One of these forks has been found at Lachish, in an excavation there;

The priest's three-pronged fork with which he took his share of the roasting sacrifice.

the drawing gives some idea of what it was like.

THE MENACE OF THE PHILISTINES

Samuel grew up during the long years of fighting between the Israelites and the Philistines, and he realized how important it was that the people should not give up hope of ridding themselves of their enemy, and—what was more important—that they should not give up their trust in Yahweh. One of their many battles was at Ebenezer, a name which means "Stone of Help." On this occasion the help they hoped for did not come. The Ark was carried into battle before them—but it was captured. This was a dreadful blow to the Israelites, who now felt that even

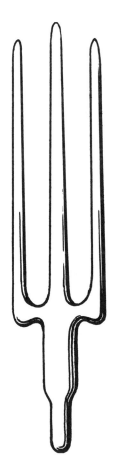

Various olive-oil lamps. Every house had its lamp, for no one dared to sleep in the dark.

Yahweh had forsaken them. They rent their clothes and piled earth on their heads, as was the custom in those days, to show their grief.

The Philistines took the Ark to Ashdod in great triumph and put it in their own god's temple. But Dagon fell to pieces and all sorts of dreadful disasters overtook them—sicknesses, tumors and boils. After having it in Ashdod, Gath, and Ekron, the Philistines decided to return the Ark to the Israelites, for they were convinced that it was the cause of their troubles. They came only as far as the border of their own and Israelite territory, at Beth-shemesh; it was the time of wheat harvest and the men were reaping. With the Ark, the Philistines brought guilt offerings as compensation for stealing property; these were golden images of mice and tumors, for these things had worried them most. The Ark was taken to Kirjath-jearim, to the house of Abinadab, a Levite. Later on, the Philistines were beaten off—at Ebenezer!

Samuel, now a judge, worked a "circuit" to Bethel, Gilgal, Mizpah, and so back to Ramah, where he lived. Mizpah was in a most central strategic position in the hills, and on one occasion when Samuel called the people to him to remind them they should worship only Yahweh, the Philistines attacked them. Samuel went on with his sacrifice, and the enemy was easily beaten.

"GIVE US A KING!"

By this time many of the soldier leaders of the people came to Samuel and asked him for a king who could lead them into battle and inspire them to defeat the Philistines once and for all. Samuel told them the king might also be a tyrant, but they insisted, so he prayed about it and felt guided to choose a king for his people.

Saul came to him by chance. He was out looking for his father's asses, and had traveled over thirty miles through Ephraim and the land of Benjamin as far as Zuph. Samuel had been supervising the sacrifice when Saul sent his servant to find him and ask for help; he sent a quarter of a silver shekel, a few cents, as a fee for the "fortuneteller's" guidance! When Samuel chatted with him, Saul, although rich and brave, followed Eastern custom in modestly referring to his family as "small, the least in Benjamin"— Benjamin being also the smallest tribe. Saul was invited to the feast and given the choicest portion of meat—probably on Samuel's fork—the priest's portion, most likely part of the shoulder. He and Samuel then had a talk on the housetop, after which, before they parted at the city gates, Samuel took his vial of holy oil, a narrow-necked bottle from which the heavily perfumed oil flowed in slow drops, and anointed Saul king.

On his return home, Saul fell in with a band of prophets. In those days there were two "schools" of prophets—the seers, that is, those with "second sight," and the ecstatic prophets, that is, those who raved and shouted in a frenzy of religious fervor to themselves and their fellows—not unlike the dervishes of today. Saul joined a group of these latter prophets.

"GOD SAVE THE KING!"

Soon after he was made king by lot at Mizpah. Then the King of the Ammonites besieged Jabesh-Gilead, a strong-walled city of Manasseh, some seven miles east of Jordan, on a ravine. Saul gathered his men on the west of the Jordan, twenty miles away at Bezek, and rescued the city. The men of Jabesh-Gilead were to remember this in later years. Following this feat, Saul was made king publicly in Gilgal, with a kind of coronation that set the seal on his previous anointing by Samuel at Ramah and election by lot at Mizpah.

SAUL AND JONATHAN

Saul now turned his full attention to defeating the Philistines, for, unless they were conquered, Samuel could not hope to see the country finally united. Jonathan struck the first blow, at Gibeah, where, at Saul's own home, there was an enemy garrison. The Philistines marched on Michmash, and Saul withdrew beyond the ravine to join Jonathan in Geba, two miles to the southeast. Many Israelites fled in panic to the caves and pits and hollows in the rocky hills. To the north of Michmash was the Bozez (shining) crag, gleaming chalk in the hot Eastern sun; to the south was Seneh (thorny) crag, studded with groups of thorny acacia trees. The Philistines were roundly defeated and were then pursued many miles down the fertile valley which sweeps from Bethhoron—where the refugee Israelites joined the army once more—to Philistia; this is known better as the Shephelah.

WHAT WAS THE ORACLE?

Saul consulted the oracle to find out if he should go farther, but something appeared to be wrong. He had given a rather rash order that no one was to eat food that day as a kind of gesture to Yahweh, and he had to find out who had disobeyed his order. Once more the oracle was consulted, and it fell upon Jonathan, who admitted he had eaten some honey without knowing of his father's command. But the soldiers were so amazed at his exploit that they would not let Saul carry out his threat to slay the wrongdoer. He, too, must have been proud of his son, and saw in him a future fighter against the Philistines. He did not know of David in those days.

In this story the oracle is called an ephod. It was in the breastplate pocket of the priest, and contained the two sacred stones, Urim and Thummim, used as sacred lots. Some people believe that the stones were black on one side and white on the other; two whites meant yes, two blacks, no; and one of each, no decision—the result of Saul's first inquiry. Yahweh was supposed to influence the results as He wished. The oracle is not unlike our own tossing of a coin; there is a good deal of chance about it, but with practice it is often possible to make the required "fall" of the coin; it was even probable that the priests—at least on occasion—would make the oracle fit their own decisions and advice.

14

Saul and David

(I SAM. 15; 16:14-23; 17; 18:1-16; 19:1-17; 20:1-30; 22:1, 2; 26; 27-31. II SAM. 1)

SAUL DISOBEYS

Some years later, Saul defeated the Amalekites decisively. These were a nomadic tribe living in the Sinai peninsula; years before they had attacked the Israelites in the wilderness and had been beaten by Joshua in a battle for the oasis of Kadesh Barnea. The revengeful order that all were to be slain was interpreted in those days as Yahweh's will, but we know it could not have been that. The Amalekites were to be "devoted" to Yahweh, as Joshua had done with Jericho. In sparing Agag and saving some of the spoil, Saul had disobeyed Samuel, who then realized that Saul would never be the fine king he had hoped; he would have to make another choice. Yahweh led him to Bethlehem.

A NEW KING

Now Bethlehem was "off the beaten track" for Samuel on his circuit, and his visit was regarded with some anxiety, almost fear; that is why Samuel assured Jesse that he came "peaceably." David was a strong, fine lad; wearing his ordinary shepherd's clothes and probably carrying his sling as he came straight from the sheepfold, he was anointed Israel's new king. As Jesse and David's brothers watched the sacred oil drop from the ram's horn which they themselves used for pouring healing oil over their sheep ("thou anointest my head with oil"), they must have been completely mystified as to what it was all about. But they must have remembered it years later when David was proclaimed king.

There are two stories of David's introduction to Saul. The more commonly accepted one is that in which David is made armor-bearer to Saul after he had played the harp to soothe the king during his fits of depression.

A FAVORITE BIBLE STORY

The story of David and Goliath is familiar. The Israelites were encamped on the hill leading down to the valley of Elah—the valley of the terebinth (turpentine) trees, along which ran the road from Hebron to Gath. Goliath was six cubits and a span high; a cubit was from the elbow to the extremity of the middle finger, eighteen to twenty inches, and a span was nine to ten inches, so his height was over nine feet. His armor was of bronze; five thousand shekels would weigh about one hundred and sixty pounds, and the weight of his spearhead was nearly nineteen pounds. In appearance the armor was similar to that worn by the Greeks.

Refusing to wear heavy armor because he was not used to it, David advanced toward Goliath with only his sling and a staff. The sling was made of rawhide or soft leather. His constant practice while guarding his father's sheep had made him an expert marksman. He had learned to sling a stone just in front of the nose of a wandering sheep to make it turn. He carried in his scrip, worn at his waist, stones for slinging, unleavened bread for a hungry boy, and possibly some odd little toys and reed pipes of his own making. Even so, he chose five special stones as Goliath jeered at him. David probably felt more than a little scared, but put his trust in Yahweh and in his own skill. Goliath was certainly unprepared for David's attack; despite his great strength and size, the stone gave him such a blow at close quarters that he was struck to the ground, where, dazed, he was dispatched by David with his own sword.

We might note here that in Judges 20: 16 we read of a corps of left-handed slingers of Benjamin whose accuracy was so good that they could sling at a hair's breadth "and not miss."

SAUL'S JEALOUSY

David returned to Saul's Court to play to him when he was suffering from his fits of evil temper. We have no description of David's harp. Some people think it was a kind of lyre-shaped instrument small enough to carry around; others think it was a long flat object with strings that were plucked as it lay across the knees. Whatever it was, it soothed Saul in his fits, until, as time went by, David became more and more successful as a fighter and a leader. Then Saul grew jealous; he was angry, too, that his son Jonathan should be so much with David, and his jealousy became so strong that he attempted to kill David with his javelin. Having failed to do so, he sent men to David's home to slay him there. But David's wife, Saul's daughter, helped him to escape. To deceive Saul's men she put the household god or teraph in David's sleeping mattress, wrapped in the blanket David usually slept in; she used goat's hair to represent David's.

Warned by Jonathan, David kept special watch. He absented himself from a special feast in order to test Saul, and Jonathan with his arrows made it clear to David that he was in real danger. He was sad at parting from Jonathan, whom he had learned to love and with whom he had sworn a covenant of friendship.

DAVID FLEES FOR HIS LIFE

But he fled to the mountains with a few loyal servants—an outlaw. David stopped at Nob, where the sanctuary then was after the destruction of Shiloh by the Philistines. The Ark was still at Kirjath-Jearim. David was given "shewbread"—the consecrated "bread of the presence." These were flat loaves of holy bread, renewed every Sabbath in the Holy Place; normally they were eaten only by the

David once moved through scrubby desert like this when he was an outlaw fleeing from Saul.

High Priests. Ahimelech, who gave David Goliath's sword for his use, was betrayed to Saul and killed on Saul's order by Doeg the Edomite. Abiathar, his son, fled, and later rejoined David, bringing with him the sacred oracle; this apparent support of the priests of Yahweh led the Israelites to believe that David had the stronger cause. The rift between David and Saul begins from this point to widen, and it continued to widen until Saul's death.

DAVID'S ADVENTURES

David sent his parents to the King of Moab for safety, for he thought Saul might take revenge upon them. As for himself, he encamped in the cave of Adullam, some twelve miles southwest of Bethlehem; he probably knew the hills well, from his boyhood journeys with his sheep. He not only kept a wary eye for Saul, but also harassed the Philistines whenever he could. Keilah, a frontier town three miles farther south, was one city he saved from this enemy. He moved through Maon, a scrubby grassland, and lived a kind of Robin Hood existence, protecting the local shepherds from marauding nomads. Betrayed by the Ziphites, he fled to Engedi, an oasis west of the

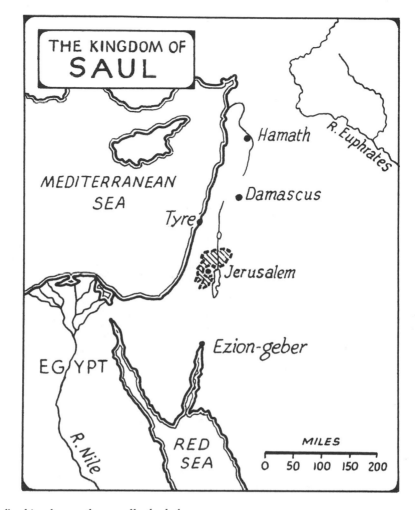

THE KINGDOM OF SAUL

MEDITERRANEAN
SEA

Hamath

R. Euphrates

Damascus

Tyre

Jerusalem

Ezion-geber

EGYPT

R. Nile

RED
SEA

MILES

0   50   100 150 200

*Saul's kingdom—the small shaded area
around Jerusalem. Compare it with the
kingdoms of David and Solomon, drawn
to the same scale.*

Dead Sea. Many psalms reflect the geography of the countryside he now lived in —the ravine, for example, miscalled valley—a dark, rocky defile, with cliffs towering overhead, hiding unknown dangers and real enemies; David knew what it meant to walk "in the valley of the shadow of death."

Once day, in the mountain fastness of the wilderness of Ziph, David had a great chance to kill Saul, who lay sleeping alone. Saul's spear was stuck upright in the ground as the distinguishing mark of the camp leader, and his cruse of water —an ever-present necessity—was near at hand. David spared Saul's life, but he knew he could no longer trust him, despite his "soft words."

David, therefore, did a strange thing; he decided to "go serve other gods," that is, go into exile. It meant, of all places, into Philistia; and in turn it implied leav-

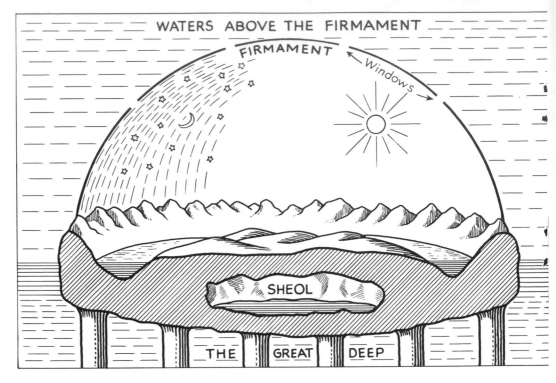

WATERS ABOVE THE FIRMAMENT

FIRMAMENT

Windows

SHEOL

THE GREAT DEEP

A model of the Hebrew Universe. The Israelites believed that the earth was supported on pillars, that the sun, moon and stars moved across a great burnished *dome, and that windows let in the rain. Sheol was the abode of the spirits, and Saul asked the witch at Endor to call Samuel from Sheol to help him.*

ing Yahweh, for it was supposed that He could be worshiped only in David's own land. The Philistines welcomed David with his strong force, and used him to fight some of their battles. He spent two years with them, with his headquarters at Ziklag, safe from Saul, and able to quell marauding enemies who were harassing his own people, too. He only just managed to avoid being sent to invade his own land. He gave the Amalekites a final trouncing after they had invaded Ziklag in his absence.

SAUL IS DEFEATED

Meanwhile, the Philistines were preparing for a mass invasion of the Israelites' land. In his desperation at possible defeat, Saul sought advice from a medium at Endor. He demanded that she should try to reach Samuel and get guidance from him through some kind of "black magic." (If you look at the drawing of the Hebrew Universe, you will see that they thought of souls going down to Sheol, whence Saul believed Samuel could come if he were called in this way.)

Saul's army was on Gilboa, overlooking Esdraelon; that of the Philistines was at Shunem. The Israelite army was utterly defeated in the valley between; Saul and Jonathan were slain on Mount Gilboa, and their bodies were taken to Bethshan, four miles west of Jordan in the plain of Jezreel, and fastened to the city gates in disgrace and shame. The men of Jabesh-Gilead, remembering Saul's bravery years before, left their mountain stronghold at night at the risk of their lives, and took down the bodies and buried them under a tamarisk tree.

Conquest by the Philistines was now so definite that "there was neither sword nor spear found in the hand of any of the people." Truly, the weapons of war had perished—for the Israelites. But David had thoughts in his mind other than of weapons when he composed his wonderful elegy to the memory of Saul and Jonathan. He called it "The Song of the Bow," for both Saul and Jonathan were expert archers (II Sam. 1:19–end).

15

David the King

(II SAM. 2:1-4, 8-11; 3:17-27; 4; 5:1-5, 17-25; 23:13-17; 5:4-12; 6:1-19; 8-11:3, 14-17; 12:1-14; 15-16:4, 15-19; 17-19:24. I KINGS 1; 2:1-4, 10, 11)

WILL DAVID SUCCEED?

Samuel did not live to see the death of Saul, and was spared the shame and bitterness of disappointment. He would have been overjoyed at the development of the nation under David. His idea had always been to unite the tribes under a fighting king and a righteous king, one who would see his people put away their feuds and quarrels and greed in a genuine desire to be Yahweh's people—a chosen people. David came very near to doing that. His story is to be found in II Samuel and I Kings 1 and 2.

David was made king of Judah in Hebron, twenty miles south of Jerusalem. He was still friendly with the Philistines, and was probably vassal to them; they seem not to have minded his being king of such a small part of the country. You will remember that Hebron was where the Cave of Machpelah was; it has figured frequently in these stories. The remnants of the northern tribes, then called Israel and mostly Benjamites, stayed loyal to Saul and put his son Ishbosheth on the throne at Mahanaim. The feud led to a battle at Gibeon, five miles northwest of Jerusalem in Israel territory. Ishbosheth was murdered, and the two warring tribes decided to unite under David, who thus became king of the whole land. This woke the Philistines to the real danger they had overlooked, and they marched on David, who used his knowledge of the Adullam district so well that he eventually drove them right out of the plain and Shephelah to the coast, where they were content to stay in their five strong cities.

CAPTURE OF JERUSALEM

Jerusalem was still one of the thorns in David's side; it was a Jebusite stronghold, reputed to be so impregnable that it could be defended, if need be, by "the blind and the lame." The story of its cap-

94

A familiar scene, even today, in the streets of Jerusalem.

Pausing on their journey, Arab traders rest their camels and exchange their news and gossip, as they have done for centuries.

ture is fascinating. Excavations reveal that there was only one water supply, from the spring beyond the city wall in the Kidron valley. Horizontal tunnels had been made from it under the city to meet the main one rising perpendicularly into the center. David explained that it was possible for men to follow this tunnel and climb up it, and so prepare the way for the entry of the besiegers ranged outside the city. Urged by the promise of high reward for the first to get inside, Joab and his men climbed the shaft (now called Warren's Shaft after its discoverer last century), pushed through the startled

women at the top, sped to the gates and let in the rest of the army. There was also a newer tunnel leading southward to the pool of Siloam which gave plenty of water to that part of the city.

David at last had the city he had longed to capture. It stood on two hills, protected by precipitous cliffs all around except on the north. It was central, neutral, and ancient, and made a fine new capital. His first task was to strengthen the city's weakest side, which he did by continuing a fortification called a Millo. This part of the city was called the city of David, and it was here that he built his palace.

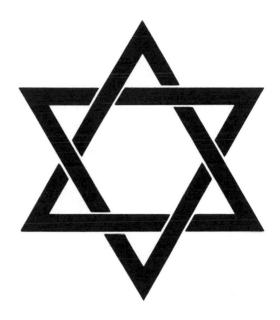

David's shield, to be seen in all Jewish synagogues.

Part of the old walls of Ammon, beneath which Uriah the Hittite lost his life.

THE BEGINNINGS OF PROSPERITY

The kings of neighboring tribes and states were already beginning to realize that here was no ordinary tribal chief; here was a king indeed, to be honored, perhaps feared, certainly to be known. So began trade negotiations with Phoenicia, especially for the materials necessary for the building of his palace. The King of Tyre, whose people were traders and merchants, exchanged cedar wood and stone and gold and metals, as well as fine linen of Tyrian hue (purple-dyed as only the Tyrians could do it, with dye from shellfish on their own seashore) for the corn, wine, and oil of the Hebrew farmers. This laid the foundation of trade that was to continue years after during the reigns of Solomon and Omri.

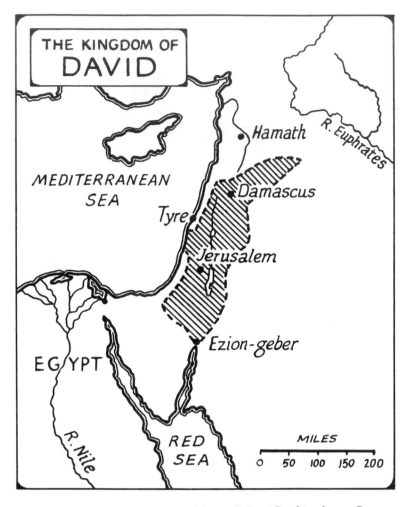

Map of David's kingdom. Compare it with Saul's and Solomon's.

THE RETURN OF THE ARK

David realized that his capital should also be the home of the Ark—and of Yahweh. He sent for the Ark at Kirjath-jearim, amid great rejoicings—music on cymbals, drums, lutes, lyres, timbrels . . . singing, dancing. Even his own wife, Michal, did not understand why David should behave in such an undignified way as to dance in front of the Ark. In great

processions in the East, a slave is made to dance wildly and caper madly, and fool about like a jester or buffoon, in honor of the person for whom the procession is held. So it was that David, the king, became like one of his own slaves and "danced before the Lord," so that he might give great honor to Him. When the Ark arrived at Jerusalem, David put on the robes of a priest and received it into the tent. Not long after this, he felt it was hardly right for him to be living in a beautiful palace when Yahweh Himself had but a tent. He, therefore, planned to build a magnificent temple for Israel's God.

ONCE MORE A FUGITIVE

But before he could do this he found himself once more a hunted man. His son Absalom had rebelled and fled to his grandfather's home in Geshur, northeast of the Sea of Galilee, in Syria. Later, he was forgiven, and returned home, where he continued to work secretly against his father. Then he rebelled openly and David fled for his life across the Jordan, probably wishing to avoid and prevent bloodshed in the city. Loyal men of his army joined him, and when Absalom took unwise advice and attacked his father, the tide turned again. Absalom, caught by his hair in the branches of a terebinth tree or thorny bushes in the forest of Ephraim, was murdered. David was heartbroken at the news (read again how he received it), but was urged by Joab to pull himself together and be what he was —a king!

DAVID'S GREATNESS

David's life was by no means without fault. It was wicked for him to get rid of Uriah the Hittite, but in those days such a thing was not uncommon. The important point of the story is that a "man of God"—Nathan—could rebuke the all-powerful king so sternly that David admitted his wrong; lesser men would have refused, but, in confessing, David showed the character he possessed.

He forgave all his former enemies, including Mephibosheth, Ziba, and Shimei. The end of his reign brings us to about 961 B.C. He left a great kingdom for Solomon to take over. His power extended not only through Palestine, but beyond, to the Red Sea, the Mediterranean, and the Tigris-Euphrates country. Tribute came from his vassals—Amalek, Moab, Edom, Ammon, Syria—and trade followed the Fertile Crescent in a wave of prosperity for those who had inherited the Promised Land. Solomon's kingdom was, indeed, from Dan to Beersheba—and beyond. (Compare the three kingdoms of Saul, David, Solomon.)

David's fame was that of a shepherd, outlaw, musician, soldier, statesman, and of a man of faith in Yahweh. The Hebrews of all the generations since have always regarded the reign of David as the most wonderful of all; and their Messiah, too, was also to be a righteous judge, a forgiving, noble "prince of peace."

16

Solomon

(I KINGS 2:12-46; 3:1, 4-28; 4:7, 20-34; 5; 8:12-21; 9:10-19, 26-28; 10; 11:1-8, 14-43. PS. 45—PERHAPS WRITTEN FOR SOLOMON'S WEDDING)

PEACE, POWER AND PROSPERITY

Solomon took the great opportunities left by his father David, and, with no extensive war to wage, developed the country and consolidated its trade and power. "Judah and Israel were as numerous as the sand on the seashore; they ate and drank and enjoyed themselves. Judah and Israel were safe, every man living under his own vine and under his own fig tree, from Dan to Beersheba . . .; for he ruled the west of the Euphrates from Thapsakus to Gaza . . . and he enjoyed peace" (I Kings 4:20-25).

He married an Egyptian princess (see Ps. 45), whose father conquered and destroyed Gezer, the Canaanite stronghold, and gave it to Solomon as her dowry. Solomon rebuilt it later as one of his "chariot cities"—Megiddo, Taanach, Eglon and Hazor. He realized the strategic importance of his country, controlling as it did the trade routes from Asia to Africa, Damascus and the Mediterranean to the Red Sea, to Arabia and the Far East.

HIS MERCHANT NAVY

He saw that a renewed pact with the seafaring Phoenicians would give him the advantage of a trading fleet westward— the Tarshish ships, carrying minerals, ore or smelted. Helped by the King of Tyre with cedarwood from Lebanon, he then built his own merchant navy, which was manned for the most part by Phoenicians, for the Jews were not good sailors. His ships sailed southward to Arabia and India, to trade in spices, precious jewels, ivory, and gold, as Masefield says in his *Cargoes*:

"Quinquireme of Nineveh from distant
    Ophir,
  Rowing home to haven in sunny
    Palestine,

cities, such as Megiddo, where forty thousand stalls is one estimate of the number of horses Solomon owned. Excavations have revealed long rows of stone pillars, each with a hole at the top for taking the halters, and stone mangers in ranks with stone-floored gangways between them, where chariots were probably stored. The horses were fed on crushed straw and barley, no doubt supplied in taxes by the hard-pressed people.

SOLOMON A TYRANT

For, despite his alliances—some even by marrying many wives—there came a time when such magnificence and luxury could not be maintained without more and more money. So the country was divided into twelve districts, each of which had its tax and tribute to pay. Solomon levied taxes of all kinds, not only in money but also in food, grain, wool, oil. To pay these taxes, the farmers sold their land and then borrowed from richer men at high interest that they could not pay; they were thus reduced to slaves, for there was little hope of redress or justice from those in power. Further, except for Judah, the fit men of the land had to serve three months every

>   With a cargo of ivory,
>   And apes and peacocks,
> Sandalwood, cedarwood, and sweet
>   white wine."

A quinquireme was a galley with five rows of oars, wielded in all probability by slaves. Ophir is believed to have been in southwest Arabia (now Yemen) on the Red Sea. It was famous for fine gold, used by Solomon in gilding the pillars of his Temple, palace, and other buildings, and also for his "plate"—the dishes on which he had his food. The chief port was Ezion-Geber, at the head of the Gulf of Akabah. It was not possible to use ports of any size on the Mediterranean coast in Solomon's territory, because of the silting up of harbors; also, there were copper refineries in the valley north of Akabah which supplied the ships of Tarshish with their cargoes; so Ezion-Geber was bound to be the main port. From here these goods were carried overland in enormous caravans to Jerusalem, and then up to the Phoenician ports for transport and trade to the West through the Mediterranean. The trading ships usually took three years for their trips.

HIS HORSES

Solomon even bought horses from Cilicia, and traded them with Egypt for their chariots (see I Kings 9:26–28; 10: 21–29). These were stabled at chariot

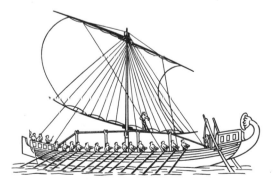

A large Phoenician trading ship, rowed by slaves; these went as far west as Spain, and even to England, perhaps around Africa, too, in search of trade.

year building and quarrying without pay. How the people hated these taxes and this forced labor; and how they longed to rebel and break Solomon's tyranny!

PLANNING TO BUILD

One wonders if any good came out of all this evil; perhaps it did, for a succession of magnificent buildings was erected, for the most part on the eastern hill of Jerusalem, at Zion. The King of Tyre sent fir, cypress, cedarwood, floated in huge rafts by sea to Joppa, then overland to Jerusalem. Skilled workmen and masons and dyers came, even Huramabi, a famous metal craftsman, who set up his foundry at Adamah, a ford in the Jordan (see I Kings 5:1–14).

For "brass" and "brazen" we should read "bronze"—an alloy of copper and tin; brass is a mixture of copper and zinc, comparatively modern in use. In return, Solomon sent twenty thousand measures of wheat and twenty measures of pure oil each year and even handed over to the King of Tyre some of the towns and villages of what was known later as Galilee. This mention of so much oil reminds us again that olive oil always has been—and still is—a staple food of the country. Later we shall read how Elisha found that the poor woman had only a pot of oil left during the famine.

SOLOMON'S TEMPLE

Solomon's greatest achievement and claim to fame was his wonderful Temple. It was oblong, with three main divisions —an entrance porch, the Holy Place, and the Holy of Holies for the Ark (see I Kings 6, 7). The Holy of Holies was a cube in shape, with thirty-foot sides and walls; it was kept in "thick darkness" except for the light from the small lamp burning in front of the Ark. (It will be remembered that it was Samuel's duty to keep this lamp burning in the sanctuary.) The Holy of Holies was hung with a heavy curtain or "veil." Two cherubim of olive wood overlaid with gold surmounted the Ark, their wings each about fifteen feet across. The Temple was finished after seven years' hard toil. It was not large—about one hundred and twenty feet long—but was exquisitely built, much of it overlaid with gold. In front were two bronze pillars over thirty feet high, ornamented with pomegranates; and twelve bulls of bronze supported a laver or bath for cleansing the sacrificial animals; this was about eight feet high and seventeen feet across. In the surrounding courtyard the festivals were celebrated. Solomon dedicated the Temple himself; you will find his poem in I Kings 8:12, 13. See how it indicates that the Hebrews still believed Yahweh dwelt only in the Temple, although they seemed to regard Him as the Creator, too.

There was much rejoicing and music on timbrels, cymbals, psalteries, and harps of all kinds, and trumpets. They may possibly have sung Psalm 136. This Temple has not been excavated, as it probably lies under sites and ground sacred to Moslems.

Below the Temple Solomon built his palace, which took thirteen years. (Here, we learn, thirty measures of flour, sixty of meal, thirty oxen, a hundred sheep, harts, roebuck, deer, and fowl were supplied every day. So it is not surprising that the people smarted under the oppressive rule meted out to maintain such magnificence. But Solomon went on building—the Hall of Pillars, the Court of Justice (although we wonder how much justice his ordinary people were given), and the House of the Forest of Lebanon—in which he had an ivory throne overlaid with purest gold. It had a rounded back, and was flanked by two lions of gold, while at the ends of each of the six steps were more golden lions.

SOLOMON'S WISDOM

When we think of Solomon we also

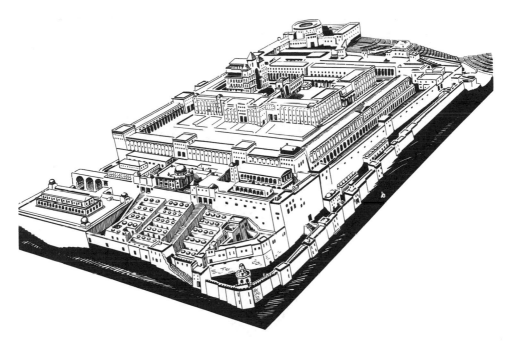

Solomon's Temple; a drawing of a reconstructed model.

remember his wisdom. His fame as a great king, wealthy and wise, spread far and wide. Foreign rulers came to visit him to see his fabulous luxury and to talk with and listen to the king whose wit and shrewdness were proverbial. (The Proverbs are attributed to him, but not all of them are entirely his own; his courtiers and counselors also said wise things on occasion.)

THE QUEEN OF SHEBA

One of these foreign rulers was the Queen of Sheba, whose kingdom may have been in southwest Arabia, near Ophir, and even more probably where we now find Ethiopia. She was so staggered at what she saw that "there was no more spirit in her." She found that what she had heard of Solomon in all his glory was indeed true: that he was wiser than her own soothsayers and magicians, that his knowledge of the creatures of the earth was limitless, that he knew the answers to riddles (a favorite pastime of those days), that he spoke proverbs of wisdom, and wrote poems and songs. She brought presents of camels and spices, gold, precious stones, but probably felt that her gifts were paltry in the face of so much splendor. As a ruler, too, she may have tried to make trade pacts, and no doubt she and Solomon talked long about prices and goods and methods of exchange.

REBELLION!

Tired of paying forced levies and taxes in wool and food, some of Solomon's vassals at last rebelled. Two in particular—both princes—Hadad of Edom, where Solomon had much of his mineral wealth, and Rezon of Syria, broke away. This meant that Solomon lost his port of Ezion-Geber—a great blow to his merchant navy trade—and also Damascus,

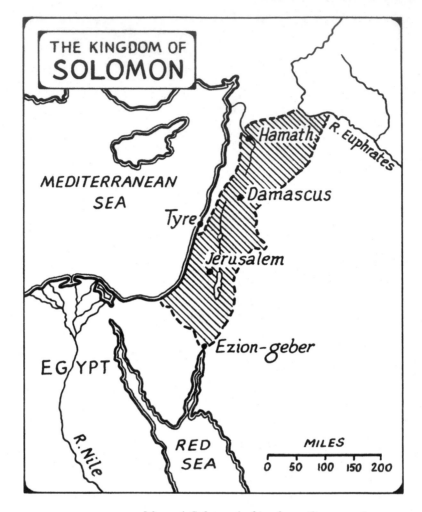

Map of Solomon's kingdom. Compare it
with that of David and of Saul, drawn to
the same scale.

one of the biggest trading centers in Syria.
These rebellions were signs of growing
dissatisfaction in the country, and just
before Solomon's death Israel was at the
point of revolution.

THE REBEL LEADER

Jeroboam had been noticed by Solomon during the period of the strengthening of the millo fortification that David
had begun and his son found necessary
to continue. Jeroboam seemed a likely
leader, and was put in charge of the
workers. But, urged on by Ahijah and
growing powerful, Jeroboam rebelled; he
was not strong enough, however, and,
defeated, fled to Egypt, whose new Pharaoh, Shishak, was glad to see the signs
of trouble and civil war. Egypt was once

more eyeing the prosperous Palestine as a prey—and now she had a rebel through whom she might succeed.

WHAT IS FAME?

Solomon died in 930 B.C. He had been an absolute king, almost a dictator; he was a seeker after power and control, quite regardless of how his methods affected his people, for whose social conditions he had no thought whatsoever. All he gloried in was his wealth and fame. He is remembered for his "glory," but Jesus Himself set it at nought when he "considered the lilies of the field"— the little wild anemones—and saw how wonderfully they were made by His Father (see Matt. 6:28, 29).

Jeroboam then returned to his home town, Zareda, while Rehoboam, the son of Solomon, next in line of succession, went to Shechem to be elected king. Both towns were in Ephraim—in Israel, the Northern Kingdom. How these rival kings and their country fared is the story of our next chapter.

Part II

PROPHETS and RULERS

ASSYRIAN EMPIRE

• Khalab

Euphrates R.

S Y R I A

Orontes R.

Assyrian power in Syria at this time was limited, allowing minor states to flourish unmolested until the coming of Tiglath Pileser III.

• Karkar

HAMATH

Hamath

CHITTIM (CYPRUS)

• Salamis

• Kition (Phoenician colony)

The Great Sea (Mediterranean Sea)

• Arvad

• Tadmor (Palmyra)

Kadesh

Zedad •

Hazar-enan •

Jeroboam restored the borders of Israel from the entry to Hamath to the Dead Sea as prophesied by Jonah.

Gebal (Byblos)

Berytus

• Berothai

KINGDOM OF DAMASCUS

PHOENICIA

Sidon

Mt. Hermon

• Damascus

Damascus, weak from the Assyrian invasion of 805 B.C., was defeated by Joash of Israel and his son Jeroboam II.

Tyre

Abel

Ijon

• Dan

Kedesh

Hazor

Accho

Sea of Chinnereth

• Karnaim

• Aphek

I S R A E L

BASHAN

Gath-hepher •

• Edrei

• Ramoth-gilead

• Dor

• Megiddo

Taanach

• Ibleam

GILEAD

River Jordan

Israel enjoyed outward prosperity and success but, as Amos depicted, was inwardly corrupt and wicked.

Samaria ⚜

• Shechem

Joppa •

AMMON

Jabneh •

• Ekron

Bethel •

Gilgal •

Rabbath-ammon •

Ashdod •

Gath •

Jerusalem ⚜

Tekoa •

• Heshbon

The Philistines were conquered by Azariah (Uzziah) King of Judah.

Ashkelon •

Lachish •

Medeba •

Gaza •

Gerar •

Hebron •

Dead Sea

JUDAH

PHILISTIA

Raphia •

Beer-sheba •

Ar •

M O A B

Kir-moab (Kir-haresheth)

EGYPTIAN

River of Egypt

KINGDOM

• Kadesh-barnea

Punon •

• Bozrah

E D O M

Arabah

• Sela

Azariah regained control of the Arabah and fortified Elath.

Elath •

ISRAEL AND JUDAH
AT THE TIME OF
JEROBOAM II
c. 785-745 B.C.

Copyright by C. S. HAMMOND & CO., N.Y.

Scale of Miles

0   20   40   60   80   100

Perennial Rivers ⌇⌇⌇   Seasonal Rivers & Streams ⌇⌇⌇

Capitals .... ⚜

Limits of territory under political or economic control of Jeroboam II ▬▬▬

Introduction to Part II

Part II of this book is called *Prophets and Rulers;* it covers the period of Jewish history between the Divided Kingdom and the Coming of Christ.

In Part I we saw how the Jews gradually learned that Yahweh was more powerful than other gods; but perhaps the most they grasped was that He was at least as good as the best of themselves. It was the prophets who led them into a closer understanding of Him; some of the rulers also had a good deal to say and do in this matter. The people felt that Yahweh, having brought them out of Egypt, had made them a chosen people, so nothing harmful could happen to them; they did not see that other nations might have felt like that about their gods, nor did they appear to give all their chief worship to Yahweh who had been so good to them. Having settled in Palestine, the Jews, learning from the Canaanites the ways of agriculture, had accepted also the Canaanite gods of fertility, in the belief that this would enable them to obtain good crops; these they worshiped alongside Yahweh at their "high places" and shrines in the open countryside. It was a common custom for tribes—and even nations—to take over any god of another people that might be expected to show special favor or power.

In this next period of the great prophets the people were to learn that Yahweh was not like these other gods; He did not need sacrifices, special gifts and payment. He wanted only trust and faith and goodness (see Is. 1:11–17; Mic. 6:6–8). Up to this time, as we saw in Part I, the kings—Saul, David and Solomon—had followed in the steps of the patriarchs and judges as spiritual leaders of the people. To a large extent they had failed, for the Jews were still quick to accept false gods and slow to believe entirely in Yahweh as the one true God. The duty of bringing them back to Him was now in the hands of the prophets.

Some people would say that a prophet was a foreteller; it would be truer to say that he was a *forth*-teller. He saw events as they were and told the truth about them. Although often humble and uneducated, he spoke for God with a strange understanding of events that urged him to proclaim what would certainly happen to the people if they did not give up their wrong ways of living and return to Yahweh. As God's spokesman he denounced their wickedness as being the opposite of what God wanted; it did not matter how correct they were in their forms of worship, how elaborate were their rituals and gifts; what was needed was kindness and justice to all men and absolute obedience to Him. God's spiritual laws could not be ignored or broken, and, if necessary, to teach them this lesson Yahweh would go so far as to allow the destruction of the whole nation, although He would save a handful of loyal servants to begin the rebuilding of a new Israel. In other words, if Israel would not listen, she was doomed.

Some advisers and leaders of the nation have already been met in Part I. There were Aaron and Miriam and the unknown prophet in the story of Gideon; Samuel and Nathan in the story of David. There were also groups of "ecstatic prophets," so called because of their habit of working themselves into a frenzy; Saul joined a band of these prophets. But we do not meet any really great prophets until the middle of the ninth century B.C., when the events of the time brought forth those fearless speakers who made great efforts to bring the people "back to their senses."

Some of these great men had followers, professional prophets or guilds, who lived in groups. Elisha joined one of these bands. Some of them retained and wrote down the fiery words and warnings of their leaders, and through them and the scribes we have had preserved for us their very words uttered in denunciation, encouragement, and advice. How powerful and moving these words sound in our ears today. Through them we see God and His people in times of great dangers and tragic events. The prophets knew God as individual, obedient servants; their duty was to bring the nation into obedience too; but how hard a task that was we shall now see.

TIME CHART

(*c.* = *circa* = about)

DATES B.C.	THE LAND AND THE PEOPLE	THEIR LEADERS AND RULERS	PEOPLE OF OTHER LANDS	EVENTS IN OTHER LANDS
c. 3000 –2350	Palestine a highway in the FERTILE CRESCENT for movements of people between Egypt and the Ancient East	NOMADIC leaders	ANCIENT CIVILIZATIONS in the valleys of the Nile and Tigris-Euphrates	
c. 2100 –1700	Hebrews leave Ur for Palestine	*Patriarchs* Abraham		Ancient Babylon now great
		Joseph	Hammurabi and Code of Laws	Tell-el-Amarna letters
c. 1700 –1600?	Hebrews in Egypt			
c. 1350? 1300	The EXODUS	Moses		Hittites powerful
	Philistines settling in Palestine			
	Hebrews enter Palestine	*Judges* Joshua, Deborah, Gideon, Samson	Philistines growing strong	Babylon weakening
1030	Tribes being united	Samuel		Assyrian power beginning
1010	War against Philistines	*Kings* Saul		
		David		
970	1st temple built	Solomon		Phoenicia important

936	**DIVISION OF THE KINGDOM**			Damascus and Syria strong
	(SOUTHERN KINGDOM) JUDAH	(NORTHERN KINGDOM) ISRAEL		
	Kings *Prophets*	*Kings* *Prophets*		
	Rehoboam	Jeroboam	Shishak invades Judah	Assyria powerful
		Omri		Moabite stone
874	(J narratives)	Ahab Elijah		
841	Elisha	Jehu	Shalmaneser (853 B.C.)	Karkar
786	Uzziah	Amos		
		(E narratives)		
760	Ahaz	Hosea		
740	Isaiah		Tiglath-Pileser III	Damascus falls
	(J and E combined)			
725	Hezekiah Micah			
721		**Fall of Northern Kingdom** Ten Tribes taken to Assyrian captivity — the "Lost Ten Tribes"	Sargon captures Samaria	
696	Manasseh		Sennacherib	Assyria weakening
639	Josiah (Law Book found)			
612	Nahum			Fall of Nineveh (Assyria)
605	Zedekiah Jeremiah			Fall of Egypt (Carchemish)
597	First Exiles to Babylon			
586	**Fall of Southern Kingdom** **EXILE** and **DISPERSION**		Nebuchadrezzar	Chaldean (Babylonian) Empire strong
	J and E stories being edited by Priests Synagogue worship beginning			Persian Empire beginning
549	Ezekiel			
	Second Isaiah		Cyrus, King of Persia	

TIME CHART

DATES B.C.	THE LAND AND THE PEOPLE	THEIR LEADERS AND RULERS	PEOPLE OF OTHER LANDS	EVENTS IN OTHER LANDS
	Judah and the Jews			
537	RETURN of the Exiles	Under PERSIAN RULE		Cyrus captures Babylon
		Haggai		
		Zechariah		Cambyses captures Egypt
516	2nd temple built		Darius, King of Persia	Persian Empire powerful
444	Walls of Jerusalem rebuilt	Nehemiah		Book of Ruth written
	Samaritan "split"	Malachi		
397	Law "published" in Jerusalem	Ezra		Book of Job written
	Synagogues established			
331	Written O.T. history of Jews now ends	Under GREEK RULE	Alexander the Great	Greek Empire rising: conquest of Persian Empire — "Hellenistic Age" begins
320	Conquered by Ptolemy	Under EGYPTIAN RULE	Ptolemy, King of Egypt	Greek Empire divides into Ptolemaic Empire and Seleucid Empire
			Seleucus, King of Syria and Asia Minor	Book of Jonah written
198	Conquered by Antiochus IV	Under SELEUCID RULE		Rome rising
170	Antiochus Epiphanes desecrates Temple			
167	Maccabaean Revolt	Judas Maccabaeus		
165	Temple rededicated	Under HASMONEAN RULE		Daniel being written
121	Priest-King set up	John Hyrcanus		
112	Pharisees and Sadducees quarrel			Seleucid Empire weakening
63	Pompey in Jerusalem	Under ROMAN RULE		Roman Empire powerful
49			Julius Caesar	
37	Herod in Jerusalem	Herod the Great, ruler under Rome		
20	3rd Temple begun			
4	Death of Herod		Augustus Caesar, Emperor of Rome	
6–4	**BIRTH OF CHRIST**			

I

The Divided Kingdom

When Solomon died in 930 B.C. his son Rehoboam went to Shechem to be anointed king. There he found waiting to talk with him Jeroboam, who had fled to Egypt after the failure of his rebellion against Solomon (Part I) and had now returned from exile in order to lead the people against the new king. The people certainly had much of which to complain —taxes, forced labor, injustices of all kinds: Jeroboam now asked that Rehoboam should be less of a tyrant than his father had been and so ease the people's burdens.

Rehoboam missed the opportunity of winning the support of the people, for after three days—having taken the worst possible advice from the young men—he threatened to rule even more harshly than his father had done; he would drive the people with whips tipped with spikes that hurt them as painfully and cruelly as the stings of scorpions. The people shouted their defiance and rebellion and stoned to death Adoram, the hated officer in charge of forced labour.

"A LAMP IN ISRAEL"

Rehoboam fled to Jerusalem, which was in the territory of Benjamin, which now united with Judah and remained loyal to the throne. This loyalty was fortunate for the king. It had been prophesied that these tribes would remain true followers of the "line of David," and that David would have "a lamp always before me." This strange reference reminds us of the great fear of darkness these people always had. In the desert they had been grateful for the "pillar of fire by night" to drive away evil spirits; if there were no light in a house it was a sign of emptiness, death and destruction. When Jeremiah speaks of threatened devastation from Babylon he uses the same idea—"I will cause to perish from them . . . the light of the lamp." David had been promised

Ashur-nasir-pal II, King of the Assyrians in the ninth century B.C. *Omri made an alliance with this very cruel king.*

a lamp in Jerusalem; the prophecy was fulfilled when Rehoboam established himself in the city (see also II Kings 8:19; I Kings 15:4; Prov. 13:9).

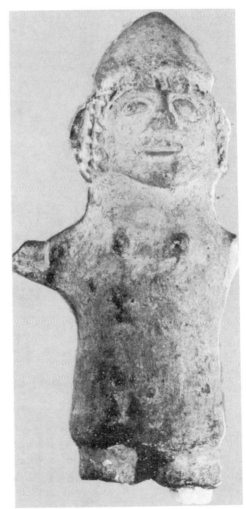

These are figurines or teraphim—little models of false gods, worn or used to bring their owners "good luck." The Bible calls them baalim. These two probably represent Astarte, the goddess of fertility. (I Kings 11:5; Isa. 44:10.)

THE TWO KINGDOMS

The land was now split in two; it remained so until its final destruction. The two tribes forming the Southern Kingdom of Judah remained loyal to Rehoboam; the other ten tribes forming the Northern Kingdom of Israel (sometimes called Ephraim) went over to Jeroboam. This division was to some extent due to the fact that Palestine had never been a complete whole. The Jebusites and Canaanites and other tribes had from the

*A lamp with seven pinchings for seven
wicks. One of the simplest kind, it dates
from the period of the two kingdoms.*

first separated the Hebrews (as they were
then called) from one another, so there
was no national unity; there had been
rivalry between the two parts even in
David's time (see II Sam. 19:40–43).
The formation of the country, with its
hills and valleys and the Jordan rift, had
also prevented real geographical union.
There was jealousy, too, for Judah had

never been called upon to pay taxes and
do forced labor in the quarries, and the
northerners had been angry at the king's
favoritism. Above all, the two kingdoms
had different interests and occupations.
Judah had difficulty in obtaining food, and
made the best of her poor soil in agriculture—farming, sheep raising, vineyards,
and olive orchards; her communities were,

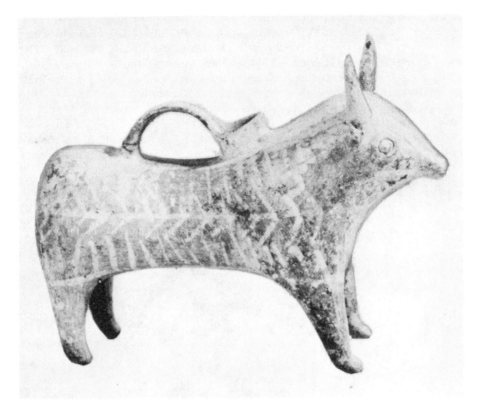

A vase shaped like a bull idol. This gives us some idea of the golden bull idols set up by Jeroboam in Dan and Bethel.

for the most part, small, in villages and walled cities. Israel, to the north, was more aware of her neighbors—Phoenicia, Syria, Assyria—and trade with these countries flourished; wealth came from taxes paid by the caravans that had to pass through the main routes of the kingdom, and there was normal trading in large cities like Samaria, Bethel and Damascus.

BULL WORSHIP

To make sure of full control of his new possessions, Jeroboam would not let the people go up to Jerusalem to worship at their feasts; he set up for them two metal bulls—"golden calves." Bull worship was familiar in Egypt and Syria as the symbol of nature worship and the Canaanites used it too. For the Israelites to worship golden calves representing Yahweh was a dangerous link with heathen worship, and with his bull idols at Dan and Bethel Jeroboam encouraged the people to drift away from the true worship of Yahweh. Even his priests were no longer Levites, whereas it had been laid down by the Law of Moses that members of the tribe of Levi were the only people who could be priests of Yahweh; this breaking of the Law made the rift even wider. Jeroboam betrayed his people with the very words Aaron had used when the Hebrews had worshiped the golden calf in Sinai— "Behold thy gods, O Israel, which brought thee out of the land of Egypt." Division of the kingdom was now complete—

Israel in the north and Judah in the south.

It is not surprising that the Northern Kingdom went over to the worship of false gods and idols (see I Kings 15:34; 16:26). But so did the Southern Kingdom (I Kings 15:23). Nor are we surprised to learn that the two kingdoms warred with each other and caused great hardship and bitterness throughout the whole land. Shishak of Egypt who had befriended Jeroboam invaded Judah. He forced Rehoboam to pay tribute and took away golden and silver vessels from the Temple itself, even though the king had his bodyguard to help him. Some scholars think he may have destroyed the Ark, for it is not mentioned again in these accounts. Shishak recorded his victories and also his invasion of Megiddo and Lachish—which Rehoboam had evidently fortified—on the walls of the temple of Amon (Amen-Ra) at Karnak. We shall hear more of these places later.

A whip of scorpions. The pieces of metal in each thong were meant to cut into the flesh. Nine hundred years after Rehoboam, Christ was scourged with whips like this.

A "city on a hill." Samaria was situated like this.

SAMARIA, THE CAPITAL

Jeroboam fared badly also. Invasion from the Syrians brought treachery and bloodshed. When he died there was much fighting for control of the kingdom, and kings followed one another in quick succession. Then Omri, seizing the throne in 880 B.C., became king. By trade and war he brought great power to the Northern Kingdom. He built as his capital city Samaria—a "city on a hill." It overlooked the Plain of Sharon; we are told that the entrance to the city was a single gate let in the walls on the steepest side of the hill and protected by a special tower. The walls of the city were ten feet thick and

the only means of conquering it was by starving out the defenders; it was well named "watch tower." Even the Assyrians called the Northern Kingdom "Omriland." The building of Samaria is the only thing about Omri that is mentioned in the Bible; the city has been excavated and in the palace beautiful ivory furnishings have been found, both solid and inlaid. But Omri must have had great success in his other undertakings, for the famous Moabite Stone (found A.D. 1868) gives a long list of lands conquered and held by him; the stone tells of the conquests of the King of Moab, serving his god Chemosh (this was Ruth's god, you will remember). Part of the inscription on it reads: "And Chemosh said unto me, Go, take Nebo against Israel. . . . And I fought against it . . . and I took the vessels of Yahweh. . . ." In 876 B.C. Ashur-nasir-pal—perhaps the cruelest of the kings of Assyria—marched through the Fertile Crescent and took tribute from Phoenicia; so Omri formed alliances between neighboring kingdoms to prevent Assyria from becoming too dangerous. His son Ahab followed his example and eventually united Phoenicia, Syria, Israel, and Judah —but much was to happen before this.

Meanwhile Samaria was growing in importance as a fine trading city, and Ahab inherited considerable wealth and power when he became the new King of Israel.

2

Elijah

(I KINGS 11:26-40; 12; 16:23-33; 17; 18:1-46; 19:1-18; 21:1-19; 22)

Ahab had married Jezebel in order to ally Israel with Phoenicia (see map). Jezebel was the daughter of the priest-king and a worshiper of Baal; baal means lord or spirit-owner. It was believed by many of the people of those days that a spirit lived in a spring or by a well, and "owned" it; this meant that the spirit had to be worshiped to make sure that it was helpful and good to the people who lived near the spring or well and needed to use its water.

A WICKED QUEEN

Domineering and cruel, Jezebel brought with her the Phoenician Baal-Melkart, a sun- and sea-god; his image was placed in the Temple in Samaria itself; Ashtart (Astarte) was already being worshiped as the goddess of fertility alongside the bull idol representing Yahweh. But Jezebel was not content to have her god worshiped as one of two or three; Melkart was to be the chief god, and worship of Yahweh was to be stamped out altogether. She even brought her own Baal prophets—four hundred and fifty of them —introduced child sacrifice once more, and persecuted or murdered the prophets and followers of Yahweh, who fled and hid in the caves outside the city; these men were secretly looked after by Obadiah. Jezebel wanted baal worship to be the national religion and was prepared to go to any lengths to make it so. Jeroboam "had made Israel to sin," but she was on the point of blotting out completely the spiritual life of the Northern Kingdom. Ahab, a brave soldier but a weak king, let her do exactly as she pleased.

It was just as she seemed to be succeeding that she was suddenly and dramatically challenged by one of the greatest men in the Bible—Elijah.

Elijah comes into the Bible narrative quite unexpectedly. He was a Tishbite

A Phoenician war galley, carved on a bas-relief at the time of Sennacherib. The Phoenicians were expert sailors and traders.

Jezebel brought her false Phoenician gods to the Northern Kingdom. This is a terra-cotta model of her favorite—Melkart.

An example of Israelite pottery of this period. It was always much better formed and finished than was the pottery of Judah.

(or Jabeshite) from the desert highlands of Gilead, across the Jordan. His name means "My God—Yahweh." It was evident that Elijah was not going to stand by and see his people forsake Yahweh; nor would he hide in the caves with Obadiah's prophets. He knew that without Yahweh, Israel could not exist as a nation, and he was determined to save her.

ELIJAH AND THE WIDOW

Elijah was sure that the threatened famine was a sign of Yahweh's displeasure, and the prophet foretold drought and distress unless and until the people turned to Him. Elijah then moved to a quiet spot by Brook Cherith, and there he was

able to live, because—according to the First Book of Kings—the voice of God had told him "I have commanded the ravens to feed thee there." He decided to go to Phoenicia, the land of Baal-Melkart. So we follow this gaunt, sunburnt man; as a man of God, a prophet of Yahweh, he wore his hair long and flowing beneath his headdress, and over his shoulders was slipped the simple sheepskin or goatskin cloak (his mantle) which, later, he was to hand to Elisha, his faithful follower. He crossed the Jordan, having moved along its eastern bank, and travelled westwards to the coast near Sidon. At a little village, Zarephath, he paused; a woman came near him and he asked for water—a common request in the east when travelers were hot and thirsty. She was gathering sticks—possibly pieces of acacia bush—"at the gate," just outside the village. She must have recognized Elijah as coming from Israel by his dress and perhaps by his dialect, for she spoke to him in the name of Yahweh—"As Yahweh, thy God, liveth . . ." She did as Elijah told her, despite her first doubts, and shared her food—meal and oil. The meal was barley meal, in a pot—not a barrel as we know it. The cruse was a small earthenware jar, the oil, olive oil. The raising to life of the child is a gentle, moving and happy incident in the life of this fierce, stern prophet.

The famine had come, despite the wailing prayers of the priests of Melkart to their god who was the "spirit-owner" of the rain. With the drought had come anxiety and fear; nearly three years had gone by and there was starvation and desperation. The ground was brick-hard, the waterless wadis were cracked deeper than they had ever been, and the hillsides were brown with scorched vegetation; cattle and sheep and people died. . . .

MOUNT CARMEL

Ahab put the blame on Elijah; but

Elijah was to prove to him that he himself was very much to blame for allowing Jezebel to do so much wrong. The prophet made his challenge to the king. Mount Carmel was well chosen; it was a sacred mountain, overlooking the sea to the north and the Plain of Esdraelon to the east. Its hillsides would normally have been covered with growing crops, and sheep and cattle would have been grazing on its soft grass. On a small plateau near the top (the spot, called "the place of burning," is still to be seen, 1,600 feet up the mountain) Elijah faced the people, crowded among the rocks, weary, frightened, staring at the parched ground and wilting under the hot sun. Near by the prophets of Baal waited, unaware of the disastrous defeat that was to be theirs by the end of the day; already they were fingering their knives and calling on each other in fierce excitement. The altar to Yahweh had been destroyed and one to Melkart put in its place.

THE GREAT CHALLENGE

The Bible describes the scene that followed in wonderful language. Elijah heightens the drama. Water was precious enough at any time, but just now it was beyond price. Yet he told the people to pour it into the ditch and on the altar—on the twelve stones he had reared to represent the twelve tribes. Then from sudden storm clouds came fierce streaks of lightning—always in the Bible called "the fire of the Lord." The fire of the Lord and the prayer of Elijah did what the Baal-Melkart and his screaming prophets could not do. Then came the dramatic challenge to the people. Read it aloud, in I Kings 18, and feel the exciting climax. How long were they "to halt and totter, first on one knee and then on the other"? (This probably referred to the steps in some of the heathen dances around the altars of the false gods, and even more closely to the very dances of

the frenzied prophets of Baal.) The people must make a decision for or against Yahweh. And they shouted, "Yahweh, He is God! Yahweh, He is God!"

Elijah's calm confidence in Yahweh stood out boldly against the foolish frenzy of the prophets of Baal. The storm had ended the drought. The Kishon overflowed its banks, as it had done many years before when Sisera's army threatening Deborah and Barak had been caught and drowned; and now Ahab's chariot was almost swamped as it plowed through the boggy marshland, heading for Jezreel, his summer capital. Elijah, in the excitement of victory, ran in front of the chariot for the whole seventeen miles. Wells and streams and wadis filled up—the rain had come! Yahweh, He was God!

THE "STILL, SMALL VOICE"

Jezebel was furious. Realizing his immediate danger, Elijah fled—through Beersheba and on to Horeb, the place of Moses. This was where the Covenant between the people and Yahweh had been made—and where, for Elijah, it might now end. We are not certain if Horeb was indeed Sinai, or whether it was perhaps Mount Hor, south of the Dead Sea. By now, Elijah was dejected; he wanted to die. He had forgotten the prophets in hiding awaiting a leader. He was asking where was Yahweh, after all? Not in the hurricane, or in the earthquake, or in the lightning; God was in the "still small voice" speaking to Elijah in that strange inner way that we sometimes call "conscience." The real translation of this familiar phrase is "a sound of gentle stillness"—which makes it very clear that God comes to us in moments of quiet. Elijah was learning that Yahweh was not just another god; He had a purpose and claimed obedience from His people. And Elijah was to see to it that this was made clear to them also. He heard, too, the judgments of Yahweh upon Ahab and the nation: then he returned to Israel to continue his work for Yahweh.

NABOTH

The story of Naboth's vineyard is another familiar incident in the life and work of Elijah. Ahab's summer palace at Jezreel overlooked the vineyard; the king must many times have seen Naboth mounting his watchtower, looking out for marauders or signs of rain and generally supervising his property. The vineyard must have been in Naboth's family for years, since the Israelites had come to Palestine. It was an inheritance that he

A Hebrew seal (I Kings 21:8). This is a sacred beetle-shaped one, called a scaraboid, sometimes used as an ornament or bead. Probably brought from Egypt to Palestine during the time of the Hyksos kings (Part I).

Here is an impression such as Jezebel made with Ahab's seal. It says "belonging to Shemac, Servant of Jeroboam, King of Israel, 786–745 B.C.*"*

could never give up except to a kinsman (Num. 36:1–8; Lev. 25:27, 28). But Ahab wanted the vineyard; it was so handy alongside his own garden, and he had only to make a new gate into it. Yet, though he was king, he recognized Naboth's right to refuse; he made a fair offer for exchange, but Naboth held out; so Ahab sulked on his ivory-backed divan and behaved like a spoiled child.

JEZEBEL'S PLOT

Jezebel found him in this mood. Ahab

told her what had happened; he had wanted the vineyard for a herb garden where he could grow lettuce and chicory, water cress, even onions and garlic, and —so that Jezebel might be sure of having spices for seasoning her food—cinnamon, dill, and mint. But he could not have it. Jezebel saw Ahab's sense of justice as nothing but weakness. She determined that the king should have the vineyard and made a wicked plot to get it. She sent letters to the chief men of the city, written on skins and bearing the king's seal; two lying witnesses were to bring false evidence against Naboth. As a result, Naboth was accused of treason and murdered.

So Ahab obtained his vineyard, but at mortal cost. When he went to take possession of it, there at the gate he found himself confronted by the figure of Elijah, awful with the wrath of God. Ahab shrank back before him. "Hast thou found me, O my enemy?" he said. And the prophet who dared thus to bring a king to judgment answered, "Yea, I have found thee; because thou hast sold thyself to work evil in the sight of the Lord." And he pronounced upon Ahab and Jezebel their coming doom. Both of them should die by violence; and as for Jezebel, her body should be torn by scavenger dogs, as had been the body of Naboth, whom she had murdered.

ELIJAH CHOOSES ELISHA

Elijah had to find a successor; he could not carry out all the work necessary to restore the nation to Yahweh. He probably already knew Elisha and found him handling a plow as one of a team of twelve (I Kings 19:19ff.). He threw his mantle of goatskin or sheepskin over Elisha's shoulders to show that he was choosing the young man as a disciple and follower. A father frequently passed on to his son his simlah, his striped outer jacket, and Elijah was making it clear that Elisha was to take over his work. Elisha then burned the plow, yoke, and goad—"the instruments of oxen"— to make a fire on which he roasted the oxen. As a mere servant he "poured water on the hands of Elijah"—a common duty in those days. Although evidently a rich young farmer, he was now prepared to follow his new master and to learn what was needed of him in the service of Yahweh.

3

Elisha

(II KINGS 2:1-15; 4:8-37; 5:1-16; 6:8-23; 13:14-20)

Elisha's special work was to carry out the other two orders of Yahweh—to anoint Jehu, a ruthless soldier who would rebel against Ahab and root out the false Phoenician worship of Melkart; and to go to Damascus to meet a Syrian captain, Hazael, who would be the future ruler of Syria when he, too, had rebelled against his king.

ELIJAH'S LAST JOURNEY

The prophet journeyed with Elijah from Gilgal to Bethel. At Bethel they met a group of young men training to be prophets who warned Elisha that he would soon lose his beloved master. Elisha felt that this was true and insisted upon staying with Elijah, through the Jordan valley to Jericho, where they met yet another group who gave him the same warning. They came to the Jordan at the "place of baptism"—a ford over the river; this was possibly the ford across which Joshua had

passed many years before, when the Hebrews began to enter Palestine. Across the river loomed Mount Nebo where centuries before, Moses had left his people.

Here it was that the two prophets now paused, and in answer to Elijah's question, Elisha asked for "a double portion" of the older man's spirit. He did not want to be twice as great as Elijah; he was merely asking for the share of the firstborn, which was twice that of the rest of the sons; for Elisha was to succeed Elijah as a son did his father and as the man responsible to Yahweh (Deut. 21:17).

Elisha's test of worthiness was to see the chariot and horses of fire in what may have been a furious storm of lightning. His exclamation, "the chariot of Israel; the horsemen thereof," appears to be a proverb or saying; Elisha meant that Elijah was of greater worth to the nation than all its horses and chariots. And to him, too, it meant that the horses and

127

This is a N. Syrian god or baal, made of bronze and dating from the time of the Exodus (see Part I, Ch. 9).

chariots of the Lord of Hosts were the true defense of Israel (Ps. 20:7).

Thus Elijah passed from the great events of this time. But the Jews have always remembered him. We recall that he was one of those at the Transfiguration of Christ (Matt. 16:14; Luke 9:8, 19, 30; John 1:21). Even today, at every Passover Feast, a chair is placed for Elijah and every so often someone goes to the door to see if he is waiting to come in.

ELISHA BEGINS HIS WORK

When Elisha—whose name means "God is Salvation"—finally put on his master's mantle he showed his willingness to continue Elijah's work; the "schools of prophets," or prophet guilds, also accepted him as one of themselves having special authority as a leader, and frequently he sat with them "round the great pot" at Gilgal (II Kings 4:38–41).

Elisha, bald (II Kings 2:23) and weather-tanned, was a friendly man. Unlike Elijah, he had grown up among the people; he was the son of a rich farmer and knew what it was to move amongst his neighbors. He visited the walled cities (II Kings 6:13–19, 32), and even had his own house in Samaria. He "went about doing good," and the stories about him are for the most part warm, kind and human. One cannot imagine Elijah having any interest in music, but Elisha seems to have enjoyed it (II Kings 3:15).

THE SHUNAMMITE WOMAN

The story of the Shunammite woman reveals much about the prophet. You will find it in II Kings 4:8–37. Shunem lies in the north of the Valley of Jezreel, high in the hills, facing south, some fifteen miles from Carmel. The woman was the wife of a wealthy farmer whose fields lay terraced on the hillsides; she herself had connections with rich people too. The "lit-

tle room" made for Elisha was reached by an outside stairway of stone steps; it contained a thin mattress or pallet that could be rolled up by day, a table, a stool and the all-important olive-oil shoe-shaped or seven-pinched lamp—for even Elisha would not sleep in the dark if he could avoid it. Gehazi was Elisha's servant and disciple; we do not form a very high opinion of Gehazi. The woman's son, whose birth Elisha had foretold, caught sunstroke in the fierce hot noonday sun. His father was in the harvest field reaping and threshing corn. He was watching the heavy threshing instrument, a board studded with flints and pieces of iron, dragged by oxen over the reaped corn (see Isa. 41:15). He wondered why his wife should want to go to Elisha; it was not a feast day or a new moon, not even a Sabbath. She rode on an ass, probably a white one, as wealthy people always did, her servant urging it along with his right hand on its flank and in his left a stick or goad to encourage speed. The journey was quite twenty miles and her anxiety on arrival made Elisha act quickly.

He told Gehazi to "tighten up his belt" —that is, to tuck into his girdle the folds of his cloak so that he could hurry. He was not to stop to speak to anyone. This seems discourteous, but what Elisha really meant was, "Be as quick as you can." Greetings and salutations in Palestine, even today, are most elaborate; there are certain routine phrases and actions that must be observed, and to cut them short would certainly be rude; the only way to avoid offering them would be to hurry along with eyes to the ground. Jesus had much the same idea in mind when He told His disciples to "salute no man by the way" (Luke 10:4).

In II Kings 4:29–31 we read that Gehazi failed to revive the child with Elisha's staff, despite the fact that he may have believed it was the sign of authority; it is evident that he had no real faith in Elisha—perhaps not in Yahweh either.

Elisha had faith and we are glad that he brought happiness to the Shunammite woman who had been so kind to him.

THE SLAVE MAID

The story of Naaman is set against a historical background (II Kings 5). The Syrians (see map) were frequently at war with Israel and whenever possible in their forays had dragged off men, women and children to be their slave workers. That is how the little girl in this story came to be a waiting-maid to the wife of Naaman, a captain in the Syrian army. Naaman was a leper. Leprosy was a dread infectious disease for which in those days there was no known cure. Soon Naaman would have to leave his wife, home and companions, and live alone in some wild corner of the hills—an outcast.

The serving-maid remembered Elisha in Samaria and Yahweh, her own God. She must have been fond of her master and mistress, who had evidently treated her kindly from the first. Perhaps Naaman agreed to go to the man of God as a last hope. The King of Syria gave Naaman a letter of introduction—probably written on a skin and sealed with the royal seal—to the King of Israel, who was perhaps startled to see the captain in his war chariot. He was suspicious of the letter, for he missed the point of what the little girl had said. "Behold Naaman . . .," said the letter, "that *thou* mayest recover him of his leprosy." But it was not the king who could do it; it was the prophet. Elisha reassured the king and gave Naaman instructions that he did not like. He refused to dip himself in Jordan. There were at least two other rivers, the Abana and the Pharpar, flowing eastwards from Damascus, both clear and clean—why could he not bathe in one of those? But in answer to the pleadings of his servants, who were anxious to see their beloved master healed, Naaman went down to the muddy waters of Jordan, entered them and came out with his skin like "that of a little child."

NAAMAN TURNS TO YAHWEH

The captain's request for two mules' burdens of Israel's earth seems strange until we remember that in those days it was a common belief that a god of any country could be worshiped only on the soil of that country. Even the Jews in Exile believed at first that Yahweh had forsaken them when they were taken to Babylon. So if Naaman wanted to worship Yahweh, as he now said he would, he must rear an altar to Him on the soil of Israel. He would have to continue at least lip-service to Rimmon, the thunder-god, whom he had worshiped all his life. It is possible that he set up his new altar on the earth he took with him at the temple in Damascus and alongside the altar to his Syrian god. Perhaps you wonder, as many people do, what happened to the little serving-maid; no one knows, although it seems difficult to believe that she was not rewarded in some very wonderful way.

The story of Naaman ends with the dreadful punishment of Gehazi, which some people think gives a wrong impression of God. Probably Gehazi became a leper through contact with Naaman or through handling some of the gifts he took from the captain, but his cunning was given as the reason. The old writers often looked for some kind of sin or wrong action to account for a misfortune, and the scribes probably felt that Gehazi had deserved his leprosy. We shall see how the friends of Job told him his sorrows had come because of some secret sin in his life. But Jesus has something to say about this idea, as you will find in John 9:3 and Luke 13:1-5.

OUTWITTING THE ENEMY

A third familiar and popular story of Elisha is that in which he outwits the

Syrians at Dothan (II Kings 3:9–20). Dothan was ten miles north of Samaria, lying in a valley followed by the great caravan routes connecting Egypt and Assyria through Damascus. We have heard of this town before, in the story of Joseph (Part I). Ben-hadad, King of Syria, often found that his invasion plans made "in thy bedchamber"—that is, in secret—were known to the powerful King of Israel, and eventually decided that the "culprit" was Elisha, who must be captured without delay. He sent an *army* to Dothan—for one man! They surrounded the city by night, planning to starve it into surrendering Elisha to them. The "blindness" of the Syrians may have been due to their bewilderment at having lost all sense of direction; Elisha led them by unfamiliar tracks and byways, so confusing them until, terrified, they found themselves in the heart of Samaria. Elisha showed his servant—and this is a lesson for us too—that the "hosts of Yahweh" are a heavenly protection if only we have faith. The prophet may, of course, have used his hypnotic power on the will of the Syrian captain, whom the soldiers would follow as a matter of discipline. The clever ruse ended in a surprise feast for the Syrians, who returned more than ashamed at their experiences, and "came no more into the land of Israel" (II Kings 6:23).

Elisha still had the task of carrying out orders given by Yahweh to Elijah. First, at Damascus, he talked with Hazael, who was then on a mission from Ben-hadad, King of Syria; on his return Hazael rebelled and took the throne. His wars against Israel were fierce, but Elisha seems to have known they would be and regarded them as a means of bringing Israel to her senses.

Before he died Elisha told the king, Joash, to shoot his arrows eastwards towards Damascus, the capital of Syria: to do so was to declare war upon Syria. Later the king recovered his captured cities, as the prophet had said he would.

PROPHECIES COME TRUE

The death of Ahab is told vividly in the Bible story. Recent excavations in the city of Samaria have revealed much of the palace built by Omri and extended by Ahab. It was of yellow limestone, laid out with a central courtyard; in the rooms were housed the king's bodyguard and slaves, and in the stables were his magnificent war and chariot horses. The truth of the Bible story is borne out by the discovery of an artificial pool; this was probably the very one in which his servants washed Ahab's chariot and by which the pariah dogs gathered to lick at the blood-stained wheels.

Meanwhile, to complete his task, Elisha had persuaded Jehu to rebel against his king, Ahab's son. Jezebel, now an old woman, who had done so much harm with her false gods, was murdered, the pariah dogs pouncing madly upon her body, broken in its fall from the lattice window. The priests of Baal were slaughtered. By this terrible bloodshed Jehu drove out false idol worship and returned the country to the worship of Yahweh.

A DANGEROUS ENEMY

But it was not long before the Assyrian hordes were sweeping across the lands of Syria and Israel and threatening Judah. On the Black Obelisk of Shalmaneser the cuneiform inscriptions and pictures include some of Jehu and Hazael, as well as the names of Ahab and Ben-hadad; it shows much of the history of this period (see also I Kings 20:34 and 22:1). The record gives a vivid picture of Assyrian cruelty: "Karkar, his royal city, I destroyed, I devastated, I burned with fire. . . . I rained destruction upon them. I scattered their corpses far and wide . . . the plain was too small to let their bodies fall . . . with their bodies I spanned the

Orontes (a river) as with a bridge." This was in 853 B.C., an important date for us, as it is the first date in our history of the Jews to be accepted as accurate by the majority of Biblical scholars; from this, other dates both before and after the Battle of Karkar may be calculated, although dates earlier than that of David—about 1000 B.C.—are difficult to fix with exactness.

To the very end Elisha was anxious that the king and the people should remain loyal to Yahweh, who would save Israel from her enemies. But they did not learn their lesson either then or later.

4

Amos

(AMOS 1:1; 2:6-8; 3; 4:6-13; 5:4-15, 15-27; 6:1-8; 8:8-14; 9:1-8)

In 786 B.C. the King of Israel was Jeroboam II. Syria was at war with Assyria and Israel was free from attack for a number of years. She grew strong, her trade flourished and her power extended even to Damascus. For fifty years both Israel and Judah enjoyed peace and prosperity.

But, as in Solomon's time, power and trade brought luxury and splendor to the few and suffering and hardship to the many. The people kept their feast days and offered sacrifices and outwardly appeared to be serving Yahweh; but there was slavery, oppression and injustice that made their worship seem a mockery.

HIS HOME LIFE

This is when we hear of Amos, the first of the writing prophets. He lived at Tekoa in Judah, about six miles south of Bethlehem. As a herdsman he looked after the hardy sheep that were able to exist on the thin scrubby grass of the wilderness; these sheep produced a fine quality fleece however, and at certain times of the year Amos would take his wool into the bigger cities of Bethel, Gilgal and Samaria to sell at the markets. At other times of the year he grew sycamore figs—fig-mulberries. These must not be confused with the fine figs with which we may be familiar. It is possible that Amos took to market branches and parts of the fig tree for fuel, altars, burnt-offerings, yokes and so on. The tree grows even today on the hillsides of this bleak district of Judah (Amos 7:14).

It was a wild, desolate area; on three sides reared gray limestone hills and to the east fell away four thousand feet of lowlands, brown and parched; wild animals roamed by day and by night—wolves, jackals, panthers, leopards and hyenas. Amos scanned the wilderness around him and in its vastness saw the wonder of Yahweh; especially at night when the sky was bright with stars did he feel the majesty and might of the Creator; and by day when he caught glimpses of the water of the Dead Sea glinting in the hot sun he must have felt that surely here Yahweh reigned.

HIS WORK

His life was hard (see Ps. 63:1). The scanty rain had barely fallen before hot suns dried the brooks into caked wadis; freshly springing flowers and grass quickly shriveled under the heat; stony patches of ground seemed hardly worth the labor of tilling. Amos had learned to seek shelter for himself and his flocks; he spoke the language of a shepherd, using his sling as had Jacob and David to guide his wandering sheep, carried his club to protect them, his rod to check them, sought and found water in the most unlikely places to refresh them.

In June he must have handed the care of his flock for a short time to a friend or relative, for he had to see to his wild fig trees. He then put on one side his staff, reed pipe, sling, rod (club) and staff, and with only his flint knife in his girdle he set off. Probably a few hundred feet above the Dead Sea were small oases where the trees would grow; he would scramble down narrow gorges to reach them. The trees were often fifty feet high, but their branches spread out horizontally and offered easy movement for the agile Amos. It was tiring work, this "dressing," but it had to be done. Each fig was cut or pinched sufficiently to make it soft as the bitter juice was squeezed out; this encouraged the fruit to ripen more quickly, but as the crops were gathered by hand the work had to be done frequently. In the markets only the poor people bought these wild figs, so there was little profit.

TO THE CITY

With this life behind him Amos felt strangely alone in the towns he visited to sell his wool and figs and wood. There was bustle and argument and noise; dogs, pigs, sheep, children fell over one another in anxiety and fear; women sat outside their mud-brick hovels, grinding their corn, kneading dough and spinning wool or flax; some stood to talk, balancing gracefully on their heads pots of precious water fetched from the well outside the city walls. The men seemed to have more time; they filled the market place at the entrance gate, talking over their business with gestures and much shaking of heads. A great deal of what he heard made Amos shudder. Who were these well-dressed men? Who were these ill-clad slaves cowering before them?

IN THE MARKET PLACE

He stood and watched the merchandise as it passed into the town on heavily burdened mules, asses and oxen; the booths were stacked with wares—wool from Moab, tools, garments of sheepskin, goat hair and camel hair; jewelry from Egypt; perfumes, knives, swords, weights and measures from Damascus; Arabian spices; African ivory; gold from Ophir; vases from Greece; silver, pottery, ivory and silks from Phoenicia. Here there was wealth, but here, too, there was poverty. Amos reached the Temple with its four-pronged altar bearing smoking sacrifices; harps, flutes and timbrels echoed over the town; but the priests seemed not to be interested in their duties. The rich paid their dues with a swagger, then returned to make more money in the markets, and the poor found it wellnigh impossible to get near the House of Yahweh at all.

When Amos moved to another part of the market the noise offended him even more. Frequently he heard the hoarse cry of a beggar and the shrill song of the water carrier—"Ho, everyone who is thirsty!" But it was the cheating that horrified him—the use of false measures and weights below standard; moldy and rot-

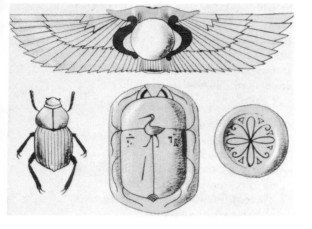

Scarabs and an Egyptian amulet representing the sun-god, in precious stones and ivory. The Egyptians believed that the beetle (scarab) had the power of eternal life and wore these charms for protection against evil spirits.

ting grain being offered at prices the poor could not afford. He saw, too, money-lenders forcing the last coin of interest, rich men accepting children in payment for debts, men and women being bought by Philistine slave traders, poor men fighting to the death for scraps of bread dropped near the baker's booth. Through the open courtyards of the big houses he could see the rich reveling in their luxuries (6:4, 6). The women, in their paint and perfume, encouraged their husbands in this selfish and cruel extravagance; as Amos looked at them he scornfully compared them with the "kine of Bashan" (4:1).

What was happening to the people of the Northern Kingdom? They were Yahweh's, as he of the Southern Kingdom was Yahweh's; they were all of the Promised Land, they were His chosen people; they were brothers—the rich *and* the poor.

CALL OF AMOS

Amos returned to Tekoa, but his mind was not on his sheep or his figs; it was on what he had seen and heard—on the scenes of cruel injustice he had found. But what could *he* do about it—he, a poor Judaean shepherd? Suddenly he knew! Yahweh was calling him; he was not trained as a prophet, he was not even a member of a prophet guild—but he must go and speak out against these evils. Humble and uneducated though he was, he must become Yahweh's spokesman (3:8; 7:15). Amos was stunned at the thought but knew it was true; and his spirit gave him power to do what Yahweh told him. And when he spoke it was with his Tekoan background behind him; his words, stern and simple, were vividly illustrated by his experiences and knowledge of country life—just as Jesus was to draw His lessons from everyday scenes of life in Palestine. Examples of this teaching are seen very clearly in 3:4-8, 12; 4:2, 13; 5:8; 6:12; 7:14; 9:13.

"The Lord God [Yahweh] has spoken, who can but prophesy?" Amos went to Samaria, the capital city. It was there that he heard of the approach of the Assyrians; he talked with the traders in the caravans from Damascus; they told him how the captured city had been foolish enough to rebel against her conquerors, who were even then advancing toward her gates once more to subdue her utterly. It could not be long before Samaria, too, would be besieged; it was only a matter of time before the whole kingdom would be overrun—and defeat by the Assyrians would surely be punishment for Israel's wrongdoing, disobedience and injustice.

To make sure the wall is upright, the builder uses a plumb line (Amos 7:7–9).

AMOS PREACHES

In Bethel, Amos spoke sternly to the people; his message can be found in 2:6–16. The rich, he said, were oppressing the poor, whose lives were now so cheap and worthless that they could be exchanged for the cheapest thing in any market—a pair of shoes (2:6; 4:1; 5:11; 6:4–6; 8:6). Paying temple dues was not enough, attending services was not enough (5:14 ff.); Yahweh could not, would not, accept their worship while there was cruelty; the "day of the Lord" for which they all hoped would never come while bitterness and bribery and slavery went on. They could not even be certain that Yahweh had no thought for any other nation; was He not Creator of

the whole earth? (1:3, 6, 9, 11, 13; 2:1, 4, 6). Yet He must punish them for this wickedness as He had punished other nations. Syria had been punished, as had Ammon, Moab and Judah—and the people rejoiced. Now—Israel would suffer,

"For you sell good men for silver, the
   needy for a pair of shoes,
You trample on the heads of the weak
   and deny justice to the poor.
Above all nations I have blessed you
   with knowledge and freedom;
Therefore I will punish you for every
   last one of your sins!"

Amos had seen baskets of fruit, luscious summer fruits, in the courtyards of the rich—grapes, apricots, pomegranates, figs. Soon they would become overripe, unfit, dead. That would happen to Israel. He saw the workman handling his plumb line to test the straightness of a sloping wall, and told the people that Yahweh would test Israel for her uprightness too —"With a plumb line I am testing my people."

AMOS IS STOPPED

Needless to say, this was not the kind of prophecy that the prosperous schemers wanted to hear. Even Amaziah at Bethel (7:10–13) missed the point of the prophet's words and declared him to be a plotter against the king, Jeroboam II. "Get back to your fellow prophets," he sneered. Amos retorted that he was not one of those, nor even a seer; he was the spokesman of Yahweh the Creator, the Lord of Hosts. Tradition says that Amos was beaten and thrown from the Temple courtyard and forbidden ever to preach there again. He then knew that to reach the people he must write his words; it is possible that some friendly scribe did this for him, which is why to this day we have his fiery words and reproaches in our Bibles.

Over his heavy white linen ephod, threaded with gold, blue and purple strands, Amaziah the High Priest slipped his blue linen robe with its border of embroidered pomegranates and tinkling golden bells. As he did so he may have thought more deeply about Amos. Passing over his head the jeweled breastplate, he may have paused to look at the gems that represented the ten tribes and to think wistfully of the other two tribes now divided from Israel. And he may have wondered if the division of the country meant that not only were the people separated from one another, but that they had drifted far from Yahweh Himself.

Amaziah did not dream then that within a few years Samaria would fall to the Assyrians as Amos had said it would, and that he, the High Priest, would—too late—regret his scorn of the prophet from Judah.

5

*Hosea and the
Fall of the Northern Kingdom*

(HOSEA 1:1-3; 2; 3; 4; 6; 8:4-6; 11; 14:1-18. THE EXILE—II KINGS 17:1-20, 24-29)

Following the death of Jeroboam II there was strife, murder and bloodshed. Six kings came to the throne in quick succession, and of these four were conspirators and usurpers.

CALL OF HOSEA

Hosea belonged to the Northern Kingdom; he was well-educated, friendly and human. As a boy he may have seen and heard Amos in the market place of Bethel or Samaria. Amos had been roused by the injustices he saw—the unfairness between man and man—and he had preached that Yahweh was a just and righteous God. Hosea, whose ministry took place nearly a generation later, during the years 750–735 B.C., taught the lesson he learned bitterly in his own life.

Hosea's wife had left him and his three children. She sank eventually into squalor and even slavery; but Hosea loved her so much that when the chance came at the slave market he bought her back. He paid fifteen pieces of silver and an omer (approximately three quarts) of barley. Hosea saw his message in this. If he could love his wife so much that he forgave her, then Yahweh would forgive his beloved Israel. However low she sank He would take her back; He would be merciful if she repented and was sorry for what she had done. Note how like the message of the New Testament this is—that God is a Father, kind and loving.

Hosea was so much concerned with the fate of the people that he even gave to each of his children a name that carried a message; thus, Jezreel—to remind him of Jehu's massacres and bloodshed in Israel; Lo-Ruchamah—"for I will no more have pity on the house of Israel"— that is, the unpitied one; Lo-Ammi—"for ye are not my people and I will not be your God"—that is, not-akin-to-me. Eventually these names were changed—Jezreel to mean "God sows"; Ruchamah, "pitied"; Ammi, "my people."

Hosea may well have had this intent expression as he listened to Amos. Notice the scrip (wallet) on his belt.

HIS MESSAGE

Although he seems to have some close knowledge of the priesthood, Hosea's messages, like those of Amos, were built on things of the countryside that his hearers understood. Some verses—for example, 2:22; 6:4; 11:10, 11—show how well he knew the landscape. He knew how the leopard prowled and then lay in wait for its prey, and saw Yahweh "like a leopard," like a bear, a lion, a wild beast (13:5-9). There were rare occasions when Israel did obey the will of Yahweh, and then, Hosea said, "Your goodness is as a morning cloud, and as the early dew it goeth away." The Hebrew word for "dew" is the very lovely phrase, "summer-sea-night-mist," which refers to the misty fine rain that comes in from the Mediterranean in silvery clouds to freshen the countryside—a precious rain in times of drought.

In these passages Hosea shows how well he knew Samaria and Bethel—7:1; 8:5; 10:5-7; 4:15; 12:14. We read of their idolatry in 2:8; 4:13, 17; 8:4-14; 10:8; 13:2; 14:8. His knowledge of farming is seen in 4:16; 8:7; 10:10ff; 13:3; 6:3, 4; 9:10; 10:1. Hosea reveals that he is well aware of the danger from neighboring countries and of possible invasion, in such verses as 5:13; 7:11; 8:9; 12:1. He spoke of Ephraim (Israel as a "cake not turned" (7:8). His hearers knew what he meant: with their simple ovens they had often known how a cake could be burned on one side and underdone on the other—half-baked. Israel was neglecting one side of her life—the spiritual side (see 7:4, 6, 7).

Hosea's messages were unpopular, of course, especially to the priests and the rich, who kept the poor in ignorance of the law and in poverty as well (4:6; 12:7, 8).

Hosea announced that Israel would be devastated, and through her desolation and destruction would be made to realize that Yahweh did indeed love her; she would even be sent into captivity and exile, and her suffering would make her turn to Yahweh. His message is to a large extent contained in 11:1-4 and 14:1-8.

ISRAEL A "BUFFER STATE"

Look again at the map and see how Israel lay between the great nations— Babylon and Assyria to the north and west, Egypt to the south—waiting for the chance to conquer the "buffer state," the land of trade and war routes. These three nations were watching each other like wild animals, waiting to attack. The whole of Palestine lay between them and complete power over their enemies. Already the land was divided within itself, torn by civil war, aggression and rivalry. Time and again its people had been invaded and countless numbers of them had been carried away. Now the might of Assyria was on the very borders of the Northern Kingdom. Like Amos, Hosea saw how dangerously near was the aggressor, and he knew that before long Samaria must fall a prey to the invader.

In about 738 B.C. King Menahem, in an effort to secure his own position as ruler, decided to pay tribute to Assyria, and sent to Tiglath-Pileser III one thousand talents of silver (a talent would be worth more than $1400). But the enemy could not be bought off. Some of the king's courtiers advised friendship with Egypt, with gifts of olive oil, wood and wool. Hosea told them they were wasting their time and produce; the One to turn to before it was too late was Yahweh. . . . "Ephraim [Israel]," he said, "is like a silly dove, without understanding; to Egypt they cry, and hasten to Assyria. They strike bargains and carry oil to Egypt!" Hosea was reminding them of the Eastern proverb which says, "There is nothing more simple than a dove." Like the dove, Israel was heading for the snare (7). Yet, if she would return to Yahweh and not trust in the idols of these countries, He would forgive her and look after her once more (14).

THE ASSYRIANS AT WAR

Six years later, in 732 B.C., Tiglath-Pileser, having captured Gilead and Galilee, took Damascus, the great city of Syria. Five years later still the danger became very real; serious raids were made on Israel and captives were taken by the Assyrians. We shall hear much of these invaders, but we must try to picture them early in our story. They were warlike, cruel and determined; they showed no pity for their captives; they destroyed, burned all and spared none. Carvings in stone (called bas-reliefs) show them wearing long-fringed robes, usually tucked up or shaped to free their legs for movement in fighting; their long hair and square beards were closely curled and plaited; on their feet they wore leather sandals, on their heads helmets—probably of bronze. They carried bows and arrows and rode to the city walls on siege towers or tanks, from the tops of which —protected by wicker screens—they showered iron-tipped arrows upon the defenders of the city. On many of the bas-reliefs in the British Museum in London —and some of these are reproduced in the pictures in this book—Tiglath-Pileser himself can be seen riding in his two-wheeled chariot. Some of his men are rearing a battering-ram from a kind of armored horse truck. The prisoners are also shown, some impaled on stakes, others roped together or falling prostrate before the Assyrians or bringing tribute and gifts of food and animals and golden vessels.

An Assyrian king before a besieged castle wall. The battering-ram is breaking down the wall and the archers are high enough to attack the defenders.

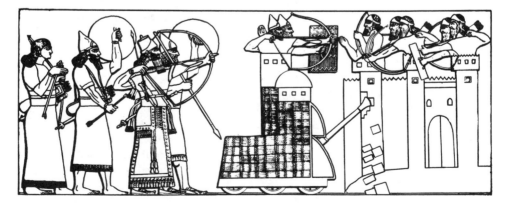

THE ASSYRIANS AT HOME

At home these people lived in luxury, for they were strong and powerful and demanded food, money and tribute of all kinds from the nations they conquered or frightened. Syria sent wood and bronze and articles made of these; Egypt sent gold, ivory, golden and jewelled vessels; Phoenicia sent dyes and silks and pottery.

Even when not fighting, the Assyrians spent much time in dangerous sports like hunting wild bulls and lions; the king kept these animals in captivity so that they could be released for hunting at any time. Their god, Nergal, was a god of hunting and war; he is shown as having an Assyrian human head on the body of a four-footed animal—usually a bull or a lion. The Assyrians had other gods, like Nebo and Bel; these, too, demanded cruel worship (II Kings 17:29). There is no doubt of the skill and power of these people; there is even less doubt of their bloodthirsty, cruel and swift conquests. And yet Israel hesitated.

SAMARIA FALLS

Some years later Shalmaneser decided to extend his kingdom to the Mediterranean. He demanded more tribute from Israel, who went on paying it for a time— and then refused. Shalmaneser promptly laid siege to Samaria. His successor, Sargon II, took over and after three years Samaria gave in; starved into surrender, her leaders opened the gates to the enemy (II Kings 17). The Assyrians loved to portray their conquests and to record their campaigns in their own wedge-shaped cuneiform script. Sargon wrote: "I besieged, took and captured the town of Samaria and carried into captivity 27,280 persons who lived in it."

THE END OF THE
NORTHERN KINGDOM

The Assyrians were utterly ruthless and believed in exterminating their conquered peoples. Thus, we are told, the majority of the population of the Northern Kingdom was carried away beyond the Jordan to Nineveh in Assyria—never to return. Despite the warnings of Elijah, Elisha, Amos and Hosea, the "Lost Tribes" of Israel, as they are called, were gone forever.

Sargon replaced the captives with those of other tribes he had conquered, and soon Samaria was occupied by strange people with strange tongues and strange idol worship. These mixed races intermarried with those few Israelites left behind by Sargon; their descendants became the "Samaritans," of whom we shall hear more later.

From this time, 721 B.C., which marks the fall of Samaria, we are concerned no longer with the Northern Kingdom, for it ceases to exist; we follow now the fortunes—and misfortunes—of the Southern Kingdom, Judah, with her capital Jerusalem and her people the Jews.

THE "BEGINNINGS" OF OUR BIBLE

This chapter ends in the destruction of the Northern Kingdom, but it is as

Nergal—the winged man-headed bull god of the Assyrians.

This shows how the massive bull god was moved with rollers, ropes and levers by hundreds of slaves. Compare it with the moving of the Rameses statue in Part I.

well for us to remember that from this sad end came a wonderful gift to the whole world. It is obvious that at least a few of the Israelites of the Northern Kingdom were anxious and able to flee the country in fear of the invading Assyrian army; they made their way to Judah in the south. They took with them precious manuscripts, the chronicles and stories of their land and ancestors, that were then being written down for fear they should be altogether forgotten. Scholars have since named these the E documents—E standing for Ephraim and Elohim, a Hebrew name for God in the Northern Kingdom. In the Southern Kingdom there were already in existence similar documents called J—standing for Judah and Jahveh, another spelling of Yahweh. These stories were similar to those of the Northern Kingdom, but differed in detail and style of writing. These two narratives of familiar stories were woven together in later years, and became the basis of our present Bible. You can trace these two different accounts in many of the early Bible stories, for example, the creation in Genesis 1 and 2, and the stories of Joseph, in which the differences are indicated in Part I of this series.

Thus we owe the preservation of these wonderful stories to the refugees from the Northern Kingdom who brought for safekeeping their precious documents; their loyalty to Yahweh brought for ageless possession the stories of the people and their God.

6

Hezekiah

(II KINGS 18; 19; 20:1-7. II CHRON. 29; 30:1-15; 32)

The history of the Jews now centers in the Southern Kingdom of Judah. By the time Hezekiah came to the throne, about 725 B.C., there had been many bad and good kings. The "bad" kings were those who did "that which was evil in the sight of the Lord"—those who allowed and encouraged the worship of baals and idols and neglected Yahweh; the "good" kings were those who "did right in the sight of the Lord"—those who destroyed the groves, shrines and high places used for idolatry and insisted that Judah should worship Yahweh as the one true God of the people.

HIS GOOD WORK

Hezekiah was a good king. He came to the throne a few years before the final attack of the Assyrians on the Northern Kingdom. It must have seemed to him only a matter of time before Judah too would be invaded.

Judah itself lay to the east of the trade routes and could even be by-passed by marauding tribes and armies anxious to come to grips with one another for complete power; but Egypt to the south and Assyria to the north had no intentions of leaving Judah unconquered and possibly a thorn in their flesh. Besides, Uzziah had made the country prosperous once more, and it was now a kingdom worth capturing for its own wealth.

The father of Hezekiah, Ahaz (not to be confused with Ahab of the Northern Kingdom), had been an idol worshiper, he believed that the Syrian gods—like Reshef pictured on p. 141—could help him. When he was sent for to pay homage to Sargon he not only accepted his enemy but also his enemy's gods. On his return to Jerusalem he erected an altar like the alien one he had seen, showing that he would pay tribute to Assyrian gods as well as to the Assyrian king. This would

The countryside of Judah, with its terraced slopes and fertile valleys. Not far away are the wilderness and rough hill country and desert.

have meant a return to child sacrifice too. Hezekiah cleared away this altar and all others used for the worship of false gods; he had the Temple cleansed, reopened, and reconsecrated. The people welcomed these changes, sudden as they were, and Hezekiah decided to celebrate Passover, which had been neglected since the time of Solomon. You can read about Passover in Part I. The feast was held to remind the Jews of the last meal the Children of Israel had had before their release from Egyptian slavery. Invitations were sent through the length and breadth of the land—"from Dan to Beersheba"—and by so doing Hezekiah was trying to bring the people back to Yahweh. It

is probable that Isaiah helped him to word the invitations. Read what he said in II Chronicles 30:6–9. It is sad to find that so many of the tribes "laughed them to scorn and mocked them." But the feast was attended by many loyal Jews and lasted fourteen days instead of seven.

SAFEGUARDING THE WATER SUPPLY

By now Israel, the Northern Kingdom, had fallen and the frontiers of Judah stood as a final challenge to the conquering Assyrians. Hezekiah knew the danger, and having repaired the Millo earthworks built by David and strengthened by Sol-

On the carving is inscribed "Reshef, god of the wind, the Great One, may he give you light and life every day."

omon, turned his attention to one of the key factors of an army's existence in the land—the water supply. If he could cut off or diminish that he might stave off invasion. Asking, "Why should the kings of the Assyrians find much water?" he and his people set about the control of all water supplies, fountains, and streams. There are references to this in II Chronicles 32:4; II Kings 20:20; Isaiah 22:9,

Excavations have revealed his wonderful feat of engineering. Wells were more often than not outside the city walls, whence the women fetched water in pots and jars and skins, and where the shepherds watered their flocks more easily because there was more room than in the

city itself. Other water supplies within the city were available, of course. From Gihon, the Virgin's Spring, where the natural spring supply was, Hezekiah had dug a tunnel through 1,750 feet of solid rock. It led into the Pool of Siloam. Evidently dug in a hurry, it is not by any means a perfect piece of work, being uneven and unequal. But it does represent a remarkable task, for, boring from opposite ends, the workmen met almost exactly as planned. Here is part of the inscription cut in the rock: "While yet they plied the drill, each towards his fellow . . . there was heard the voice of one calling unto another . . . on the day of the boring through the stonecutters struck, each to meet his fellow, drill upon drill, and the water flowed from the source to the pool for a thousand and two hundred cubits." (Remember that a cubit was eighteen to twenty inches.)

The Syrian storm god Reshef in bronze.

145

The outer end of the tunnel—shown in the picture—was disguised and hidden so that the Assyrians would not find it. It was rediscovered A.D. 1880 by two inquisitive and adventurous boys.

HEZEKIAH'S FOOLISHNESS

Soon after this work was completed, Hezekiah fell desperately ill. He probably had some poisonous abscess which, neglected, would prove dangerous. It is at this time that we meet Isaiah, of whom we have so far heard little. He treated the king's illness with a poultice of figs; an ancient remedy for a sick horse, it certainly cured Hezekiah.

The king recovered and received gifts and kind greetings from no less a person than the prince of Babylon. Hezekiah was delighted and invited him to Jerusalem, where he was shown the king's treasures and the wealth of the Temple. This was an unwise, even a foolish, thing to do. Babylon was an enemy to Assyria and might prove a welcome friend to Judah, but having seen all the splendor of Judah the prince was sure to report to his father, who might decide that Judah was worth capturing too. Isaiah (39:6) reproved Hezekiah for his lack of foresight.

THE THREAT OF SENNACHERIB

Meanwhile, the Assyrians were getting uncomfortably nearer. Isaiah 10 tells vividly how swiftly Sennacherib moved westward, conquering as he came; one after another, the little kingdoms fell, until in Judah itself forty-six cities, including Lachish, were taken by storm. A tremendous tribute was demanded from Hezekiah, who had to strip his palace and the Temple of all their gold and rich hangings to meet it; he even gave up a captured Philistine king as part of the ransom. Like other kings, Sennacherib recorded his campaigns on his own cylinder of baked clay, which is now in the British Museum. It is called the Taylor Prism. In Part I is a copy of some of the sentences in the account of the siege of Jerusalem, in cuneiform script. In the inscription on the six-sided cylinder are these words: "As for Hezekiah, King of Judah, who did not submit to my yoke, forty-six of his strong-walled cities I

Assyrian archers behind a screen of wickerwork — interlaced reeds strengthened with leather.

besieged by escalade, by bringing up siege engines, by storming, by mines, tunnels and breaches. I took two hundred thousand people . . . horses, mules, asses, camels, cattle and sheep. . . . As for Hezekiah himself, I shut him up in Jerusalem, his royal city, liked a caged bird. . . . The Arabs and his mercenary soldiers . . . deserted him. Thirty talents of gold, eight hundred talents of silver, gems, antimony, jewels, precious stones, ivory couches and chairs, elephants' hide, ivory, maple, cedar . . . his daughter, his harem and his musicians, he had them brought after me to Nineveh, my royal city."

ASSYRIAN WARFARE

There is no doubt that Sennacherib launched his attack from Lachish, which he had made his headquarters and center

An Assyrian siege-engine followed by spearmen. Compare the helmets and armor of the fighters.

Slingers. They hurled stones over the walls of the besieged city with remarkable skill and accuracy.

from which to control the way to Egypt as well as to Jerusalem. Lachish has been excavated and has revealed many historical facts. The bas-reliefs showing the siege—that once adorned the palace at Nineveh, the capital of Assyria—are now in the British Museum. (See II Kings 18:14, 17; 19:8; Isa. 36:2.) These show thirteen slabs carved with scenes from the siege, the assault and capture of the city of Lachish, the prisoners and plunder. The title reads: "Sennacherib, the mighty king of the country of Assyria, sitting on the throne of judgment, before the city of Lachish. I give permission for its slaughter."

ATTACK!

What had happened at Lachish now seemed likely to happen at Jerusalem. The Assyrians set up mounds of mud bricks, soil, rocks and trees; up these were to be rushed the siege engines or battering-rams. These were mounted on four wheels and were leather-covered for the protection of the invaders—three in each, one to handle the ram, one to shoot iron-tipped arrows, one to put out firebrands hurled from above by the defenders on the city walls. Looking closely at the bas-reliefs you can see kneeling archers backed by rows of standing men, protected by others holding shields of leather-covered wicker-work. The Assyrian bowmen wear conical peaked helmets, but those of the shield-bearers and spearmen have crests or combs not unlike those on firemen's helmets.

Imagine the scene; there are slingers, spearmen, horsemen, and charioteers. The prisoners are pathetically kneeling—men, women and children, even babies. The king sits on his rich throne, in his right hand two arrows, on his lift a bow. A slave carries his parasol to protect him from the sun. The slave in a turban is clean-shaven and is probably a Canaanite; the Assyrians themselves all have long, square-cut beards, their long hair curled at the ends; the Judaeans wear short, curled beards, more rounded at the corners, and their hair is curled all over the head. The landscape is filled with olive and fig trees and clusters of grapes.

SURRENDER!

Hezekiah knew what to expect and the murderous revenge likely to befall him for his refusal to give in. Probably Sennacherib, with his eyes on Egypt as well, did not want to risk either losing too many men or a stab in the back from Egypt. So he sent someone to try to talk the king into surrender.

Acting on Isaiah's advice, Hezekiah told the people in the city that Yahweh would save them. The Assyrian chief officer, the Rabshakeh, came to the walls and shouted up to the besieged people. He accused them of trusting Egypt—"this bruised reed" (II Kings 18:21). Read his speech aloud and see how full of taunts, flatterings and accusations it is; see how cunning and furious he is at getting no answer to his bluff—especially when he jibes that he will provide two thousand horses if the king can produce the riders. Hezekiah had already asked Egypt for cavalry. The Rabshakeh's threat that they would die of thirst and famine was wasted on the Jews as they thought of their strategy in securing a safe water supply. The nations the Rabshakeh mentions were some of those overrun by the Assyrians on their way to Palestine; many of the captives had been deported to other lands, just as had been those of the Northern Kingdom.

The chief officer returned to Sennacherib, who advanced his army up the slope toward the city walls; he brought up his deadly siege engines, began piling up the mounds near the walls, and lined up his men according to the weapons they used. Before long, thought the fearful watchers, it would be Lachish all over again; not even Yahweh could save them now. Still Sennacherib hesitated; his main army was toward Egypt—ought he to attack? He wrote to Hezekiah. Surrender —or . . . ! Hezekiah then did a wise thing; he talked to Yahweh about it. You will find his fine prayer in II Kings 19:15–19. Isaiah gave his good advice, for he was quite sure that Yahweh would save Jerusalem, even at this late hour. Isaiah had, of course, previously told the king not to break with Assyria, but once the king had done so the prophet remained loyal to him. Remembering that the sign of

Assyria was a fierce bull, he said that "this raging bull shall be tamed and driven back," with a rope through the ring in its nose! In other words, the Assyrians would never succeed in their siege of Jerusalem.

DESTRUCTION OF SENNACHERIB

That night the Assyrians were deployed against the city walls; the blow would fall at any moment, perhaps that night. It did—but not against Jerusalem. A strange event took place in the besieging army. No one is quite sure what it was;

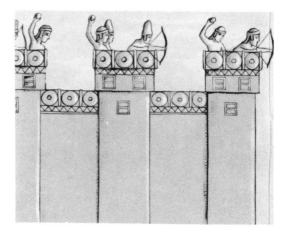

Some of the Jewish defenders.

some say a plague broke out, brought and spread by hordes of field mice (rats and mice do spread diseases); they even gnawed through the bowstrings of the bowmen. In the morning light the anxious defenders saw the army—dead. To the Jews this Assyrian disaster could mean only one thing—Yahweh's Angel of Death had passed over the camp (Isa. 37; II Kings 19). Dismayed by this unexpected catastrophe, with his army weakened and Egypt near enough to make a decisive attack, Sennacherib retired and made his way back to Nineveh. His famous records say: "As for Hezekiah himself, the fear of my royal armies cast him down"; but there is no reference to his failure to take Jerusalem!

The city was saved once again and her people felt more secure than they might have done could they have known what the future held for them. Many believed that after this great escape Jerusalem would never fall to a conqueror; they did not foresee the victorious armies of Babylonia, whose prince had seen the treasures of the palace and the Temple a few years before.

7

Isaiah, Micah, Josiah

(ISA. 1:1-20; 2; 5:1-24; 6:1-13; 7:1-7; 9:2, 6, 7; 10:20-24; 11:1-9; 28:23-29; 31:6; 35:3-10; 36; 37. MICAH 2:1-3, 8-11; 3:1-8; 6:6-12; 7:1-7. II KINGS 21:1-6, 16; 12; 23:1-8)

ISAIAH

Without Isaiah, Hezekiah would probably have given in to Sennacherib and failed in his kingship. Who, then, was Isaiah? And why had he such a fine influence on the king?

It is not easy to find this merely by reading the book bearing his name. For one thing, scholars tell us that not all the book was written by one man, but that there may have been three authors; also, the chapters are not in chronological order, so the prophecies do not follow one another correctly. But Isaiah was certainly a historical character, a real person. His call to serve Yahweh and be a spokesman is given in chapter 6:1–13; he had most to do between the years 740–700 B.C. Isaiah himself was unlike any of the prophets of whom we have already heard. They were of ordinary birth and background. Isaiah was a statesman, well-educated, rich, familiar with the king's court, and adviser to Hezekiah.

ISAIAH THE STATESMAN

Isaiah knew of the dangers arising from military alliances and did not want Judah dragged into war. Ahaz, King of Judah, was being encouraged to join the Syrian and Israelite kings in fighting the Assyrians; these two kings even attacked Jerusalem in an attempt to force him; but Ahaz wanted to "buy" help from the very enemy who swept over the other two countries and was left to pay (II Kings 16:7). Isaiah said this was foolish but Ahaz ignored him. When, in the same way years later, Hezekiah wanted to buy help from Egypt, Isaiah advised him against that too. The prophet said, "Keep away from these warring nations; stay neutral." Not only was this wise for political reasons (20; 21) but also from the religious point of view. Other gods

Isaiah must have seen this view many times; it is one approach to the city of Jerusalem.

had failed their nations but Yahweh would save Judah, for He was in the Temple at Jerusalem, the City of God; this would prove Him to be the one true God.

HIS CALL

The prophet had felt his unworthiness (Isa. 6), but his, "Here am I; send me" gave him great courage and confidence. He had received his call in the Temple itself, while in some kind of trance. What most impressed Isaiah was the holiness of God. He felt sure that his country would one day fall to an invader, and his message therefore centered on the "remnant of Israel," who were to be a holy people serving a Holy God.

"SONG OF THE VINEYARD"

This belief sent him out to do God's work—to forthtell. It was probably at a vintage festival when the people were happily celebrating the year's good grape harvest that he sang his song of the vineyard (5:1-7). He sang as a minstrel and

the people gathered around him. He told of the preparation of the vineyard, in a sunny spot and in fertile soil. The vineyard was cultivated by hand, since a plow could not be used on the hillside, and the stones were cleared away; strong plants were put in. Next came protection —a watchtower such as that used by Naboth to look over his vineyard, a hedge and a stone wall to keep out thieves and goats; and a vat in which to trample the grapes was hewn out of the limestone at harvest time. But the harvest failed, and there grew only wild, sour grapes. Here Isaiah turned to his hearers and there was a change of rhythm in his song. Judge, he said, what should be done. The vineyard must be destroyed. Down must come the hedge and the wall; the cattle and goats should devour the vines. The vineyard must be left to rot and shrivel, untended, unpruned, undug. Ah, sang Isaiah, "the vineyard of the Lord of hosts is the house of Israel, the men of Judah his pleasant plant; and he looked for judgment, but behold oppression; for righteousness, but behold a cry" (5:7). In the original Hebrew tongue the prophet makes a play on words here; he meant, "He looked for rule and found misrule; for redress and behold distress."

The people had condemned themselves; they were indeed a neglected vineyard that should be destroyed. Yet, said Isaiah, a few should be saved—a remnant to whom Yahweh's majesty and holiness would be powerful guides for living. Isaiah even called his son Shear-Jashub, meaning "a remnant shall return to God."

WARNING

On another occasion, Isaiah carried around with him a kind of notice board or poster; it was a clay tablet bearing the words MAHER-SHALAL-HASH-BAZ, which meant "swift-spoil-speedy-prey." He was trying to make it clear that Judah would one day be the prey of the swift Assyrians; he gave this strange name to his second son.

To Isaiah the promise of a Messiah was to be the reward of the "chosen people," the remnant. His words are familiar to us as part of the Christmas story and in Handel's *Messiah*. Note especially 9:1–7 and 11:1–9. Amos had seen Yahweh as a God of justice; Hosea, as a God of love; Isaiah was positive that He was a God of righteousness and holiness, who would accept nothing that was wicked or impure. To this end He would forgive (1:18), if they would give up their sins, injustices and idolatry. . . . "His hand is stretched out still."

"A LODGE IN A GARDEN"

There came a time when there was much distress and confusion in Jerusalem. News of disasters came in daily; refugees crowded into the city, workmen strengthened the walls and prepared to secure the water supplies; beaten soldiers straggled back with their vivid stories of defeat and death at the hands of the invaders. Not a few people flocked to the Temple in their panic and anxiety; others were reckless and carefree, seeking what they thought to be their last pleasures before the siege of the city and its fall. Isaiah watched all this; in imagination he saw the victorious armies conquering village after village and city after city in their advance upon Jerusalem, left isolated "as a booth in a vineyard, as a lodge in a garden of cucumbers" (1:8). The prophet recalled the booths or shelters of brushwood and branches built on the hillsides during the Feast of Tabernacles; he knew, too, of the even more flimsy and loosely made shelters that the worker made for himself in the fields or vineyard or orchard for protection against the rain and sun. Frequently such structures were left until they fell to pieces in the rain and wind, when they presented pictures of ruin and desolation. That was how "the daughter of Zion" would be left because Jerusalem had disobeyed Yahweh. Yet Yahweh would lop down their enemies as a woodman cut down trees—if the people would heed His words. But His words fell on deaf ears.

ISAIAH'S MESSAGE

His message was one of confidence and hope and trust (31:5). Just as Amos had done, he said he was certain that Yahweh would look after any nation with real faith in Him (26:2), and that other nations might be His instruments (8:7 and 10:5), despite their power to conquer (10:15 and 37:29). Amos had pointed out the folly of lip service and mere ritual in worship; Isaiah now said that what God really wanted from everybody was righteousness, charity and fairdealing (1:11–18: compare Ps. 51). Like Amos, he, too, was angry at social wrongs, especially those brought on by the luxuryloving women. Amos had called them cows of Bashan (4:1); Isaiah has a bitter passage about them too (3:18). There were other injustices towards the poor (3:14 and 5:8, 9).

HIS ADVICE

Like the prophets before him, Isaiah tried to help his hearers by referring to things they knew about. Thus, in 28:23–29, there is an excellent description of farming; in 17:6 and 24:13, he talks of the olive berries left on the tree after the beatings at harvest and compares them with the "remnant" of holy people. He mentions the potter in 29:16 and 30:14; the "potter's vessel beaten down" refers to the crushing of broken pottery to powder for making cement. When a pot is broken in the home the larger pieces are saved for "taking fire from the hearth," as we might use a dustpan; curved pieces called "sherds"—hence, "potsherds"—

The potter's work is much the same in many Eastern countries. He works the bottom wheel with his feet and the top one spins; with his free hands he shapes his jars and bakes them hard in a nearby oven.

Isaiah poured much scorn on Judah's false idols (Isa. 2:8). The bird-faced one was made by hand in Mesopotamia, but was found in Palestine. The "mother-goddess" has a feathered headdress and is Canaanite.

were laid beside the well or brook so that thirsty travelers could use them for scooping up water to drink. The prophet says that the crushing of Yahweh's disobedient people would be final and total destruction—like the grinding to powder of the pieces of the potter's vessel (compare Jer. 19:11).

Isaiah refers to homely things like using a razor (7:20), robbing birds' nests (10:14 and 16:2), beds too short for comfort (28:20), faithfulness like a firm nail (22:23). Note how clearly these references must have carried messages if only the people had bothered to think about them. When they jibed at him he retorted that they would be taught in a foreign tongue—the tongue of the invader (28:9–13). His words about molten and graven images—those made in the melting pot and those carved from stone—remind us that false worship was still common in the land; the people were loath to give up the gods that they could see in order to trust in a God they could not see.

What happened to this great statesman-prophet? Tradition tells us that by the Pool of Siloam he was hideously murdered—Hebrews 11:37 says "sawn asunder"—by the evil king Manasseh, in whose reign Judah returned once more to her sinful and wicked ways.

MICAH

Micah was a contemporary of Isaiah; that is, he lived at about the same time; his preaching covers the years 715–701 B.C. Because of the power and work of Isaiah, Micah was to some extent overshadowed by his older friend, although some of his messages were at times identical with those of Isaiah. This you can see if you compare, for instance, Isaiah 2:2–4 with Micah 4:1–3. None the less, Micah had much to say about Judah's religion and fate. He, too, complained of injustices (2:2 and 3:10); about the greed of the wealthy (2:1–4 and 3:1); about mere lip service in worship (6:6–8; 3:11 and 4:3, 4).

One hundred years after he had made his prophecy about Jerusalem in 3:12, his words were repeated by Jeremiah (26: 18, 19). The book bearing his name is probably a collection of prophecies by at least three writers, but contains some fine passages and noble thoughts. Chapters 1–3 are Micah's, 4 and 5 relate to a later period; 6 and 7 refer to the Babylonian captivity rather than to the Assyrian conquest.

THE PROPHET'S BACKGROUND

Little is known of the prophet; he was born at Moresheth, a village in the Shephelah district near the Philistine border and twenty miles west of Tekoa, the home of Amos. He must have watched the caravans along the trade route to Egypt and he had seen too often the armies of the invaders; obviously country-bred, he saw and knew of the oppression and starvation of the poor—he saw it in Judah as Amos had seen it in Israel. He heard about the destruction of Damascus and Samaria and knew that Jerusalem would eventually fall because of her social wrongs. Strangely enough, he has little if anything to say about idolatry; he seems more concerned with justice.

He knew that some of the rich landowners stole their poorer neighbors' ground by moving landmarks and boundary stones; no one could prove that the stones had been moved, and the wealthy farmers gained by this cheating. They even lent to their victims the corn grown on this stolen land and charged such a high rate of interest that when the farmers could not pay they had to give up the rest of their little farms: some had to give themselves when their property was gone, and they and their families became servants and slaves to their rich cheating neighbours.

Micah watched the oxen trample corn on the threshing-floor and felt that Jerusalem would one day be trampled by a powerful enemy.

But the prophet preached a message of hope and peace and joy in the land; and, like those prophets who had before him said similar things and given the same warnings, Micah was laughed at by the very people he most wanted to help.

JOSIAH

MANASSEH—A BAD KING

On the death of Hezekiah, Manasseh —an evil king—came to the throne and once more encouraged idol worship. He was only twelve years of age, so the responsibility really falls upon the shoulders of those ruling for him; but as he grew older he continued their wrongdoing and rebuilt the high places, shrines and altars. He even introduced sun, moon and star worship; he paid tribute to Assyria and took over the Assyrian gods. The chief of these was Astarte (called Ishtar by the Babylonians), the Mother goddess of these Eastern nations. She was often called the "Queen of Heaven," and all sorts of cruel sacrifices, mainly of children, together with superstitious beliefs, were connected with the worship of this goddess. Shamash, another god, was supposed to ride in a horse-drawn chariot, for he was the sun-god; his chariot was placed in the Temple itself. In place of the prophets and priests, Manasseh had sorcerers and wizards; he persecuted and murdered all believers in Yahweh whom he could find; Isaiah was one of these. In II Chronicles 33:12, 13, and in the Apocrypha, is the Prayer of Manasseh, which some writers say proves the king's final repentance for all his wrong-doing; but history does not agree and what II Kings 21:16 says is probably nearer the truth.

JOSIAH—A GOOD KING

It is good to know that his grandson Josiah, only eight, was the next king, ruling from 639 to 608 B.C. He was a good king, guided by better advisers and faithful followers of Yahweh. Once again, like Hezekiah, he set about ridding the country of idols and worship of false gods. The power of Assyria was waning and this made his reforms the easier to carry out. Again the Temple was cleansed and repaired; money for this was collected

In the mason's yard today, cutting and shaping stone for building, much as it was done in the time of Isaiah.

and spent on the wages of carpenters and masons, as well as for their materials—timber from Lebanon and stone from the quarries of Solomon.

A GREAT DISCOVERY

It was when cleaning out rooms and wall niches that Hilkiah the High Priest made his startling discovery of a roll of the scriptures which had most probably been hidden during the persecutions of Manasseh's cruel reign. This roll is believed to have been part of the Book of Deuteronomy; even in those days such a roll would be a great treasure. Shaphan, a scribe whose duty it was to keep copies

of the scriptures, took it to Josiah, who read the words now to be found in Deuteronomy 28:1–6, 15–17. He was horrified at what the words of the Law of Moses revealed; Judah had indeed sunk low, she had forgotten her holy Covenant (Deut. 26:16–19).

REPENTANCE AND REFORM

Josiah rent his robe and garbed himself in sackcloth, and put ashes on his head; this was the usual sign of grief and sorrow. He sent for advice and Huldah, a prophetess, brought him messages from Yahweh. She told him that for her sins Jerusalem would be punished by captivity, but he, Josiah, would be spared that disgrace in his own reign. The roll was read to the people, who agreed to reform. As a sign of their conversion they destroyed everything connected with idolatry—the idols, shrines, vessels, the horses and chariots of the sun-god, the pole Asherah, altars. . . . These were burned or broken to pieces by the Brook Kedron outside the city. An order went out that from then on sacrifice was to be made in Jerusalem and nowhere else, and all village sacrifice had to cease. Then, like Hezekiah, Josiah called for a celebration of the Passover for rededication (see Deut. 12:1–7). It is helpful to note here that Deuteronomy contains the words of Moses spoken during his last days before the Israelites crossed the Jordan, together with a collection of laws. The book teaches that God expects us to love and respect our neighbors as ourselves—the teaching of Jesus Himself. We should remember, too, how much Jesus used the words of Deuteronomy, especially in the account of His temptations and also in His teachings (see Matt. 4:1–11, especially verses 4, 7, 10).

FALL OF NINEVEH

Meanwhile, a new threat was clearly

A roll of the Law. Hilkiah found one and brought it to Josiah.

on the way, this time from Egypt. To the far north Scythian hordes had swept in their fierce attacks across the Fertile Crescent, and had taken heavy toll of the power of Assyria. Assyria was weakening and could not face these new attacks and hold on to her many conquests as well. In 612 B.C. the capital city Nineveh fell. Chapter 3 of the little book of Nahum is a shout of exultation at this event; part of it, in modern translation, says:

> "Hark to the whips, to the rumbling of
>   wheels;
> Horses are prancing,
> Chariots leaping,
> Cavalry charging,
> Swords flash like flames and spears as
>   the lightning;
> There's abundance of slain and a mass
>   of dead bodies; . . ."

It is a vivid description of the kind of bloodshed the Assyrians had in former battles brought upon other nations.

DEATH OF JOSIAH

Egypt, strangely enough, was moving northward in an effort to help Assyria;

perhaps she was anxious about the possible downward sweep of those Scythian marauders. At Megiddo, where Solomon had had his stables in days gone by and where Sisera had been routed by Deborah and Barak, the good Josiah was executed as a disloyal vassal. II Kings 23: 28–37 gives a different impression that is not confirmed by Egyptian records. Pharaoh Necho put a new king over Judah, but three years later was himself defeated by the Babylonians in a decisive battle at Carchemish, in 605 B.C. (Jer. 16:2).

By this time all Josiah's good work was undone. It was now the turn of yet another prophet to sound the alarm. This he could do with a great deal of experience behind him. He had heard of the attacking Scythians when he was but a youth; news of the fall of Ninevah came to Jerusalem at the time he began his preaching and prophecy; he knew full well that before he became an old man he would see the fall of his beloved city of Jerusalem unless . . . So he, too, warned his people; and they laughed at him as they had always laughed at their prophets. The name of this prophet is Jeremiah.

8

*Jeremiah and the Fall
of the Southern Kingdom*

(JER. 1:1-16; 5:1-6, 15-19, 25-31; 7:1-15, 21-24; 18:1-12; 20:1-6; 22:13-19;
23:5-8; 24:1-10; 26:1-16; 28; 31:29-34; 34; 36:1-32; 37:11-21; 38:1-13
39:1-10. LAM. I)

Jeremiah was born in about 650 B.C. at Anathoth, just to the northwest of Jerusalem, on the edge of the wilderness, where he learned what it was to experience intense heat and bitter cold, darkness and light, rain and drought, famine and plenty, danger and safety. All these experiences are seen in his teachings and preachings, for like the prophets before him, as a prophet-spokesman of God he explained things to the people in parables and events that were familiar to them. Like most of the prophets, he did not want to answer his call; he was timid and gentle, and shrank from the task of speaking in public against the wrongs he saw.

"WAKE UP!"

Early in his book we find him looking at the beautiful almond tree in blossom —the first tree to do so, in February. It spoke to him of the awakening of nature;

it was the "wake-up" tree, and he thought of Yahweh's watchfulness and wakefulness over His people (Jer. 1:11, 12). Read the verses in the Bible and then compare them with this translation: "The word of Yahweh came unto me, saying, Jeremiah, what seest thou? And I said, I see a branch of a 'wake-up tree.' Then said Yahweh unto me, Thou hast well seen; for I am wakeful over my word to perform it." Little did Jeremiah know what a hard task lay before him, how obstinate and stubborn would be his hearers, how persecuted, lonely and miserable he himself would be.

JEREMIAH'S BACKGROUND

In order to understand his preachings and words we need to see how keenly he saw and remembered his home life. He had watched the migrating birds (8:7) and thought of their wonderful homing instinct; he knew of the ways of the partridge (17:11). In the wilderness he had known the dangers of wild animals (4:7; 5:6); there were bears, lions (no longer found in Palestine), leopards, hyenas, jackals and wild boars. Leaving the wilderness, Jeremiah had sometimes entered the depths of the Jordan gorge —the "pride of the Jordan." When he spoke of the invasion of the Babylonians he said, "Behold, he shall come like a lion from the pride of Jordan" (49:19). And again (in 12:5) he asked, "In a land of peace [safety] how wilt thou do in the pride of Jordan [danger]?" Like Hosea, he had seen the leopard with its yellow spots ringed with black, high in the craggy rocks waiting for sunset; he had known of its stealthy descent, its hunting for prey, and the deathly silence that reigned when it was on the prowl. For three nights it would wait motionless until an unsuspecting villager or sheep or even wild beast was near enough for its swift, deadly leap. So Jeremiah speaks of distrust—"Does an Ethiopian change his skin, or a leopard his spots?" (13:23) —and of the danger of the watching, waiting enemy—"a leopard shall watch over their cities" (5:6).

HIS MESSAGE FOR THE INDIVIDUAL

For all this knowledge of the countryside, Jeremiah was evidently born into a priestly family, among the priests of Levi, and was a descendant of Eli (see Part I). He therefore knew much of the early writings and stories of his people, and may even have read some of the accounts of the Northern Kingdom that were brought to Judah when the scribes of Israel had fled before the conquering hordes of Assyria in 721 B.C. Like Amos and Isaiah, he knew only too well how unfit and weak he was, but felt sure that Yahweh would always help him in his bitter duty of challenging his own people (15:15–18; 23:18, 22).

His message was straightforward but startling. If Judah continued to disobey Yahweh, the people would be punished —they had heard that from the other prophets. But Jeremiah had different ideas. He said that they would be punished both as a nation and also as individuals. This was a new teaching, the responsibility of the individual. The people had been used to the idea of being represented by a great leader—like Moses, for example—who could speak with God for the nation; but Jeremiah was now saying that Yahweh was concerned with each and every one of them separately, and looked for a change of heart in each individual, not merely in the nation or their leader (31:31–34).

There was a proverb in Israel: "The fathers have eaten sour grapes and the children's teeth are set on edge" (31:29: compare Ezek. 18:2, 3). Other prophets had said Yahweh would bring disaster upon the Jews because of their wicked history; but the people now said this was not fair, they ought not to be punished for their fathers' sins. Jeremiah told them that they themselves were wicked enough to deserve the punishment that was expected. Each one of them must be judged for his own sins and wrong-doings. Josiah had tried to make them good with his reforms, but his work had been "from the outside." What was needed was something "inside"—a change of heart. This is often spoken of as Jeremiah's New Covenant—and new it certainly was in the ears of the Jews.

FORBIDDEN TO PREACH

Knowing from their past history how easily the nation switched from evil to good and back again to evil, Jeremiah decided that only exile—as had happened to Israel—would teach them that Yahweh meant what He said (27:1, 2, 7–11). He proclaimed this in no less a place than the Temple courts and was promptly seized by his enemies (7:1–16; 26:1–16: compare Luke 19:46). The Temple priests rescued him; some of his relations may have been among them. They felt sure that his message was from Yahweh, but

Into a brazier of this kind Jehoiakim threw the pieces of skin bearing the prophecies of Jeremiah.

they forbade him ever again to preach in the precincts of the Temple. So he dictated his message to a young friend who became his secretary; this was Baruch, who took Jeremiah's words to the Temple and read them for all to hear. The prophet was hurried away to a place of safety, but the king—Jehoiakim—had the message read to him. It was the ninth month, November, and the winter had set in. The king therefore sat by a brazier, a fire of charcoal (not coal as we know it) burning in a copper pan mounted on a. stand about two feet high. The charcoal was probably from the root of broom (Ps. 120:4 and Job 30:4); sweet-smelling chips of pine might have been added to give the smoke a pleasant tang. The king listened to Jeremiah's prophecy of exile, and as he did so, with his knife he deliberately slashed pieces from the scroll and

watched them shrivel in the "coals of fire" (36:22, 23). He sent for Jeremiah and Baruch, but they were safely away, ready to start all over again the message that the king had destroyed but which the prophet knew he must tell to the king's people (36:28, 32).

It was at this time that a lesser prophet named Uriah had prophesied against the king, had fled to Egypt and was brought back to Jehoiakim, who had him murdered. Letters about this man, written on pieces of pottery called "ostraca," have been found at Lachish; they tell of the arrest and trial of Uriah and give interesting information about the people of the time. Jeremiah was more fortunate than Uriah, though he must have despaired of ever getting the people to listen to him.

A KING OF ASSYRIA

Meanwhile, if Judah's lesson could be learned only through captivity which na-

Pieces of pottery like this are called "ostraca." On such a piece might be written notes, receipts, letters, etc., instead of on papyrus or skin. This one reads: "For the King, a thousand and one hundred [measures?] of oil [from?] Hiyahu," probably an Israelite customs officer.

Ashurbanipal and his Queen are feasting in their garden, with throne, divan, slaves and musicians.

in Babylonia the nation into whose hands Judah would fall. Yahweh's will was that Judah should be a god-fearing nation rather than a mighty one; and if the people went on worshiping baals, op-

tion would be her conqueror? Assyria, weakened by her battles with Egypt and the Scythian hordes, had fallen. Ashurbanipal had become king—the most powerful of them all—but even he had not been able to hold together the whole empire. Besides, he was a scholar rather than a fighter; he had an enormous library of clay tablets and cylinders in cuneiform script—histories, stories, lists of plants, mathematics, chemicals, prescriptions (one of these recommends liquorice root crushed in beer as a cure for a cough). There were dictionaries, too, and translations of old Babylonian stories, including the Babylonian legend of the Creation. Perhaps the king became too much interested in his learning or spent too much time feasting with his queen; his kingdom dwindled and it was soon after his death that Nineveh was destroyed by the Babylonians, now more correctly called the Chaldeans.

JUDAH IN DANGER

Babylon also subdued Egypt once more; Nebuchadrezzar now looked at Judah, a pearl by the wayside between Babylonia and Egypt. History repeats itself over and over again. Jeremiah saw

pressing the poor, ignoring true worship, then they must be carried away from their land and in the loneliness of exile become sorry for their wickedness and prepare to return to Him. Bravely, Jeremiah came out of hiding. He went to the home of a potter and saw a message in the potter's work.

The potter was a familiar craftsman. He had his store of clay, a simple kiln or clay oven, and a rough shelter, even a rocky cave, for his booth. Having kneaded the clay to a soft consistency, he placed it on a small wheel connected to a larger one beneath it by a strip of strong leather or a post. With his feet he turned the bottom wheel, which revolved the small one, and as it began to spin so he shaped his jars and pots and water vessels. If the jar broke or a flaw appeared in the making and it was spoiled, he stopped the wheel, took off the imperfect jar and remolded the clay in order to begin again. From the imperfect he would make the perfect article. This, said Jeremiah, was what Yahweh would do to His people. They were like clay in His hands; they had become imperfect and He must now reshape them into the vessel He wanted them to be; He would remold them to His purpose (Jer. 18:1–12).

In the Valley of the Son of Hinnom, at Potsherd Gate, the scene of child sacrifice in the cruel reign of Manasseh, Jeremiah gathered the people around him and held aloft a potter's vessel.

Jeremiah proclaimed the words of Yahweh—that because of their sins and refusal to listen to His prophets, Jerusalem would be made desolate and the people would be given over to their enemies. Yahweh would break them as Jeremiah would break the potter's vessel, into so many pieces that "it cannot be made whole again." Whereupon the prophet dashed it to the ground, where it broke into smithereens. Not a sherd of any size was left for use in the house or by the well or for writing on, and for the most the fragments were fit only for grinding into powder and dust. This, said Jeremiah, was what Yahweh would do to His rebellious people—"dash them in pieces like a potter's vessel" (Ps. 2:9; Isa. 30:14; Jer. 19).

JERUSALEM SURRENDERS

Jeremiah's enemies were furious and put him in stocks at the mercy of those who jeered and sneered at him and pelted him with citrons and pomegranates. Meanwhile the king tried to "buy off" Nebuchadrezzar by paying tribute; he could not continue this, so he allied himself with Egypt and refused to pay any more. Nebuchadrezzar laid siege to Jerusalem in 597 B.C. The city surrendered; the king, his court, the principal leaders, craftsmen and smiths were taken to Babylon. Among them was Ezekiel, who was taken to Tel-abib on the River Chebar, near Babylon. Jeremiah's prophecies were beginning to come true. Jeremiah described this captivity in his parable of the baskets of figs: the good figs were those who had been carried off—they would learn their lesson and return to Judah determined to become servants of the true God; the future of Judah was in

their hands. Those left behind were the bad figs (24:1–10); they would merely be cast away as useless.

EXILE

The captives were not treated cruelly as had been those of the Northern Kingdom taken by Assyria; they were able to live among their captors, to work, to trade and even to rule. Yahweh did not wish them to be utterly destroyed as were the ten lost tribes. They were encouraged by a letter from Jeremiah, who advised them to settle down and accept their foreign yoke. Yahweh would be with them. This was difficult for some to accept, but through Jeremiah Yahweh had said, "Ye shall seek me and find me when ye search for me with your whole heart . . . and I will turn again your captivity" (29:1–18).

THE PROPHET'S OWN FAITH

Jeremiah was so certain of the return that he bought a piece of land in his own village—a risky chance, seeing that it was occupied by the enemy; he paid seven shekels and ten pieces of silver. At the time of the transaction he was in prison! In the Court of the Guard the deeds were drawn up; two copies were placed in an earthenware jar for preservation and given to Baruch for safekeeping (32:11).

The new king, Zedekiah, was changeable and weak-willed, eager to accept guidance from false prophets but equally sure he ought to listen to Jeremiah. Having angered Nebuchadrezzar by joining Egypt in yet another rebellion, he secretly sent for Jeremiah. Because of the siege little food was available, but the king gave him bread in the Street of Bakers, a short street in which the booths were all of the same trade.

JERUSALEM FALLS

But Zedekiah was strangely indecisive and even gave way to Jeremiah's enemies to the extent of letting them throw the prophet into a pit, waterless and slimy, from which he was rescued by a kindly Ethiopian court official; the king then promised Jeremiah safety if he would guide him in his difficult position. Jeremiah wore a yoke like that used on the necks of oxen when plowing. "Bring your neck under the yoke of the king of Babylon; serve him and live," was his answer (27:12). But Zedekiah, again accepting the advice of false prophets, revolted. Nebuchadrezzar moved southward a second time, destroyed Lachish which the king had rebuilt, then laid siege to Jerusalem, as Jeremiah had said would happen. With their enormous siege engines and skilled fighters the Babylonians swiftly captured the city, razed the Temple and palace to the ground. Zedekiah had to watch his sons and courtiers killed; then his own eyes were put out, and, chained, blinded, and defeated, he was sent to Babylon. This was in 586 B.C.

JEREMIAH'S CHOICE

Jeremiah was set free and given his choice—safety and comfort in Babylon or hardship and disappointment in Judah. He decided to stay where he felt he could do most good, among his own folk; the "good figs" could look after themselves. Once more the strong and useful Jews were taken away, beyond the Euphrates; those left were poor, inefficient, old and lazy; it would be as much as they could manage to till the soil and tend the vineyards (39:1–40:6).

At last Judah was in captivity, as Jeremiah had prophesied, and—as we should say—"for her own good." See how Psalm 74 fits in here.

Meanwhile, the prophet worked with the Babylonian governor Gedaliah, a Jew put in charge by Nebuchadrezzar. Many of the Jews who had fled from the invasion into the hills now returned, and then rebelled. They killed the governor and forced Jeremiah to go with them to Egypt, where they went to escape the revenge of the King of Babylonia, and where they hoped to find help and protection (40:1–5; 42:2–10, 19–22; 43:1–7; 44:29, 30).

Did Jeremiah finally escape to Babylon, or was he stoned to death in Egypt? We do not know. We do not know how far he succeeded in his difficult task, but we know with what courage he faced it. He was rejected, laughed at, hunted, thrown into prison, put into the stocks, dropped into a well, taken by force to a foreign land. Read what Paul says of his own experiences whilst serving God as a missionary and a preacher (II Cor. 11: 23–27).

9

The Exile: Ezekiel and Second Isaiah

(EZEKIEL 1:1-3, 7, 8, 11; 2:1-7; 3:10-13; 6:8; 18; 20:12, 13; 34:11-16; 36;
37:1-14; 44:24. ISAIAH 40:1-31; 42:1-15; 41:5-39; 43; 44:9-28; 45; 49:1-16;
50:4-9; 52:1-15; 53. EZRA I. PSALM 126; 137)

THE JEWISH DISPERSION

For the next fifty years (586–539 B.C.) the history of the Jews is a blank; the national life of Judah seemed to be extinct; its peoples were scattered far and wide through the then known world. This is known as the Jewish Dispersion. As we examine the movements more closely we can see three main groups. There is one settlement in Babylon, consisting of the more wealthy and intelligent leaders and craftsmen taken captive after Nebuchadrezzar's first siege of Jerusalem. These Jews we shall consider later in this chapter, for they were being taught their lesson —in Babylon, as Jeremiah had said they must; they were preparing, in Yahweh's own good time, for the return to their homeland.

A second group was made up of the peasants and poorer people, the "bad figs" left behind after the second devastation of the city. They had no leaders, no craftsmen, no farmers; they allowed Judah to become a wilderness, for they were without hope, miserable and beaten; their Temple was gone and they believed that Yahweh had forsaken them.

The third group is not easy to see. It consisted of scattered communities and settlements. To one of these, in Egypt, Jeremiah was taken against his will. Places like Assuan and Memphis had these groups; fugitives from home, they remembered their God and built temples. Later events indicate that among them were soldiers and leaders, for papyrus records written in Aramaic, the Jewish dialect, and belonging to such a community, have been found at Elephantine in Upper Egypt. They seem to have worshiped Yahweh, but also served two other gods; the Egyptian priests appear to have interfered with their worship too. Other colonies were in Damascus (I Kings 20: 34), in Persia, Rome and Pontus (Turkey) (Acts 2:9–11).

The city is long since devastated, its glory is gone. Here are excavated walls and a gateway as it now is.

CAPTIVE IN BABYLON

In Babylon, the first captives came quickly to the notice of the king and were allowed considerable freedom in their worship and ways of living; they took a share in education and commerce, and before long their national unity began to reassert itself. If Judah was to recover, it must be through the exiles, whose faith was being sorely tried. The elders and priests resumed their former rôles and took over the communities as they had done in Jerusalem. Others, like Nehemiah and Zerubbabel, did so well that they entered the king's court; some stayed when it was taken over by Persian rulers —as is shown by the stories of Daniel and his three friends.

THE WONDERS OF BABYLON

What did the exiles find in the city of Babylon? In II Kings 18:32, we are told that Babylon was a land of corn, wine, vineyards and olives; to the exiles it was "a land like their own land." Its fertility depended on the two great rivers whose wide, flat valleys formed much of the Fertile Crescent, and as the Egyptians controlled the Nile waters for the fertility of Egypt, so the Babylonians had to harness the waters of the Euphrates, the "soul of the land," and the Tigris, "bestower of blessings." A network of canals irrigated the country and the peasants worked the shadufs and water-wheels to provide the water necessary for their crops. It was a hot land but the air was clear, and the nights must have been beautiful, brilliantly lit with stars (Isa. 47:13).

The buildings were for the most part of bricks made from clay and bound with natural bitumen or pitch found near the city. Larger buildings such as those of Nebuchadrezzar were built of stones brought from Mesopotamia. The king is known to have been a great builder, and the Jews, accustomed though they were to the magnificence of their own city, its Temple, palace, and chief buildings, must have been amazed at the wonderful sights they now saw. The Hanging Gardens (one of the seven wonders of the world) reared high before them; over vaulted chambers or cells the gardens were built in tiers or terraces watered by shafts sunk deep into the Euphrates. Here, too, were the great temple of Merodach (Marduk), "Lord of Heaven and Earth," flanked by winged figures, and the enormous Tower of Babel or Ziggurat (see Gen. 11:1–9 and Part I, Chapter 1). This was the "House of the Foundation of Heaven and Earth," of which Nebuchadrezzar wrote, "I raised the summit of the Tower of Stages so that its top rivaled the heavens."

When pinnacles toppled down, as they sometimes did, it was said that the gods were very angry and must be appeased.

On New Year's Day, Marduk was taken out of his temple, put on a ship and drawn along red-stoned Babel Street into white-paved Procession Street, and through the huge gold-covered city gates, for worship at a special shrine. The king in his royal robes attended and the crowds —including open-mouthed, awe-struck Jews—thronged the Ishtar Gate or climbed the walls to watch. And such walls they were—two hundred cubits high, fifty wide, moated all round. Houses lined the top, with room for four-horse chariots to turn; over a hundred gates, fronted with solid brass, gave access to the city. Such massive strength seemed impregnable, yet Cyrus of Persia entered

One of the seven wonders of the world.
An artist portrays the Hanging Gardens
described on this page.

easily, and Alexander of Greece died in one of its brilliantly adorned palaces two hundred years after that.

KEEPING FAITH WITH GOD

Psalm 137 makes it clear that many of the Jews in Babylon now felt that Yahweh had forsaken them as they had forsaken Him. These turned to their conquerors' gods, which now seemed so much more powerful than Yahweh and worship of which was so much more splendid and realistic. But some remembered what Jeremiah had said, and his message assured them of Yahweh's presence with them even in a foreign land. It was these who met and devised plans whereby their Jewish home and religious life should be maintained. They began to prepare for their eventual return to Judah; this meant detailed lists of names and families; rules and customs, rites and ceremonies—especially of Temple worship—were drawn up. The Jews found that one day each week was already kept by their captors as a kind of day of rest or sabbath; this enabled the Jews to keep the same day for attending to their own worship, to talk over the scriptures and prophecies which they now read more frequently. These meetings were the beginnings of the synagogue worship that was to be the accepted form of Jewish worship down to the present day.

PRESERVING THE SCRIPTURES

During this period, too, priests and scribes interested in the stories and histories of their ancient land compiled and revised these records—the J and E documents referred to in Chapter 5—and wrote down those that had been handed on hitherto by word of mouth; these scribes, as they were called, tended to alter as they wrote, often to please themselves or to give reasons for events and happenings. (Remember that Gehazi's leprosy was given a "reason.") They revised the Books of the Law, especially Deuteronomy—found in the reign of Josiah—and the histories of Joshua, the Judges and Kings. They were determined that the nation's life and faith should not die. The records called P documents were written in Hebrew, which was the language of the Canaanites among whom the Jews had settled when they first entered Palestine, under Joshua. This tongue was retained while the Jews were in captivity, but later, under the influence of Greece —after the conquests of Alexander the Great—the upper classes spoke Greek and Latin, and Hebrew dropped out of use except in the synagogue and Temple worship. The ordinary folk also developed among themselves during this time the dialect called Aramaic. Some of the Book of Ezra is in this language. If you look closely at the typical examples of Hebrew writing you will notice the strange shapes of the symbols. They are all consonants; the dots and dashes represent the vowels. The original word we know as YAHWEH was YHWH; the vowels are from another Hebrew word for LORD, and when this occurs in the Bible in capital letters it should be read as YAHWEH. But when the scribes wrote the scriptures during their exile, they wrote only in consonants; the vowels were a later addition to make the accounts more easy to read and to understand.

Two men felt they must do a great deal for their fellow men while they were in Babylon. One was Ezekiel, before and during the exile itself; the other was Second Isaiah, at the time the Persians were about to take over the Babylonian (Chaldean) Empire.

EZEKIEL

Ezekiel certainly knew Jeremiah well; he may have been one of the friendly priests who rescued Jeremiah from the

Temple, and was probably among the first Jews to be taken into captivity. His writings are difficult to understand. The early part of his book contains the messages he preached before the fall of Jerusalem, warning the people of what might happen to them. In 33:21, the fall of the city is announced; then the book continues with messages of hope and thoughts of the return. Ezekiel says much of what Amos and Isaiah had already said; he sees the danger of Babylonian idol worship. He condemns and warns the exiles that it is no use for them to excuse themselves or blame their forefathers. Like Jeremiah, he was unpopular, but he brought hope to those who believed that because Yahweh was interested in them as individuals they could worship Him wherever they were—even in Babylonia. In this way Ezekiel helped to preserve the Jewish religion and he had much to do with the rites and ceremonial aspects of the sanctuary, priesthood and laws (see Ezek. 40–45).

In chapters 1 and 2 Ezekiel describes his call and vividly portrays his wonderful vision, trying to explain his thoughts of Yahweh's majesty, power, strength, and speed through pictures of the winged faces of a lion, a man, an ox, and an eagle. This call came six years before Jerusalem fell, and for those six years he seemed to have worked in vain.

HIS MESSAGE

In the second part of his book he describes in pictures the restoration and return of the Jews. Chapter 34 tells of the good shepherd, a figure familiar to the exiles; compare it with the account given in Matthew 18:12–14 and Luke 19:10. In chapter 36 he tells of the ruin of Moab, Edom, and other nations which had closed in on the defenseless Judah that the exiles had left behind; he goes on to tell of the return to their simple agricultural life in Judah. This, says Ezekiel, will prove to idol-worship nations that Yahweh, the God of Judah, is a strong God. An even more striking picture is found in chapter 37, in which Ezekiel describes his vision of the Valley of Dry Bones. It was not unusual on a journey to pass the remains of armies or the dead of caravans that had been attacked, and the Jews had seen the bones whitening in the hot sun. Ezekiel uses this memory to make it clear to the Jews that the nation, now dead in exile, is to be given new life: "I will bring you into the land of Israel and ye shall live." This seemed impossible at the time to everyone except Ezekiel. The prophet adds a symbol of unity; the two sticks stand for the two kingdoms of Judah and Ephraim (Israel); they are now seen as one nation with a covenant of peace between them and with Yahweh's sanctuary "in the midst of them for evermore."

The new covenant is to be a new stage in their history, for Yahweh would return to His Temple and to them; they would be a holy people in a holy city under the care of a Holy God. It is with this thought that Ezekiel echoes the teaching of Isaiah that the "remnant of Israel" would be a holy people; he also strengthens the teaching of Jeremiah, who taught the responsibility of the individual. Ezekiel says that individuals must worship *together* for the full spiritual benefit of each person. This is nowadays an accepted belief, that individuals best serve in a community, whether it be a church or a school or other group, in which the people have the same ideals of life.

Before any of the exiles returned to Judah, the priest-prophet died, but his influence continued throughout the years to come; for not only did he establish a formal type of worship, but he also kept together the small number of Jews who were really anxious to return, when the time came, to begin their nation anew.

SECOND ISAIAH

The really great prophet of this period is Second Isaiah, living from about 550 B.C. We do not know his name. His writings are in the Book of Isaiah, chapters 40–55; he is called Second Isaiah (in some books, Deutero-Isaiah) to distinguish him from the Isaiah of the first chapters of the Book and of whom we have already read in Chapters 6 and 7 of this book. His writings are at least two hundred years later than those of the first Isaiah. He speaks to the exiles of hope and deliverance. Most of the original exiles were dead by then, and their children and grandchildren knew of Jerusalem only by name and story. They were now prosperous and did not particularly want to return to this city of their fathers, where it might be difficult, even dangerous, to live; it was far distant, too, and to reach it they would have to make a hazardous journey. In any case, it seemed foolish to return to this place when Yahweh could be worshiped equally well in Babylonia. Jeremiah had said so, and they would accept his word (29:5–7); and many of them certainly had proved the truth of this in their own lives.

HIS MESSAGE

Second Isaiah makes it clear that Cyrus is to deliver the Jews by conquering Babylonia; he is the "Lord's anointed" and his "shepherd" (44:28; 45). Isaiah reasserts the teachings of the earlier prophets, that Yahweh is Creator, that He loves, that He may be worshiped anywhere, that to worship Him is a personal matter.

The exiles had suffered but had learned to trust Him; for the second time in their history they were to move into the Promised Land, and they and their scattered kinsmen were to be united and restored to their homes. Even the Gentiles (people of other nations) would see and acknowledge Yahweh's power (49:6 and 42:6); and they would accept Him as Lord God. This duty—revealing God to the Gentiles—was one that the Jews were reluctant to carry out. These are familiar chapters, read and sung in our schools and churches throughout the year. They all speak joyously, even exuberantly, of the exiles' future—provided the people give up their idol worship and wickedness.

THE FOOLISHNESS OF IDOL WORSHIP

In chapter 44:9–20, Second Isaiah writes an almost amusing jibe at idolatry. There were many idols in Babylon, many gods, too—Marduk, Shamash, Bel, Nebo, small ones, great ones, gods in gold, bronze, stone, and wood; it was easy to worship these figures that could be seen and difficult to worship Yahweh who could not be seen. Second Isaiah says: Look at this idol; watch the craftsman making it; he chooses the tree, cuts it down, shapes the figure, burns the wood chips and shavings, carries it around and stands it up—and then, bowing down before it, expects it to help him! How stupid this is, says the prophet. "Deliver me," says the man, "for thou art my god." Read 46:6, 7 and Psalm 115:4–8. There can be no other God but Yahweh, says Second Isaiah. Now, choose. Leave your comfort, your money, your position; return to the flock of righteousness and peace, with Yahweh as the Great Shepherd, for you are His chosen flock, His people. Both Ezekiel (24:12) and Isaiah (40:11) use the familiar idea of the shepherd, as Jesus was to do many years later.

THE "SERVANT SONGS"

Second Isaiah is certain that God's purpose will be fulfilled (55:8 ff.), and he writes some wonderful poems which are now called the Servant Songs. These are found in 42:1–7—his call; 49:1–6—his failure, 1, 4–9—his trust; 52:13–53

—his faithfulness. Some scholars say that the prophet was foretelling of Jesus and His Crucifixion; if he was not, neverthe- less Jesus in His service and suffering could well be described by these verses; He could easily be the Servant.

10

The Return: Haggai and Zechariah,
Nehemiah and Ezra

(HAGGAI 2:1-9. EZRA 1:1-11; 8:21-36; 10:7-10. ZECH. 2:1-6; 7:8-14. NEH. 1; 2; 3; 4; 6; 8:1-8)

CYRUS

Babylon had lost her great king Nebuchadrezzar in 562 B.C., and, despite various campaigns in Edom and Syria, her last king had begun to feel the pressure from Media; then, almost without warning, about 550 B.C., an unknown king of Persia appeared on the scene and became king of the western empires of Media and Persia, obviously set upon extending his conquests even further. Second Isaiah spoke of him as the deliverer of the exiles. Egypt, Lydia, and Sparta joined Babylon in an attempt to stop Cyrus, but Croesus of Lydia (known to us for his great wealth and first use of coins for money) was defeated and Cyrus was master of a growing empire that was to last for two hundred and fifty years. Look at the maps and see how he advanced through these nations—Babylon, Western Arabia, Mesopotamia, Asia Minor. The maps of the Assyrian and Babylonian Empires are on the same scale and should be compared closely with the map of the Persian Empire.

PERSIAN RULE

Having taken control of the irrigation system of canals on which life in the city depended, Cyrus marched into Babylon in 538 B.C. This is recorded on a broken cylinder of baked clay called Cyrus' Cylinder, now kept in the British Museum. Cyrus says that the conquest was "without battle and without fighting," but see Jeremiah 25:12; 51. Cyrus introduced a new idea of rule over conquered nations, probably because as a boy he had learned much about justice and honor. He learned, too, "to ride, to use the bow, and to speak the truth." Although he was a dictator, he was a noble one and a fine statesman. On his tomb are written these words: "I am Cyrus, who won the empire for the Persians. Grudge me not therefore this handful of earth which covers me."

The Assyrians had believed in complete extermination of the nations they defeated; the Babylonians took their best captives to their own land and allowed them to continue their own way of life; but the Persians did not believe in either oppression or captivity; they wanted the nations they ruled to be happy and content, realizing they would accept conquest the more easily. Cyrus set up local governors and rulers of their own race, encouraged their religion and made it easy for them, if they were already captives in a foreign land, to return to their homeland if they wished.

JUDAH

For the Jews this meant that they could continue their own religion and mode of worship and think about their return "home" with even greater freedom. Cyrus knew that Judah needed attention. During the fifty years of the exile it had been ravaged and invaded by surrounding nations and had become a wilderness (Hag. 1:5, 6, 10, 11; 2:15–19). Even the language had changed and instead of Hebrew the Jews were speaking a Syrian dialect called Aramaic; Jesus spoke this tongue nearly six hundred years later (see II Kings 18:28; Mark 5:41 and 7:34). Jerusalem had been leveled to the ground; armies had swept through the land where the people had tried miserably to build and rebuild their poor homes with debris from the ruined cities and villages. In the south Edom had advanced, to the north was Tyre, to the west Philistia, to the east Moab; they were closing in—and who could save Judah?

THE RETURN

It was with high hopes that some of the descendants of the exiles at last prepared to return to Jerusalem, in the first year of Cyrus, King of Persia, in 536 B.C.

Won over by Second Isaiah's enthusiasm and encouragement, they looked forward with great joy to the task and duty of rebuilding their fathers' city. For their further help, Cyrus allowed Sheshbazzar, a prince of Judah, to lead the returning Judaeans; he gave them gold, silver, cattle, horses, mules, asses, camels, and even the Temple vessels that Nebuchadrezzar had taken from Jerusalem for the House of Merodach—for it was the Temple of Yahweh that they were planning to build; houses and homes could come later. We are told that 42,000 people journeyed in that great caravan, but this is probably an exaggeration. Many of the Jews stayed in Babylon, perhaps to await news of the first return, and very likely because of their prosperity which they wanted to keep; but they later sent money to help the work that was being done in Jerusalem. It is not clear which way the caravan went, probably northward through the Fertile Crescent, by Nineveh, Haran, with its ziggurat outlined against the sky, Carchemish, where Pharaoh Necho had been defeated by the Babylonians, across the Euphrates, and then southward along the "Royal Road" as Abraham had gone so many years before them. They were very anxious to see for themselves the Jerusalem about which they had heard so much.

DISAPPOINTMENT

But in Judah they found desolation and destruction, famine and wasteland. The "bad figs" were antagonistic, there was jealousy and fear—which was not surprising after all those years. New religious centers had been set up at Mizpah, Jericho, and Bethel, for Jerusalem was in ruins and it had seemed pointless to build another center of worship in a devastated city. However, the returned exiles began to rebuild the Temple, but they had no real heart in the work; the people of Jerusalem watched them, refused to help, and even hindered them, so that during the next sixteen years very little was done. Their disappointment crushed them; they had hoped for so much when they were in exile, but here there was only bitterness and opposition and failure.

DARIUS RULES

The Persian Empire tottered somewhat on the death of Cyrus, but when Darius took over from Cambyses, who had added Egypt to the empire, he strengthened his control by dividing the whole empire into twenty-eight "satrapies" or provinces, each under a satrap or civil governor who was responsible for law and order, raising taxes and collecting tribute. Each governor was placed in a principal city, and was watched by officials called the "Eyes and Ears of the Great King." Only Darius could make a decision, and once it was made it was final—the "law of the Medes and Persians." He kept in touch with his satraps by means of couriers, whose horses were stabled along the many roads he had built to link up his provinces. His capital cities were at Persepolis, Babylon, Susa, and Ecbatana; he also issued his own gold coins bearing his image and called "darics" (Ezra 2:69; Neh. 7:70). Tribute from conquered nations kept him in luxury; we know that from Arabia came frankincense, from Ethiopia gold, ebony, ivory—and every five years, five children!

Egypt again rebelled and Darius subdued her; then he marched into Asia Minor, conquered Scythia to the north of the Black Sea, and continued westward until he was checked at Marathon.

Darius also encouraged the Jews in building the Temple. Having found the decree of Cyrus, he gave further gifts of all kinds (Ezra 6:1–5; 5:8).

HAGGAI AND ZECHARIAH

At this time a new prophet arose—Haggai. He was a very practical man, anxious to get things done. In 520 B.C. he preached in favor of rebuilding the Temple. With the help of Darius, a second caravan of exiles had come to Judah under Zerubbabel the governor, a prince in the line of David. Read Esdras 3 and 4 (in the Apocrypha) and find how Zerubbabel obtained permission to come to Jerusalem. With Zechariah, Haggai declared that it was wrong of the people to build "paneled houses" for their own comfort, that the Temple must be built first; then the country would blossom plentifully once more—but not until. We find that on the site of the destroyed altar of Solomon's Temple a new one had been erected on their arrival in 536 B.C. The Feast of Tabernacles was then celebrated (see Part I). To remind them that the Children of Israel had once lived in tents in the wilderness, the people set up in the open air little booths or shelters made of branches of trees and lived in them; they offered their sacrifices on the new altar. Again cedar trees from Lebanon were floated from Tyre to Joppa and brought by camels overland to Jerusalem; carpenters and masons and other craftsmen began to put into practice the crafts they had learned from their fathers while in Babylon so as to be ready for the rebuilding, already delayed for sixteen years.

THE SAMARITANS

Haggai and Zechariah preached encouragement and worked hard; and at last the foundations of the Temple were laid. Meanwhile, the worshipers at Bethel offered to help. They were the descendants of the Israelites who had intermarried with the people of other nations brought in by the Assyrians; they even worshiped Yahweh alongside the gods of those nations. Haggai spoke bluntly to them and said they were unclean; he refused their offer of help, so making them bitter enemies. These people were later called the

Samaritans, and in their home at Shechem (now called Nablus) they never forgot Haggai's snub. This explains the many jibes and bitter references to the Samaritans during our Lord's time, for the Jews "had no dealings" with them. They evidently built a temple for themselves on Mount Gerizim, and there is a Samaritan community there to this day.

THE "NEW JERUSALEM"

Both Haggai and Zechariah hoped that Zerubbabel would restore the line of kingship and so fulfill the prophecies of Isaiah 11 and Jer. 23:5 and 33:15; but he disappears, probably recalled by a suspicious Darius. Zechariah's book is mainly one of visions, foretelling Yahweh's return to Jerusalem and the establishing of righteousness (8:16, 17). He looks forward to the time when the Temple would be the center of the Jewish faith all over the world (2:10–13; 8:20–23). His vision of the "New Jerusalem" (8:4, 5) is well known. Ezra records (6:15) that the Temple was finished in the sixth year of Darius, from which we date the dedication as being in 516 B.C. Passover was immediately celebrated (6:20).

NEHEMIAH

Darius had tried and failed to conquer Greece, having been stopped at Marathon. His son Xerxes also tried, and though defeating Leonidas at Thermopylae was himself checked at Salamis. Then came Artaxerxes; under him the exiles made a second attempt to return to Jerusalem. The story in Ezra is rather confused, but scholars tell us that Nehemiah, a Jew, came to Palestine before Ezra, in 445 B.C. From Hanani, whom he calls "one of my brethren," he had heard how the exiles had been hindered in their building of the walls by raiders and tribes bearing down on the unprotected city. As cupbearer to the king he was much in his master's company. His duty was to taste the wine before handing it to the king to drink—poisoning was not unknown in those days. He was also the king's friend; so, urged by the sad news he constantly heard from merchants traveling from far-off Palestine into the markets of Babylon, he dared to plead that he might go to Jerusalem. He was a loyal Jew bound in exile, but longing to help in rebuilding the city. The king was sympathetic and gave him leave of absence and the official governorship of Jerusalem for a limited period; he also gave a grant of timber for rebuilding the walls.

NEHEMIAH AT WORK

Nehemiah found the Persian satraps Sanballat and Tobiah jealous of him; they stirred up strife. But in his capacity as governor Nehemiah was the equal of the two satraps and went about his work without fear, although he was well aware that they would even murder him in an effort to get rid of one of the king's "Eyes and Ears."

By night he examined the walls and planned how best to repair them. He divided the workers into groups, each to work on a given section of the walls. Despite sneers and active hindrance—mainly from the satraps and the Samaritans—with half his men working and half watching (4; 6:1–14), Nehemiah saw his task completed in fifty-two days, "because the people had a mind to work." The walls were dedicated in a religious ceremony (12:30–40). The story is vividly told in his book; see also Ecclesiasticus 49:13.

Nehemiah found that there was oppression of the poor (5:1–19) like that found and denounced by Amos hundreds of years before. Money-lenders, in particular, were overcharging at high interest in their dishonest trading. He called the rich men together and made them promise not to force their claims on the poor

In exile, the Jews met to read their precious scriptures; today, the Jews of the Dispersion still meet to do this in their synagogues all over the world.

who had lost their lands and property so soon after returning from exile. He set them a personal example by paying for the freedom of slaves and by not accepting taxes due to him from poor people who could not afford to pay. He then returned to Susa, twelve years having elapsed since he had left his master.

HIS SECOND VISIT

Artaxerxes gave him permission to return to the city as governor. When he did so, twelve years later, he found that his old enemies were strong and in powerful control. The sabbath was being desecrated, buying and selling were going on as if it were an ordinary day of the week. Nehemiah took swift action: he turned out the offenders neck and crop. Some were literally chased out, had their furniture thrown out of the city and their hair pulled. (See 13:25.) He made every-

body pay charges and taxes for the upkeep of the Temple and insisted that there was to be no sabbath trading there or anywhere else. He made laws forbidding intermarriage with Ammonite and Moabite women, for the children of such marriages were speaking a foreign tongue and following foreign gods. The Book of Ruth (see Part I) was written to challenge such a policy as this, for it tells how Ruth, a Moabite, married Boaz, a Judaean, and they became the great-grandparents of David, King of Israel. However, Nehemiah wanted to keep the race of Jews all of one blood and he felt that it was wrong for them to marry into other nations.

A group of seventy of the chief Jews promised Nehemiah to keep the Law and to see that others did also. These seventy became the Sanhedrin, of whom we hear more in the New Testament; their leader eventually became the High Priest, the most important person in Jerusalem.

"MY MESSENGER"

We note here the Book of Malachi—about 400 B.C. The name is usually accepted as that of yet another prophet, but it is only a name meaning "My Messenger" given to a roll of scriptures, especially to 3:1 and 4:4–6. In this book foreign marriages are denounced; it challenges the Jews on their injustices (3:5) and on the careless way in which they follow the rules of worship. The writer also points out that some of them are so mean as to offer blind, lame, and sick animals for sacrifice (1:6–8); this was the very sin the Israelites had committed in the time of Amos. One wonders just how much the people had learned from these great prophets. Chapter 3:1–3 contains some words familiar to those who know Handel's *Messiah*.

EZRA

Thirty-five years were to pass before yet another band of exiles returned, this time under Ezra, in 397 B.C. Ezra was a priest, ever anxious to teach the Law. Accepting the fact that the common tongue was now Aramaic, he made sure that the people understood the Law—the Pentateuch—by having it read in their own tongue. Some of his book is written in this language too.

When he had made clear to them what was expected of loyal Jews, he ordered the celebration of the Feast of Tabernacles, and they solemnly promised to keep the Law. Some of his own company broke both Nehemiah's and his own rules against marrying non-Jewish women and caused Ezra great bitterness and anger. But, unlike Nehemiah, he merely pulled his own beard!

As a scribe, Ezra insisted upon restoring the rules and rites they had practiced in exile and with which they were all familiar. Synagogues were set up in towns and villages; schools were begun so that the children could learn their Jewish history and religious faith. Wherever at least ten males could meet (women did not count!) and there was a copy of the Law, there they could have a synagogue. This gave rise to many synagogues throughout Palestine and in the surrounding countries where there were Jewish communities. It also made the scribes important, for it was their duty to write out the scriptures and to explain the details of the Law. By the time of Christ they held very high positions.

The Temple was made more beautiful, though the Ark was no longer there; we do not know what happened to it. Some say that Shishak took it when he invaded Judah under Rehoboam, soon after the division of Palestine; others say that Jeremiah hid it just before the destruction of Jerusalem and it was never found.

PROPHECY DIES

So began the new community in Jerusalem. The outlook of the people was as narrow as their religion, but they fought bravely against all sorts of difficulties and dangers. Their loyalty was to Yahweh, who became for them the God of Jerusalem rather than the God of Creation; which is probably why the Temple itself continued to be the center of Jewish thought and life as well as of worship. A coldness of ritual had now come to their religion; and in the priestly atmosphere of what is known as Judaism, the fiery challenge of prophecy seemed to die. It was not to blaze again for four centuries, when the fiery words of John the Baptist proclaimed the old cry of the prophets—Repent!

The Greek Empire and the Maccabees

(I MACC. 1:1-9; 2:1-48; 3:1-4:61. II MACC. 4:1-17; 6:12-7:42)

For the next great influence on the history of the Jews we have to go to Greece and to trace briefly the rise and power of Alexander the Great. His father had begun to unite the Greek cities that for many years had existed as separate centers of rule, even fighting one another for control of the country; but he was murdered a short time after the first Olympic Games, in 336 B.C. Alexander's tutor was no less a person than Aristotle, a Greek philosopher and thinker whose teaching about kingship and government, learning, art, and beauty had a lasting and deep influence on Alexander, whose ambition was to conquer the world and spread these ideals by means of the Greek language, thought, and culture.

ALEXANDER'S CONQUESTS

He decided to begin with the Persian Empire. In Daniel 7:6, Alexander is pictured as a winged leopard, swift and deadly. He won battle after battle. Through Asia Minor into Syria, through Tyre and Gaza, he marched to Egypt; then back he came, northward into the Fertile Crescent, through Mesopotamia, conquering Babylon, Susa, Ecbatana (see map). Darius III, King of Persia, fled and was murdered many miles from his capital; Alexander's empire now reached from Greece to India.

He was a noble ruler, intent on being "law-giver to all and to reconcile humanity . . . in a single fatherland." He made no objection to continued worship of the gods of the nations he defeated—Amen-Ra of Egypt, Melkart of Phoenicia, Merodach of Chaldea (Babylonia) and even Yahweh of the Jews. He founded many cities—Alexandria, Kandahar, Samarkand, all self-governing and settled by Greeks, Jews, and Persians alike, but Greek in pattern and ideals. This introduction of Greek customs and culture is called "hellenizing" the cities and land.

Every city had its public baths and gymnasium and theater, its senate or political assembly for governing the people, its feasts, and its philosophical discussions and arguments. Greek was the common tongue, at least for trade and learning; it was easy to read and write. So began the Age of the Hellenes—the true name for the Greeks, used even today.

Alexander died in 323 B.C. at the age of thirty-two, in Babylon, having in thirteen years conquered the known world. But the result of his campaigns was the spread of Greek culture throughout the conquered nations as far as Rome.

THE GODS OF GREECE

Many are the stories of heroes, poets, philosophers and orators, but we have no space to tell of them. Their gods and goddesses were known to the Jews and even worshiped as Greek influence spread through the country—Zeus, the father of gods; Athene, goddess of wisdom; Aphrodite, of love; Apollo, sun-god of light and youth; Pan, of nature, goat-footed and playing his reed pipes; Ares, of war; Artemis, of hunting. The gods lived in power and majestic beauty on Mount Olympus. The Greeks had no room for ugliness; they worshiped beauty in all its forms—beauty of thought as well as of body. On the gods depended their crops, their safety on long journeys by sea and on land, their victory in war. Every house had its shrine and altar at which daily prayers and gifts were offered. Four times a year feasts and holidays were celebrated before the shrine of Zeus, and every fourth year the famous Olympic Games were held. The Greeks' intense love of games, athletics, drama and pageantry led to the building of huge theaters and arenas, circular and tiered so that everyone could see and hear; many of them were built in Palestine.

A DIVIDED EMPIRE

The story of Greek rule after the death of Alexander does not, however, make pleasant reading. When news of his death came, the two chief leaders of his armies split the empire between them. Ptolemy I took over Egypt, with his capital at Alexandria, and ruled the Ptolemaic Empire. Seleucus took Asia, with his capital at Antioch, a new city fast becoming important in Syria; he changed his name to Antiochus I and ruled the Seleucid Empire. Ptolemy and Seleucus soon quarreled over Palestine. Once more the land lay between two great nations, like a lamb between two hungry lions. In 312 B.C. Ptolemy captured Jerusalem and his empire held Judah for over a hundred years; then the Seleucid Empire completely defeated the Egyptians (see Dan. 11) in 198 B.C., and Judah came under the rule of yet another nation.

There were feuds, wars, and murders until Rome overtook both empires. The Jews had stayed submissive under Greek rule; Jerusalem had become the cultural and religious center for the Jews scattered throughout the land, and the scribes and writers had done much to continue the records of the country's history.

THE SEPTUAGINT

Some of the Jews of the Dispersion, it can be recalled, were in Egypt, where they had forgotten both their native Hebrew and colloquial Aramaic. They spoke Greek. (We remember here that the New Testament was written in Greek.) It soon became necessary for them to have their Law in Greek too. In Alexandria, Ptolemy II invited seventy scribes (or so the story goes) to come and translate the five books of the Law—the Pentateuch—into Greek. The High Priest sent six men from each of the twelve tribes. There are several accounts of the magical way in which each of the seventy-two scholars produced on the Island of Pharos identical translations, but the main thing to remember is that this work gave us the Septuagint—often written LXX and meaning Seventy. This was done in 250 B.C. and as time went on other parts of what we now know as the Bible were added, until this Greek Bible came to be read in all the synagogues outside Palestine. In this way it is to Alexander the Great that the world owed the Holy Scriptures in a tongue that everybody could understand. It meant that people who were not Jews—that is, Gentiles—could read and hear about God in the Greek tongue, and they could even become members of the synagogues if they believed in Yahweh. Paul found many of these Gentile believers in his missionary journeys when he visited synagogues in cities of Asia Minor and in Greece itself.

THE ROSETTA STONE

It is a later Pharaoh—Ptolemy V—to whom we owe further light on the history of this time. In about 196 B.C. he approved a decree proclaimed by the priests of Memphis. To make sure that everybody understood it he had it inscribed on a huge slab of black basalt in three languages—in Egyptian hieroglyphics or picture-writing, in the common written language of the people, and in Greek. It was discovered, A.D. 1799, at Rosetta, to the west of the Nile delta, and from this famous Rosetta Stone scholars have been able to translate all the Egyptian hieroglyphics for the first time, because they could read the Greek and compare the two (see Part I, p. 49). It is a wonderful experience to stand quietly in front of this stone—not unlike a rather chipped black gravestone—and to think about the people who wrote it, read it and discussed it; and we are glad that Greek became the "official" language of the people in those days, for we realize that because of this we can also read unknown tongues which our scholars for so many years could not interpret.

RELIGIOUS DIFFERENCES

The Jews were not long left to their quiet existence. There had been some disagreement over taxes, and quarrels quickly broke out over these. But there were differences of opinion in their worship too, and a certain amount of bitterness resulted from religious arguments and beliefs. Surrounded by Greek colonies, some of the Jews began to accept Greek thought and religion, including new conceptions of "another world," and life after death, or "immortality." In Part I there is a drawing of the Hebrew Universe showing Sheol, the abode of the dead. Most of the Jews had believed that when people died their spirits went to this place and were forever lost (see Ps. 6:5). Now the Greeks were making them think about a place where life went on; Greek legends of spring have this thought behind them. Of course, these ideas were not as clear then as they were after the teachings of Jesus, but one can see how the people would certainly argue over the possibilities and beliefs about life after death, as they do today. Two sects of Jews were already showing differences in their religion—the Pharisees and Sadducees: the Pharisees held that the really important part of worship was keeping the Law; the Sadducees, although priests, refused to have anything to do with the idea of an after life.

DESECRATION OF THE TEMPLE

Then came a disastrous event. In 168 B.C. Antiochus Epiphanes, a hated Syrian king and overlord of Palestine, found some of the Jews plotting against the High Priest whom he had chosen to be in charge of the Temple. Then and there he decided to stamp out altogether the worship of Yahweh and to hellenize (make Greek) the Jewish religion. He even called himself a god: "Epiphanes" meant "the god manifest" or revealed. He made up his mind to introduce Greek gods to replace Yahweh and to force the Jews to accept *his* religion whether they liked it or not. He murdered the priests, entered the Temple, plundered its contents and burned the Law books; he even walked right through the Holy of Holies, desecrating it in the eyes of the Jews. He carried away the Temple vessels of gold and silver, the seven-branched candlestick, the golden altar and the rich draping curtains of scarlet, together with the priests' garments. I Maccabees 1:20 ff. describes this, and in 4:38 we read that the sanctuary was laid desolate, the gates were destroyed, the priests' apartments were razed until there were "shrubs growing in the courts as in a forest or as on one of the mountains."

Most dreadful deed of all, the king offered swine—an insult to the Jews themselves—to himself in the form of Zeus the Greek god, on Yahweh's altar. Orders went out to all cities and villages in Judaea (as it is now called) to do likewise, and the Jews in their desperation looked for someone to lead them. Antiochus was anxious about the nearness of Roman legions at this time and with his armies prevented Jewish people from free movement, trading, and even worship; he did not realize that because of his tyranny he was not breaking Jewish opposition, but, in fact, strengthening it into a revolt for religious freedom.

REVOLT!

The spark was kindled in a tiny village called Modin, lying in the hills between Jerusalem and Joppa. An old priest named Mattathias refused to obey the command to sacrifice to the Greek gods; he slew another priest who was willing to do so, as well as the Greek officer on guard, then destroyed the defiled altar and fled with his five sons to the hills. There they began a guerrilla war. On a sabbath some of them were caught and, according to their laws, refused to fight; they were massacred (I Macc. 2:36). From this time the rebels fought for their religious faith even on the sabbath. Antiochus thought that this kind of rebellion would soon be put down, but he did not realize the kind of people he was attempting to destroy. The Jews now had a new leader, Judas Maccabaeus—the "Hammerer" (I Macc. 3:1-4), who believed that "with heaven it is all one, to save by many or by few, for victory in battle standeth not in the multitude of a host; but strength is from heaven."

He made his center at Mizpah and prepared to stand against much larger and stronger forces of Syrian soldiers. With his four brothers, he harried the enemy and gained considerable ground, even defeating an army supported by troops of elephants. By 164 B.C. he was in a strong position, and although he could not take the Acra, a fortress near the Temple, he entered Jerusalem, cleansed the Temple and restored it, then rededicated it to the worship of Yahweh. The Jews still celebrate this great event, calling it the Feast of Dedication or the Feast of Lights (John 10:22). Freedom for the Jewish religion was almost won. But Judas was not satisfied. He was very ambitious and he wanted to extend his conquests, and embittered not only his enemies and those Jews who had accepted the Greek form of worship, but also some of his own people who were satisfied with what had so far been achieved; among them the Pharisees, also called the Chasidim or "The Separated."

THE STRUGGLE CONTINUES

The rulers of the Seleucid Empire also distrusted the success of Judas, although at first he was officially recognized as the governor of Judaea. Wars continued and four years later Judas was killed. His brothers went on with the struggle and somehow through all the strife managed to throw off taxes and get rid of military control in the Acra, which was razed to the ground (I Macc. 13:41 ff.).

A new line of priest-kings had by now come into Jewish history; descended from Mattathias, they were called the Hasmoneans. But a new Seleucid king took a firm hand and besieged Jerusalem yet again; he destroyed its walls, demanded tribute, and turned out the High Priest. The great hope of the Hasmoneans had been to extend Judaea to the sea coast, but Judaea was once more a vassal state and under the Seleucids for the next ten years. Then the High Priests seized new chances and for sixty years gave religious and political freedom to the Jews. The dream of power was revived and the Hasmoneans extended their kingdom by forcing their neighboring states one by one under the rule of Judaea. The Seleucids were anxious about Rome at this time, and were too much concerned with their northern lands to worry much about the Jews.

PHARISEES AND SADDUCEES

The High Priest, John Hyrcanus, nephew of Judas Maccabaeus, was now openly calling himself king; he even had a bodyguard as David had when he was king. There followed a bewildering series of squabbles and fightings among the king's family, and religious differences grew stronger than ever as the Pharisees and Sadducees argued about how the people should worship. The Pharisees kept strictly to the Law, especially its teachings interpreted by the scribes; they paid their Temple dues regularly and in the same formal way set up rules and regulations of their own making. In later years it was these petty laws that aroused the scorn of Jesus (Matt. 23). But they did try to serve Yahweh honestly and they also believed in the resurrection—or, at least, some kind of after life. The Sadducees, on the other hand, held to the Law of Moses only and denied an after life. They were inclined to accept Greek rites in their worship and this angered the Pharisees, who wanted to keep the worship of Yahweh traditionally Jewish and free from any kind of change.

CIVIL WAR

There came a day when a new High Priest so angered the people by his slackness in carrying out his duties that they pelted him with the citrons and lemons they had brought with them as part of their offerings. He brought out his bodyguard and there was fighting and bloodshed. For six years civil war continued; then the Pharisees asked the Seleucid king to come and help them; but some of the army deserted and the Pharisees were defeated. The Sadducee High-Priest-King took control once more. Tradition says that he crucified Jewish captives—mostly Pharisees—and murdered their families while the Sadducees looked on. This was an almost unbelievable cruelty to be ordered by a High Priest of the Temple. The people were in utter dejection and weary of war. More than ever did they long for a divine leader, someone sent from God—a Messiah. We should remember that this Messiah did come; and many who watched Him on the cross must have recalled stories that their parents had told them—of those eight hundred crosses bearing Jewish captives; and there was a High Priest concerned in both events.

THE SYNAGOGUE

Strange as it may seem, the Pharisees came into power a few years later, during the reign of a woman ruler (she could not be a priest, of course). They set about educating the people in the Law by building synagogues and schools. Whereas the Temple had been the place for priests and sacrifice and ceremony, the synagogue could be used by everybody—including women, who sat behind a kind of lattice hidden from the men. There was no altar. A rabbi—a teacher rather than a priest—led the service; he had to know a great deal about the Law and its teachings. The service consisted of a psalm (all joining in), prayers, two lessons—

Some coins of Alexander the Great, Seleucus I of Syria, and Ptolemy of Egypt. These were known and used by the Jews under these three rulers.

one from the Law and one from the Prophets—and a spoken explanation of some of the passages, a kind of sermon. The chief work of the scribes was to interpret the Law in such a way that it meant something to the people in any country or province where there was a synagogue; we must not forget that originally the Law had been given to the Israelites when they were in the Wilderness, and now that the people were living in villages and cities some parts of the Law did not really apply to them. The Law itself is often called the *Torah*. Some of the scripture passages were translated from the Hebrew into the common Aramaic tongue so that the people could understand them better; these translations were called *Targums*.

THE SYNAGOGUE SCRIPTURES

We recall how the priestly writers had guided the scribes in weaving into history the familiar stories of the patriarchs and judges and kings. Not caring to leave out any of the old stories, they took all the accounts written in the Northern Kingdom in about 750 B.C. (the time of Amos) and called E, because E stands

for Elohim, a name for God, and joined them, story for story, to the similar accounts written in the Southern Kingdom in about 850 B.C. (the time of Elisha) and called J, because J stands for Jahveh, another way of spelling Yahweh.

These accounts had undergone all sorts of changes and alterations through the years, especially during the Exile, when the Priests revised them to fit their own ideas and way of thinking about God and His people; these were the P documents —P standing for Priests, or Priestly Code. The scriptures, as given by Ezra to the people, then consisted of the Law and the Prophets, plus stories of their leaders. The Writings, a third section of the Old Testament as we have it, came when the Psalms and similar collections of poetry were added. These were the scriptures of the Pharisees of the Dispersion in Palestine, Egypt, and Asia Minor, translated into the Greeks' Septuagint (LXX); they were written on papyrus rolls or prepared skins and kept in a special cupboard called an ark. (Do not confuse this with the Ark of the Covenant.)

Next to the synagogue was a school in which boys were taught to read and learn by heart passages of the scriptures; this explains why Jesus had such a full knowledge of the "Law and the Prophets."

The power of the Pharisees came to an end when the Sadducees, who had been jealous of their rule, of course, supported a new High-Priest-King who tried to take control and to rule over not only Judaea but also Edom, Galilee, and Samaria. Both sides now had armies and before long the country was again plunged into civil war.

12

The Roman Empire and Herod the Great

(I MACC. 8. Selected Psalms. I CHRON. 16. ECCLUS. 1, 5-21)

The struggle between the Pharisees and the Sadducees continued. By now, Roman legions were marching into Syria as the kings of the Seleucid Empire had feared would happen; Pompey took over the empire. He set up his headquarters at Antioch and later went southward to settle the quarrels between the two Jewish sects. Suspicious of the Sadducees, who supported their own Priest-King in any attempt at rebellion against the ruling power, Pompey, in 63 B.C., besieged Jerusalem. He attacked on a sabbath day and the defenseless priests went on with their normal duties, knowing full well that they would be murdered as they did so.

Pompey did not defile the Temple, nor did he interfere with the religious freedom of the Jews. But he joined Judaea to Syria and demanded both tribute and loyalty from the people. Strife continued between the High Priest's party and the Pharisees, however, and there were minor outbreaks against the Romans too. At last, in 54

B.C., the rebellions were crushed by Cassius (afterwards one of the assassins of Julius Caesar) and many thousands of Jews were sold into slavery, some being taken to Rome: this indirectly extended the Dispersion to Europe.

ROMAN WORSHIP

But Caesar allowed more freedom to the Jews than had Pompey; he reduced the taxes and agreed to the rebuilding of the walls of Jerusalem. There is no doubt that the soldiers and citizens of Rome who settled in the district brought with them their own gods and forms of worship. Like the Hebrews of old, they had their terra-cotta teraphim or household gods—you will remember that Rachel stole hers when she and Jacob left Laban. The gods that looked after the farm were called lares; those that preserved the home, penates. They could bring good or bad fortune and unless they were given the honor due to them the family fell on evil days. Therefore, in every house there was a shrine on which were offered fruit, flowers and wine; then prayers were said. There were special occasions too, when the gods were taken round the fields and sacrifices were offered. Jupiter and Juno were the chief gods; Minerva, goddess of wisdom; Mars, god of war; Vesta, goddess of fire. Many of these were Greek gods with Roman names; thus, the Roman Jupiter and Zeno were the Greek Zeus and Hera. The Jews were tempted to worship these gods, as their forefathers had been when under the influence and power of Assyria and Babylonia; and since the Romans themselves had a strong sense of loyalty to their gods, it is more than likely that these Jews accepted Roman gods alongside their own Yahweh. Mithras, god of light and strength, was worshiped even in England, and a temple to this god has been excavated in London. We shall hear more of both Greek and Roman gods and their influence on the Jews of the Dispersion in Part IV.

ROMAN WRITING

We owe our letters to the Romans too; the print at which you are now looking is Roman lettering. They gave us, too, their numerals, most of which are easy to read with a little practice. The use of C, D and L often gives more difficulty. The Romans showed 1,000 by a circle O, 500 by a half a circle Ɔ D, 100 by a half-circle without the diameter C, and 50 by the lower half of this, ᴜ, which soon became more like an L. The 1,000 later became shown as twice 500, that is, by two semicircles—D and D; if you put these two close together they make ƆD or OD = M. Instead of writing four Xs (XXX) for 40, they made it ten less than 50—XL; for 60, ten more than 50—LX. It will be remembered that the Septuagint, written by seventy scholars,

was and still is shown as LXX.

Roman boys at school did their writing in a way similar to that of the Greeks. A wooden tablet was covered with wax and with a pointed instrument—a sharpened reed, for instance—they wrote or scratched their work into the wax. Warming the wax would enable them to "rub out" and prepare the tablet for further work. Longer exercises or letters were done on parchment made from papyrus —of which we read in Part I. A reed pen was sharpened and dipped into ink made from soot-black and gum. The ink bottle was a small cylinder with a conical top. The writing was done in columns and the papyrus was unrolled to the right and rolled from the left as it was read. Rolls to be kept—those of the great orators like Cicero—were put into a kind of drum-shaped box with a hinged lid.

The Jews learned bitterly to recognize a Roman soldier; (read Ephesians 6:13–17).

THE CALENDAR

An interesting story of Roman origin concerns the calendar, the first of which, made by Romulus, contained ten months relating to the periods of the moon. The names of the months were those of Roman gods and goddesses. Julius Caesar improved on this in 46 B.C., and July was named in his honor. We also have the month of August, after Augustus Caesar of whom we shall hear shortly. But the story of the calendar must be followed elsewhere.

ROMAN RULE

Caesar's grant of freedom to the Jews probably arose from the fact that the Romans believed in allowing conquered nations to manage their own affairs so long as they remained loyal to Rome and did not join with other nations to rebel; they were to regard themselves as Romans and could earn the right to be Roman citizens, with all the advantages of such freedom. We know that Paul was proud of the fact that he was "free-born" (see Part IV).

In order to encourage the conquered people to become Romans, all sorts of

The High Priest wearing his breastplate and carrying a censer. By the time of Jesus he was absolute ruler of the religious lives of the people, and his friendship with Rome made him powerful even in their civil lives.

An example of Roman work—an aqueduct. Note the Roman arches.

Roman ideas were introduced to them. We have already seen the influence of the Roman gods and language—though we must admit the greater influence of the Greek tongue, which continued to be used in trade and argument. Fine roads were made to take the place of the winding caravan routes, cities were walled, aqueducts for water transport were raised, heating and drainage were improved. Even more important, perhaps, was the setting-up of Roman customs of rule, by which the Jews had the right to consider, discuss and pass laws benefiting their own people. But the Romans had little time for beauty as loved by the Greeks. They were hard-headed, practical, disciplined, and to some extent unimaginative. The art they did practice was for the most part copied from the Greeks.

HEROD THE GREAT

We now hear about Herod the Great In 40 B.C. Rome found that Syria was being invaded by the Parthians, who had promised to help the Jews too if they wished to rebel against Caesar. Herod had been in power for some time, even then, but now fled to Rome. He returned three years later, in 37 B.C., with an army, captured Jerusalem and became the first King of the Jews. His rule was difficult, for the Jews hated him, as they did all foreigners. He was an Edomite, whose father Antipater had left his country to the south of the Dead Sea (once the home of Esau) to lead the Jews through an anxious period of their history; but the Jews had shown no gratitude, and so far as they were concerned Antipater could have gone back to Edom, and Herod with him. Herod did not receive much help from Rome either. Antony, who had now come to power in Rome, was under the spell of Cleopatra, the last ruler of the Ptolemy dynasty of Egypt, and had little interest in the rule of Herod. But Herod made no secret of his plans to be absolute king; he was determined to be without a rival, to the extent of murdering all his enemies, including the High Priest, and took sides with the Pharisees, as most of the successful rulers before him had done.

On the defeat and death of Antony and Cleopatra in a Roman civil war, Octavian became the new ruler of the Roman Empire and, under the name of Augustus, the first Emperor of Rome. Peace seemed likely to last for many years and during this period—known as the *Pax Romana* (Roman peace)—Herod went over to Augustus to make sure of Roman protection and help should he need it. The emperor accepted Herod, seeing in him a man on whom he could rely for firm control of Judaea. Herod was thus certain of Roman support, and continued to strengthen his own position in the country.

HEROD'S TROUBLES

It is not surprising to learn that he had a good deal of trouble in his home and palace, for he had ten wives! They seem to have spent a great deal of their time in fighting, quarreling and plotting. Herod met these troubles with murder and execution—even of members of his own family. He was determined to let no one, not even his wives, interfere with his rule over the Jews.

Yet Palestine began to grow powerful once more. Herod built good roads and stamped out robber bands. New cities, like Caesarea and Samaria—which had been razed to the ground years before—were built; others were fortified. He made Samaria his northern capital and built there a Roman amphitheater like the one described in Part III. More important to our story than all, however, was the rebuilding of the Temple.

THE TEMPLE

Begun in 20 B.C., it was not finished even in Christ's time (John 2:16–20 and Mk. 13:1). The architecture was Grecian, in white marble, "like a mountain covered with snow." Gates and pillars were overlaid with gold, and as it glittered in the bright sunshine it must have given every Jew a great sense of pride and happiness and even love. It is not surprising that the Jews scattered throughout the then known world returned to Jerusalem whenever they could to see their Temple and to worship there the God of all Israel.

ITS EXTENT

In order to make sure that the Temple

had a sound foundation, the top of Mount Moriah was built up, so that underneath the Temple were large crypts and rooms for storage; even horses were stabled there.

The whole site measured about 440 yards by 330 yards. The main entry was through the Golden Gate; the doors were massive and covered with brass, twenty men being needed to open and shut them. This gate led to the Court of the Gentiles, beyond which any who were not Jews could not go; across it was a wall of

A Jewish lamp, showing the Menorah (seven-branched lampholder)—see Exodus 17:12; 25:31, 32. The shofar and a shovel depicted here were used in Temple sacrifices.

marble, 4½ feet high, on which in Greek and Latin were the words: "No foreigner may enter within the screen and enclosure round the Holy Place. Whosoever is caught so trespassing will himself be the cause of death overtaking him." A polite way of saying: "Trespassers will be executed!"

Through the Beautiful Gate was the Court of the Women, where was also the Treasury, containing thirteen trumpet-mouthed chests for offerings; each chest was for some special purpose and the giver could chose any one for his gifts. This Court was as far as women were allowed to go. Beyond this was the Gate of Nicanor, leading into the Court of the Men; thence to the Court of the Priests, where the service and sacrifices of the priests at the four-horned Altar of Burnt Offering could be seen, and where the Temple choir and musicians led the psalms and singing.

The Temple itself was small, beautiful and sacred. No actual service took place within it. Before it reared a huge porch 172 feet high and broad; the Holy Place was 120 feet wide, its double doors being covered with a veil of rich Babylonian material in purple and blue. The priest entered only during the hours of duty; here were the Table of Shewbread, the Menorah—a golden candlestick with seven branches—and the Altar of Incense. Beyond was the Holy of Holies, empty except for a stone representing the lost Ark of the Covenant (see Part I). The Holy of Holies, separated from the Holy Place by only a veil of beautiful material, was entered but once a year, and then only by the High Priest on the Day of Atonement; on this occasion he spoke aloud the Sacred Name of Yahweh.

ITS MUSIC—THE PSALMS

During the period of the Maccabees, the hymn-book of the Temple was being put together—compiled, as we say. Psalms had been written for many years before this time, some of them by David himself; these were in Book 1 and consisted of Psalms 1–41. Then, about 300 B.C., Books 2 and 3 were collected, containing Psalms 42–89. During the last two hundred years B.C., and including the time the Temple was begun, other psalms were written, and put into Books 4 and 5. The collected psalms are called the *Psalter*.

A selection of Roman coins. These had to be exchanged for Temple shekels when the Jews paid their religious dues.

They tell in beautiful language the story of the Jews—their fears and hopes, sadness and joy. There are psalms of thanksgiving, praise and worship in honor of God the Creator who is righteous and just and holy. These psalms were sung in Temple worship, and varied according to the day of the week. In the intervals between the groups of verses, the priests blew their trumpets and the people fell prostrate before the altar (Ps. 150). The Temple orchestra played on wind instruments like rams' horns and pipes, stringed instruments like psalteries and harps, percussion, such as cymbals, timbrels, and tambourines. In Herod's Temple there was an organ with thirteen pipes and two bellows. Both men and boys sang in the choir and there was also dancing (Ps. 149). Some of the psalms contained responses sung by the choir and people in reply to the leader or priest, as Psalms 145 and 150. These are called antiphonal psalms.

Special psalms were sung on special occasions, for example, Psalm 135 at the Feast of Dedication. The "Songs of Degrees," Psalms 120–134, were probably sung by pilgrims on their way to Jerusalem for the feasts.

When reading some of the psalms you will come across the word "selah." It marks the end of a group of verses and is believed to indicate in the singing of the psalms some change in musical accent, rhythm or tempo. It certainly should not be read aloud when you are reading the psalms in school or church, any more than you would say "period" at the end of this sentence.

In Psalm 150 is a list of musical instruments used in the Temple. The psaltery was a harp, and the harp then used was more like the lyre.

Haggai 2:9 summed up the feelings of the Jews about their Temple of 516 B.C. Herod's Temple was even more glorious, especially when we realize that it was the Temple into which Jesus went for worship during His life and ministry.

Nearby was the Castle of Antonia, a stronghold for the Roman soldiers whose duty it was to keep guard over the city and to deal with possible riots and signs of rebellion. They had also to enforce law and order in the collecting of the hated taxes and levies demanded by Caesar.

"IN THE DAYS OF HEROD THE KING"

Despite the great care Herod took over the building of the Temple, he was not popular with either the Jews or the Romans. He had hoped to reconcile the Pharisees and the Sadducees, but angered them all when he reared over the Temple the Roman eagle itself. The deeply religious Jews openly sneered at him—"this foreigner"—and the Romans thought of him as an upstart. He loved pomp and ceremony and probably saw himself as

A silver shekel dating from 138 B.C. It bears the façade of the Temple and the word "Simon." On the reverse is a lulav— a bundle of palm branches, and an ethrog —a citrus fruit; these were symbols of the Feast of Tabernacles. The words are: "For the Freedom of Jerusalem."

another Solomon. He imitated the Greeks by introducing their athletics and pageantry; this further upset the religious sects, which held that such things were wicked and against the laws of Yahweh. Some of the older members, too, must have been horrified at seeing the younger priests hurry over their duties at the Temple in order to rush to the arena and gymnasium to join in the excitement provided there. Herod also built fortresses to strengthen his position, but this made the Romans suspicious that he was plotting against them. He then tried to win favor by calling one city after the emperor him-

self—Caesarea. His reign was full of murders and cruelty of all kinds, for he was constantly afraid of his enemies. A dread disease (we do not know what it really was) took hold of him and this made his fear even more frightening to him; he became so brutal and savage that he could order the deaths of tiny babies.

He died in 4 B.C., a sullen, miserable man. But into the world, "in Bethlehem of Judaea in the days of Herod the King," had come the Child he could not kill, the Child sent by God Himself to become the King of all mankind—Jesus Christ our Lord.

13

Stories of Babylon and Persia:
Daniel and Esther

(DANIEL 1:8-21; 2:1-19, 25-49; 3; 5; 6. ESTHER 3-10)

DANIEL

At the time of the persecution by Antiochus Epiphanes in his effort to destroy the Jewish people and obliterate their religion (see Chap. 11), there was desperate need for the leadership in resistance which was furnished by the Maccabees. There was equal need for a voice which could encourage the rank and file of the people to endure. So about 165 B.C. appeared the book known as the prophecy of Daniel, with its stories of heroes who had stood firm under persecution, its representations of earlier tyrants who had come to disastrous ends, and its pictures—in apocalyptic terms that the agents of Antiochus Epiphanes might not recognize but that the Jewish people would understand—of the doom that awaited all new tyrannies. In Ezekiel 14:14 there had been mention of Daniel as one of the great souls remembered in the tradition of Israel; and now the writer

of the book to which Daniel's name was given set forth, as though having been exemplified in the days of Babylonian persecution by Daniel and his friends, the kind of courage which had to be striven for by his own contemporaries in face of the cruelties of Antiochus.

THE FOUR FRIENDS

After the first siege of Jerusalem in 597 B.C., Nebuchadrezzar, King of Babylon, had carried off the courtiers, leaders, and craftsmen of the city. The Book of Daniel begins with a story of four of these captives, one of whom was Daniel, and the others of whom were Shadrach, Meshach, and Abednego. They were selected by the king for special training and education in the Babylonian arts of war, hunting, and leisure. They learned the Chaldean tongue and how to read and write the wedge-shaped cuneiform script. They learned how to count. The

Babylonians counted in 60's rather than in 100's, and from them we have today our 60 seconds = 1 minute, and 60 minutes = 1 hour.

The friends learned, too, how to behave in the king's court. However, whatever they learned of Babylonian idol worship, they held to their own Jewish faith in Yahweh and in the promise of Jeremiah that one day the people of Judah would return. It was because they wanted to keep their own laws that Dan-

The Babylonians were much interested in astronomy and astrology. Here are their signs of the Zodiac.

iel persuaded the king's steward to let them have water and vegetable foods rather than strong wine and meat that had been offered to idols or killed not in accordance with their laws (see, too, I Macc. 1:41–53).

KNOWLEDGE OF THE STARS

In chapter 2 we learn that Daniel had a special interest in astrology and magic, as had Moses and Joseph years before. It was quite a common training for those who showed interest in the stars. In Babylonia the clear night skies were filled with brilliant stars that attracted the curiosity of scholars and lesser men

like sorcerers and magicians, who, as members of the king's court, were expected to interpret movements of the stars as well as strange dreams.

Apart from the belief that fortunes could be "told from the stars"—astrology—there was in Babylonia a considerable knowledge of the stars and planets as a science—astronomy. Of course, the stars were linked with many legends of the Babylonian gods. The moon was the father of the Sun and stars which shone and gleamed in the dry atmosphere of the country. The Sun's path was divided into twelve and stars were grouped in each division. Each month was controlled by a group of these stars, as October by Scorpio (scorpion), April by Taurus (bull). Merodach was believed to have put the gods in their stations "as the stars of the Zodiac" (Zodiac probably means "animals"). The Signs of the Zodiac have come down to us through the Phoenicians and the Greeks; they were certainly known by the Babylonians and by Daniel in his studies. More about the Zodiac can be found in reference books and encyclopedias.

THE KING'S DREAM

When Nebuchadrezzar had his strange dream it was natural for him to send for his astrologers and soothsayers for an explanation of it; he made their task more difficult by forgetting what it was about. Daniel eventually interpreted it for him; he said that it was about an image and that a stone crashed on the feet of the image and broke it. The stone became a great mountain which filled the whole earth. This, said Daniel, meant that the dream foretold the rise and fall of many kingdoms but that in the end the kingdom of God would be supreme.

The king rewarded Daniel and his three friends, giving them high positions: Daniel was made a judge "at the gate"; he told the king that it was Yahweh who had helped him to tell the king his dream, and Nebuchadrezzar was tremendously impressed, so much so that he said, "Your God is the God of gods."

THE BURNING FIERY FURNACE

You will recall how the Jews refused to worship the figure of Zeus that Antiochus Epiphanes had raised on the altar of Yahweh. Chapter 3 of the Book of Daniel refers to the persecution of those who suffered for their faith and encourages them to resist a heathen religion. Nebuchadrezzar set up a golden image— probably of wood and covered with gold, standing sixty cubits high (a cubit was eighteen to twenty inches). It was most likely erected to the glory of Merodach (Marduk), god of the wind, sun, thunder, and life, his own god and "great lord." Daniel was away from the court on this occasion, perhaps on some ambassador's business for the king, but his three friends heard the herald's announcement and the king's decree that at the sound of music everybody had to worship the image; the three refused. (Among the listed instruments are the sackbut and psaltery, both triangular; the dulcimer was a stringed instrument; see drawing.)

Nebuchadrezzar did not like to be disobeyed, but gave them another chance; they again refused. Then he threw them into the "burning fiery furnace." We know what happened and how even the king cried, "Blessed be the God of Shadrach, Mesach, and Abednego!" when he learned of their safety. In the Apocrypha is the Song of the Three Holy Children which the three friends sang while in the fiery furnace. Its rightful place in the narrative appears to be between verses 23 and 24 of Daniel 3. You will also find this song as the Benedicite, in in the Book of Common Prayer.

THE WRITING ON THE WALL

The desecration of the Temple by Anti-

ochus Epiphanes was still very much in the thoughts of the writer, and in chapter 5 we find him foretelling disaster for those who defile the Holy Place. He tells of the King of Babylon drinking and feasting from the vessels stolen from the Temple; and he says that the nation will certainly meet destruction. The message to the Jews is clearly this—if such a king and his people are to be punished for stealing and defiling the vessels of the Temple, how much more certain will be the punishment of Antiochus Epiphanes who had committed sacrilege and even offered swine on Yahweh's altar.

The chapter as we have it is not strictly true history. Cyrus, not Darius, captured Babylon, and Belshazzar was son of the king then reigning and therefore a prince: but some scholars say that the prince may have been acting as regent at this time.

In the story the prince is horrified at the fingers of a hand that appear so strangely and write on the wall MENE, MENE, TEKEL, UPHARSIN. It is not certain what the words really meant; some say "counted, counted, weighed, divided"; others, "amina, amina, a shekel and half a mina," these being three weights representing the values of different kings of Babylon. Whatever they meant, they carried with them the threat of doom. Babylon would fall, as Isaiah had foretold in 34:11–14.

Once again the message to the persecuted Jews is clear: they were to keep their faith and wait patiently for the fall of their enemies and the returning power of Yahweh.

DANIEL IN THE LIONS' DEN

This is yet another story familiar to most of us (6). Again there is a special message behind it for the Jews. Following his desecration of the Temple, Antiochus tried to stamp out entirely the worship of Yahweh. He was determined to make all Jews worship Greek gods, and murdered the priests, and ordered all Jews everywhere to do as he commanded. But this story tells the Jews quite clearly that whatever happened they must worship Yahweh faithfully, for He is the one true God.

The king's courtiers, jealous of Daniel, prepared a cunning plot into which the king fell. Having given an order, he could not change it; the "law of the Medes and Persians" was a decision that could not be altered. He therefore had to do as he had decreed, even though it meant the death of Daniel, who had been caught worshiping Yahweh at dawn, in the afternoon, and at sunset, the Jews' hours of worship.

The lions' den was not far from the palace. Lions were kept in captivity ready to be released whenever the king wanted to go hunting, probably to make sure that he did not waste weary hours searching for them. When his seal—imprinted on wax or soft clay and sun-baked—had been fixed to the entrance, it was not possible for even the king himself to break it and release Daniel. But when he found that Daniel was still alive, he lost no time in getting the door to open. As rulers of nations often did, he thereupon accepted Yahweh as a great God, and ordered his peoples to worship Him. Daniel was promoted to a high position.

ESTHER

The Book of Esther is a very fine story of plots and counterplots in the Persian court. It should not be taken as actual history and must be seen rather as a story that dramatizes the unconquerable resistance of the Jewish people to the heathen forces by which so often they were persecuted. There is little that is religious in it; it does not even mention God; and the Feast of Lots (Purim) it tells about is not written of anywhere else in the Bible.

It is not easy to say why the book found its way into the Old Testament. Perhaps because it helps to explain the belief of the writer and the people that Israel could never be entirely destroyed while every Jew did his duty in standing up for his country—even if it meant risking his own life to do so.

BACKGROUND AND PLOT

The story is set in Persia during the reign of Ahasuerus (Xerxes) about 485–465 B.C. The Feast of Lots (II Macc. 15) became a yearly feast to keep in memory the deliverance from the Persians of the Jews then living in Persia; it may once have been a heathen feast adopted and altered by the Jews to fit their own celebrations. The author of the story lived about 130 B.C., when the successes of the Maccabaeans were filling the Jews with pride in their country. Judas Maccabaeus, it will be remembered, had led the revolt against Antiochus, and for the next thirty years or so the Jews, despite feuds and quarrels among themselves, had thrown off much of the power of their rulers; the borders of Judaea had even been extended by conquest. But there was always the fear of being conquered again, and the Roman eagle was stretching out its wings. Is was necessary for every Jew to fight and risk death for his country.

The plot of the book tells how Queen Esther prevented the success of a cruel scheme planned by a courtier named Haman. He had made up his mind to destroy the Jews living in Persia. Haman, "a strutting little peacock," was furiously angry when the Queen's Jewish cousin Mordecai refused to bow to him or to pay him special respect. So Haman went to the king and, promising to pay 10,000 talents of silver, obtained the king's permission to slaughter the whole Jewish race on a day that he, Haman, would himself decide. The actual day was, in fact postponed so that it fell on the 13th of the Jewish month Adar; this was the very day on which the Maccabees had defeated the Syrians in 135 B.C.

It is obvious that at the time Ahasuerus did not realize that his queen was a Jewess, or he might have thought twice about Haman's strange request. Haman erected an especially high gallows, hoping to see Mordecai swing for his "insults" to him. Esther knew it was a daring and dangerous thing to go to the king and ask him to change his decision. Once the king had made a decree it could not be altered. But she risked her life and pleaded for her people.

Haman gloated in the belief that he stood high in power with the king and that the king was about to show it publicly.

Instead of that, disaster struck. Ahasuerus decided to look into the court records, and found that he already owed his life to Mordecai, who had never been rewarded for saving it. Next morning, Haman, seething with anger, was obliged to lead Mordecai clad in royal garments and on horseback through the city streets; for "thus shall it be done unto the man whom the king shall delight to honor."

Then Esther begged for her people's safety and denounced Haman. Whereupon the king ordered that Haman be strung on the gallows he had raised for Mordecai, and Mordecai received the high honors he had deserved (Ezra 2:2; Neh. 7:7).

FEAST OF PURIM

But the king's decree was a "law of the Medes and Persians" and could not be changed. So he issued another decree in which the Jews were given permission for two days to defend themselves against the Persians who had been commanded to slay them. In so doing they slew 75,800 Persians. The Feast of Purim was held to commemorate this deliverance. The word *purim* means "lots," Haman had cast lots to decide on the day of the slaughter. From this time, all Jews were required to attend their synagogue and join in the reading of the Book of Esther from a roll—"The Roll"—containing just this one book; the feast following was one of rejoicing, mirth, and revelry, in celebration of their ancestors' fortunate escape from cruelty and death.

14

Job and Jonah

(JOB: R.V. advised—selected passages: 1:1-3, 6-22; 2:1-7, 11, 13; 3:1-19; 4:7, 8, 17; 5:17, 18; 8:3, 5, 6, 20; 11:6, 9; 13; 22:5, 7, 9, 10; 31:7-40; 38:1-12, 36; 39; 40; 42:1-12. JONAH 1; 2, 3; 4. CF. JER. 16:19; 18:3-12. LK. 11:29, 30. ISA. 42:6, 7; 45:14, 15. II KINGS 14:26)

JOB

The Book of Job was written about 500 B.C. We do not know the name of the author, but he was certainly a very fine poet. Like our own Shakespeare, he took as a framework an old story and turned it into a drama. Like some of Shakespeare's plays, it has a prologue, a main plot, and an epilogue. Its language is often beautiful.

The background of the story is the time of such patriarchs as Abraham and its theme or subject is the age-old problem: Why do good people suffer? Or, as we sometime say: Why do cheats seem to prosper? or, Why do the wicked get on better than the good?

In the old story, Job was so good that one of God's "ministers," a kind of prosecutor called Satan (not the Tempter or the Devil, as he is sometimes called), asked God if he could test Job. He said Job was righteous merely because God

was good to him and that if he were tried with many sorrows and losses he would turn against God. But Job bore his sufferings patiently and the Satan had to admit defeat; Job became even richer and worthier.

THE DRAMA

Let us see what the poet makes of this old story. Job is "perfect and upright and one that feared God and shrank back from evil." ("Feared" does not mean that Job was afraid of God; rather, he regarded God as great and wonderful and worthy of worship, and Job longed to serve and work for Him.) Job is a wealthy sheikh or farmer in the Land of Uz—possibly on the borders of Syria, or even Edom down in the south; wherever it is, the hero appears not to be an Israelite, which makes the story even more powerful, for Job is not one of the "chosen people." Everything so far has gone well for him, and he is prosperous and happy. Then comes the Satan to God and says that Job is good only because he has all he needs. . . . "But touch all he hath and he will renounce thee to thy face," says the Satan. That is your task— to prove it, says God. So the Satan sets to work.

Everything now goes wrong for Job— murder, fire, storm, destruction of his servants, camels and home. He is ruined. Yet he does not blame God—that is the remarkable thing about Job. The Satan comes again to God, who now gives him permission to make Job suffer physically, so long as he does not actually kill him. It is then that Job suffers dreadful boils— a form of leprosy; his wife turns against him and against God; his friends come one by one and try to prove to him that he must have done some wicked thing in his past or secret life for God to punish him in this manner—in other words, that Job is getting what he deserves. This is almost a modern argument, that we get "what we deserve," but the kind of thing said usually by rather thoughtless and self-satisfied people. Job knows this is not true; he has no secret sin of which to be ashamed, and he is patient in his miseries. But the doubt is put into his mind that God is not being very fair to him; at least He might have told him *why* he has to suffer all these things, then they would have been easier to bear; perhaps his faith hasn't much foundation after all. He reaches the depth of disappointment and pessimism (9:23 and 14:1, 2).

"JOB'S COMFORTERS"

His friends are "miserable comforters," which explains why today we speak of "Job's comforters." They are the kind of people who seem to enjoy the sorrows and sufferings of other people and feel how very good they themselves are; they are not very pleasant people. Job longs for someone to plead with God on his behalf, if only so that he can find out what is wrong and then put right. This someone he calls a redeemer or vindicator —someone who will speak up for him. "I know that my redeemer liveth," he says. We are familiar with this cry because we have heard it sung in Handel's *Messiah*. This has perhaps altered its meaning for us, or at least the original meaning. Christ redeemed or saved us from *sin,* from wrong-doing, but Job had no sense of sin whatsoever, so he could not have been thinking of the resurrection as we think of it. In any case, he still believed in the old idea of the Hebrew heaven and Sheol, and had no thoughts of an after life such as we learn from the life, death, and rising again of Jesus. That idea had come very slowly to the Jews; the Pharisees, you will remember, began to believe in it, although the Sadducees refused to do so, and Jesus finally made it clear with His resurrection for all to believe.

WHAT IS MAN?

Job then demands: Has God really been fair to me? And God answers him, not in so many words, but by asking Job questions. One after another they come, all leading to the main demand: What can man do? Read 40:6–14 and see that the only answer Job can give to all these questions is to admit that man is not really important, that he is very small and that God is very great. All creation is witness and proof of the wisdom of God, and man ought to trust Him at all times.

THE TEST OF FAITH

The drama ends almost too happily, for Job becomes even more prosperous than he was before his trials and temptations. Such an ending may mislead us in our final thoughts, if we are not careful. The poet is anxious to reward Job and to prove that by standing up to his test he received even greater riches. But real-life stories do not always end "happily ever after," as we well know. The real point of this story is Job's own faith and belief—that he has learned to trust God when everything goes wrong. It is easy enough to trust Him when "God's in His heaven; all's right with the world"; it is a much harder lesson to learn that He is just as near and ready to help when the "world is upside down." We may never have to suffer as Job did, but we all have to learn that sorrows and bitterness come to the best of people, and that the best of people stand strong in their faith in God and overcome them all.

JONAH

It used to be thought that the Book of Jonah must be read as literal history, and so there sprang up the endless arguments whether the "great fish" could swallow Jonah, and whether Jonah could live for three days in the great fish's belly and at the end of that time come out in good condition. But the Old Testament does not have to be all literal history. It has poetry in it; it has the drama of Job; it has parables and allegories. And the vivid meaning of the Book of Jonah comes to light when it is realized that *this* is what it really is: a magnificent plea for evangelism cast in the form of a symbolic story. There were two tendencies among the Jewish people. One was the impulse to a narrow and exclusive nationalism, as expressed in the Book of Esther. The other was the awakening realization that Israel's mission might be to give light to the Gentiles also. And that is what the Book of Jonah represents. It is a picture of the purpose of God that was greater and more compelling than the prophet— who symbolized the stubbornness of Israel —wanted to express.

The author knew that one of the tasks given to Judah was to make Yahweh known to all the world, that is, to the heathen peoples, or as they were often called, the Gentiles. He also knew that the Exile had been in some part the punishment for not doing this task. He probably lived about 300 B.C., placing his story before the fall of both Assyria and Babylon. The story, as a kind of parable, seems to show that Jonah is the Jewish nation, Nineveh the tyrant city representing the whole world, and the "great fish" the Exile or Captivity, from which Israel is "disgorged" in the Return.

Jonah tried to flee from Yahweh by boarding a ship from Joppa to Tarshish across the Mediterranean Sea. The cargo ship was Phoenician, like this. Read Ezekiel 27.

JONAH TRIES TO ESCAPE

Jonah is told that he has to go to Nineveh, the capital of the dreaded Assyrian Empire, to tell them about Yahweh, He refuses to go and, terrified, tries to get as far away from God as he can; this he does by boarding a cargo ship at Joppa, hoping to make for Tarshish (Tartessus), right across the Mediterranean in Spain, the farthest point of the then known world. Yahweh could not possibly reach him there. In the storm he learns that even the heathen are his brothers, despite their beliefs in gods other than his own; he is thrown overboard by the kindly yet fearful sailors, and then taken by the great fish "prepared to swallow up Jonah." There is nothing unusual in the Bible idea of being swallowed by a great fish; it is mentioned in Jeremiah 51:34, 44; Isaiah 27:1, and Psalm 74:13, where "dragon" = sea monster. Here it is the swallowing up of the Jewish nation by Babylonia. The author uses the phrase "three days and three nights," which is a Hebrew expression meaning "for a short time," after which Jonah is disgorged or thrown out; this is the release of Israel from exile.

JONAH OBEYS

Ordered a second time, Jonah now obeys Yahweh and goes to preach in Nineveh. He is extraordinarily successful; even the king turns to Yahweh, who tells Jonah that He forgives these people their wickednesses. But Jonah is angry at this; these people are not Yahweh's "chosen people," they cannot be spared from punishment. He has not yet learned that God loves all His people, however wicked they are and wherever they happen to live.

Jonah then builds a shelter or booth of branches as a protection against the hot sun. A gourd (possibly a wild vine) grows over it and serves for shade. It shrivels and dies, and Jonah is sorry to see that happen. God then says: "Thou hast pity for the gourd for which thou hast not laboured neither madest it grow; which came up in a night and perished in a night; should I not have pity on Nineveh, that great city?" That is, you are sorry for a plant that without any help from you grew and then died; don't you think I should be sorry for my people of Nineveh whom I brought into the world and whom I love? We are not told what Jonah said in reply, if he did reply; it is more than likely that when he saw what Yahweh meant he hung his head in silent shame. Perhaps, like the elder brother in Christ's story of the Prodigal Son, he had begun to learn that God came not to seek the righteous but the lost. The real question is: will Israel carry out her task of bringing the heathen into God's Kingdom?

A LESSON TO BE LEARNED?

But even by the time of Paul, the Jews had not learned this lesson; they still refused to listen to his plan to preach to the Gentiles (Acts 22:21 ff.). Isaiah had told the Jews that through them the Gentiles would be brought to Yahweh. But they remained jealous of their belief that having survived the Exile they were God's elect—His chosen people—and that no other nation could be as important as they. When would they learn that He was God not merely of the Jews but of the whole world?

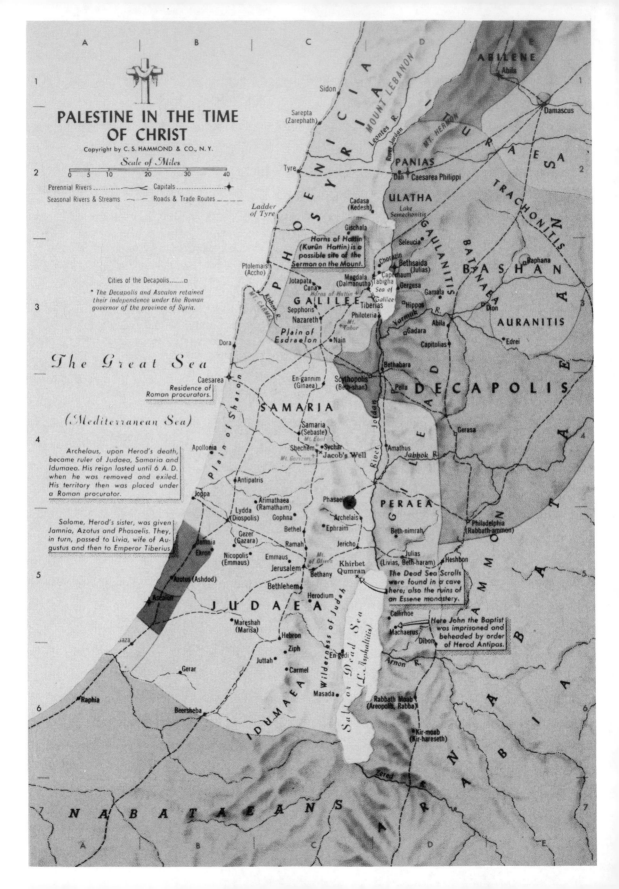

PALESTINE IN THE TIME OF CHRIST

Copyright by C. S. HAMMOND & CO., N.Y.

Scale of Miles

0 5 10   20   30   40

Perennial Rivers .... Capitals ....
Seasonal Rivers & Streams ---- Roads & Trade Routes ----

Cities of the Decapolis ......□

*The Decapolis and Ascalon retained
their independence under the Roman
governor of the province of Syria.*

Archelaus, upon Herod's death,
became ruler of Judaea, Samaria and
Idumaea. His reign lasted until 6 A.D.
when he was removed and exiled.
His territory then was placed under
a Roman procurator.

Salome, Herod's sister, was given
Jamnia, Azotus and Phasaelis. They,
in turn, passed to Livia, wife of Augustus and then to Emperor Tiberius.

The Great Sea

(Mediterranean Sea)

Residence of
Roman procurators.

Horns of Hattin
(Kurūn Hattin) is a
possible site of the
Sermon on the Mount.

The Dead Sea Scrolls
were found in a cave
here; also the ruins of
an Essene monastery.

Here John the Baptist
was imprisoned and
beheaded by order
of Herod Antipas.

Part III

THE PALESTINE of JESUS

ABILENE

Sidon

Damascus

MOUNT LEBANON

Leontes R.

PHOENICIA

Tyre

MT. HERMON

PANIAS

Panias • Ulatha and Panias were
placed under Herod's
control in 20 B.C.

TURAEA

TRACHONITIS

The Great Sea

(Mediterranean Sea)

Cadasa
(Kedesh)

Ecdippa

Gischala • Lake
Semechonitis

Herod's first territory
was Galilee, given to him
by his father, Antipater.

ULATHA

GAULANITIS

BATANAEA

Raphana

Ptolemaïs

GALILEE

MT. CARMEL

Taricheae (Magdala)
Arbela

Sepphoris •
• Gaba

Nazareth

Philoteria

Sea of
Galilee

Hippos

Gamala

Dion

AURANITIS

Kanatha

Plain of
Esdraelon

Yarmuk

Abila

R.

Gadara

Edrei

Dora

Hippos and Gadara were
cities of the Decapolis given
to Herod by Augustus.

Bostra

Caesarea
(Strato's Tower)
City and port were
rebuilt by Herod.

SAMARIA

Scythopolis

Pella

DECAPOLIS

Plain of Sharon

Herod rebuilt Samaria,
giving it the new name
of Sebaste.

Gerasa

River Jordan

The Decapolis was a league of neighboring city districts united for mutual
protection against marauding tribes.
It was not a compact geographical or
political unit with definite boundaries.

Apollonia

Sebaste
(Samaria)

Shechem

Mt.
Gerizim

Amathus

Jabbok R.

PERAEA

NABATAEA

Antipatris

Joppa

Thamna

Gophna

Alexandrium

Phasaelis

Lydda

Modin

Jamnia

Ekron

Gazara

Bethel

Jericho

Beth-nimrah

Philadelphia

AMMON

Emmaus

Beth-horon

Azotus

Jerusalem
Mt.
of Olives

Khirbet
Qumrân
×

Livias
(Beth-haram)

Heshbon

Herod gained control of Jerusalem
in 37 B.C., defeating Antigonus, and
became King of Judaea.

Hyrcanium

Ascalon
Birthplace
of Herod.

Bethlehem

Herodium

JUDAEA

Beth-gubrin

Callirhoë

Marisa

Beth-zur

Machaerus

Anthedon
(Agrippium)

Hebron

Gaza

En-gedi

Salt Sea
(Dead Sea)

Dibon

IDUMAEA

Arnon R.

THE DOMINIONS OF
HEROD THE GREAT
37 to 4 B.C.

Copyright by C. S. HAMMOND & CO., N.Y.

Scale of Miles

0   5   10   20   30   40

Beersheba

Masada

Kir-moab
(Kir-hareseth)

Perennial Rivers ....
Seasonal Rivers & Streams ......

Capitals ....
Cities of the Decapolis □

NABATAEANS

Zered R.

Introduction to Part III

How and Why the Gospels Were Written

Our introduction really begins with the last paragraph of this Part. After the Day of Pentecost, the first followers of Jesus began to preach about Him, especially that He had risen from the dead as He had promised. This was their Good News—the Gospel of Jesus Christ.

The first Christians believed that Jesus would return and set up His Kingdom quite soon, and that the world would then come to an end. This did not happen, as we know. But, as time went on and the first disciples—Peter, John, Philip and the others—grew older, it was realized that soon there would be left no eyewitnesses of the wonderful life of Jesus. The best thing to do would be to write down all they could remember about Jesus. Besides, the Good News had been taken by Paul and his companions to places far from Palestine, and written records were necessary for the Christians in heathen cities in other parts of the Roman Empire. There were false teach-

ers, too, who were using the words of Jesus to suit themselves, and true records would help Christians to recognize which preachers were genuine and which were not. All these reasons made it obvious that accounts of the life, work, and resurrection of Jesus should be written down.

Although it stands second and not first in the printed New Testament, the oldest Gospel is the brief "Gospel According to Mark." A very early tradition in the Church, handed down first in specifically written words by Papias, Bishop of Hierapolis, about A.D. 140, is that this Gospel was written by Mark, "who became the interpreter of Peter," apparently in Rome shortly before the year 70. This Mark may have been the John Mark of whom the Book of Acts tells as a companion of Barnabas and Paul in their first missionary journey toward the West (Acts 12, 25; 13, 13; 15, 37–39).

"The Gospel According to Luke," and the Book of Acts, appear to have been the work of Luke, "the beloved physician" (Col. 4, 14), and friend of Paul. Luke knew the Gospel of Mark, and he incorporated almost the whole of Mark into his own Gospel, together with other material, including some of the most precious of Jesus' parables (such as those of the Good Samaritan and the Prodigal Son) and traditions of Jesus' birth and infancy, which he had gathered from other sources. He used also the collection of the sayings of Jesus contained in a document which present-day scholars refer to as "Q"—from the German word *Quelle,* meaning source.

"Q" dates from perhaps as early as A.D. 50, or even slightly before that, when someone gathered together what many remembered and were repeating of the teachings of Jesus. There is good reason for the belief that this someone was the Apostle Matthew. "Q" no longer exists as a separate document, but it is identified as the source of large and almost exactly similar blocks of material in the Gospels of Luke and Matthew.

In the completed form in which it appears in the New Testament, "The Gospel According to Matthew," like the Gospel of Luke, includes practically the entire narrative of Mark, and the contents of "Q"; and priceless additions of Matthew's own, such as the story of the coming of the Magi, the Sermon on the Mount, the parable of the Wise and Foolish Virgins, and the parable of the judgment. The whole Gospel as we now have it bears the name of Matthew; but if it was the Apostle Matthew who gathered the material of "Q" it may be that some other and unknown early Christian was responsible for the completion of what now goes under Matthew's name.

Both Luke and Matthew appear to date from the latter part of the first century, probably not earlier than the '80's. As to where each Gospel was written there are various conjectures, but no sure evidence.

So the Gospels are made up in this way:

> St. Mark = stories from Peter.
> St. Luke = St. Mark + Q sayings + his own stories.
> St. Matthew = St. Mark + Q sayings + his own stories.

These three, although they differ in many details, give essentially similar accounts of the life and work of Jesus, and therefore are called "the Synoptic Gospels." Here is a diagram to show how they are linked:

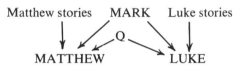

"The Gospel According to John" is different from the Synoptics: more meditative and more mystical, less concerned with narrative and more intent on reflecting what Jesus had meant to a soul that loved him. It has been an almost unanimous belief of New Testament scholarship that this Fourth Gospel was the latest of all, dating not earlier than about A.D. 100, but the surprising fact that some of the Dead Sea Scrolls, discovered recently in the Wâdí Qumrân near the ruins of the pre-Christian Essene monastery, have forms of expression remarkably like some of those in the Gospel of John have made some scholars think that the Fourth Gospel may belong to a period in advance of what had been supposed. But there is no way of fixing its date with certainty, nor any way of knowing surely whether the Gospel was written— as ancient tradition affirmed—by John, "the Beloved Disciple" who outlived the others of the Twelve and, at a great old age, in Ephesus, wrote his final witness. Whatever be the fact of its authorship, the Fourth Gospel has come down through the centuries as perhaps the most moving of all the testimonies to Jesus as "the Way, the Truth, and the Life."

The following chapters are based on

the Gospel of Mark, with material from the other Gospels also—but mainly on Mark, the shortest of the three and written in the everyday Greek speech of Roman slaves and workmen. Since none of the ·Gospel writers tried to give a "Life" of Jesus in any sense of chronology, it is impossible to give more than a suggested order of the events in His life. But the important point is that Mark, in vivid, impetuous, almost blunt speech, announces itself as "the Gospel of Jesus Christ, the Son of God," and it is this Good News and its background that we shall be trying to understand.

TIME CHART

DATES	THE EARLY CHURCH	THE NEW TESTAMENT	RULERS OF PALESTINE	RULERS OF THE EMPIRE
B.C. 6–4	Birth of Christ		Herod the Great (40 B.C.–4 B.C.) Archelaus (4 B.C.– A.D. 6) [Judaea, Samaria, Idumaea]	Augustus Caesar (31 B.C.–A.D. 14)
	Ministry of Jesus		Antipas (Galilee) (4 B.C.–A.D. 39) Philip (Ituraea) (4 B.C.–A.D. 34) Roman Procurators (Judaea) (from A.D. 6)	
A.D. 29	Crucifixion and Resurrection		Pontius Pilate (A.D. 26–36)	
31/2	Stoning of Stephen			Tiberius Caesar (14–37)
32/3	Conversion of Saul			Caligula (37–41)
34/5	Paul's 1st visit to Jerusalem		Agrippa I (39–44)	
46	Famine in Judaea		Judaea under Rome (44)	
	Paul's 2nd visit to Jerusalem			
47–49	First Missionary Journey	Galatians 48/9 or 52		
49	Council of Jerusalem			Claudius (41–54)
	Paul's 3rd visit to Jerusalem		Agrippa II (50–100)	
49–52	Second Missionary Journey	Thessalonians 51/2		
52	Paul's 4th visit to Jerusalem		Felix (52–58)	
53–56	Third Missionary Journey	Corinthians 55		Nero (54–68)
56	Paul's 5th visit to Jerusalem	Romans 56		
56–58	Paul in Caesarea		Festus (58)	
58–59	Journey to Rome			
59–61	Paul imprisoned in Rome	Colossians, Ephesians, Philippians, Philemon } 59/66		
61	Probable release of Paul Preaching in Asia Minor			
64	Fire of Rome Persecution of Christians Peter and Paul martyred	Timothy 1, 2 Titus 64/5 Mark 64/5 1 Peter ?		
70	Fall of Jerusalem Persecution of Jews			Civil Wars (68–69) Vespasian (67–79) Titus (79–81)
80		Luke 80		
82		Acts 82 Hebrews ?		
85		Matthew 85		
95		Revelation 95		Domitian (81–96)
100		John 100 (Other Books at turn of Century— John 1, 2, 3, James, Jude, Peter 2)		Trajan (98–117)

I

The Land to Which Jesus Came

Herod the Great died in 4 B.C. One of his last and most cruel acts, according to the Gospel of Matthew, was the murder of baby boys in an attempt to destroy the Christ-child born to be King of the whole world.

THE HISTORICAL JESUS

Concerning the life of Jesus we can know the great crucial facts, but we cannot be sure of specific dates. We celebrate his birthday on December 25, but observation of the event and the time set for it apparently began in the Church only in the fourth century. No specific record of the date of Jesus' birth had been handed down. Inferences were drawn from this or that reference in the Gospels to the comparative time of the birth of John the Baptist; but perhaps the strongest influence in the acceptance of December 25 was the fact that in the Roman world there had long been celebrated at that time the festival of "The Birthday of the Unconquered Sun"—the joyful marking of the winter solstice, the emergence of the earth from darkness, and the beginning of the period of lengthened days. So with instinctive spiritual appropriateness the Church made that festival the time at which to commemorate the coming of Him who was to be the Light of the world.

And as it cannot be said categorically that it was on December 25 that Jesus was born, so neither can we say certainly that our calendar is right in reckoning the beginning of the Christian era—the year which because of Christ's coming is marked for all subsequent time as A.D. *(anno domini)*. If Jesus was born before the death of Herod, then He was born not later than what has been reckoned as 4 B.C. There are other details, too, that cannot be positively established. Some evidences in the Gospels point to the belief that Jesus' active ministry, after

He came out of Nazareth to John's baptism, lasted only one year; but other indications make the time seem more likely to have been two years or three. Consequently, the date of the crucifixion cannot be fixed unquestionably. It may have been 29 or 30, or even as late as 33.

If we were writing modern history we should wish that we could be more precise. But the Evangelists to whom we owe the Gospels were not concerned with satisfying our academic interest. To set down exactly *when* this and that occurred so that a calendar could be established, was not in the framework of that which to them was of importance. It was with *what* had occurred that they were interested. And *this* is the overwhelming fact they were proclaiming: that in Palestine, when Augustus Caesar was Emperor of Rome, began the life that was more important than any other life that has been on this earth. In Jesus—in what He was and what He did and what He taught, in His ministry among real men and in His death and resurrection—the eternal meaning of God for all the world had been made known. *That* was the great reality.

THE COUNTRY

Into what kind of country was He born? Look at the map of Palestine. The country is little more than one hundred and fifty miles from north to south and only fifty miles at its widest in the south. It lies between the sea and the Rift Valley, its ranges of mountains and narrow plains running in parallel bands the length of the country. In Judaea the mountains spread out to form wide plateaux, sloping gently to the west through the foothills of the Shephelah and falling more steeply and often suddenly to the Dead Sea on the east. Beyond the Jordan valley rises yet another range of hills, extending to the Arabian Desert. Because of the extreme height of the mountains and the tremendous depth of the river valley, there are great changes of climate. There are hot, sandy deserts, temperate valleys and steaming jungles.

THE JORDAN

The river itself rises in the foothills of Mt. Hermon, snow-capped and magnificent in the north. Passing through Lake Huleh (the Waters of Merom) it enters the Sea of Galilee some 680 feet below sea level. The Sea of Galilee is, of course, a lake; it is about thirteen miles long and seven wide. Because it was shaped like a harp it was sometimes called Chinnereth; sometimes it was given the name of the plain lying along the western shore—Gennesaret. The Jordan— whose name means the "Descender" —sinks deeper and deeper, rushes faster and faster in its rift valley, winding like a great green snake until it empties itself into the Dead Sea, a huge lake from which it cannot escape. Its waters evaporate in the terrible heat and leave behind a salty sea in which there is no life whatsoever (see Part I, Chapter 1).

GALILEE

In following the life of Christ we shall travel much in Galilee and Judaea. Galilee was a land of fertile plains, valleys and rich terraced slopes where crops of all kinds, olive groves and vineyards grew easily. Rain was plentiful, pasture was easy to find. The country and its twelve largest towns had been bartered a thousand years before by Solomon to Hiram, King of Tyre, for cedar needed for the Temple. The name means "circle"; its population included Gentiles and foreigners. The people lived either in farming villages on the hillsides or in the busy little fishing villages or busier towns on the shores of the lake. They were kindly and friendly, but often impetuous, with a keen sense of freedom; they had never forgotten that under Judas Maccabaeus many non-Jews had been forced to accept the religion of the Jews. Nor were they glad that at Tiberias, where their ruler Herod Antipas lived, there was also the palace of the Roman Governor reminding them of Roman control of their land. Galilee was crisscrossed with trade routes, and caravans of burdened camels, laden donkeys and pack mules wended their way through the land. The people themselves traded in their fish—fresh and salted; their fruits—fresh and dried; their corn, olive oil, wine, and wool. Industries in weaving, dyeing, pottery, and the like grew up.

JUDAEA

But Judaea "was on the road to nowhere." If you look at the map you will see that the main trade routes passed down the coast through Philistia (the Way of the Philistines) and by-passed Judaea except for those routes to and from Jerusalem itself—and there were very few of those. Judaea was, as we say, "off the map," and this, coupled with the fact that her land was mountainous, desert and difficult, made her a country very different from Galilee. In some parts, her farmers had to make the best of the thin dry soil of the narrow valleys and steep hills; sometimes rain was scarce and had to be stored in cisterns or dug wells, and in summer much of the land was cracked into dried-out wadis. The peasants were in the main poor, scraping a living with their sheep and by sowing crops whose harvesting they watched with anxious eyes. They terraced the slopes to save what soil there was from washing into the valleys during the sudden torrents of rain; they tended their olive and grape orchards. For the most part they lived in small villages; trade with outside countries—except with the traders who came to Jerusalem at special times of the year—was almost unknown.

This hard existence made them self-centered, even cunning and proud; they were cold toward strangers, especially to those from the north, from Galilee. They had no warm feelings towards Galileans, of whom Jesus was the greatest. Their whole life was centered in Jerusalem, where stood their magnificent Temple, the symbol of their religion.

SAMARIA

Look at the map again. You will see that between these two countries lay a third. This was Samaria, hated and despised by the Jews, to some extent feared by the Galileans. The people were, for the most part, descended from a mixed race. After conquering the Northern Kingdom, the Assyrians transported captives from other conquered lands to what was then Northern Israel; in time they intermarried with the Israelites who had remained in their own country. Their descendants were the Samaritans. At the time of Haggai, when it was proposed to build the second Temple (Part II), they were snubbed after offering to help. Told they were unclean, they began a hatred of the Jews that was returned throughout the centuries (II Kings 17:1–6, 24–41). Pilgrims from the north on their way to Jerusalem usually avoided Samaria; they crossed the Jordan at its borders and traveled along its eastern bank through Peraea. We shall see how Jesus deliberately moved through the country and tried to show the Jews that Samaritans also were children of His Father.

These, then, were the three main divisions of Palestine at the time of Jesus. When not at the mercy of invading armies the land was the highway for trade between these same nations; it was part of the Fertile Crescent, the highway of the East. Goods of all kinds came into it and went from it—perfumes, gold, silver, ivory, silks, spices, jewelry. This merchandise came on camels, horses, mules,

The ruins of Jerash give some idea of the noble pillars and buildings familiar in the days of Jesus.

donkeys—driven by traders anxious to buy and sell, to exchange news, to spread rumors. And these people all used the common tongue of the East—Greek. Alexander the Great, with his great conquests, had left behind him a culture and a learning that was to remain strong for many years, but, most important of all, he left a language that all could learn and speak and understand, one in which were written our stories of Jesus and His life in this land of Palestine.

RULE IN PALESTINE

But at this time Palestine was divided into three other districts, under the rule of the three sons of Herod the Great, who, in turn, were responsible to Caesar Augustus. Herod Antipas—"that fox" (Luke 13:32) was tetrarch of Galilee and Peraea; Philip was tetrarch of the land east of the Jordan, and Archelaus was ethnarch of Judaea, Samaria, and Idumaea. Archelaus showed himself to be such a brutal ruler that at the people's request he was removed by Rome in A.D. 6. Rome then sent a governor or procura-

A Roman bridge.

tor to rule in his place. The fifth of these procurators was Pontius Pilate—A.D. 26–36.

This reminds us that the real ruler of Palestine was, of course, Rome; the three rulers of the parts of Palestine were responsible to Rome only for law and order. Palestine was an occupied country, one of many such in the Roman Empire (Map, Part II). The headquarters of the Romans was at Caesarea, on the coast.

The Praetorian Guard—bodyguard of the Caesars.

There were garrisons in the chief cities to insure control and safety of the trade routes. At the time of Jesus there were four legions in Palestine (a legion was six thousand men). There were foot soldiers, cavalry, slingers, archers, bridge and road builders and a camel corps. In the main these soldiers were Roman, but there were also some from non-Jewish areas like Northern Syria, who were given the more menial tasks, like beating and scourging and crucifying criminals, and the heavier army duties, although it was possible for a non-Jew of this area to rise

to a higher position—such as a centurion. The Jews themselves were excused from war service, mainly because their Law and religion forbade their use of arms on the sabbath.

The Praetorian Guard, the bodyguard of the Emperor, was but rarely garrisoned in Palestine, but couriers from Rome were often seen galloping between Caesarea and Tiberias. The Jews hated the sight of the Roman eagle, the standard borne by these armies. The Dead Sea Scrolls speak of the worship of their standard by the Romans, probably because they had been seen saluting it, or at least showing it the great regard that soldiers throughout the ages have shown for their flags and banners.

The Galileans resented this Roman rule and frequently rebelled, with bitter results. But it chafed the Jews of Judaea even more. They were a chosen people and could not live peaceably with anyone who prevented their realizing this belief about themselves. They hated the Samaritans and they hated the Galileans, and they hated the Romans. But they also hated each other, for the poor hated the rich, the Sadducees despised the Pharisees, and the Zealots were willing to kill all who accepted Roman rule. This hatred flared constantly into fighting, rioting and bloodshed, quelled only by ruthless Roman forces. That is why immediately alongside the center of Jewish worship was the stronghold of Antonia from which the Romans could keep a watchful eye on the Jews of the city at the times most likely to produce rebellion.

The Jews had had mixed feelings about Herod the Great, the first King of the Jews. He had given them the amazing Temple, their fine roads, sanitation, heating, magnificent buildings, safe traveling . . . but he also had kept well in the favor of his masters at Rome. In trying to please both the Jews and the Romans he had lost the favor of both. The Jews disliked him for his cruelties, his leanings toward Greek (hellenistic) forms of worship, and his extravagance; in any case, to them he was a foreigner, having come from Idumaea.

THEIR TAXES

After his death in 4 B.C. the Jews realized still more the ruin he had brought on the land. Even the Temple he had begun for them now had to be their own responsibility for upkeep and further building costs. And, with the Romans in power, they had to meet innumerable taxes as well. This meant religious and civil demands; paying both was a bitter grievance. Let us examine these taxes a little more closely. Payments had to be made for the expenses of Temple sacrifices, to the priests who represented Yahweh and who must be kept in luxury and magnificence. The priests saw to it that they lacked nothing. Every male Jew over twelve (when he became a "son in the Law") paid a half-shekel as poll tax or Temple tribute. He also gave a tithe of his possessions—on crops, cattle, even garden produce (Matt. 23:23). Of these "first-fruits" there were seven—wheat, barley, vines, figs, pomegranates, olives, and honey. There were all kinds of dues at special festivals, thank offerings—five shekels for first-born sons and male animals, sin offerings, meat offerings, trespass offerings and special requests of the Temple rulers. Little did the people know that the Temple vaults were rich with food and gold. Yet it is probable that few Jews really grumbled at these demands, for they were deeply religious.

But the Roman taxes were a different matter. So far as the Jews were concerned these went not only for good roads, bridges, theaters, but also to the hated Emperor to whom, in Sebaste (Samaria), Herod the Great had even built a temple! There was a poll tax of one per cent for everybody, a water tax, road tax, property tax, village tax, city tax; there were tolls in the markets, duties on goods coming in or going out, death duties. There was even a purchase tax, which was introduced by Augustus to provide pensions for retired soldiers; Tiberius reduced this tax from one per cent to a half per cent A.D. 17, and it was finally abolished by Caligula A.D. 39.

Worse still, the taxes on Jews for Rome were collected by people of their own nationality, who were usually dishonest, and cheated the public by overcharging. The Revenue officials in Rome were called *publicani,* a word that soon became transferred to their agents throughout the empire; we hear of Matthew and Zacchaeus as publicans. (The word, therefore, has nothing to do with men who keep inns or taverns.)

THE JEWS' MESSIAH

Neither religious nor civil taxes could be avoided, and in meeting them the people were kept poor. Food was scarce and prices were high for what little food there was. Some of the poorest peasants could not even find work, for the fortunate rich employed slave labor at cheaper rates. It is interesting to note how well aware of all this was Jesus. No fewer than fourteen of His parables are connected with money, and it is easy to see why. The people were anxious about their daily bread—tomorrow's bread, and about their future; they were unhappy, bitter, restless. They looked for a leader as their forefathers had done in the days of Antiochus Epiphanes (Part II, Chapter 11). Some wanted a new Judas Maccabaeus, or a David—a Messiah who would rid them of the yoke of Rome and make them the chosen nation they had been led to believe they would one day be. They longed to be a prosperous nation in a peaceful land. Others looked for the sudden appearance from Heaven of the Son of man; their Messiah would establish the nation magically and peacefully.

A fragment of the Dead Sea Scrolls.

Pharisees. We recall that after the Return of the Exiles prophecy died out. At the time of Jesus there had been no great leader like Elijah or Amos or Jeremiah for four hundred years. The people had therefore turned more and more to the Temple and the synagogue, and a religious life that was increasingly formal and stereotyped had developed.

As we read the New Testament we observe that the Pharisees—and the Sadducees also—almost always appear as antagonists of Jesus. It was men from these two groups whose opposition to Him became so bitter that at the end they brought about His crucifixion. Because they were Jews there may come the impression that the Jews as a whole were guilty of rejecting Jesus, and that Jew and Christian must always be thought of as opposite and hostile. But such an idea is false and hurtful. Jesus Himself was a son of Israel, and all His first disciples were Jews. If it was by Jews also that He was rejected and brought to His death, it was not because of their blood and lineage. It was because in a particular situation their interests and their prejudices were jeopardized, and they responded, not peculiarly as members of a special race, but as blind and sinful human beings generally.

In their inheritance and in their loyalties the Pharisees especially had much that was honorable. They were the descendants of the "separated ones" who had joined Judas Maccabaeus in his first fight against Antiochus Epiphanes (175–165 B.C.), but who had withdrawn their help when Judas had wanted to extend his conquests by force (Part II, Chapter 11). Their religion was now the supreme passion of their lives. Everything they did was connected with it—their speech, their reading, their culture, their day-to-day way of living, their education; but the

Both groups looked for a deliverer from their enemies. It is not hard to see why they could not accept Jesus and His Kingdom.

These things must be borne in mind as we follow the life and teaching of Jesus, for how He lived and talked and worked among these people can be understood only against this background. So far we have thought mainly of the peasant people, especially those burdened with their double taxation. We must now consider other groups—the Pharisees, the Sadducees, the Zealots—although these probably included many of the poorer Jews.

THE PHARISEES AND SCRIBES

In Part II we learned something of the

unhappy fact was that their religion had become more and more negative and shrunken. They detested anything Grecian; to them, Greeks and Gentiles were one and the same people. Despite the prophet Isaiah who had proclaimed that the destiny of the Jews was to be "a light to lighten the Gentiles" (Isa. 9), they had come to regard Yahweh as exclusively their own God and themselves as His people. They numbered several thousands at this time and included members with no Temple connections at all—those we would call "laymen." Some of the more wealthy were on the Sanhedrin, the ruling council.

The scribes are first heard of during the Exile. Originally, they were the men who helped the priests to write down the records of the Jewish nation, the stories and the laws. As time went on, they became better known as teachers. Not only were they copyists but also interpreters of difficult passages; soon, they became rabbis. The word "rabbi" means "my teacher"; sometimes the Bible uses the word "lawyer" or "doctor of the law," both of which mean the same as "rabbi." Since their work was always connected with the Scriptures they became the authorized or qualified teachers of the Jewish religion, not only of the Law but especially of the "Tradition" (below). If any difficulty about a ruling of the Law arose only a rabbi could solve it; his word was final. Because of this the power of the rabbis or scribes became very strong, and wherever they went they were both respected and feared.

Some of them had their own schools and taught their own particular interpretations of problems in the Law. Others toured the country (Luke 5:17); they were welcomed at the synagogues to lead discussions on the Scriptures. Naturally, they were fond of arguments and debate, often just for the sake of arguing their own ideas. We shall meet one scribe who started an argument with Jesus and lost it when Jesus made it clear to him who was his neighbor.

THEIR RELIGION

By the time of Jesus, the Jews—except the Sadducees—were beginning to accept some kind of belief in an after life, with a vague idea of immortality and resurrection. They were losing their acceptance of Sheol (Part I). The Law represented the bond between Yahweh and the people and they believed that if they kept it, then Yahweh would look after them. This was a strong bond of unity in the Jewish nation, which is one cause of their survival from conquests throughout their history.

Unfortunately, in their great desire to be the perfect nation, the Pharisees added to the Law so many rules and regulations, called the "Tradition," that their religion became an artificial keeping of instructions and petty rules which the common people found almost impossible to carry out; they were what Jesus was later to call a "burden" too heavy to bear. The ordinary people were treated with contempt and dislike by the strict Pharisees. Time and again we shall find Jesus at loggerheads with the Pharisees over sabbath healing—what they called working on the sabbath.

We read of a sabbath day's journey, for instance, which was the exact distance a man might walk on this day. It was laid down at 2,000 cubits (about 1,000 yards); but if he really wanted to go farther, he had only to measure the distance from a distant tree or from the gate of the city. If on a sabbath a man carried a needle in his cloak—he was sewing; if he dragged a chair through a sanded floor —he was plowing; if he carried his mattress—he was bearing a burden; if he plucked corn and rubbed it in his hands —he was reaping and threshing. And in doing all these things he was breaking the Law. It was even argued that it was wrong to eat an egg laid on a sabbath because the hen had been working! The "official" sabbath burden allowed was the weight of one dried fig.

JESUS AND THE PHARISEES

These examples give some idea of the exaggerations and details that had been made by the scribes in their interpretations of the Law. Ever since Ezekiel had laid down his first rules of conduct based on the Law, more and more rules and regulations had been thought out and added. The Pharisees believed that if they kept every one of these rules they were living a life pleasing to God. Later on, these rules were collected and made into a complete book, called the *Mishnah*.

Such petty and trivial instructions as those listed seem foolish and even laughable to us. To Jesus, too, they were foolish, but He did not find them in any way funny. He saw them as rather unfortunate and perhaps sad rules, for they were the very things that prevented the people from accepting His own teachings. They hindered the people's understanding that "the sabbath was made for man, not man for the sabbath"; God went on working, so would He. In Matthew 23 we find Him speaking out against the Pharisees and scribes who made such impossible rules, and we find Him doing His best to show them—and those who were expected to keep them—just how foolish this "Tradition" of rules and ceremonies really was.

His outspokenness caused much hostility, but not all the Pharisees were against Him (Mark 12:34; Luke 7:36; 11:37). Nor were they all hypocrites (the word means "play-actor"—putting on a part and pretending to be someone else). True, some of them loved to show off and make out that they were perfect in their religion; but many of them were respected leaders ready, if necessary, to die for their beliefs—as Pilate learned when he first entered Jerusalem. Among the Pharisees were people like Simeon and Anna who had blessed Jesus in the Temple,

The scrolls were wrapped in linen and put in pottery containers like this one.

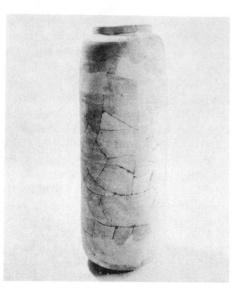

and there must have been many others as sincere, hoping for their Messiah. But the majority were quite blind to anything else than keeping these rules, and it was this blind belief that Jesus found so sad. In their spiritual pride they were quite incapable of seeing that they might be wrong; and it blinded them to accepting anything else.

THE SADDUCEES

The fact that Jesus could not agree with the Pharisees did not mean that He could accept the beliefs and religion of the Sadducees, or that they could accept Him. For although they refused to live by the "Tradition" of the Pharisees and believed only in the actual words of the Law itself (thereby making enemies of the Pharisees) they also denied the possibility of an after life. There was no mention of such a thing in the Law, therefore they could not accept it as possible; they used this argument as a catch question for Jesus, as we shall see. They had no belief in angels or evil spirits, ideas which had come into the Jewish religion from Persia.

Of high-priestly background, and therefore of wealthy families, they lived in luxury and extravagance at the expense of the Jews who starved themselves to pay their Temple taxes in obedience to the Law. They had originally accepted the Greek forms of worship, ways of life and culture; now they were pro-Roman. The reason is clear to see. They were anxious to keep their wealth and their power, and the only way to do this was to accept their new masters and avoid at all costs any trouble that would bring upon them the displeasure of Rome. Their numbers were much smaller than those of the Pharisees, but their power was unquestioned and their attitude toward any who dared to oppose them was brutal and final. Their real power lay in the Sanhedrin, the Council of seventy-one members who had full rights—civil and religious—over the Jewish people. The leader of the Sanhedrin was the High Priest, who was chosen by Rome as the people's representative. So long as he maintained law and order Rome was content to leave him as the religious leader and ruler. The only decision the Sanhedrin could not carry out was a sentence of death; they could decide on it but it could not be carried out without the agreement of Rome. That is why the Sadducees had to bring Jesus before Pilate.

THE ZEALOTS

The Sadducees had many enemies within their own ranks, not the least being the Zealots. These were fiery nationalists who spent much of their time secretly plotting to overthrow their rulers by force. Simon Zelotes, one of Jesus' disciples, was one of these ardent fighters. Judas Iscariot was not perhaps a Zealot, but in his desire to force the hand of Jesus to proclaim Himself the Leader of the people against Rome, he showed the same feelings. It was the open rebellion of the Zealots that eventually led to the wars in which Jerusalem was razed to the ground in A.D. 70.

THE ESSENES

Another group of people at this time were the Essenes. They were dressed in white garments and kept themselves apart from the rest of the Jews. They faced the sun at prayer and lived in lonely places in the hills around Jerusalem. They were not unlike the stricter sects of monks today. It is believed that the famous Dead Sea Scrolls—found by chance in 1947 by a Bedouin shepherd in a cave north of Engedi and near the northern shores of the Dead Sea—were written or collected by the Essenes. These Biblical scrolls are of leather; they were wrapped in linen and placed in cylindrical earthenware pots for preservation. The oldest manuscripts in existence, older by a thousand years than previously known Old Testament manuscripts, they contain parts of Isaiah 53, 59, thanksgiving Psalms by one of the leaders of the sect and fragments of Essene organization. At the place of discovery, Khirbet Qumran, archaeologists continued their search and have found a library of manuscripts in papyrus and leather. It will be many years before definite reports or results are made known, but we do know that we have the remains of seventy different scrolls, thirty-eight of which are Old Testament books. These are written in Hebrew, Aramaic, and Greek, some in the earliest form of Phoenician script.

The Essenes responsible for this library were living in this wild district many years before the coming of Jesus. It is possible that John the Baptist knew them and may have lived with them before emerging to preach to the Jews. When, later, Roman persecutions forced them to flee, they left behind their wonderful library in the sad hope that one day they might return to find it again. But this they could not have done, for nineteen hundred years later the scrolls have been found as they were left—preserved in jars or stacked in caves, or lying on the floors of the caves where they had been thrown hastily by the fleeing Essenes.

BEDOUIN

The people of the land belonged to three main types or groups, as they do even today. There were the Bedouin, the fellahin, and the belladeen. The Bedouin were the Arabs of the desert, nomads and herdsmen. Descended from Abraham and Jacob, they roamed the desert, living in their "houses of hair" (Part I), wandering from place to place with their flocks and herds in search of pasture and food and water. Often they swept upon defenseless villages, especially at harvest time, and stole all they could; they would allow their cattle to graze on the villagers' land and help themselves to their crops. Thus quarrels and feuds arose in the land and were continued from one generation to another. Yet the Bedouin have always had a fine reputation for their hospitality and when entertaining strangers and guests would never dream of asking their names lest their blood feuds become involved and they be forced thus to be discourteous to their visitors.

They wore black goat-hair cloaks and gay silk or cotton headdresses held on by two-inch thick ropes of goat's hair. The women wore long cloaks, headdresses, and veils, usually of indigo blue, the color given to the material by the dye obtained from the rind of pomegranates.

FELLAHIN

The fellahin were the agricultural workers—farmers, shepherds, weavers, potters, etc., living in small communities wherever the soil could be tilled and crops could be grown. Abraham settled at first like this, after deciding to give up his Bedouin life. All members of the same family lived in the one mud house. These people wore a white cotton shirt girded at the waist with a leather strap into which were tucked the ends of the shirt, so that "girded" they could work without hindrance. There was an outer ankle-length cloak of goat or camel hair. This cloak was both heatproof and waterproof and was slept in at night. The harshest moneylender would not take this cloak in payment for debts. It was not unlike a sack in shape, its stripes always being perpendicular; the stripes were made by weaving alternately camel and goat hair. As protection against the hot sun the fellahin wore a turban with a neck covering, or a simple headdress held on with a coil of rope. On their feet were sandals, although often they went barefooted (Matt. 3:11; Mark 1:7; Luke 3:16; 15:22; 23:35). Some possessed red shoes, turned up at the toes (Mark 6:9; Acts 12:8), but they or their servants often carried them to save wear and tear! (Mark 7:7).

The women wore a blue cotton ankle-length cloak with long wide sleeves in which they carried their personal property; all of them wore a long veil. (In Part I we read of Ruth carrying home her gift of corn from Boaz in her veil; she shielded her face with the flowing sleeves of her undergarments.) Across their foreheads they wore their precious bridal coins.

BELLADEEN

These people lived in the towns—the walled cities. They were of the richer group, merchants, traders, craftsmen, scribes, boothkeepers, and the like. Their clothes were of finer material and more colorful; even the girdle—of bright silk from Arabia—was fully five yards long, wound round and round the waist to keep the folds of the silk gown overlapping. This gown was often striped in beautiful colors. When loose pantaloons were worn, they were tied in at the ankles. Centuries before the time we are now studying, the belladeen were mostly to be found in the courts of the kings, denounced by prophets like Amos for their luxury and extravagant living; but at the time of Jesus such people were still holding important posts in connection with the king's palace or even with the Temple.

Jesus belonged to the second group. He was a fellah, for although a carpenter and a craftsman, He left this work and lived in Capernaum and similar villages which were communities without walls. He avoided town life for most of His ministry and found His friends among the fellahin class—country folk.

In this chapter we have spoken mainly of Jews and Arabs. Mention of the Romans and Greeks reminds us of other inhabitants (foreigners and Gentiles) at this time. There were Egyptians from the south, Persians from the northeast, Africans, Indians, and representatives of countless other nations in Palestine, the Holy Land. But so far as the Jews were concerned, there was but one nation— the Jewish.

2

His Nativity and Childhood

(MATT. 1:18-25; 2:1-23. LUKE 1:5-2:52)

JOSEPH'S HOME

Joseph and Mary lived at Nazareth, in Galilee, a little town some fifteen miles from the Lake. The town itself lay in a hollow high in the hills rising 1,650 feet north of the Plain of Esdraelon, so that to see across the hills people had to climb five hundred feet out of the fertile valley and beyond the clusters of houses that crawled up the slopes all around. Then they could see for twenty miles in the clear air of the mountain tops, across to Mount Carmel in the west, to the Jordan valley and hills of Gilead in the east; farther north lay Mount Hermon, snow-capped and majestic. And to the south, below the foothills, through the vineyards and olive groves, ran one of the main highways between Caesarea and Damascus.

The carpenter's home was much like those of other folk in the village. Probably situated in the part of the town where lived most of the carpenters—just as elsewhere there would be the Street of the Bakers, of the Shoemakers, of the Weavers, etc.—it was of mud and straw, white and flat-roofed. Joseph's may even have been strengthened with limestone blocks hewn out of the hillside or with beams of wood. There the houses stood side by side, the narrow, dusty, stuffy streets between them noisy with bleatings of sheep and lowing of cattle and echoing with the shouts and shrieks of men and excited children. Behind his house there may have been a kind of courtyard where Joseph could do his heavier work and lay out his yokes and wheels, tables and troughs, for prospective buyers to see. His tools were those of his ancestors (Isa. 44:13)—a saw, an adze and a drill; the wood he used was varied—fig, olive, wild fig, oak, pomegranate, though on his richer work he would use cedar from the famous trees of Lebanon.

We are told that the word translated

Inside, showing the stable and raised platform.

as "carpenter" really means "builder" (Mark 6:3; Matt. 13:55) so it is likely that Joseph designed and made shelters and houses, too, using stone as well as wood. He was later to teach his trade to Jesus; fathers taught their crafts to their sons. Judging by the wide knowledge shown by Jesus, Joseph must have been a very good craftsman (Matt. 3:10; 7: 24–27; 6:19; 11:29, 30; 21:33, 42, 44; 24:1. See also Luke 12:16–21; 14:28–30; 23:31).

Joseph could not have been very rich and more often than not, payment for the work he did was made by gifts of corn, olive oil, wine, wool, and wood.

THE HOME

Inside the house was only one room; this served as living and sleeping quarters for both family and animals. The front part at street level was occupied by the ox and ass, chickens and goats, kept for their work and food. Their presence gave warmth in winter. Two or three steps led to a kind of upper platform where the family lived. At this level there was a trough of crushed straw for the animals. On this raised part only the essentials for their simple lives were found. There was little furniture—well-made in Joseph's home, we may be sure—a chest for their belongings, stools, waterpots (por-

ous to keep them cool), oil jars (glazed to prevent oozing), bins for meal; cavities in the wall were used for the sleeping mattresses and various utensils. In the floor was a covered hole where corn was kept; the millstone for grinding it was in another corner and not far away, on a carefully-made wooden tripod, was the precious olive-oil lamp, always alight, for, it will be recalled, no one in Palestine slept in the dark and even by day the room was gloomy without it. Cooking was done outside over a charcoal pan when and where possible. A flat stone or metal lid was placed over the fire until it was hot, then the dough was placed on it and turned so that both sides were done; the loaf was a kind of pancake about eight inches across, but the village baker often made much larger ones. In the winter the indoor oven was used (Matt. 6:28–30). The bread was usually unleavened, but was sometimes fermented with yeast to leaven it (Matt. 16:6; Luke 12:1; I Cor. 5:6–7.

The droppings of the animals were always carefully collected and dried in the sun; these were then used in the brazier as fuel for cooking and heat in the winter when acacia sticks could not be found. Joseph was able to add shavings and bits of wood to his supply.

Coins showing Augustus 27 B.C.–A.D. 14 and Tiberius A.D. 14–37.

Outside, stone steps led to the roof. Here the children played and the family rested in the cool of the day. Sometimes a small room was built on it; there was a parapet all around to prevent accidents (Deut. 22:8). Neighbors could chat to one another and it was easy to shout things "from the housetops."

THE PROMISE

It was into a home of this kind that Joseph was to take Mary. He was engaged to her although she was much younger than himself. According to the custom of the land, the betrothal had been arranged by her parents and the wedding had been planned for the following year. Part of our lovely Christmas story tells how Mary was promised by the Angel of God that she should bring into the world a son, Jesus. This message is called the *Annunciation*. Joseph took Mary into his house and in so doing indicated to his friends and neighbors that he already accepted her as his wife. It had come to Joseph in a dream that he would be the one to bring up as his own son Jesus, the Saviour of the World. The name Jesus is the Greek form of Joshua and means "Yahweh is Salvation"; "Immanuel" means "God with us"—the hope of the Jewish nation.

It was soon after this that Joseph and Mary had to prepare for their long, tiring journey to Bethlehem. The Roman Caesar Augustus wanted to take a census of the inhabitants of Palestine so that he could be sure of taxing everybody under his rule. This counting was done every fourteen years. The people were ordered to their birthplaces or home towns where the census would be taken. Joseph was born in Bethlehem, the city of David (I Sam. 17:12), so he had to go there, with his wife, on the orders of Quirinius (Luke 2:1–5).

THE JOURNEY

Mary rode on a donkey, Joseph walked. The three-days' journey took them across the boggy Plain of Esdraelon (the Greek name for Valley of Jezreel) to the Hills of Samaria; they crossed the valley east over Jordan in order to avoid Samaria and so down the Jordan valley and into the high Judaean plateau to Jerusalem. They must have fallen in with other travelers and this gave them company and friendship and protection, for the hills were infested with robbers and thieves as well as with fierce jackals and hyenas. Six miles to the south, but involving a climb of many feet into the hills, was Bethlehem, in one of the few fertile spots of Judaea. Its name means "House of Bread," probably because grain grew there easily and well. Ruth, an ancestress of Jesus, had gleaned grain in the fields of Boaz near by.

NO ROOM AT THE INN

The town was crowded with travelers, cattle, camels, mules, and donkeys. Joseph searched in vain for lodgings. The inn or khan was probably a building with a central courtyard. Caves at street level served as stables for the pack animals, and over them was a chain of rooms for pilgrims and travelers. But these rooms were all full of weary folk glad to lie down on their thin mattresses which had served as saddles on their journeys.

There was no room at the inn, at least in the guest rooms. In any case, Joseph was anxious to have some privacy, for Mary was likely to become a mother at almost any moment. So it was that he accepted the opportunity of bedding down with the animals in the lower stable. He tethered his donkey near the feeding trough of the ox. In this rough stable Jesus was born. Mary washed Him in salt water (Ezek. 16:4), swaddled Him in yards and yards of white cotton or linen cloth until He looked like a small Egyptian mummy. This was to make sure that His bones grew straight and that He breathed through His nostrils! Then, for warmth and safety from the feet of the animals, He was laid in their manger on the soft crushed straw. Later, He would be slung in a hammock cradle.

Over the cave where Jesus is said to have been born now stands the Crusaders' Church of the Nativity.

The coming to earth of Jesus, the Son of God, as a tiny babe that was to grow into a man is called the *Incarnation*. This is the central truth of our belief in God and Jesus, and of what we call today—Christianity (Phil. 2:5-11).

SHEPHERDS AND WISE MEN

We know how the shepherds, guarding their sheep (probably those to be sacrificed in the Temple) from wolves and jackals, learned of the birth of Jesus (Luke 2:8-20). Even today, some two miles beyond the town of Bethlehem, there is a cavern in which the Angels are said to have appeared to the shepherds in the Field of the Shepherds.

We know, too, that the Wise Men—the Magi—came from beyond Arabia, probably from Persia. Tradition calls them Melchior (who was old, with a white beard), Balthasar (dark and middle-aged) and Caspar (a strong youth). They, like Moses and Joseph and Daniel (Parts I and II), had studied the stars and were learned in both astronomy and astrology. Having seen a bright light, due, we believe, to the closeness of Jupiter and Saturn at this time, they were certain that someone great was to be born. They had heard of the hopes of the Jews for a new king who would reign as David had done in Jerusalem (Mic. 5:2-4). He had long been awaited—and perhaps this was the King they should now seek. So they made their way to the capital city, where, naturally enough, they expected to find this King. It is not surprising that Herod the Great should be so much interested in their visit! They brought gold, frankincense, and myrrh—wealth, worship, and healing. The gold probably came from

Africa, perhaps Ophir; the frankincense was a gum obtained from the bark of a resinous tree in Central India and had a fragrant smell when burned; the myrrh was a healing medicinal gum that relieved pain—it was obtained from a shrub growing in Arabia. Having worshiped Jesus, the Wise Men went home "another way."

IN THE TEMPLE

A week later Jesus, according to the Jewish Law, was circumcised; and after forty days Mary had to make a special offering and take Jesus to be dedicated to God (Lev. 12:2-8). She and Joseph decided to do these things at the Temple in Jerusalem before returning to Nazareth (Luke 2:21-39).

In the Court of the Gentiles, at the money-changer's table, Joseph changed his Roman money into Jewish currency. The Law said that the first-born son belonged to God and that if he were not to be trained as a priest he must be "bought back" by the parents; the price for this was five shekels (nearly fourteen dollars in our money). Mary, in the Court of the Women, brought her offering also according to the Law. The Law expected a lamb and a dove, but those who could not afford the lamb were allowed to bring an extra dove; so Mary bought two turtle doves to offer. She stood at the top of the fifteen steps leading to the Court of Israel, which was as far as she was allowed to go. She then presented her offering to the priests and Jesus to the Lord God.

It was here that Simeon took Jesus and spoke of Him as the Messiah, the promised Leader and Saviour. His words are sung every Sunday in churches all over the world as the *Nunc Dimittis*. Simeon and Anna belonged to the more sincere Jews who looked for the coming of the Messiah in quiet hope and strong faith.

TO EGYPT

Returning to Bethlehem for their belongings, Joseph and Mary prepared for the long trek to Nazareth. But by this time, as we know, Herod had heard of Jesus. Having dreamed of danger, and feeling that was a warning, Joseph—according to the Gospel of Matthew—took Mary and Jesus to Egypt (Hos. 11: 1; Jer. 31:15; I Sam. 1:11). From Bethlehem two ways lead southward: one through Hebron and Beersheba, the other through Gaza and down the Way of the Philistines. By one of these they went, in anxious haste, one hundred and fifty miles, pausing for rest at oases where they also obtained water and food—palm nuts and dates. They heard that Herod had issued his cruel order to kill the babes of Bethlehem. But safe in Egypt (II Kings 25:26), possibly at Heliopolis (On) in the Jewish community there, Jesus grew into a sturdy child.

BACK TO NAZARETH

Herod died and it was now safe to return northward to Nazareth (Matt. 2: 20; cf. Exod. 4:19). On the way back, Joseph heard of the dreadful massacre of three thousand pilgrims at Passover time when they had rebelled against Archelaus, the new ruler of that district. So Joseph hastened anxiously along the sea coast from Gaza, past Caesarea—with its magnificent harbor built by Herod—round the foot of Carmel where Elijah had challenged the priests of Baal, over the Kishon whose waters had drowned the enemies of Israel, and so into the foothills of his beloved Galilee and upward to the high mountain cup where Nazareth lay.

THE BOYHOOD OF JESUS

Joseph and Mary made their way to the carpenter's home, where, no doubt, they were greeted joyfully by their neighbors and friends and customers. There Jesus was brought up in the knowledge of the Law and in the love of His parents. We know very little of His boyhood beyond His visit to the Temple at twelve years of age, after which there is a long gap until He is thirty.

But from His own words and our knowledge of the times we have been able, to some extent, to fill in this unknown period. From His teachings and parables we learn much of what He noticed during His life in Nazareth. In the home he watched His mother at work, baking her loaves (Matt. 13:33), mending clothes (Mark 2:21), sweeping (Luke 15:8), searching for lost articles (Luke 15:8, 9), grinding corn (Luke 6:38; 17:35); the latter was done by pouring into the central hole handfuls of grain sifted to remove dust and chaff (Luke 22:31) and turning the top stone by a handle so that it rotated over a lower larger stone. The flour was produced between the two stones. It was usual for two women to work at this grindstone.

Like most healthy youngsters, He probably spent much of His time out of doors. When a small lad He would perhaps go with Mary to the spring to fetch water in the jars she would gracefully balance on her head; the well is to this day called Mary's Well. Climbing the hills He would see the wild flowers He loved—the lilies of the field as He called them (Matt. 6:28; Luke 12:27); these were probably anemones. He would watch the eagle soaring and circling overhead (Luke 17: 37), and track the foxes to their lairs (Luke 9:58). He probably helped the farmer (Mark 4:3 ff.; Matt. 13:24 ff.) and shepherds (John 10:1–14; Luke 15: 6; Matt. 18:12). Boylike, He probably loved games (Luke 7:32) and to wander alongside the shore of the Lake. Here He learned much of the fishermen's work and His knowledge is clearly shown in His later life (Matt. 4:21; 13:47; Mark 1:16, 17; Luke 5:2).

Down in the village He would stand

at the booths and watch the potters and weavers at work. The Galilean weavers were famous for their cloaks woven in one piece, and Jesus probably longed to have one of these for Himself. The weaver produced sacks for goods and nose-bags for the pack animals. Women sitting outside their homes would be twirling wool or flax fibers into strands for weaving. And near by were the vats (possibly made by Joseph) in which the linen and cotton fabrics were dyed; blue with the rind of the pomegranate, red with the stain from an insect found in oak trees, and purple with the dye from crushed shells obtained from the shores of Phoenicia. On these beautiful cloths other women would be embroidering intricate designs with colored cottons and silks.

Across the way was the smith, blowing sparks joyfully to the skies and turning out plowshares and sickles, cooking pots and candlesticks; sometimes he would design and make delicate silver and gold trays and dishes fit for a king.

On occasion Jesus would make His way downhill, often slipping from the path in order to track across the hills until He reached the main road, long and straight as far as the eye could see—a Roman road. It was alive with traffic: caravans of camels and pack mules, Roman couriers galloping on their important errands for Caesar—the sunshine flashing on their spears and shields, uniformed cavalry four abreast, marching Romans of the 10th Legion. Sometimes He might see Herod Antipas riding or driving to or from Tiberias, with his wife Herodias and daughter Salome borne in litters by Greek slaves, followed by courtiers on their camels and slaves driving baggage mules and pack asses. On special days He would go with His father to Capernaum and watch the traders there. Like Amos, years before Him, He would see them cheating and overcharging (Luke 6:38); he heard moneylenders exacting high interest from people who could not afford to pay. There were those who traded, bought and sold (Matt. 5:33, 37); some wanted a pearl of great price (Matt. 13:45); others, cattle (Luke 14:19); land (Matt. 13:44; Luke 22:18); oil (Matt. 25:9); weapons (Luke 22:36). He stood by the hated tax-gatherers and learned of robbers and thieves, kindness and hospitality, wasteful spending, fair play—as is revealed so clearly in the Gospels.

CHILDREN'S GAMES

Jesus had four brothers—James, Joses, Jude, and Simeon, and two sisters whose names we do not know (Matt. 13:55; Mark 6:3. With them He played the usual children's games in the village square and narrow streets (Matt. 11:16, 17; Luke 7:32)—funerals, weddings, schools, building houses and so on, imitating their parents and elders. One of their games is well known to us. Twelve stones (perhaps representing the twelve tribes of Israel) were thrown gently into the air and as many as possible were caught on the back of the hand; the one holding most was the winner. This game was called "Gap." A kind of "Blindman's Buff" was called "Jacob and Rachel," in which the boy had to guess the name of the girl he caught.

No doubt the boys and girls chased one another through the hot dusty streets, dodging the donkeys with their heavily laden panniers of goods, frightening sheep and goats into doorways, daring each other to bestride a kneeling camel. They hid in the shadows, splashed in the puddles, sang and shouted happily—and sometimes quarreled and cried. When exhausted with play they sprawled behind the rocks near the village spring and lowered the bucket for long drinks. Or they made mud pies and baked them in imaginary ovens. Perhaps the older ones told the youngest stories—of Joseph and his brothers, of Moses, David and Goliath, Daniel in the lions' den, of Mattathias, of robbers, thieves, superstitions, proverbs. And sometimes the older boys would take out their slings or arrows and practice their shooting.

HIS FATHER'S TRAINING

Like all boys of His time, Jesus was early taught a trade—his father Joseph's (cf. Acts 18:3). We sometimes forget the part played by Joseph in training Jesus as a person. It was his duty to see that Jesus was brought up in a full knowledge of the sacred Scriptures (II Tim. 1:5). He taught Him to touch gently the little wooden box of papyrus (the *Mazuzah*) fastened to the doorpost and kiss His fingers as He came in and out of the house. On the papyrus was written the "Shema"—the Hebrew word for ·"Hear," which was the first word of the verses to be found in Deuteronomy 6:4–9 and 11:13–21; Numbers 15:37–41. God had commanded, "Ye shall teach them your children."

For special prayers, Joseph tied to Jesus' arm a little black box or leather case containing the Scriptures; this was a phylactery. The strap was wound round the arm, hand and middle finger, to bring heart and mind to God's service; another phylactery was worn on the head. Later on, Jesus was to find that some of the Jews wore very large phylacteries to show how good and religious they believed themselves to be. From Joseph, too, he heard the stories of the great leaders, warriors, prophets and kings and of their past history.

SCHOOL

When He was about six, He went to school. It is probable that the synagogue school—"House of Books"—had not yet been set up in His time, but He certainly joined a group of young boys for special teaching by a local rabbi ("my teacher"). He sat cross-legged on a thin mat on the ground at the feet of His teacher. They chatted in their local Aramaic tongue and wrote words on the stone floor with lumps of chalk or in the sand with the finger. He learned in the Hebrew tongue the passages of the Law and the prophets. As part of His learning were the special texts that all Jewish boys had to learn and also certain verses which contained the same letters as His own Hebrew name, or whose first and last letters matched the first and last letters of His name. Up to the age of ten He was instructed in the stories of His nation. From ten to fifteen there were the Law and special ceremonies and rites connected with the festivals and worship in Jerusalem. All through His life He remembered these passages and met dangers and temptations and made decisions with the words of the Scriptures. We believe He must have asked many searching questions that His father could not answer and that His rabbi found difficult; probably they told Him that when He went to Jerusalem He would be able to ask the learned doctors and rabbis to be found in the Temple there. His whole education was religious.

THE SABBATH

The sabbath was a very important day of the week. Just before sunset on Friday would come the loud, clear call of the trumpet warning all that it was time to stop work, whatever they were doing. (Gen. 2:2). A prayer was said in the doorway and wine was blessed and drunk in turn by the family. Hands were washed and bread was eaten. Fathers went to a special evening service. Next morning (our Saturday) everybody went to the synagogue. Only the men and boys were allowed in the main hall, where they sat on mats all wearing their fringed cloaks. The synagogue officials sat on the chief seats (Matt. 23:6; Mark 12:39). The women had to sit in the galleries behind a lattice or screen.

After the singing and reciting of the

Shema, accompanied by a strange rocking to and fro in time with the rhythm of the words, the Ruler of the synagogue chose seven readings from the sacred scrolls kept in a special cupboard call the ark (*not* to be confused, it will be recalled, with the Ark in O.T. stories). Any man or boy of thirteen who knew Hebrew might be chosen to read, and either he or the rabbi added explanations of the passages chosen (Acts 13:15). For the benefit of the local and less well-educated people he did this in Aramaic so that they could all understand. (You will recall that Ezra introduced this—Part II, Chapter 10.) Then there were questions and discussions about the passages and their meanings. Two Hebrew words used by us today are "Hallelujah," which means, "Praise ye Yah" or "Praise the Lord," and "Amen," which means, "So let it be."

REBELLION

Jesus was probably just a lad of twelve when the Galileans rebelled against the Romans who wanted yet another census for further taxing. They were cruelly defeated by the Roman legions, and the capital city of Sepphoris, seven miles from Nazareth on the western shore of the Lake, was razed to the ground. Thousands of Jews—even boys and girls—were shipped to Rome as slaves; two thousand young men were crucified. The threatened taxation came; and the people looked for a second Judas Maccabaeus to overthrow their enemy, Rome. When Jesus was beginning His ministry Herod Antipas built a new capital at Tiberias, and it is interesting to note that in His journeys Jesus never set foot in what appears from history to have been a city of wickedness and false worship. Yet, strange as it may seem, Tiberias became the center of Jewish rabbis who fled there A.D. 70, after the fall of Jerusalem; there they wrote the *Talmud*, a collection of in-

structions and traditions relating to the Law.

A "SON IN THE LAW"

Jewish boys reach manhood early, and at twelve Jesus was as grown up as a boy of sixteen. So, after His twelfth birthday He had to join the family in His first Passover Feast at Jerusalem; this was the most wonderful event in a Jewish boy's life. He was to be a "son in the Law," as it was called later in the history of the Jews; what it meant was that He was now old enough to make His own decisions and take responsibilities in life. His mother Mary gave Him a "talith"—a robe or cloak with fringes (Num. 15:38, 39; Deut. 22:12). Nowadays the talith is a scarf or shawl with fringes. We may note here that Jesus probably attended Passover every year during that period of which we know nothing; John gives three occasions in His ministry—2:13; 6:4; 12:1.

THE JOURNEY TO JERUSALEM

It was an exciting three-days' journey in the long caravan of pilgrims from far and near. The pilgrims had eighty miles to go in mid-spring greenness and sunshine. Bread and dried fruits and nuts were packed, thin mattresses on which to sleep were spread on the donkey with other goods, leaving just enough room for Mary to sit. The starting point was most likely at the spring, where the waterskins were filled and the animals watered. Then, at the signal, off they went, chatting to friends, waving to those left behind. Here soon was the Plain of Esdraelon; in the distance before and behind were thousands of pilgrims, all making for the same way—from Damascus, Persia, Antioch, Caesarea. The Jews of the Dispersion were "going home" to Jerusalem. Many of them lived within ninety-days' journey of the city and were therefore expected by the priests to attend Passover; some came by sea in sailing and trading ships from Greece, Gaul, the Danube lands, and Spain, others from the ports of Alexandria and Caesarea in litters and gigs or on camels.

In larger numbers many of the pilgrims risked the journey through the land of the hated Samaritans, who would not have hesitated to attack them like bandits and robbers; others preferred the safer way through the Jordan jungle road to Jericho. Here they had to climb the fifteen miles of winding rough roadway that Jesus was to be familiar with many years later. Those who did go through Samaria passed between Mount Ebal and Mount Gerizim, the latter being the mountain sacred to the Samaritans, who would be preparing their own Passover.

The town of Samaria (rebuilt by Herod the Great and called Sebaste) was a city on a hill (Part II). It had been the stronghold of Omri and Ahab who had built a wonderful palace of ivory and gold within its walls, but had been starved into surrender by the Assyrians in 721 B.C. Roman soldiers clanked down the roadway prepared for riots between the pilgrims and the Samaritans. If Jesus came this way He would have had his first view of Sebaste, with its colonnades and pillars and magnificent temple to Augustus; when years later He paused at the well of Sychar not far away to talk with the Samaritan woman He would have remembered this.

THE ARRIVAL

By whichever route He came at this time, suddenly before Him, high on the hills, Jerusalem came into view. The pilgrims burst into the Song of Ascents (Hallel, or "Praise," Ps. 93-98). They beat their drums and clanged their cymbals as they started the mountain climb to the city itself. The caravan halted, and on the slopes of the Mount of Olives Jesus and His parents camped for the night. Tomorrow they would find lodgings in the city. Fires twinkled on the mountain and the noise of voices and animals filled the air.

THE TEMPLE

In the early morning sunshine the Temple gleamed white and golden, high and stately—even though only half built —above the flat roofs of the newly whitewashed houses. This "city of gold and snow" was the center of the Jewish faith. It stood 2,500 feet above sea level on a group of hills, including Mount Moriah, jutting from the plateau of Judaea. A deep, narrow valley ran right through the city itself; this was the Tyropoeon valley or ravine, the Valley of the Cheesemongers. It was spanned by a bridge connecting Herod's palace with the Temple; part of this bridge, called Robinson's Arch, stands today. The Temple's importance as the center of Jewish religion began in the time of David, who for fifty shekels of silver bought the threshing floor of Araunah, a flat rock high in the hills where the farmer threshed and winnowed his corn, and made it a sacred altar to Yahweh. True, this Temple was only a tabernacle like a large tent (Part I, pp. 5 and 8), but when Solomon decided to build his magnificent Temple in 966 B.C. he did so over the same altar rock. Even this was small by comparison with some buildings, being only one hundred feet long by thirty feet wide; it was destroyed by Nebuchadrezzar in 586 B.C. (II Kings 25:8–9).

On their return from Exile (Part II) the Jews under Zerubbabel rebuilt the Temple, dedicated in 516 B.C., but it was again destroyed (I Macc. 4:38), having suffered considerable damage throughout the Maccabaean period. Then, in about 20 B.C., Herod the Great began yet a third Temple, in shining white marble and gleaming gold, in a series of courts wonderfully lined with cloisters and colonnades and pillars. This Temple was destroyed A.D. 70, and today the site no longer belongs to the Jews. In the pictures you will see that there is a Moslem mosque built over the shrine of the altar rock; it is called the Dome of the Rock. The ancient rock is still there, and the channel down which the blood of sacrificed animals was run to an underground chamber may still be seen. All that remains to the Jews today of their ancient center of faith is a few yards of outer stone wall, their Wailing Wall, where, for centuries, outside the precincts which now they may not enter, they have meditated on their past glories, kissed the stones, prayed, and wept.

THE CITY

The city had been subjected to sieges and destruction throughout the centuries before Jesus; the ravines were filled with rubbish and debris and bridged with Roman arches. To the south was the Valley of Hinnom (remembered for its hideous child sacrifices to Moloch in the reign of cruel King Manasseh (Part II) and often referred to as Gehenna or Hell); it led into the Valley of Kedron and rising from the eastern bank of this ravine was the Mount of Olives, whose slopes hid the view of the Dead Sea farther east in its rift valley 4,000 feet below. On the slopes were olive orchards, one of which was the Garden of Gethsemane. On the steep downward road to Jericho lay Bethany; across the city to the north and outside the wall was a hill—the Place of a Skull, Golgotha.

ON THE WAY TO THE TEMPLE

We have already described the Temple with some detail in Part II, but must now try to see it through the eyes of Jesus. It was there He would be going for His first Passover, His first sacred service. He could not help seeing to the northwest of it the stronghold where Roman sentries paced to and fro, their armor glinting in the sun; then He remembered that His people were not really free, but were under the heel of Rome, a foreign country. These people had come to stay, He felt, as He gazed over the city and noted other enormous buildings—the gymnasium, the games amphitheater, the public baths. He longed for the liberty of everybody in the land. Years hence He would be regarded as the One who could lead them to this very freedom if He would use His powers in the way they wanted; and at His last Passover He would give to all men the Passover of remembrance, our Holy Communion (I Cor. 11:23–26). And He himself would prophesy the destruction of this very Temple (Matt. 24:2).

But He was a mere lad now, and His one idea was to get there. With His parents, he excitedly made His way to the city walls, entering by one of the massive gates. The streets were narrow, stuffy, and dark; they seemed like long, vaulted tunnels with gaps in the roof. Often they descended in a series of steps, overhung with latticed windows and linked with supporting arches of limestone blocks. Sheep and cattle for the Temple sacrifices were being brought in and He had to stand on one side to let them pass, bleating, bellowing, frightened. On either side of the streets were the booths, now closed but promising much of interest later when they were open to passers-by with their wares stacked outside—shoes and sandals in one street, pancake loaves in another, cloaks and headdresses in another, pots and jars and lamps in yet another. We can believe that traders arguing over prices and quality of their goods had always attracted Jesus, for He was interested in people and their rights and wrongs.

IN THE TEMPLE COURTS

This day, however, Jesus hurried on and at last passed through one of its enormous gates into the Court of the

Gentiles. The Temple itself was a small building in the center of a series of courts to which certain people were allowed entry according to their race and position. These courts were open to the sky and people thronged into them. Men and boys were allowed to go into most of them but only the priests could enter those nearer the Holy Place. Services and sacrifices went on all day. Priests were allotted special duties, and choirs of Levites, musicians playing flutes, cymbals, and trumpets, kept up a continuous sound. In the Court of the Gentiles—the only place where non-Jews could pray, traders, money-changers, sellers of doves, had set up their booths; there was noise and smell and excitement that seemed to Jesus unfitting in the precincts of the Temple. He moved forward and stooped to read the warning to the Gentiles; they could not go beyond that point without endangering their very lives! And this must have seemed wrong to Him, too, for surely all people might go to worship His Father.

On He went to the Court of the High Priests where He could watch the altar sacrifice; and we may dare to think that the words of Micah came to Him as He did so (Mic. 6:7, 8).

THE PASSOVER FEAST

It was here that Jesus had to wait while Joseph took the lamb he had bought in the Court of the Gentiles. There Joseph slew it, the priest catching the blood of the animal in a silver bowl and throwing it upon the altar rock, whence it trickled into the channel of rock below. Special parts of the lamb were then offered for sacrifice and Joseph took them back after they had been blessed. Then he returned to Jesus and the two went to their lodgings in the city.

Gathered there were ten to twenty people who joined for the meal of Passover lamb, which was roasted on a spit of pomegranate wood; there were bitter herbs — parsley, lettuce, endive, horse radish dipped in vinegar — to remind them of the troubles of the Children of Israel in the Wilderness and the crossing of the Red Sea (Part I); there was also wine. As the youngest present, Jesus might have asked, "Why is this night different from all other nights?" And in reply Joseph must have told the old, old story of the Israelites, their escape from bondage in Egypt and their settling in Palestine, the Promised Land. The Feast represented the "passing over" of the Angel of Death in Egypt and the haste in which their forefathers had left (Exod. 12:21–51). At one time the meal had been eaten standing up, but later the people reclined or sat cross-legged around a communal dish of unleavened bread, herbs, and fruit. Wine was drunk at certain points in the ceremony and parts of the Hallel, Psalms 93–98, were sung. Now and then someone would look outside to see if Elijah were waiting to come in, and there was always a special chair left for him.

"ASKING THEM QUESTIONS"

Next day, to let our imagination continue, Jesus drew near to the famous rabbis and learned doctors, fascinated by their explanations of the Law. We are wrong when we think *He* was teaching them. What this passage (Luke 2:46, 47) means is that He stayed and began to ask questions—the questions to which He had received no satisfactory answers from Joseph and the Nazareth rabbis. The doctors realized that here was a lad, intelligent and quick, who was seeking information, who had a remarkable understanding of what they said and who wanted to know more.

Jesus lost all count of time; He probably was not the only lad left behind by anxious parents. Joseph and Mary had begun their downward journey to Jericho. They thought, naturally enough, that

Jesus was with friends somewhere in the caravan, and it was not until evening when they paused for food and rest that they discovered He was nowhere to be found. Back to Jerusalem they toiled; they spent the next day in the city inquiring and searching in the bazaars and booths, but were unable to find Him. Then, on the third day, in the morning, they found Him, in the Temple "asking questions." We are not surprised that they spoke a little crossly and firmly—what parents would not have after so much anxiety and delay? But Jesus' answer to His earthly parents showed that He now knew He was no ordinary boy—He must be about His "Father's business" in His Father's house. He knew what He was going to do when He grew up.

They returned to Nazareth. Although the Angels of God had told them their Son was to be the "Son of the Most High," Joseph and Mary did not yet understand.

We can only guess at what Jesus did in those eighteen years that followed before He left home at the age of thirty. He must have continued His trade as a carpenter-builder, and when Joseph died, as the eldest son He had to take care of the family. That He was popular, attractive, and gracious is borne out by the words of Luke (2:52) "and Jesus increased in wisdom and stature, and in favour with God and man."

3

John the Baptist: Jesus Begins His Ministry

(MARK 1:1-15. MATT. 3:1-12. LUKE 1:5-25, 39-80; 3:1-18. JOHN 1:6-37. MATT. 4:1-11. LUKE 4:1-13. JOHN 2:1-11; 3:1-13; 4:1-43)

Three months before Jesus came into this world His cousin John, called the Baptist, was born in a Judaean town near Jerusalem. His father Zacharias, a priest in the Temple on duty with his allotted task of carrying the fire from the Altar of Incense to the Holy Place, was promised a son. Note that Elijah (Mal. 3:1) was to be the herald of the Messiah, and in Luke 1:17 Elijah and John the Baptist are indicated as one and the same person. This implies that John was to be the "forerunner" of the long-promised Messiah, who, in the words of Zacharias, was to give "salvation from our enemies, and from the hand of all that hate us" (Luke 1:71).

In the passages given for study you will recognise the *Magnificat* (Luke 1: 46–55) which some scholars say should be the Song of Elizabeth, not of Mary, and also the *Benedictus* (Luke 1:68–79) spoken by Zacharias. These consist largely of quotations from Old Testament scriptures which may be traced from the references given in your Bibles. Both are sung in Anglican churches as part of the service of worship, and may be found in the Prayer Book.

John (his name means "God's gift") could have been a priest like his father, but he left home when a young man, and, like Elijah, spent much of his life in lonely desert places — Jeshimon ("Devastation") between the Dead Sea and the plateau of Judaea—away from towns and people. It is surmised that he may have studied and lived with the Essenes in their settlement north of En-gedi. He was planning and thinking and preparing his fierce prophecies. We are not told whether the two boys ever met, but it is very likely that they did, for they were relations; but Jesus and he had very little in common except perhaps the feeling that the world was "all wrong" and that one day when they were grown up they would do something about putting it right. But Jesus grew up among His people, whereas John withdrew himself from them.

IN THE DESERT

John's food was wild honey, gathered from the nests—in hollow tree trunks—of wild bees, and locusts. The locusts

Ain Karen, birthplace of John the Baptist.

were a variety of those insects that in Eastern countries swarmed in myriads on crops and vegetation and left the land ravaged and bare; even today the Bedouin eat a kind of locust boiled in salt and water. John was a Nazarite, for his parents had dedicated him to the service of God; Samson was a Nazarite (Part I; Num. 6:1–8). Artists often show John half-naked, clad only in the skin of some wild animal. But he was clothed with "camel's hair" (Mark 1:6), which more likely means that he wore a long outer cloak woven of camel's hair, like any peasant (fellahin) of the district, with a leather belt at his waist (cf. Matt. 11:8). Probably he was more rough and unkempt than some fellahin, but he was not so wild or mad as some people think.

HIS PREACHING

About A.D. 26, when He was about thirty years of age, Jesus left His mother in the care of His brothers and sisters who were now grown up. He had heard that John had suddenly appeared at Bethabara ("House of the Ford"), a place on the east side of the Jordan, south of Galilee and about thirty miles from Nazareth. John had come from the Wilderness of Judaea as unexpectedly as Elijah had come to Israel some nine hundred years before. In fact, people thought he *was* Elijah. Like him in dress, he preached angrily against the wrongs he saw and told his hearers that they must give up their wrong ways of living—they must repent and live better lives. There had been false prophets and leaders whose calls to revolt had ended in dreadful massacres by the Romans and long, lingering deaths by crucifixion for the rebels. But John the Baptist was different. Even Annas and Caiaphas, the High Priests, sent for a report on him; Herod Antipas sent spies; but young men left their homes to join him. He was the first great prophet for four hundred years—with the figure

John the Baptist emerged from the Wilderness; this is the gorge of the brook Cherith.

of Elijah, the power of Amos and the message of Micah (Part II). The Jews believed that they were a chosen people, but the passage of time had hardened their idea of the Messiah. Isaiah had said He would be a Prince of Peace and righteousness (Isa. 9:1–7; 11:1–10); Jeremiah had said that Yahweh looked upon them as individuals and each one of them must keep faith with Him (Jer. 31:31–34). The prophets of the Exile had encouraged them, too, but time had shown one conquest after another and even the freedom gained by Judas Maccabaeus had been short-lived. There could now be only one Messiah — and He would free them from Rome by force and make them the chosen nation of God.

But they must first give up their sins and wickedness and change their hearts toward God. They must *repent*! This was a great shock to the people, especially to the Pharisees, who thought that they were perfect enough to be above such advice. John called them vipers — snakes that fled from burning brushwood or stubble. He spoke of the Messiah as the expected king. They all knew that when the king was on a journey through the country the roads were examined and made level, rough roads were made smooth, holes were filled in. Ahead of the king's cavalcade ran a slave shouting, "Make way for the king . . ." John was that voice (Isa. 40:3, 4).

So, drawn by His cousin's fame, news of which had reached Nazareth, Jesus came over the foothills southward into the valley of the Jordan, to Bethabara; He knew His own time had come.

WHAT WAS JESUS LIKE?

Many artists have tried to picture and paint Jesus for us. Their paintings are beautiful and make us think more about Him, and most of us in our own minds have been influenced by the pictures we have seen. The earliest portrait of Jesus was found in a Roman catacomb—an underground passage in which the persecuted Christians buried their dead. It shows Jesus much like other men of His time, with long hair parted in the middle

The earliest known portrait of Jesus painted on the ceiling of a first century Roman catacomb.

to fall in waves on His shoulders, a short beard, a firm mouth and penetrating sad eyes. The fact that Judas had to point Him out to the Roman soldiers in Gethsemane seems to show that Jesus was not greatly different from His followers in either build or dress. Artists usually show Him bareheaded, but He must have worn a head covering as protection against the hot sun; this was the headdress commonly worn by the fellahin. His cloak is almost always shown as white, clean and unstained; but His Galilean seamless tunic or robe was woven in one piece, probably the usual blue or perhaps of white and brown stripes, girded at the waist with a belt. On his feet were sandals.

THE BAPTISM

John recognized Jesus as the Messiah whom he had come to herald. He regarded himself as lower than the slave whose menial duty was to carry his master's sandals. Despite his protests, Jesus said, "Suffer [let] me be baptized." John baptized his followers as a sign that they had agreed to repent of their sins and make a new effort to live honestly and faithfully to God. But Jesus had no need to repent, for He had no sin of which to be ashamed. True, He had been tempted, but unless one gives in to temptation one does not sin (Heb. 4:15). Therefore, His baptism by John was rather an act of dedication to His new work; it was an act of sharing the needs of men. He ac-

A Roman sandal as worn in the days of Jesus.

cepted the fact that He was a human being and made it clear that He also accepted what John was saying about Him—that He was sent by God. In this way Jesus was ready to begin His own ministry in the service of God His Father.

Jesus heard the voice of God (Matt. 3:17): "Thou art my Son, the beloved," and knew that He had been sent to preach—not with the angry fury of John, but with the gentle persuasion of love that wins men to God (Ps. 2:7; Isa. 42:2). He was to preach, not John's message of repentance and doom, but His own message of a Kingdom of God in men's hearts and lives through dedication to their fellow men.

But how was He to do this? He must be alone to think it out. He must plan.

For many years now He had sought His Father in the hills around Nazareth, inspired by the majesty and awe of the quiet places. Like Moses at Sinai, and Elijah at Horeb, like John in the Wilderness—and like Paul years later in Arabia—Jesus now sought a place of solitude where He could talk with and listen to God. So we find Him making for the vast hot desert of Judaea, climbing from the ford of Bethabara in the steaming jungle eight hundred feet to the scorched limestone edge we now know as the Mount of Temptation.

CHRIST IS TEMPTED

How do we know what happened on this arid, bleak mountain side? Only Jesus could have told His disciples, later in His life, for He was alone in the Wilderness (Matt. 4:1–11; Mark 1:12, 13; Luke 4:1–13). It was a tremendous challenge to Jesus at this time to accept the prophecy of John that He was the expected Messiah. He could put Himself at the head of the Jewish nation and with His wonderful God-given power rid the country of Roman rule and set up the new nation of God's chosen people. His temptations came to Him to test that sense of vocation He had felt as a boy long years before and as a man more aware of His calling. They came to try out His belief in Himself and in God. Some people accept the three temptations as really happening as described in the accounts; others say they are Jesus' picturesque ways of describing them to His disciples so that they could understand. Whatever beliefs about them we may hold, the result is the same, for Jesus overcame His temptations.

Jesus was tempted to *prove* that He was the son of God—"*If* thou be the Son of God . . ." He could give food to His starved people. Then in imagination He saw Himself on the pinnacle of the Temple. He knew that many of the Jews expected the Messiah to come on the clouds of heaven in unexpected suddenness (Mal. 3:1; John 7:27). He could jump into the Valley of Kedron, nearly 500 feet below—and God would miraculously protect Him—and it would show the people that He was their Messiah and so win them to Him. And then, in fancy, He saw the kingdoms of the world; He could rule them all — "if thou wilt . . ." — *if* He used His power. . . . It was an easy short cut. . . . Jesus met all three temptations with the words He had learned as a boy; the Scriptures gave Him His answers, as they might so often do for us in our temptations. You will find the three answers in Deut. 6:16; 8:3; 6:13; they show His obedience to and trust in God. He had made up His mind. His only power and force would be the miracle of love, even if it led Him to His death.

Jesus left the stony desert and dropped once more into the hot "pride of the Jordan," as the jungle was called; he left behind the jackals and moved among the lions and leopards. Six weeks had passed. He looked for John and found him with his disciples (John 1:35–51; Mark 1:14–20). James and John were there, and Andrew, who throughout the Gospels appears as the one who introduces people to Jesus. He brought Peter (or, as he was then known, Simon) of Capernaum, saying, "We have found the Messiah." Philip joined them and brought Nathaniel (Bartholomew), who seems to have been surer than any that he was meeting the Christ and in whom Jesus recognized an extraordinary faith. These disciples now left John the Baptist to follow Jesus although John retained many of his followers (Acts 18:25; 19:3).

RETURN TO GALILEE

It was spring A.D. 27, and Jesus began a brief ministry in Judaea before moving north to His own home. He was to preach until the spring A.D. 29, two short years

(to the Jews, three) and in that time, like His disciples after Him, to turn the world "upside down." The Galilean disciples went with Him, for they were anxious to return home to their families and perhaps to their fishing. It must have been a great joy for them to leave arid Judaea and the tropical Jordan valley for their own land of fertile plains and terraced foothills. Herds of black goats and flocks of sturdy sheep spread over the hillsides within call of the shepherd; vineyards and olive groves stretched green and fruitful toward the east where they knew lay the beloved Lake. The Galileans greeted them in friendly tones—the women bearing their heavy water jars, grinding corn in the spring sunshine, making butter in goatskins set spinning on pieces of rope, baking sweet-smelling bread; the men tending their crops, driving heavily laden donkeys or a surefooted camel. Jesus and His disciples took the main highways going east–west, north–south. East–west to and from Damascus and the sea, through Capernaum (Sepphoris, too, before it had been devastated), Tyre and Sidon; it was level and straight, a Roman road. North–south ran the route from the Fertile Crescent to Egypt, through Esdraelon and Jaffa or through Samaria and Jerusalem.

CAPERNAUM

But they were glad to leave the highways and climb into the hills and down again—to the Lake, their Lake. Jesus was made welcome in Capernaum, the home of Peter; Andrew returned to Bethsaida across the waters, to the "House of Fishing."

Mark tells us that Jesus made His headquarters at Capernaum and from there began His Galilean ministry. In 1:21–45 we find a typical day at this period of His work. The city was important as a center of trade. A Roman garrison was stationed there; and taxes, customs, duties, market charges, and so on were collected by Matthew (Levi). Its streets were crowded with people of all kinds — fishermen, farmers, merchants, traders, soldiers, rabbis, elders of the synagogue. They were proud of their fine white stone synagogue built by their friendly centurion. Even today a village called Tell Hum stands there; the ruins of the original town are marked by piles of volcanic black basalt, while the remains of the synagogue that have been unearthed have been raised again to show at least part of the fine building it was in the time of Jesus. We are told that it was oblong in shape, 80 feet by 60 feet; the pillars were Corinthian (Greek) in style. On the ground level and facing south toward the Lake and far-away Jerusalem were three doors covered with reliefs of animals and birds and foliage. There were eagles and palms, vines and flowers, even centaurs that remind us of Pan who was worshiped by Herod. On the lintel was carved a pot of manna (Part I, Chapter 9; John 6:31–58), and clusters of grapes (John 15:1 ff.). One stone bears the five-pointed star of David. The Jews of Jerusalem would have been horrified to see all these figures and "graven images," but the Galilean Jews, upon whom their religion had been forced many years before, were not so strict in keeping the Law (Exod. 20:4). Around three sides ran a kind of balcony for the women and a dais stood against the fourth wall. Ten steps of the original way to the upper platform now remain.

The Roman centurion (captain of a hundred soldiers) was evidently a Gentile who had accepted the Jewish idea of worshiping one God; when we realize the dozens of deities that the Romans accepted as controlling their lives (Part II, Chapter 12) this is a surprising fact.

AROUND THE LAKE

This part of Galilee was busy with its fishing towns ringing the northern and western shores. On the Lake itself were ships of all kinds, small fishing vessels with single mast and sail, decorated Court pleasure boats and even Roman galleys. The king had his palace and center of government at Tiberias, where the hot medicinal springs were a great attraction. We have already seen how Capernaum was the center of trade at the crossroads of trade routes throughout the land. Besides the exchange of goods from countries far and wide, there was local buying and selling of farm produce, wool, milk, cheese, and the like, as well as of the products of industries such as weaving, pottery, carpentry, and other crafts. There was dyeing at Magdala and fish curing at Tarichaea—the "pickling place" —from which town loads of salted fish in coarse sacks and boxes were sent to Jerusalem and other large cities. The Fish Gate at Jerusalem was probably the main way in for this Galilean export, and the crowds assembling in the city at every festival found the fish a welcome food. It has been suggested that the opportunity for John to enter the household of the High Priest during the trials of Jesus was due entirely to the fact that as a fisherman engaged in this work he was well known at the house.

All around the shores the hills were wooded (today they are bleak and bare). Wherever the Greeks and Romans had settled there were long straight roads and aqueducts and bridges, fine buildings with soaring columns and arches, arenas, theaters for gladiatorial shows and athletics. When Jesus looked across the Lake on a particularly fine day He could see easily the outlines of the Greek cities of the Decapolis. The three main peoples of His world met at the Lake—the Greeks, with their love of art, beauty, and language; the Romans, with their hard discipline, firm government, practical outlook on life; the Jews, with their hopes and their belief in the One God who would one day send a leader to rid them of the Gentile Greeks and Romans.

We are not told whether Jesus returned

to any form of His carpenter's work, but there is no doubt that He used His craft to help His fisher friends; He must have mended their boats, the oars, the landing places, and may even have helped to repair, with stone from the hillsides, the house in which He lived with Peter.

THE WEDDING AT CANA

To the northeast of Nazareth was a little village called Cana. Mary and Jesus had been invited to a wedding of one of their friends or, possibly, relations. It is pleasant to find that His first miracle was performed to bring happiness to a young couple who might have been so easily disgraced.

This is a familiar story, and it is easy to feel the great anxiety in the home. The six stone jars were for holding water used in Jewish ceremonial washings; each held twenty gallons. The reply Jesus made to His mother—"What is that to me?"—loses some of its apparent sternness if we think that what He meant was, "It's not my wedding," with a twinkle in His eyes—and that is what many scholars now tell us may have been His answer. "Woman" is a term of respect. Jesus could have made very inferior wine, but His was better than the first; He not only saved the family from embarrassment, He added to their joy. If the quantity of wine seems a great deal, you need to remember that the festivities lasted a week at least, and guests and visitors—even casual passers-by—all received hospitality.

The wedding ceremony took place at midnight, toward the end of the rejoicing. The bridegroom came in procession, dressed in gorgeous robes, with music on drums, lutes, and flutes; a little boy dressed exactly like him followed him like a small shadow. The guests went out to meet him (Matt. 25:6) and brought him to his bride's home. The bride was young—perhaps only twelve. She was adorned with "jewels of gold and raiment," wearing them like Rebekah (Gen. 24; Ezek.

16:12), and riding under a silk canopy on a camel. The bridegroom then received her into his own house, lifted her veil, and saw her face for the first time—for their parents had arranged the wedding many months before. He placed her veil over his left shoulder to indicate that he took her as his wife. The Jews have a saying that "love comes after marriage"; it is easy to see how this saying originated.

NICODEMUS

Soon after this incident, Jesus went to Jerusalem for Passover. There He was visited by Nicodemus, a rich Pharisee and a member of the Sanhedrin. Nicodemus felt that Jesus had the secret of true life and living, but was cautious enough to avoid notice, for he came to see Jesus by night, probably with his face hidden and his cloak wrapped around him. He talked with Jesus on the roof of the house in which Jesus was staying, which may have been the home of John Mark. The house may have been the one in which the Last Supper was held. Nicodemus called Jesus "Rabbi," which means "My Teacher"—a strange form of address from a well educated man to a peasant preacher. But Nicodemus learned that the Kingdom of God was for all believers—in the hearts of men who accepted His rule. We hear of him again later in the story of Jesus.

Jesus stayed in Judaea for a while, His disciples still baptizing as they had learned from John. Then they moved through Samaria. In the Plain of Mukneh the grainfields were springing green. It was about six in the evening when Jesus and His disciples arrived at the Well of Sychar—Jacob's Well (Josh. 24:32) at the crossroads of routes from Jerusalem to Galilee and Samaria to Peraea and half a mile from Shechem (Nablus). Shechem stood at the entrance of the pass between Mount Ebal (Mount of Cursing) and Mount Gerizim (Mount of Blessing). Since John gives us this account it is possible that he was in the vicinity, but the other disciples had gone to find food—dates, olives, bread, and dried fruits. Jesus was thirsty, but the well at the foot of Mount Gerizim was a hundred feet deep and nine across; travelers usually carried their own buckets of leather, but Jesus had none.

His request for a drink was an accepted opening for brief conversation, even to a woman (you will remember how Eliezer began his conversation with Rebekah in the same way), but this particular woman, who had come some distance from the village well in order to avoid gossip and scandal about her from the other women, was surprised that He should go on talking. He revealed to her that He knew all about her, and told her He was the Christ of whom she spoke. In her haste to spread the news to the other women, she forgot her waterpot. The disciples on their return disapproved of His chatting with a woman, especially a Samaritan. We may note here that all through His ministry Jesus had special regard for women. He raised them from being mere chattels and servants to an honored position of respect and equality with men.

The Samaritans had a deep faith in their own forms of worship. On Mount Gerizim they had their own altar and followed out their own version of the Law (Pentateuch); they worship there still (Part II) and claim to be the true descendants of the Israelites. They still hate the Jews and still hold Passover. By His words, "God is a spirit . . .", Jesus opened the Kingdom of God to these people and to the whole world.

A Jewish synagogue lamp of the time of Jesus.

4

Galilean Ministry—Capernaum

(MARK 1:29-45; 2:1-17; 6:1-6. LUKE 4:16-37. MATT. 9:9-13. JOHN 4:44-5:18)

Two days after the incident at the Well of Sychar, having been given kindly welcome by the Samaritans, Jesus and His disciples moved northward into Galilee. His friends were glad to see Him again (John 4:45) for many of them had been with Him in Jerusalem during Passover. At Cana a Government official—possibly Herod's steward whose wife Joanna knew Jesus (Luke 8:3) and His mother—begged Jesus to go to Capernaum to heal the official's son, who was probably suffering from some form of malaria, for parts of the town lay near marsh land where malarial mosquitoes could breed. Jesus told him (John 4:46 ff.) he would find his son cured when he arrived home. His friendship with this official may well have helped Him in His ministry at Capernaum.

Then, in the local synagogues and villages, He began in real earnest His teaching of the Kingdom of God. It is not surprising that we find the people attracted not only by His power to heal but also by His words of grace (Luke 4:22) and authority (Mark 1:22).

ON THE LAKE

After a brief visit to Nazareth, Jesus went to Capernaum down by the Lake shore (Isa. 9:1, 2). Crowds followed Him. Simon and Andrew were mending and cleaning their nets. Zebedee and his two sons were there also. Jesus climbed into Peter's boat and they pushed out a little way. From this lake pulpit Jesus spoke to the crowds. Near by were other boats of the little fishing fleets. Each was pointed at both ends and carried four to six men. The boats were equipped with a single sail attached to one side of a long pole drawn up high on a short mast, the sail lowered in bad weather; then the boat was rowed. Along the shore were wooden frames over which the nets were hung so that they could be picked clean of weed and rubbish, washed and mended (Matt. 4:21; Mark 1:19).

FISHING

The Sea of Galilee was notorious for its dangerous storms and fishing was done mostly late at night when the winds were light and least likely to stir up tempests (Mark 4:35, 41; Matt. 8:23-27; Luke 8:22-25). The Lake, even today, is full of fish easy to catch. The most common are bream, carp, eels, perch (Matt. 4:18; Mark 1:16).

Various nets were used, according to the type of fishing. There was the seine or dragnet (m'batten), a kind of curtain net weighted and sunk between two boats so as to encircle shoals of fish; it was marked by floats or corks (Luke 5:5-9; Matt. 13:47). In modern times a banging noise is set up to drive the fish into the net, and it is very probable that this was done in the time of Jesus, for in Palestine customs in such matters have changed but little. Because of the heat and the occasional need to dive overboard to attend to the net, the fishermen often worked naked (Mark 14:51, 52; John 21:7). Some of the fish, especially those without scales, were regarded by the stricter Jews as "unclean" and, if caught, were thrown away; these were picked up by boys and poor people beachcombing on the shore.

Then there was a large cast net (diktuon or jurf) which was lowered from the boat's side over a shoal (Luke 5:4-5; John 21:6-11). A smaller net of this kind could be handled by one man. This was the cast net (shabakeh), rather like a fine mesh bag tapering to a point, to which a long rope was tied. The outer edge of the mouth, which was a yard across, was weighted with heavy stones or pieces of lead which caused it to swing wide open as the net was flung into the water. It then sank mouth downward, swallowing the fish which were shut in as the weighted edges closed; the net was then hauled in by the rope. In order to reach deeper water the fisherman often waded, with his cloak or tunic tucked in his waist (girded), a few yards from the shore. Peter and Andrew were using this kind of net when Jesus called them to be "fishers of men" (Mark 1:16).

On occasion the fishermen used a baited hook, especially at the point where the Jordan enters the Lake at its northern end. In Matt. 17:27 we read how Jesus told Peter to fish in this way; the fish caught was probably a musht, in whose mouth was the coin with which the Temple tax was paid. Travelers tell us that it is not unusual to find this fish carrying in its mouth its young or other large objects.

The most favored spot for fishing seems to have been near the two "places of fishing," one called Chorazin, the other (rebuilt by Herod Philip and renamed) Bethsaida Julias, in honor of the daughter of Augustus (Mark 6:45; Matt. 11:21; Luke 10:13).

All fish had to be taxed, of course, and probably it was Matthew who dealt with these dues. He must have known Jesus very well before he joined Him (Matt. 9:9-13; Mark 2:13-17; Luke 5:27-32).

After His talk to the people, Jesus told Peter to throw out his net, the diktuon, and the haul of fish was so great that others had to come to his aid to drag it in. The fact that the net "did not break" indicates their anxiety lest their precious net be torn on the rocky bottom of the Lake.

"ERE THE SUN WAS SET"

On Jesus' return to Capernaum it was the sabbath (Mark 1:21-45). He went to the synagogue as usual. It was here that He healed the epileptic. People suffering from fits and certain illnesses were believed to be in the grip of evil spirits or demons. That Jesus Himself accepted this idea is shown by the fact that He spoke to the demons in His healing—"Be quiet! Come out of him!" (Mark 1:25). Later He cured Peter's mother-in-law; she, too, was ill with some kind of malarial fever. By sunset the sabbath was over and people suffering from all sorts of diseases and sicknesses were brought to Him; they had not come before, since it would have offended the Pharisees if they had been moved on the sabbath—that would have been working!

REJECTED AT NAZARETH

Jesus knew that the crowds wanted Him for His miracles rather than for the Good News—and He left the district. But He wanted to give His news to His own people as soon as He could and therefore went home. As always, He went to the synagogue which He had attended so many times as a child and as a youth. He had often read the Scriptures and it was not unusual for Him now to be handed by the chazzan or minister the sacred scroll taken from the holy cupboard. Jesus turned to a passage from Isaiah 61:1, 2, which He read in Hebrew and then in the local Aramaic so that everybody could understand. The congregation had heard of His preaching and now expected the usual sermon that rabbis gave after the reading. But His words stunned them into amazement. He said quite plainly that the prophecy referred to *Him*. His boyhood friends looked at one another—this was the carpenter's son! What nonsense was He saying? At first they were awed, then they grew annoyed and scornful, especially as He spoke of the worthwhileness of foreigners and the wrongs committed by their own forefathers. He told them He was well aware that a prophet was appreciated anywhere except in his own district where he was well known. The angry Galilean Jews determined to drive Him out and throw Him over the cliff

Casting the shabakeh.

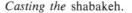

where He must have stood many times as a boy; but He evaded them and calmly left them in their anger. They had expected Him to prove His power by miracles, but He had been unable to do anything great "because of their unbelief" (Mark 6:6). His own people had rejected Him and we are not told that He ever went again to His home town of Nazareth.

BETHESDA

Soon after this, Jesus made His way to Jerusalem to attend a festival. Again on a sabbath, He was near Sheep Gate, a small cistern or pool called Bethesda. Here was a spring of healing waters and when it bubbled the sick, blind and lame hurried to enter it in the belief that the first there would be cured. Jesus saw a man who had been ill for thirty-eight years, unable to get to the waters. He said to the man, "Get up and take your mat with you." This the man did and was promptly stopped by the Pharisees, who said that because he was carrying his mat he was working. They were angry with Jesus because He had worked on a sabbath too. But Jesus pointed out that His Father went on working on sabbath days. This made them more furious, for He was putting Himself on a level with God—and that was blasphemy.

ARREST OF JOHN THE BAPTIST

It was at this time that Jesus received news of the arrest of John by Herod Antipas, the governor of Galilee. Herod was anxious lest John should be acclaimed a leader by the people and stir up a rising; and John had also told Herod that he was a wicked man for breaking the Jewish law in marrying his brother's wife Herodias. (The account gives the impression that Herodias was the wife of Herod's brother Philip, but this is wrong. She was the wife of another half-brother of Herod Antipas, and Philip actually married their daughter Salome.) Herod was strangely afraid of John, knowing him to be a good man, but for fear of the people he merely imprisoned him, for he dare not at this time kill him.

John was put into an underground dungeon in the fortress of Machaerus (see map) "the Watchtower of Arabia." The fortress was at the northern end of the Dead Sea and 4,000 feet above it; it stood guard over the bleak hills of Moab and the waterless wadis, ravines, and desolation of the desert; today its ruins provide a shelter for Bedouin cattle. Perhaps John wondered why Jesus did not lead a band of Zealots from Galilee to try to rescue him. We do not know; but he was allowed to see his disciples, who brought news to him of what Jesus was doing.

HEALING THE LEPER

Jesus now decided to go to Galilee, where once more He was surrounded by people from the whole region around—Galilee, Decapolis, Jerusalem, Trans-Jordan, Syria. They came in litters, wagons, on donkeys; there were old women, wizened men, sick children, cripples, epileptics; all were wretched, miserable, pain-ridden. And among them were rich, haughty, curious people, anxious to see this Jesus but afraid to admit even to themselves why they wanted to see Him —which was because their minds and hearts were sick.

Jesus healed many people. One was a leper. The word "leprosy" covered all forms of skin disease, from ordinary scaliness to the dangerously infectious kind. Note that Jesus touched the leper —something no ordinary person would have done. Then He told the sufferer to report to the priest to offer the necessary sacrifices and to obtain a health certificate according to the Law (Lev. 13, 14). Despite Jesus' wish that he was to say nothing more, the man was so overjoyed that he spread the news of his cure. People thronged into the village and Jesus had to withdraw to a lonely place in the wild hills to pray.

He often went to quiet places for prayer, and found strength and courage for His work after talking with His Father, God.

HEALING THE PARALYTIC

On returning to Capernaum He was followed by the crowds that came even into Peter's house. Among them were Pharisees, ever anxious to watch Him. Remember that houses were flat-roofed and that people could get on top by means of the stone steps outside (see pictures). It was a simple matter for the four men to remove part of the roofing reeds and plaster or brushwood and earth (Mark 2:4 says they "dug out" the roof). They then let down by the four corners of the mat the paralyzed man— right in front of Jesus. Jesus saw that he had a sick mind as well as a sick body. He healed both, though the people were more interested in the fact that the man was able to get up and walk away. But the Pharisees seized upon this new challenge of Jesus—that He had the right to "forgive sins." Once more, to them this was blasphemy.

5

The Hostility of the Pharisees

(MARK 2:13-3:19. MATT. 9:9-17; 5; 6; 7. LUKE 5:27-32; 11; 12)

Jesus made for the Lake Shore at a point where ran the frontier between the territory of the Herods Antipas and Philip. Here, as might be expected, there was a customs house. Matthew Bar-Alphaeus (Levi) was there, at his work; Jesus called him. That Matthew had been waiting for this call is shown by his readiness to answer. He must have planned it over a long time, for his papers were in order and ready to be handed to his assistant at a moment's notice. We cannot imagine that he merely got up and left everything as casually as the story suggests; he would have had to render some kind of an account to his Roman employers.

Matthew, we remember, was one of the hated Jewish agents who collected the Roman taxes on fish and salt and the general trade of the Capernaum market. He had probably made a good deal of money for himself in the process; but Jesus must have recognized him as an

honest man and it is likely that Matthew had been one of the few honest publicans who dealt fairly and justly with the traders and charged only his rightful interest and commission. This was certainly unusual, for, having obtained the post by offering to do it for the lowest commission, the publican usually proceeded to cheat, overcharge the poor, and accept bribes from the rich to such an extent that he very easily made money over and above what he had to send to Rome.

Matthew was certainly rich. He gave a dinner for Jesus in Roman fashion. The Roman dining-table was called a *triclinium*. The prefix *tri* means three. There were three tables and couches or divans were ranged alongside them at right angles to each. The fourth side was open to allow servants to move freely. Usually, the men ate first, which meant that the women could serve, as they were expected to do; they dined afterward on what was left. The guests reclined on their left sides, on the divans, dipping the fingers of the right hand into the common dish, sometimes using a small piece of bread as a spoon. Jesus must have sat

Here is a Jewish priest sounding the shofar (*ram's horn*) *for worship* (*Gen. 22:13*).

next to Matthew as the guest of honor, and Matthew would have offered Him a tasty morsel on a piece of bread. Servants or women brought water to pour over the hands, and towels for drying them.

Following criticism by the Pharisees and scribes at His dining with "publicans and sinners", Jesus spoke to them in a series of parables or picture thoughts which they could not fail to understand. He spoke of the folly of mending old cloth with new material, of putting new wine into old and cracked skins. His teaching was that a new faith like His could not be grafted on to the old Law by which they were bound in all they said and did.

IN THE GRAIN FIELDS

On yet another sabbath, in late April or early May, Jesus and His disciples were walking through the grainfields, happily chatting. But they were hungry, and idly plucking heads of corn, which they rubbed together in their hands. Then blowing away the chaff, they ate the ripe grains left in their palms. They were allowed to take the corn, as was any Jew (Deut. 23:25), but this was a sabbath and no work of any kind was allowed. In the eyes of the Pharisees they were guilty of reaping, threshing, and winnowing grain. How absurd this sounds to us, but these Pharisees really believed it (Exod. 34:21). It was just this kind of nonsense that Jesus found difficult to accept. See what He thought about it, in Mark 2:27. The Pharisees could not find fault with their national hero David, and Jesus used the story you can find in I Samuel 21:1–6 to show how even David had ignored the Law in a time of need. Note that Mark refers to the priest in the story as Abiathar, whereas he was, in fact, Ahimelech; this error is due to a lapse of memory or a mistranslation.

FURTHER HOSTILITY

You will have realized that most of the incidents so far recorded happened on a sabbath. The Pharisees were not slow to note this and made it their special business to watch Jesus on the sabbath day. By now there was another group interested in what He was doing, but for a very different reason. These were the Herodians, anxious to see that no harm from popular risings came to Herod and his power. They were suspicious of this new prophet from Nazareth and what He might do in attracting crowds in opposition to the king.

As usual, Jesus went into the synagogue and preached. In the congregation was a man with a withered hand—Luke says it was his right hand, the one needed for his living, and tradition says he was a stone mason. Jesus knew what was in the minds of his enemies and silenced them with questions—Was it better to do good or harm on a sabbath? Then he healed the man. The Pharisees were furious, of course, for they themselves had been trapped; they began to plot against Jesus, who again moved to the Lake shore, where thousands of Gentiles gathered around Him. He preached to them from the prow of the boat as He often did, the people sitting and standing in the horseshoe-shaped bay to listen.

THE TWELVE

Needing quiet time for thought and rest, Jesus went alone to talk with His Father (Luke 6:12). After much prayer, He chose His group of twelve disciples, some of whom had been with Him for some time. These were more truly "apostles" or preachers, for they were to extend His work. But they were also learners and, indeed, Jesus found it difficult to teach them anything during the next few months. Their names may be found in the following passages: Mark 3:13–19; Luke 6:12–16; Matthew 10:2–4. See also John 1:35–42; Matthew 4:18–22; Mark 1:16–20.

These men were: Simon, later called Peter; Andrew; James; John, the beloved disciple; Matthew, the publican; James, son of Alphaeus; Thaddaeus; Philip; Bartholomew or Nathaniel; Thomas the doubter; Simon Zelotes the Zealot; Judas Iscariot. Eleven of these were Galileans. Since Judas was the only Judaean, from Kerioth, he was to some extent among strangers, and, apart from his strangely bitter and selfish nature, he must have found himself very much alone in such company. Even the love and friendship of Jesus may not have made up for the lack of understanding in the disciples. Yet he stayed on. Was it in the hope of some future high position when Jesus was King and Rome defeated?

THE SERMON ON THE MOUNT

The crowds followed Jesus into the hills to a point where a wide valley or plateau lay in the basin of the highlands. In such a place His voice would carry a long way without tiresome echoes. Here he preached his wonderful words that have come down to us as the Sermon on the Mount, beginning with the Beatitudes found in Matthew 5 and Luke 6:20–49. The sermon comes from Q, which we discussed in the Introduction; it may not have been given all at one time and is probably a collection of His sayings. (Cf. Deut. 28:3–13.)

These are very lovely words and are worth close study. Read them often. In the first verses Jesus says, "Blessed are . . ." The word "blessed" means "it is well with" or "happy." Modern translators now give us more exact meanings to other words; thus, "comforter" means "strengthener" and "meek" means "gracious and kindly"; the "pure in heart" are not those without sin, they are those who have learned to control themselves. These Beatitudes speak of the character of the good Christian (Rom. 8:14), and underline the difference between the teaching of Jesus about the Fatherhood of God and the "Law and Tradition" religion of the Pharisees, who were more concerned with keeping every "jot and tittle" of their Law than with love and friendship and service.

THE "NEW" TEACHING OF JESUS

It was in these things that Jesus broke away from the teachings of John the Baptist. John had suggested changes in their mode of living that were practical and reasonably acceptable—sharing their possessions, paying their taxes, accepting discipline and government, and being satisfied with their wages (Luke 3:10–14). Even the Pharisees could accept these things. When Jesus began He followed in the footsteps of the great prophets. He stressed the need for social service in the community—which was what Moses had done; He demanded social justice for all—as Amos had done; like Jeremiah, He taught that outward show was useless while the inward heart was wrong. This, too, the Jews had heard— and had ignored. But Jesus was now preaching something new—a gospel of service through love. They could not grasp that at all. They were so hardened to their own selfish beliefs that when Jesus said, "Yet a little while I am with you, and I go unto Him that sent me," they thought He meant that He was going to the Jews of the Dispersion. They were spiritually blind and deaf. Even the Romans sent to arrest Jesus were so affected by His teaching that they returned without Him. But the Jews were not ready to give up their religion of sacrifices and obedience to the Law of Yahweh in order to accept the new Law of self-sacrifice brought by the Son of Yahweh.

Much of His sermon made it clear to the people that the Jewish Law was good and useful as a guide for living, but, He said, many of its rules were revengeful and unkind, and getting one's own back was not *His* way of Life. His teaching was harder—"Love your enemies. Be kind to those who are unkind to you." "You should be the salt of the earth . . ." He had known how easily salt became adulterated or impure when left to get damp and open to dust; it then lost its taste and power to keep things fresh. He knew how necessary it was to stand the olive-oil lamp in a position that gave best light to the little room—certainly not behind a grain measure! He reminded them that a walled city on a hilltop could be seen for miles. He knew, too, how much the Jews resented the lawful right

Many houses in the time of Jesus were like this, with flat roof, outer stairway and lower stable quarters.

of Roman soldiers to make them carry their baggage and equipment (Matt. 5:41).

Jesus said, "You worry too much about yourselves, your food and your future. Leave those things to God. He will take care of you as He cares for the birds and the lilies of the field . . ."—and as He said this His eyes must have gazed over the flower-covered plateau stretching to the mountains beyond.

Now and again we see a flash of humor in Him. He was not always serious. He attracted people, especially children, so He must have been happy, cheerful, and, at times, even amusing. He saw the funny side of life in things and people—the man with a beam of wood in his own eye trying to remove a speck of dust from his friend's eye. Life, He said, needed a strong foundation of character, as a house needed a solid foundation. He illustrated this with His fine parable of the houses built on sand and rock (Matt. 7:24–27). It was a remarkable and memorable ending to His sermon. The people, listening quietly, were amazed at His words; suddenly they realized that He was moving away, and feeling they could not let Him go, they followed Him down the hillside, to Capernaum.

6

Teaching by Miracles and Parables

(MARK 3:20-26; 4:1-41; 5:1-43. LUKE 7:1-35; 8:26-33. MATT. 8:5-13; 13:24-53)

In Capernaum Jesus healed the servant (Luke called him a slave) of the centurion who had built for the Jews the fine synagogue in which they worshiped. He was probably a Syrian, serving under Herod Antipas with his Roman band of one hundred men. He was a believer in the One God, Yahweh, and showed his fine character not only in having provided the Jews with their place of worship but also in his attitude toward both Jesus, whose authority he accepted, and to his servant, whom he evidently loved. He did not wish Jesus to be made "unclean" by coming into his Gentile home; in fact, he was a very different person from the kind of proud and overbearing captain that we might have expected.

NAIN

Moving into the countryside, Jesus reached a little village eight miles southwest of Nazareth. There he met a funeral led by the widowed mother of the young lad who had died. Wailing women and professional mourners moaned and played dolefully on their flutes as they walked by the bier—a kind of stretcher made of wickerwork or perhaps just a plank of wood. Because of the great heat, swift burial after death was absolutely necessary. No coffin was used and the body was wrapped in long bandages and embalmed with spices, then put in a cave tomb, usually on a ledge hewn for the purpose; a large stone, like a millstone, was placed over the mouth to keep out robbers, wild animals, and other marauders. Perhaps remembering His mother, now also a widow, Jesus was moved at the distress of the woman. "Don't cry," He said, and touching the stretcher He murmured, "Rise up"—and the lad did so. The news spread fast.

JESUS AND JOHN THE BAPTIST

Meanwhile, John the Baptist, although

imprisoned in Machaerus, was allowed visitors. His disciples brought to him the news of Jesus. What the fierce prophet heard probably disappointed him; Jesus was preaching something he would never have dreamed of saying—love for one's enemies! He spoke of His Kingdom, banqueted with taxgatherers, flouted the Law when it pleased Him! Was this the Messiah of whom he had foretold? John was anxious to discover the truth. He sent two of his disciples on a special errand—to find Jesus, to watch and listen to Him and to bring news of Him to John. They arrived at Magdala on the northwest of the Lake. They watched Him at His work and returned to John with their news of His healing and teaching. Jesus in His turn spoke finely of John the Baptist; He called him as great a prophet as Elijah. When the scribes and Pharisees challenged this He was indignant with them and said that too many people looked only for miracles and were not willing to change their own lives and follow His teaching.

JESUS AND THE PHARISEES

Jesus went throughout Galilee with the twelve and some of His women helpers. It was quite usual for a prophet to be attended by women, whose work it was to look after his food and needs. The crowds still followed and it became almost impossible to have a meal in private or in peace (Mark 3:21). His mother and brothers tried to persuade Him to return home; they were beginning to think that He was mad and needed looking after. Before long the Pharisees came from Jerusalem. They were getting anxious about both the power of Jesus to attract crowds and also about His new teaching beyond the Law and its traditions; if He undermined those, their religion was gone.

They watched Him cure the blind and dumb man (Matt. 12:22, 23) of what they all believed to be his evil spirit. But they went on to say that His power over evil spirits was given Him by Beelzebub himself (beel = baal = lord of. See Part I). This was Satan, the chief ruler of the evil spirits. You will remember that Satan was originally the one who was allowed by God to persecute and test Job (Part II). In the passage of time, probably through the influence of Persian beliefs about angels and evil spirits, Satan became a more powerful tempter and finally the great enemy of God Himself. The kingdom of Satan was very real to the Jews; it held those who were in the power of evil spirits and demons and made them hate, lie, cheat, and kill; it filled them with pain and disease, it brought bad harvests, disasters, storms, death. Where these evils were strongest Satan was in power and God was ineffective. When Jesus performed His miracles and people were healed, then Satan and his demons were defeated and God and His angels had returned to power.

When the Pharisees said that Satan had given his power to Jesus to cure evil spirits, Jesus was quick to point out that such a thing was nonsense, for that would mean that if Satan gave Him power to drive out demons, Satan was fighting against himself. In any case, said Jesus (a little ironically, perhaps), some of the Pharisees themselves cured people suffering from fits—did Satan help them too? This shocked them into greater hostility and jealousy.

PARABLES OF THE KINGDOM

Later that day Jesus went to the shore to a favorite spot. As He so often did, He climbed into a boat which was pushed out a little way. The crowds sat and stood on the beach in the warm evening, some edging forward with the cool waters lapping around their ankles. Just as in the hills, Jesus let the waters of the Lake carry His voice. Looking toward the bay

"Some fell on stony ground . . ."

and over the rising slopes across the fertile valley, He could see the farming land before Him; perhaps it was then that He saw the figures of plowmen silhouetted against the sky; from the bow of the boat He told them about the Kingdom of God—the rule of God in men's hearts, and He told it in a parable—the Parable of the Sower.

They had all seen the farmer, his right hand steadying the simple plow as yoked oxen drew it through the fine soil from boundary to boundary, each marked with stones or trodden paths. The furrow was shallow. Walking behind the plowman was the sower, casting his seed by hand in a rhythmic movement born of long experience. Much of the seed fell on the stones and the footpaths, where it was quickly eaten up by the birds that flocked around the sower; some of it lay for a while in the thinnest soil, then shriveled in the heat of the noonday sun, or grew for a while until it was choked by weeds. But some fell on the good ground in which it grew to the full harvest welcomed by the farmer, who reaped, threshed, winnowed, and stored the grain. The explanation Jesus gave to His disciples is clear to us all. He continued His parables.

The Kingdom of God is like a tiny grain of mustard seed that grows to a large tree. It is like this that great things come from small beginnings. The Kingdom is also like hidden yeast in flour, working silently but leavening the whole; it is like buried treasure in a field; it is like a valuable pearl. By these pictures Jesus tried to make it clear to the people what the Kingdom of Heaven could be to them—if only they would listen and believe.

Parables should be seen in their context—that is, not merely as stories but as answers to questions and problems and as illustrations of points that Jesus wanted to make clear; in this way they become deeper in meaning for us.

STORM ON THE LAKE

Toward evening, Jesus was again by the Lake and, once again pressed by the crowds, He entered a boat. But, too tired for more preaching, He suggested crossing to the other side. Lying down wearily, He went fast asleep, his head resting on the leather cushion used by the steersman for a neck pad. Storms arise suddenly on the Sea of Galilee. In the evening, as the warmer air from the day's heat rises, cold air—borne on the western winds from snow-capped Hermon—sweeps into the Jordan valley. With amazing speed the calm surface of the Lake is lashed into a fury of waves, which even in modern times have been known to rise to thirty feet at Tiberias. The boat's journey now lay due east, but safety could be reached only by swinging to the nearer north shore. But this was impossible. Caught by surprise, the experienced sailors knew that their boat must fill and sink—unless . . . And they cried to Jesus for help. "Peace, be still," were His words to the winds and waves; they were meant for His disciples, too, for their hearts were in a turmoil of anxiety that swamped their faith in Him.

THE MADMAN

On the other side of the Lake lay the country of the Gergesenes. Three cities of similar name lay here: Gadara, seven, and Gerasa, twenty miles east of the Lake, and Gergesa (its modern name is Khersa) just off the shore, with a steep precipice overhanging the waters far below. The alternative names of Gadarenes and Gerasenes come from the other towns, but it is generally agreed that the town and people concerned in this story are Gergesa and Gergesenes. Here the hills were scorched brown; they were riven with frightening ravines and gullies in which wild animals lurked.

With these wild creatures roamed the madman. He was too strong and too

"Some fell among thorns . . ." probably acacia scrub.

dangerous to be held, even in chains; he lived in the rock tombs cut in the hillside that edged the Lake. Perhaps as a child he had been frightened, or cruelly treated, by the Roman soldiers garrisoned in the hill fortress, or he may have imagined himself possessed by many demons; so he called himself Legion. Accepting the beliefs of His time, Jesus commanded the evil spirits to leave the man, who was instantly cured. The pigs feeding nearby stampeded and rushed over the cliff into the sea. All sorts of explanations have been put forward to account for the drowning of the pigs. Some people say that they were frightened by the shouting and screaming of the madman. It was believed in those days that evil spirits could be overcome by drowning them, and the madman probably felt that he was free when the swine were destroyed in that way. The Jews have always regarded pigs as unclean animals so it is certain that their owners were Greek.

Whatever happened, it does not alter the fact that the man was made sane once more. The herdsmen were astonished and naturally grieved at their loss; and they begged Jesus to go. He entered the boat to recross the Lake, and the cured man moved through his own country of Decapolis (Ten Cities), spreading the news and fame of Jesus. In the days of Jesus these cities, the remnants of the empire of Alexander the Great, were prosperous. In their own Grecian way they continued to worship Zeus, Ares, and other gods (Part II, Chapter 11) and traded through caravan routes running between Petra and Damascus, linking themselves with Egypt in the south and Syria and the countries of the Fertile Crescent to the north; through Capernaum they were able to contact the ports of the Great Sea so as to reach their motherland Greece.

We have no record of Jesus visiting these cities but He would have found hospitality in any of them. Forty years later, before the siege of Jerusalem, A.D. 70, the Christian Jews fled from the Roman armies to Decapolis and found sanctuary in Pella, a city on the southern shore of Galilee. Today, only a few pillars and stones remain as pathetic memorials of these great cities.

A wadi—torrent in winter, waterless in summer.

JAIRUS' DAUGHTER

Near Capernaum once more, Jesus was begged by Jairus, an elder of the synagogue, to heal his daughter. On His way to the home of the child, jostled by the crowds, He suddenly realized that some power was being drawn from Him. A woman, who for twelve years had suffered from hemorrhage—internal bleeding—without any hope of ever getting better, had in her faith touched the fringes of His cloak. Her fear was probably due to the fact that, according to the Law, she was "unclean" (Lev. 15:19); by touching Jesus she had made Him "unclean" too —and that was a very serious matter. But Jesus was more concerned with the woman's faith, which to Him was a greater thing than the Law.

By now, news had come to Jairus that his daughter was dead. Already anxious at the delay caused by the woman, he agreed that it was useless for Jesus to go any farther; but Jesus knew better. In those days, as we have seen, it was the custom to hire people to come and mourn and moan and wail, and play sad tunes on their flutes—as they did at Nain. The wailing was a high-pitched howl or shriek made by moving the tongue rapidly against the roof of the mouth and varied by tapping the mouth itself with the hand. The Hebrew word for this is *yalyal* = yell. Probably the little girl herself had pretended to be one of these mourners in her games, playing at funerals. It was these people that Jesus now sent away; they were annoyed, of course, not only at the possibility of losing their payment, but also because they really "enjoyed" this professional work. They sneered at Jesus in his assertion that the little girl was only sleeping.

With her parents and—for the first time—His disciples, Peter, James, and John, He went to the child. As always in moments of great sorrow, He spoke in Aramaic, His boyhood tongue—"Talitha cumi"—"Little girl, rise up." She did so. Note how thoughtful Jesus was to point out her need for food.

Despite His wishes, the news spread like wildfire. Two blind men were cured, then a dumb man was made to speak, and the fame of Jesus increased. And as it did so, so also grew the anger of the Pharisees and the suspicion of the king's spies.

7

Continuing His Ministry

(MARK 6:7-56; 7; 8:1-26. MATT. 9:26-11:1. JOHN 6:1-15. LUKE 9:1-17)

SENDING OUT THE TWELVE

Realizing the need to extend His work, Jesus now made a new approach to His ministry. He had selected His twelve immediate disciples (learners) and had trained them for their new work. They were now apostles (messengers). They went in pairs, partly for safety, partly for company. And they went to the Jews only (Matt. 10:6, 7). They were given power to heal and preach. They went "just as they were," with no extra food, money or change of clothing. Matthew and Luke say they did not even have a stick, but Mark says they did; possibly Peter recalled that he had one.

DEATH OF JOHN THE BAPTIST

Jesus then went on His own way until He heard of the death of John the Baptist. You will recall that the prophet was imprisoned in the dungeon of Machaerus.

Herod was no doubt celebrating in his palace below the hill fortress. The events leading to the execution of John are given dramatically in the Bible account. We are told that John's head was brought in on a charger. This was a flat dish, probably of gold. We should note in addition to the story, that in dancing before the king and his Court, Salome—a princess—shamed herself in the eyes of the courtiers and captains; for only the commonest and most vulgar of women did this sort of thing. Herodias now had her revenge against John, but Herod was unhappy. Secretly he feared the Baptist and even believed the prophet lived again in Jesus. Luke tells us this, and he most likely learned of it from Herod's foster brother or from Joanna, wife of Herod's Chancellor.

RETURN OF THE TWELVE

When the twelve disciples came back

to report to Jesus, He took them in a boat to a lonely spot in the hills to the north of the Lake near Bethsaida Julias, the birthplace of Peter, Philip, and Andrew. Only basalt black ruins are to be found there today.

Jesus wanted peace and quiet, and naturally He wanted to hear all about His disciples' experiences. Besides, it was wise to be out of the reach of Herod Antipas just then lest He should be arrested and treated as John the Baptist had been; He would be fairly safe in the territory of Herod Philip. But the crowds persisted even into the hills, having walked round the edge of the Lake to find Him. To Jesus they were like lost sheep—lost and unhappy (Ezek. 34:1–15).

BE OUR KING!

Here we have the familiar story of the Feeding of the Five Thousand; it is the only miracle related in all four Gospels. Note from the Bible narratives that the people gathered on the plain between the hills (Mark 6:39) and sat on green grass; it was thick, green grass (John 6:10); so this incident must have taken place in the springtime. The five barley loaves were flat, like pancakes, about six to eight inches across and an inch thick. The fish were possibly two the lad had picked up, small ones thrown aside by the fishermen. But they were ready to eat without being cooked in any way, so it is more likely that they were pickled fish; John uses a word that means "savory." The twelve baskets in which the remains of the meal were collected were the small wicker baskets carried by the disciples on their return from their preaching tour.

The people, especially the Zealots, were now sure that Jesus was their Leader. Moses had fed his people with manna; here was One who could feed thousands with practically no food at all; He could heal the sick and even bring the dead to life. As king He could overthrow Rome, feed and heal His followers and make them a great nation. They must make Him king. This was the very thing Jesus did not want to happen, although had He accepted there would indeed have been an end to foreign rule. But one of His great temptations, you will remember, was to use His powers in this way; He had conquered it then, He must conquer it now. So He sent the people away, "constrained" (forced) his disciples to get into their boats and row off; then He went higher into the mountains—as He always did when in great distress of mind —to talk to His Father about it.

Late in the night He came down from the hills towards Capernaum. Across the stormy Lake He knew His disciples were struggling to reach the shore; he would go and meet them, walking on the water. In safe harbor at Magdala on the shore of the Plain of Gennesaret, they acknowledged Him to be "the holy one from God." But Jesus knew only too well that they, too, wished Him to be king. Simon the Zealot did; Judas did; so, at heart, did they all.

THE PHARISEES AGAIN

In the early morning, crowds, on their way back, had missed Jesus. Many had crossed the Lake by boat to Capernaum, where Jesus was in the synagogue. In the course of His preaching the Pharisees especially contradicted what He had to say. Jesus knew they would be troublesome and even plan His death, so He moved through Galilee with the crowds still at His heels.

But neither did the Pharisees leave Him. They had come from Jerusalem, together with selected Sadducees sent by the Sanhedrin, which was getting anxious at the extent of Jesus' popularity; they did not want any kind of uprising that would undermine their friendship with Rome. These spies thereupon questioned

The interior of a synagogue.

Jesus on the attitude of His disciples toward a matter of their Law. They said that the disciples were eating without first washing. This seems to us a small thing; we know it is hygienic and the correct thing to do. But the Pharisees were not interested in hygiene; they were concerned with their Law—or at least the petty rules they had added to it. The tradition of ceremony and show in washing merely indicated that they were "clean" after contact with the non-Jews or Gentiles in the market-place or in the streets. Some occasions required washing up to the elbow, others only to the wrists; not to wash, therefore, was a religious crime. Jesus rounded on them for being so finicky and hypocritical; they should be much more concerned, He said, with greater matters (Isa. 29:13–15. Part II).

Naturally, the Pharisees were much annoyed. As Jesus told His disciples, they were the "blind leading the blind"—all fell into the same ditch! What went into a man's mouth did him no harm; what

came out of it did, for it was from the heart. Paul said much the same thing— "What a man is at heart, that he is and no more." It was evil thoughts that harmed a man, not failing to keep a rule for washing his hands.

This was yet another occasion when Jesus made it clear that His teaching would not be controlled by the Law of Moses. He was not interested in rites and ceremonies; He wanted His followers to be clean in their living.

RETIREMENT

We now find Him traveling northwest so as to avoid the hand of Herod Antipas who by this time had been informed by his spies of the following this Jesus now had. He was bent on training His disciples, too, and could not do this while being pressed so closely and so frequently by the crowds. They journeyed forty miles by rocky footpaths, from 600 feet below sealevel to 2,000 feet above, and then down once more toward the coast to mingle with the hook-nosed Phoenicians of Tyre and Sidon. The two towns were famous trading ports before the time of Solomon. For centuries their ships had gone across the Great Sea in search of trade, even to England to barter for Cornish tin their silken robes dyed purple with the stain of their own seashells. They went to Greece, Italy, and Spain for copper trays and bowls, southward to Egypt for papyrus; their trade moved inland in enormous caravans of merchandise along the great trade routes through Capernaum, Damascus, or down to Jerusalem (Mark 3:8; Luke 6:17).

Jesus wanted to be quiet and to rest without disturbance; but His presence was soon noised abroad. A woman of the district, a Syro-Phoenician (Canaanite), begged Him to go and cure her daughter of an evil spirit—she was probably an epileptic. The mother was not a Jewess, but showed such great faith that although He knew it would mean the end of quiet as soon as the news leaked out, Jesus gladly did as she pleaded. His conversation with the woman sounds discourteous and even rude as it stands, but we should realize His kindly humor in this incident. He speaks of puppies, not scavenging dogs, and the woman showed such a quick wit in her answer that even the puppies had crumbs from the table, that Jesus was unable to refuse her or deny her faith. Although He was Galilean and she Phoenician they were able to converse in the common language, Greek.

RENEWED HOSTILITY

According to Mark 7:31, Jesus left the district, journeying twenty miles up the coast road, passing by Sidon, famous for its glass, and around the mountain range to Decapolis, returning to the Lake and into the hills. This seems to be an impossibly long route, which normally took several months. The Aramaic phrase better translated indicated a shorter route to Bethsaida. Near by, on the Decapolis shore of the Lake, Jesus cured a deaf mute. He put His fingers in the man's ears and saliva on his tongue and said, "Ephphatha"—which is Aramaic for "Be opened."

More and more sick, blind and crippled people were brought and Jesus healed them; the watchers were amazed. We have here the story of the Feeding of the Four Thousand with seven loaves and a few fish. The baskets in this account were large, round wicker or rush baskets.

After the meal Jesus crossed the Lake. Mark says to Dalmanutha, Matthew to Magdala—we do not know where either village was, except that both were on the western shore, where the Pharisees and Sadducees waited to challenge Jesus. They demanded a sign from Heaven as proof of whatever He claimed. As St. Chrysostom says, they wanted Him to "stop the sun or rein in the moon or hurl down thunder." He refused; the only "sign" was the change seen in men's hearts. As the boat turned eastward, He warned His disciples of the "leaven" (yeast) of the Pharisees and Sadducees and of Herod. He was not thinking of bread but of the hard, harsh rules of the Jewish scribes and of the love of worldly things enjoyed by Herod.

At Bethsaida he healed the blind man. Taking him to a quiet spot He put saliva on his eyes. The man saw "men as trees walking." This may have been his first impression of vague outlines of people, or it may have been his first sight of men actually carrying on their backs bundles of acacia thorn for fuel. Laden in this way, the men would have appeared to be trees moving along the road.

8

The Great Confession: Transfiguration: Renewed Hostility

(MARK 8:27-38; 9:2-42. MATT. 17:1-23. LUKE 9:18-48; 10:38-42. JOHN 7:3-52)

PETER'S CONFESSION

Jesus now made His way from Bethsaida into the foothills of Mount Hermon, taking His disciples to a place of quiet and solitude where He could find out how far He had been successful in their early training. Climbing higher into the mountains, they reached the cave where the first waters of Jordan sprang from the rock a thousand feet above sea level and eighteen hundred feet above the Sea of Galilee. Behind, to 9,000 feet, rose Hermon, majestic, snowtopped. Here was the heathen city of Caesarea Philippi, originally favored by Herod the Great, who had built a white marble temple in honor of Augustus Caesar; his son Philip had extended the town itself and called it Caesarea Philippi in order to distinguish it from the Caesarea on the coast. Here it lay on the plateau to the north of Galilee, and where the river burst from its grotto Herod had built an altar sacred to the Greek god Pan, whom he worshiped alongside Yahweh. The city had been called Paneas—the place of Pan—as early as 200 B.C. Its modern name Banias is not unlike the old, especially when we remember that the Arabs have no "p" in their alphabet. But Banias today is an expanse of ruins, broken pillars—and Arab mud huts.

Jesus felt He could now test His disciples' belief in Him. He asked them who *they* thought He was. Peter, always impetuous and hasty, was the first to blurt out what some of them at least were thinking—"You are the Christ," he said, "the Son of the Living God." This is known as the Great Confession of Peter. When Jesus called him Cephas He was making a play on words: Peter and rock in the Aramaic dialect are both Cephas; just as in French we might say Pierre and pierre (cf. I Cor. 3:11; I Pet. 2:4-8; Eph. 2:20; Rev. 21:14).

Christ is Greek for Messiah = the

257

Anointed One. Peter had given to Jesus the highest honor he could think of; perhaps he recalled his synagogue texts when he did so. Psalm 2 and Isaiah 9:6–7 tell that Messiah was greater than Moses, David, or any of the great prophets; He was God's chosen representative on earth. Jesus Himself knew who He was, and at long last it was to be known to His disciples. Not that Jesus wanted to be called Messiah—that name had too many suggestions of popular leadership of the Jews against Rome for His liking. He spoke of Himself as the "Son of man" (Dan. 7:13), the leader of a new community of *His* choosing, not theirs. This is probably why He told His disciples that all believers who accepted Him as their leader were united; and that not even death could break the bond—for He would rise again from the dead.

For the time being, Jesus wished them to say nothing of their discovery. He did not want to be hailed as a rebel. They would have to go to Jerusalem, where He would be rejected and killed by the Jews. All through His ministry Jesus seems to have realized that His way to win people by love must lead eventually to the Cross (Mark 8:34–9:1). He would have to suffer and draw men to Him (John 12:32). Here we have the idea of the Suffering Servant (see Part II, Second Isaiah). In Isaiah 42:1–4; 49:1–6; 50:4–9; 52:12 are poems that tell of the faithful servant of God who suffers for the wrongs of other people. Jesus is that person.

When He explained that death under Rome could mean only crucifixion—the Romans' method of execution—and that He would rise again three days later, Peter remonstrated with Him; but this time Jesus reproved him sternly (Matt. 16:23), for Peter's was the voice of the tempter and Peter the rock had become the stone of stumbling.

To follow Him, from now on they must be prepared to give up everything "and take up His Cross," even if it meant crucifixion for them too. He would concentrate on His disciples, for they were to continue His work when He had left them.

THE TRANSFIGURATION

A week later, during their wanderings and quiet walks, Jesus took Peter, James, and John, and as evening fell they climbed into the foothills of Hermon, to pray. It was springtime and in the warm sunshine the lilies of the field shone brightly, the birds sang, new-born lambs bleated. Overhead the storks flew to their distant fir trees, and across the valley the wheat fields, vineyards and olive groves lay richly green. They left the pasture land and reached the bare brown rocks darkening in the fading light; there they rested and, tired, the disciples fell asleep. When they awoke it was to see their Master clothed with a strange radiance. With Him were Moses, leader of Israel who had passed from his people on Mount Nebo, and Elijah, awakener of Israel who had passed from the sight of Elisha in the whirlwind and chariot of fire.

The three talked of what would happen to Jesus in Jerusalem. The watchers were terrified but once more Peter took the initiative and suggested building shelters of branches. Through the glowing cloud came the voice of God—and they knew, and fell to earth, overcome with fear. The vision passed and Jesus bade them get up and not be frightened. They saw that He was alone. Once again He made them promise not to tell anyone until He had indeed risen from the dead; but still they had not grasped what that really meant.

It is in strange contrast to this wonderful experience that in the dawn descent to the foot of the mountain they found the rest of the disciples unable to cure the epileptic child believed to be possessed by an evil spirit. Jesus made it clear to them that they still lacked real faith, and He must have sighed sadly at

their lack of understanding.

Try as He would, He was not able to get away from the crowds once they knew He was in their midst again, so He made a deliberate move to go to Galilee and returned to Capernaum. There (Mark 9:33–37) He showed them that only the simple childlike faith of a man or woman would enable anyone to enter the Kingdom of God.

TOWARD JERUSALEM

Some time later, in the autumn, the Feast of Tabernacles or Jewish Harvest Festival was near (Part I). Throughout Galilee grapes were being gathered, put into the winepresses and the juice run into skins and jars. The olive trees had been beaten, the fruit piled into the press, and the oil crushed out under the heavy millstone. The feast lasted ten days. On

Bethany as it is today.

the last day the people went to the Temple and told God how sorry they were for the wrongs they had done. They wore white cloaks and sacrificed white fowls (Num. 29:7–10; Lev. 16:6–10). On this one day of the year the High Priest entered the Holy of Holies and spoke aloud the name of Yahweh.

Jesus' own brothers—who did not accept Him as the Messiah but thought Him merely mad, sarcastically urged Him to go to Judaea, where He could do His miracles in full view of the Jews there. But it was not yet His time to go and they went on ahead. When He did go it was again by the less frequented route through Samaria. But when the Samaritans seemed unfriendly He recrossed the Jordan and followed the usual road through Peraea. In a village on the bor-

An old house in Bethany.

ders of Galilee and Samaria He had healed ten lepers—but only one returned to say, "Thank you."

Here and there, would-be followers came to Him but all gave excuses when asked to make the final decision. One of the men said, "Suffer me first to bury my father," and the answer given him by Jesus seems very unkind. But the man's father was in good health and what the man really meant was, "Let me wait until my father is dead; then I'll think about coming to join you." In other words, he was putting off his decision—and Jesus knew it.

AT BETHANY

Eventually Jesus arrived at Bethany— "Home of Dates"—at the eastern foot of the Mount of Olives. It was now a mass of green shelters—like a green sea—for the pilgrims had put up their booths of branches and leaves. He was given a kind welcome by Martha, the practical, busy housewife. Note that the mere repetition

of her name "Martha, Martha . . ." indicates that His reproach when she complained was gentle. Mary, quiet and thoughtful, was in complete contrast to her sister. Lazarus, their brother, of whom Jesus was very fond, was also there. The village is today called by the Arabs El Azariyeh—another spelling for Lazarus.

IN JERUSALEM

Crossing the Kedron valley, Jesus made for the city. Once there, He threw off all secrecy and preached openly in the Temple courts, where the whispering Jews were amazed at His daring. He challenged them and their plans to have Him arrested; He reminded them of His humble birth—yet He was from God; He reproved them for criticizing His sabbath miracles. And the Pharisees and chief priests of the Sanhedrin saw this as blasphemy; it must be stopped before the "common" people accepted Him.

But even the Temple officers and guard

sent to arrest Him refused to do so. Annas and Caiaphas were furious but dare not risk a riot. Even worse, so far as they were concerned, they found someone in their own group who was ready to speak up for this man. It was Nicodemus, despite their sneers that "out of Galilee comes no prophet." No one at that time knew or mentioned that Jesus, although brought up in Galilee, was, in fact, from Bethlehem of Judaea, for that was where He had been born, six miles from their Temple. But from this time there was no doubt of their plans for the future. This Jesus must be stopped.

9

The End of the Judaean Ministry

(JOHN 9; 10. LUKE 10:1-37; 11:1-13; 13:10-17. MARK 12:28-34. MATT. 6:9-13)

Knowing they would find Jesus in the Temple, the Pharisees and Sadducees made a point of stopping Him to ask Him questions about the Law. They wanted to discredit Him in the eyes of the ordinary people and hoped that they could get Him to say something careless or thoughtless that would do this. They asked Him who He was, and He made it clear that He was the Christ (John 8:28). But after an argument about Abraham, even the people wanted to stone Him—the claim of Jesus was too much for them.

THE BLIND MAN

You will recall that in those days people believed that misfortunes and serious illnesses were due to evil spirits or some wrong done by the sufferer or his parents. Regardless of such a belief, Jesus healed the man. The Pharisees made their resentment clear and argued fiercely with the man's parents. Jesus had healed him

on a sabbath, and in the eyes of the Pharisees that alone was a disgraceful thing. The parents were afraid of what the Pharisees would do. To be turned out of the synagogue meant ruin, for no one would dare to trade with them or help them. They at once put the blame on their son, the healed man. John gives a wonderfully dramatic description of the incident and the arguments and ends on a fine note of climax when he quotes the man as saying, "Lord, *I* believe." The man knew that it meant expulsion from the synagogue, but he was prepared to risk that disgrace and loss in order to accept Jesus as His Lord.

THE GOOD SHEPHERD

In Part I there is a description of the work of the shepherd and a picture of his dress; he was a familiar figure in the land and his wonderful care for his sheep was known by everybody. Jesus spoke of Himself as the Good Shepherd; He was

"Unequally yoked."

not like the hired man who would run away at the first sign of danger. He would do all that the shepherd was expected to do, and at night lie down at the entrance of the fold—"the Door" of the sheep—to protect his flock.

We find that the crowds were divided in their beliefs about Him—John 9:16, 17; 10:19–21.

THE SEVENTY

The time came for Jesus to send out more missionaries, and He now sent out seventy. They went in pairs and His instructions to them were similar to those given to the twelve. They were to take no food, no money, no extra clothes; they must manage to live on the kindness and hospitality of those they met; they were to heal the sick and proclaim the Good News. Their journey was urgent; they must "salute no man by the way." We are reminded that in the East greetings were long and ceremonious; to cut them short was discourteous. The only way to hurry was to omit them altogether, and the only way to manage this was to travel quickly and, if necessary, look at or speak to no one on the road (Part I, Chapter 3; Part II, Chapter 3).

They returned thrilled with their experiences and success. Jesus offered His thanks to God. Then He called the crowds to come to Him with all their sorrows and disappointments, to accept His yoke which was easy and His burden which was light. They knew what He meant. The yoke was the wooden harness laid across the necks of the oxen to keep them together when plowing. A heavy, roughly-made yoke was painful and even cut into the flesh of the beasts; an "easy" one was well-shaped, smoothed and polished to fit their necks without chafing. Jesus had made many in His time as a carpenter. The people had seen the porters carrying heavy burdens, too, bent almost double under their weight. The burden Jesus had in mind may have been the load of petty rules and regulations of the Pharisaic Law, the keeping of which was indeed a burden for the ordinary people.

THE GOOD SAMARITAN

Then came the lawyer's question — what must he do to obtain the eternal life about which Jesus was talking? The question may have been quite sincere, but the lawyer probably wanted to argue about the Law too. Note how Jesus upheld the Law and the second commandment. He was trying to get the lawyer and His hearers to see the heart of the matter. Following out every detail of the six hundred and thirteen additions to the Law then known, the lawyer and the Pharisees were content that they were religious so long as they managed this task. But Jesus said, "Put first things first"—love God and love your neighbor. And in saying this He linked together what to Him were the first things—Deuteronomy 6:5 and Leviticus 19:18. The New Testament meaning of the word "love" is "good will in action" or service (I Cor. 13); the Pharisees had not yet reached that ideal. It was when He claimed to speak beyond the Law that hostility swept toward Him. His hearers resented His claim . . . "*I say . . .*"

"Love your enemies" was the hardest instruction Jesus could give, for these people lived in an atmosphere of hate and distrust; there were feuds and quarrels among them all. To the Jews a neighbor could only be another Jew. So when the lawyer asked, "Who is my neighbor?" the answer given him by Jesus came as more than a slight shock. It was the story of the Good Samaritan, familiar to us all.

His hearers knew the countryside. The road from Jerusalem to Jericho seems to have been still dangerous and infested with robbers, despite the making of new roads and the clearing away of bandits accomplished by Herod the Great and the Romans. It does go *down* in literal fact for sixteen miles, and Jericho lies in the steaming rift of the Jordan, many hundreds of feet below Jerusalem. The pictures show you how bleak and mountainous is this road, even today.

In the story of the Good Samaritan the priest was a Sadducee, the Levite a Temple singer; the Samaritan was one of those people hated by the Jews. The oil used was olive oil or a healing ointment of some known herb of the times; the wine was put to the man's lips to revive him. There is an inn or khan on the site of the ancient inn to which the hurt man was brought. The Samaritan left two cents. In modern days it is difficult to give an equivalent, but perhaps it would be easier to think of it as a day's pay. The lawyer and his friends could not have been pleased when they realized the truth of Jesus' answer.

HIS TEACHING

Jesus taught His disciples to pray (Matt. 6:9–13; Luke 11:1–4), and we have His words as our great "Family Prayer."

He told them that they had only to ask, seek and knock, and His Father would attend to them. In those days, a knock on the door would be met with the opening of a small peephole in the gate or door and questions (Acts 12:12–16). Jesus said the door would be opened without any doubts and questions. It is not always clear why a father could not answer a visitor to give him bread without disturbing the rest of the family (Luke 11:7). In those days at night the whole family merely loosened their girdles, removed their sandals and lay down on their thin mattresses, covered only in their outer cloaks. The father, therefore, in order to get to the door would have to step over his children and so risk waking them. The neighbor asked for three loaves, which sounds like a great deal of food for one person until we remember that these were like pancakes and not the loaves to which we are accustomed.

On a later sabbath day He healed a woman suffering from spinal trouble. The elder of the synagogue was furious at the woman. "Come on one of the six days of the week," he shouted, "not on the sabbath day." Jesus lost no time in rebuking him—"Do you not unloose your animals to water on the sabbath? Why should not this poor woman—one of your own people—be unloosed on a sabbath?" The crowds cheered, but the elder was embarrassed and angry.

IN JERUSALEM

In John 10:22 we find Jesus returning to Jerusalem for the Feast of Dedication, the Feast of Lights. This was held in midwinter, when every lamp in every house was lit and blazing torches were carried through the streets and market. In 164

B.C. Judas Maccabaeus had fought and defeated the Syrian armies of Antiochus Epiphanes, who had desecrated the Temple by offering swine on the altar (Part II, Chapter 11). The Temple was cleansed and rededicated to Yahweh, and from that time onward for eight days the Jews celebrated the Feast of the Dedication of the Temple. Psalm 135 was sung at the Temple service.

In Solomon's Porch or cloisters leading to the Court of the Gentiles, Jesus was asked by the Jews if He really were the Christ. Jesus said, "I have told you but you don't believe me. I do as my Father wishes me; He and I are one in purpose" (John 10:24–30). To the Jews this was blasphemy, the punishment for which was stoning. Jesus prophesied the destruction of the Temple and that He would rebuild it in three days. No one knew what He meant until after His resurrection. It was a claim, however, that once and for all broke His ministry from the claims of Judaism—the religion of the Law, which had served its purpose for the Jews until now. But they were not ready to accept His new message. This period marked the end of the so-called Judaean ministry.

I 0

Into Danger

(MARK 10. LUKE 15:1-32; 18:35-43; 19:1-28. MATT. 18:12, 13. JOHN 11:1-54)

Jesus now crossed the river into Trans-jordan, to Bethany, and so up the stifling valley to Bethabara, where John the Baptist had commenced his preaching and Jesus had been baptized. Crowds followed Him and eventually He moved back again toward Jerusalem. He proclaimed the growth of the Kingdom in men's hearts. But Herod was seeking His life, and a friendly Pharisee warned Him to flee. But Jesus said, "Tell that fox that what I am doing I shall continue to do," and moved on toward the city.

THE "LOST"

His teaching throughout Peraea called upon all to give up everything and follow Him. His disciples included tax gatherers and people known to be "sinners," and the Pharisees never tired of challenging Him because of them. But to Jesus, they were the "lost" whom He had found. Here we have the three wonderful par-ables of the Lost—the Lost Sheep, the Lost Coin, the Lost Son—stories that should be familiar to us all.

The shepherd knew each one of his sheep individually, and they knew every word and sound he uttered—his calls, his commands, his directions. Even so, as sheep often do, one of them would go astray from the flock in those rock-strewn, scrubby grazing grounds. Then it was that the shepherd had to look for the sheep; frightened, bleating, bleeding, caught in the tangled briars or wedged in a rocky cleft, shivering with animal fear at the jackals' cries and the eagles' screams, the sheep would be found, rescued, and reunited with the flock—and there would be great rejoicing over the "one that was lost." The point of Jesus' words lay in the last phrase, that there was "more joy over one repentant sinner than over ninety and nine who think they need no help"—a shaft at the self-right-eous Pharisees who felt they needed no help while they had their Law and Tradition.

When a bride adorned herself for her husband she wore across her forehead a headdress of ten silver coins (drachmae). They may have been a gift of the bridegroom or part of her dowry handed from mother to daughter for many generations; they were a sacred possession she treasured all her life. To lose one coin was a tragedy, a sign that she had become careless; there may even have been some superstitious fear of bad luck at losing one. Whatever the reason for her anxiety, the coin had to be found. She took her olive-oil lamp from its three-forked stand,

The anxious woman used a lamp to find her coin.

its smoky flame giving just enough feeble light to clear the shadows in the corners of the little room as she moved the straw and rushes from the floor, lifted the stools and bins, mats and jars—until at last the coin was found! Filled with joy, out she went into the narrow street to tell her friends and neighbors all about it; and understanding her fright and happiness they sympathized and rejoiced with her.

So with the Prodigal Son. Wasteful and wilful, he spent his share of his father's money, and was eventually sunk in shame and disgrace and starvation when his "fair-weather friends" had all left him. He even ate the carob beans fed to the pigs. It will be recalled that swine were to the Jews "unclean" animals, and this was the lowest shame of all. Slowly the boy came to his senses and returned home. His father, who is really the chief "character" of the story, forgave him. Note that the father ran to meet his son. It was an Eastern mark of courtesy to go out and meet a guest. The elder brother found it hard to accept his brother's return. But the lost was found and the father was glad.

With these and other parables related in Luke 16, Jesus angered the Pharisees more and more. The antagonism was mounting on all sides. Not only the Pharisees, but many of Jesus' own followers were now hostile because He had refused to be made king (John 6:15); the Sadducees were annoyed because He attacked them on the question of the resurrection (Matt. 22:23–33) and at what He had said about the Temple (John 2:19; Matt. 26:61), and the Herodians were angry at what He had said about Herod (Luke 13:31–33). Nor would it be long before they banded together in an effort to get rid of Him (Mark 3:6; John 11:47–53). For all this, He continued His way to Jerusalem, undaunted and unafraid.

"STEADFASTLY TO JERUSALEM"

One day during the following week Jesus received news that Lazarus was seriously ill. Strangely enough, although He loved the Bethany family so much, it was two days before He told His disciples that He was going there. They had thought Lazarus was probably better, but Jesus told them He knew that Lazarus was dead, and that their faith was about to be strengthened. His disciples, knowing that Bethany was only a few miles from Jerusalem, were anxious for His safety. Arrived at Bethany, they found that Lazarus was dead and his body already laid in the family tomb for four days.

As we might expect, it was the practical Martha who met Jesus near the tomb outside the village. She showed an amazing faith in Jesus that He was the Son of God and, what is even more important, it was to her that Jesus said, "I am the resurrection and the life." She went "secretly" home to tell Mary that the Master had come, and Mary, crying, went at once to seek Him. The hired mourners believed she had gone to wail at the tomb. Note how she echoes her sister's reproof —"If only you had been here, my brother would not have died." Jesus was deeply moved and grieved. "Move the stone away," He said. Protesting, Martha said, "But Lazarus has been dead for four days . . ." But the stone was moved, and at His Master's call, Lazarus appeared, alive, still swathed in his burial bandages.

JESUS MUST DIE!

News of this miracle brought to a head decisive action on the part of the Pharisees. They now went to the Sanhedrin and sought the help of the Sadducees— who denied the possibility of life after death. Annas, deposed by the Romans in favor of his son-in-law Caiaphas, but still the more powerful of the two in the eyes of the Jews, was one of the chief priests. Already they had determined to get rid of Jesus, but now they were even more fearful of His popularity with the people. If He became a national leader as one with power over death itself (Annas did not believe the story of Lazarus), then gone would be their own power and with it their luxurious ways of living, their money, and their close connections with Rome. There was great danger, too, that their hopes of a Jewish nation would never be realized. Rome would certainly interfere if there was any suggestion that Jesus was to be a king. There was no king but Caesar. This Jesus, said Caiaphas, must die—for the nation. Orders for information as to His whereabouts were sent out. Jesus went into hiding in Ephra-

im, a small village high in the hills on the edge of the wilderness. (Do not confuse this with the Ephraim, Northern Kingdom of Israel.)

While actually outside the walls of Jerusalem, Jesus was safe from the chief priests, and over the Jordan He was safer still; in Peraea He went on teaching. On one occasion His disciples tried to prevent mothers from bringing to Him their children, but He reproved them. "Suffer them . . ." means "Let them . . ." And gently, He laid His hands on them and blessed them—"for of such is the kingdom of heaven."

THE RICH YOUNG RULER

A young sheikh heard Him and asked about His promise of eternal life and the Kingdom. Jesus set him a test that proved too hard for him, for he was rich and was not prepared to consider giving away all his wealth in order to follow Jesus. It was hard, said Jesus, for people who trusted in money and earthly things to enter God's Kingdom; it was easier for a camel to go through a needle's eye. Some people say that this referred to the small postern gate used by people after the big city gate had been closed; a camel could not get through this. Others say the word "camel" should be "cable" or ship's rope. But it is more likely that Jesus was using a proverb or saying well known to them all; it was used to indicate anything that was too hard to do. A similar saying has been found in an ancient Hebrew school book, which speaks of the difficulty of driving an elephant through the eye of a needle.

The disciples were perplexed and wondered how they would fare. Jesus (Matt. 19:16–20:16) made it clear that they would have their reward. And He told them the story of the man who employed laborers to work in his vineyard; regardless of the time at which they had started work, he paid them all the same amount

—to which they had agreed when taken on. Service, said Jesus, was done for the love of it, regardless of reward or suffering; God paid everybody equally—with a place in His Kingdom, but the greatest there was he who served the most. To serve was the joy of the Lord and that joy was the highest reward of His servants.

PASSOVER DRAWS NEAR

But Passover was drawing near. Pilgrims from far and near were already moving through Peraea on their way to Jerusalem. Among them were Galileans, many of whom knew Jesus well and looked out for Him on their way. The crowds must have been large, for we are told that at this time of the year upward of three million pilgrims gathered in and around Jerusalem for Passover. Spies and informers decided that Jesus would not come to the city and openly defy the Sanhedrin and Rome; He would not dare, they said. But He was already on His way. He told His disciples what He expected to happen, but despite their fears He set His face toward Jerusalem. It was then that the mother of James and John (the Sons of Thunder, as Jesus called ·them) came to Him to ask that her two sons might be given special places in His Kingdom. That, said Jesus, was something ·beyond His power to grant. Naturally, the other disciples were angry— possibly because they had not thought to ask first . . . And once more Jesus had patiently to explain to them that the key to the Kingdom of Love was not power, but service.

ZACCHAEUS

By now they had reached Jericho, the city of palms. The story of Zacchaeus is familiar to us. He was a chief inspector of taxes, who could "farm out" his taxgathering to other agents, but he was as much hated as they. Strangely, his name means "pure." He was a short man; he had to climb a wild fig tree whose long outspreading branches enabled him to see Jesus coming up the road. Jesus, surrounded by pilgrims who had met at the crossroads of the mid-Palestine trade routes, had crossed the Jordan where it was shallow enough to ford in the track of the caravans. High before Him reared the Roman citadel; there were the gladiators' amphitheater and the hippodrome, both the haunts of soldiers and the younger Jews. On a hillside stood the palace of Herod the Great; across the way was Elisha's Fountain. Before them lay the hot white road, winding upward from the stifling heat of the valley to the parched dryness of the Judaean plateau.

But on His way Jesus saw Zacchaeus and knew what was in his lonely heart. He decided to dine with him. Zacchaeus was delighted, but of course the people of Jericho, who knew him, were disgusted; Jesus was eating with a taxgatherer, a sinner! Jesus was in danger of losing their support, and Zacchaeus sensed their hostility. He quickly came to the defense of His friend and offered to "put things right." Under the Law (Lev. 6:5; Num. 5:7; Exod. 22:1, 4, 7; II Sam. 12:6) this meant giving half his goods to the poor and "twofold" plus "one-fifth part" to those he had wronged. But, although there was no actual charge against him, what Zacchaeus actually offered was what the Law demanded from a criminal— fourfold. This was proof of his sincerity of purpose; he wanted to make it quite clear to Jesus that he was sorry for his past wrongs and had decided to be a better man, honest and just.

With the pilgrims watching and wondering at this unexpected event, Jesus realized how necessary it was that Zacchaeus should be restored to his own faith and reinstated as a good Jew—a worthy "son of Abraham." The winning of Zacchaeus to His own cause led Him to say. that He, the Son of Man, came "to seek and to save that which was lost."

BARTIMAEUS

Leaving the city, they prepared to begin the toiling journey up the mountain road hung with craggy cliffs and dropping away in frightening precipices. At the gate, sat a blind man begging. Blindness was common in those days, most of it being due to the dust, glare of the sun, dirt and disease carried by flies. In all Middle Eastern countries even today there is the same weakness of the eyes, caused by much the same reasons.

Bar-Timaeus (son of Timaeus) called to Jesus for pity and help. The people checked him when he called Jesus the Son of David, but he knew that the Messiah-King was on His way—and Jesus realized that he knew. He called him and Bartimaeus stumbled gladly in the direction of His voice. Jesus did not reprove him as the people had done, but He gave him his sight. It is pleasant to recall that the first things the blind man saw were the eyes of Jesus, spring flowers, waving palms, and bursting blossoms. He joined the crowds who themselves believed by now that Jesus must surely be going to Jerusalem to proclaim once and for all His leadership against Rome, for He was the Messiah-King, Son of David, who was to come.

The pilgrims burst into song as they went—the Hallel, and Jesus perhaps was thinking of the prophecies He had heard as a boy—"Blessed is he that cometh in the name of the Lord" (Ps. 118:26), "meek and lowly, riding upon an ass" (Zech. 9:9), "The Prince of Peace" (Isa. 9:6).

I I

Entry Into Jerusalem

(JOHN 12:1-8; 13:3-38. MATT. 26:1-35; 21:1-11. LUKE 19:11-44; 22:1-38. MARK 14:10-30; 11:1-18, 27-12:37; 12:41-13:37)

It was on the Friday or Saturday before Passover that Jesus arrived at Bethany. He was welcomed as usual at the home of Martha, Mary, and Lazarus, and on Saturday Simon the Leper gave a banquet for his guest.

MARY ANOINTS JESUS

During the meal, when the women would be waiting upon the men, as they were expected to do, Mary brought a long, narrow-necked jar of reddish, sweet-smelling balsam called spikenard, which was a perfume from the Himalayas in India. The jar itself was not alabaster as we know it but of some kind of valuable substance. Jesus was reclining on a divan and it was easy for Mary to move to His feet. In her great emotion she could not undo the seal easily and broke the neck of the jar so that she could pour its contents over His feet. Moving along the divan she bathed His head also, wip-ing both with the long flowing hair of her own head. The disciples were surprised, even annoyed. Judas, with his thoughts on the cost in shekels of this perfume, protested. Jesus saw in her act an anoint-ing for His burial, for He knew that it could not be long to His death. When we note in Chapter 13 that His burial was so hurried that there was not time for the normal anointing and embalming of His body, we shall realize that this act of Mary's was a holy anointing.

Judas was filled with a sense of despair. He did not like to be reproved by Jesus in front of the others, but he felt in the rebuke an indication that Jesus meant things to take their own course. He evidently had no intention of becoming a national leader. It was this that led Judas to make his dreadful decision to betray his Master, in what he may have thought to be a last effort to make Jesus challenge the power of Rome. Some scholars say that his name Iscariot means "Man of

Kerioth" or "dagger man," in which case he would have been a member of "a fanatic band of men pledged to wage incessant war against the Gentiles." What he decided to do was to Judas a duty of the highest order; but it does not alter the fact that his betrayal of his Master was the most dreadful crime in all history.

PALM SUNDAY

The next day was the sabbath. Jesus continued His way to Jerusalem. At Bethphage, on the Mount of Olives, he sent two of His disciples to fetch an unbroken colt or foal. They did so with the permission of the owner, who seems to have accepted as a kind of password "the Lord hath need of him." Already the pilgrims were crowding into the city, some of them still singing the Hallel. Though they had come from all over the then known world, many had heard of Jesus of Nazareth. His fame spread through the city; more crowds surrounded Him and others came to meet Him; as they did so they spread their outer cloaks and cut down leafy branches from the palms for His royal entry into the city.

Many of them, probably the loyal Galileans, realized that Jesus was indeed fulfilling the ancient prophecy of Zechariah (9:9–11; 14:4), while they themselves shouted the words of the Psalmist and Second Isaiah (Ps. 118:26; Isa. 62:11). Hosanna means "Save now." Thus Jesus made His triumphal entry when He claimed to be the Christ—the Messiah (Mark 11:3; Matt. 21:9). It ended in anticlimax for, after going into the Temple courts and watching the people, He made His way back to Bethany, apparently unmolested and unnoticed. He must have known that He had failed to stir the crowds into acceptance of His Messiahship: but they still wanted a king of war on a horse, not a Messiah of peace on a donkey. Judas probably saw the whole affair as a farce; the time had now

come for him to take action. We may imagine him arguing within himself that if Jesus wouldn't act, he would; and if He didn't, why, then, the whole business had been a waste of time and might as well be ended. He would go to the Sanhedrin. . . .

MONDAY

Jesus and His disciples again came to the city, and on their way they passed a fig tree. Jesus is said to have cursed the tree because it bore no fruit, so that it shriveled. This is a difficult incident to explain, but some people think it may be a dramatized parable (Luke 13:6–9, and 35, 36). We are told that fig leaves often come with small green knobs, which the peasants eat and call *tagsh*; when these fall off figs grow in their place. If there are leaves and no knobs, the tree will be bare of fruit. The parable seems to say that the outward signs of the Jewish faith showed very little inward belief, that, in fact, they were a "fruitless" nation.

CLEANSING THE TEMPLE

Jesus now made His way to the Temple. The Court of the Gentiles was the only place where non-Jews could stand and worship. Yet here in the wide forecourt, open to the sky, were traders' booths, stalls, moneylenders' tables, with all the noise and bustle of a market place. He had seen these things as a boy; even then the cheating and overcharging and deceit had horrified Him. Of course, these people had a perfect right to be there; their positions had been rented to them by the priests, who themselves made a great deal of money in rents and charges. But to Jesus they were desecrating the House of God, His Father's House: they were swindlers and cheats, they were selling diseased animals for sacrifice, deceiving the Jews in the exchange of their foreign currency for Temple money. He

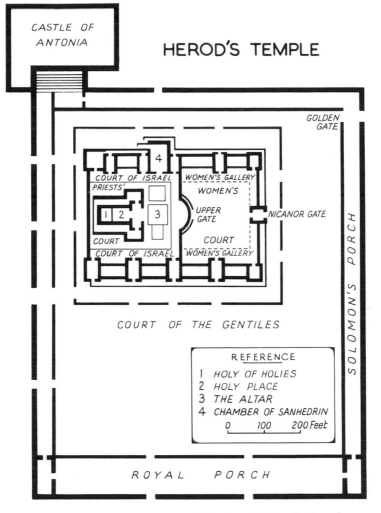

CASTLE OF ANTONIA

HEROD'S TEMPLE

GOLDEN GATE

COURT OF ISRAEL

PRIESTS'

WOMEN'S GALLERY

WOMEN'S

4

1 2 3

UPPER GATE

NICANOR GATE

COURT

COURT OF ISRAEL

COURT

WOMEN'S GALLERY

SOLOMON'S PORCH

COURT OF THE GENTILES

REFERENCE
1 HOLY OF HOLIES
2 HOLY PLACE
3 THE ALTAR
4 CHAMBER OF SANHEDRIN

0   100   200 Feet

ROYAL   PORCH

The plan of Herod's Temple.

must cleanse the Temple (Isa. 56:7; Mal. 3:1).

With His whip of rushes picked up from the floor He drove out the sheep and oxen, overturned the booths, sent the money-changers' coins rolling across the court. John makes it clear that He drove out the animals; He did not strike the people themselves; they must have been too startled to protest until it was all over. But by His action Jesus had now brought upon Himself the final hatred of the Sadducees who would stand for no inter-

ference of this kind; He had challenged the authority of the Temple priests and He had threatened their source of income.

John places this incident (2:13–22) at the beginning of Jesus' ministry, but there is little doubt that it happened at this time, four days before His crucifixion.

Recognizing Him, the people who the day before had cheered now took up the cry again and the children joined in. They were astounded at His teaching and at His action. What right had He to do this? asked the Pharisees. "Destroy this temple, and in three days I will raise it up," said Jesus. They thought He meant Herod's Temple barely finished and forty-six years in the building. He meant Himself, but they would not know that.

TUESDAY

On Tuesday, Jesus again went to the Temple. This time, the Sadducees were waiting for Him. "Who gave you authority to do these things?" they asked. But Jesus was not so easily caught. "Whence did John the Baptist get his authority—from God or men?" he replied. And they dared not answer for fear of putting themselves in the wrong. He then preached His parable of the wicked husbandmen; the chief priests knew perfectly well that He was directing it at them. The householder was God; the husbandmen were the Jews; the vineyard was the Promised Land.

QUESTIONING JESUS

But they dared not arrest Him yet. He must first be discredited in the eyes of the people; then Rome could deal with Him. They plotted to trap Him, joining again with the Herodians. They pretended to ask honest questions, hoping for answers that would cause Him to say something either against Rome or for Rome and against the nation. This would give them the excuse for immediate arrest.

"Is it right to pay the poll tax?" they asked. Jesus was ready for them. "Show me a penny," He said. This was the amount of the tax, a common Roman denarius; it was a silver, not copper, coin, especially minted for taxation. Note that it had to be sent for; no one would have a Roman coin bearing Tiberius Caesar's image in the Temple precincts—although the enemies of Jesus may secretly have hoped that He would produce one. "Pay back," He said, "to Caesar [for the benefits of good government] the things that are his and to God [for life and creation and love] the things that are his."

In this answer Jesus threw the responsibility of decision on His questioners, and their cunning had brought them only annoyance—and the laughter of the onlookers.

The Sadducees tried to catch Him on questions of life after death, although they had no belief in it themselves. Having quoted the Law of Moses to Jesus in the hope that He would anger the people by breaking it, they were astonished to hear Him quote Moses in return (Exod. 3:6), adding that God was not the God of the dead but of the living, for to Him all were alive. Even some of the scribes saw the point of His reply and approvingly said, "Master, you have given a good answer" (Matt. 22:33).

Now it was the turn of the Pharisees—"What is the chief commandment?" Jesus answered this from the Scriptures—Deuteronomy 6:4, 5, and added Leviticus 19:18. On the lawyer's comment He added, "You are not far from the kingdom of God." And the Pharisees saw that one of their own number was at heart a follower of Jesus. Seeing this, in His turn, He asked, "Whose Son is Christ?" "David's," they said. And with His reply (Mark 12:37; Ps. 110:1) He again silenced them.

JESUS REBUKES THE PHARISEES

But the crowds were delighted with this and more so when Jesus warned His disciples in their hearing to beware of the scribes and Pharisees who, He said, made the Law difficult for ordinary people to keep. They loved men to notice them and their large phylacteries with wide borders and long fringes and tassels, and to hear their long prayers at street corners (Jews pray standing). Their demand for front seats, and their self-importance were always in evidence. They were cheats and hypocrites. Matthew 23: is full of Jesus' scorn and denunciations.

"Whited sepulchers" at the foot of the Mount of Olives.

The Pharisees forgot God and justice, kindness and love; they were blind guides "straining at a gnat and swallowing a camel . . ." (How the people must have laughed at that.) Over Kedron were thousands of tombs, sepulchers or graves, glinting white in the hot sunshine, newly whitewashed for the Passover. Within them were the bones of the dead. Like these were the Pharisees — outwardly pure, inwardly rotten.

If ever the Pharisees had hesitated in their hatred of Jesus they now determined to do away with Him. He realized their rising fury, but He did not spare them. He sat by the Treasury with its thirteen trumpet-shaped offering-boxes for gifts and Temple offerings. He saw a widow put in, as secretly as she could, two mites, the smallest Jewish copper coins—all she had; the Pharisee stood and gave lavishly for everybody to see. Jesus was quick to say who had given the more.

HE FORETELLS THE DESTRUCTION OF JERUSALEM

He rose to leave and on the way out spoke to His disciples of the magnificence of the Temple. He said that soon it would be razed to the ground. They reached the Mount of Olives and sat down on the grassy slopes, the Temple shining white and gold in the distance. Peter, James and John and Andrew pursued the discussion. When would it happen, this dreadful destruction? What warning would they have? First, said Jesus, I shall be rejected. Then Jerusalem will be besieged and those who can should flee to the hills. That would be difficult if it happened on a sabbath, for that would be beyond a sabbath day's journey of 2,000 cubits. What then? Then Jerusalem would fall to the Gentiles. (This, of course, did happen, when, A.D. 70, Jerusalem fell to Titus.) There would be false prophets and leaders. They themselves would be persecuted, arrested, imprisoned, beaten, killed; but they need have no fear, for deliverance would come with the return of the Son of man.

Just as when the fig tree's buds and leaves showed that summer was on the way, so when these signs began they would know that the Kingdom of God

Bones of the dead were stored in an ossuary.

was very near. They must not expect to be warned; only God knew when. They must watch and be ready—like the five wise virgins who made sure that their lamps would be alight when the bridegroom arrived; otherwise, like the five foolish virgins, they would be refused admittance to the house. They must use their power and opportunities for the Kingdom like men given money for trading by their master before he went abroad; the idle man was of no use to his master or to anyone. Increased powers came to those who used the powers they already had. They should serve by caring for the sick and needy, for the lonely and the stranger.

As if confirming their worst fears, Jesus added that there were but two days to Passover—and then He would be crucified.

WEDNESDAY

Even as He was talking, Caiaphas and the chief priests were discussing how best to arrest Him—and then to kill Him —before Passover began. To do so openly at the time the city was full of excitable pilgrims—loyal Galileans and nationalistic Jews—might be the signal for a riot; Rome would want to know why, and that would be the end of the rule of the Sanhedrin and the end of their own power.

JUDAS AND THE SANHEDRIN

Jesus seems to have stayed in Bethany during the Wednesday of this week, but Judas had made his plans. He wanted to force the hand of Jesus—and he would receive payment too. Thirty pieces of silver—thirty staters—was the legal payment for a slave (Exod. 21:32; Zech. 11: 12; Hos. 3:2), and for this amount Judas would betray his Master. It is more than likely that at this meeting Judas gave the priests information that led to their final charge. He told them of the Messianic secret—that Jesus was indeed the Messiah. With this knowledge, they could proceed, for whatever charges of sacrilege against the Temple or of sorcerer's powers of healing they could raise, this would prove Jesus to be a leader

and rebel against Rome—and this was treason for which the penalty was— death. But the arrest must be made in absolute secrecy, and where could that best be made? Judas knew.

THURSDAY

This was the day before Passover when preparations for the feast had to be made. Peter and John were sent to arrange the room and the meal which we now call the Last Supper. The house was probably the home of John Mark; the Upper Room was reached by the stone steps outside. It was easy for the disciples to find the man of whom Jesus told them, for only women ever carried water—except for the despised water carriers—and a man bearing a water jar would therefore be very obvious. It was most likely a prearranged plan.

The meal was prepared. In washing His disciples' feet—a courtesy to visitors in those days after a hot and tiring journey and usually done by a slave or the youngest member of the family—Jesus showed what He meant by humility of service, doing the most menial duty willingly and lovingly (cf. I Sam. 25:41).

THE LAST SUPPER

The Last Supper is sometimes confused with the actual Passover meal. Matthew, Mark, and Luke indicate that it was; John says it was held on the night before (John 19:31). There are arguments for both ideas. Many people say that if this were the Passover meal, then the Crucifixion would have fallen on Passover day, which the chief priests were anxious to avoid (John 18:28; Matt. 26: 5; Mark 14:2). Also, in Luke 22:15, 16, Jesus says He would like to eat Passover with them but His death would prevent it. Again, Judas was supposed by most of the disciples to have gone out to buy food for the feast (John 13:1, 29). There is no mention in the narrative of the Passover lamb—which had to be killed in the Temple—or of bitter herbs. An important point also is that at Passover the blessing is given at the beginning, whereas here Jesus gives it at the end of the meal.

Because of these arguments, scholars say that the meal was more likely the one called the *Kiddûsh,* which is the supper held before Passover and similar feasts. On the other hand, it must also be agreed that because at this time the Passover fell on a sabbath, when it would not be lawful to work to prepare the meal, Jesus, in common with many Jews, may have brought the Passover meal forward.

The events of the meal are clearly given in the narratives. Paintings of the Last Supper by great artists show the group seated on stools around a table; it is more probable that the disciples and Jesus reclined on their divans and dipped into the common bowls. This again would have helped Jesus in washing His disciples' feet, and it would have enabled John to lean back on Jesus' bosom and also to speak quietly across the table to Peter. Further, it enabled Jesus to honor Judas by handing him a "sop"—a special morsel on a small piece of bread, as the host did for his guest.

THE NEW MEANING OF THE LORD'S SUPPER

Eating bread and drinking wine with the blessing of Jesus gave to this meal a sacredness that has been remembered ever since. It is so remembered in our Holy Communion services, in which those who promise to try to serve Him in faith and love gain strength and power to do so, in the knowledge that His spirit is with them. This is signified in breaking the bread and pouring the wine—His body broken, His blood poured (I Cor. 5:7, 8; 11:17–34). This was Christ's New Covenant (Mark 14:24). The bond between Yahweh and the people had been made at Sinai; Jeremiah had made it a bond between the individual and Yahweh. Now Christ made it between each of us and Himself. He made it clear to His disciples that in His death was our deliverance from sin and death; He uses the word "exodus"—His "going out" and our "deliverance" (Luke 9:31). He was going to the Cross as the last act of the Suffering Servant—for Israel, and for everybody, a "ransom for many."

The chalice used by Jesus is now called the Holy Grail. The word comes from *San Greal,* a corruption of *Sang Real,* meaning Holy Blood. Tradition says that it was brought to England by Joseph of Arimathea, and that it lies at Glastonbury Abbey. It is believed to be of glass; around the edge in Greek are engraved the words "What are you here for? Cheer up!" It is significant that Jesus used words not unlike these in His greeting to Judas (Matt. 26:50). It may be thought that in doing so He was reminding Judas that but a short time before this betrayal of his master he was with Him in a last sacred meal. But by then it was too late for Judas, to withdraw from his crime. The deed was done.

JESUS' LAST WORDS TO HIS DISCIPLES

Following the Last Supper, Jesus gave to His disciples His final words of comfort, help, and guidance. These are to be found in John 14–17 and should be read at this point in the story of Holy Week. He spoke of life in the hereafter (14: 1–24) and showed how love linked them like the branches of the vine to its main stem (15:1–17). There would be trials of their belief in Him, but they were to continue in prayer and they would receive the Spirit of God, the Comforter, (14:16–27; 15:26, 27; 16:1–15).

Then He prayed (John 17:1–5) for Himself, that He might face the end in such a way that He would fulfill His promises and rise again as proof of eternal life. He prayed for His disciples (6–19) as men in great need, especially now that He was leaving them. He prayed for the Church He had now begun (20–26), for its unity and fellowship.

Then they sang a hymn and moved sadly toward the Garden of Gethsemane, on the slopes of the Mount of Olives. On the way, Peter asserted his love and loyalty for his Master; but Jesus knew well how weak would be His followers in the face of real danger and apparent defeat. Peter, too, would deny that He ever knew Jesus of Nazareth.

12

Arrest and Trials

(MARK 14:32-65; 15:1-20. LUKE 22:39-23:25. MATT. 26:36-75; 27:11-31. JOHN 18:1-19:16)

Jesus and the disciples crossed the ravine of Kedron and entered Gethsemane (meaning "Oil press" because of the olives growing there); it was a garden to which Jesus often went for peace and rest and meditation. (It is a garden still, with ancient olive trees, guarded by Franciscan friars as holy ground.) As so often before, Jesus took Peter, James, and John to a farther corner of the garden, leaving the other disciples; then He moved into the shadows cast by the trees under the Passover moon. There, in an agony of mind and heart that He could not show to His closest followers, He could be alone with His Father. He wrestled with temptation as He had done at the beginning of His ministry, and even as the three slept He rose from His feet strengthened for the final test (Heb. 5:7–10).

THE BETRAYAL

Judas guided the band of Roman soldiers (John 18:3 says a cohort of six hundred men led by a chiliarch—a high-ranking officer) and the Temple guards. They carried lanterns and torches, swords and cudgels. How little they knew Him whom they were to arrest! Behind them were the chief priests and scribes and the inevitable small crowd whose curiosity had urged them to follow this strange group. Jesus went to *meet* them, His immediate thoughts for the safety of His disciples.

He was betrayed by Judas, arrested, and bound; and all His disciples ran away (Matt. 26:56)—even Peter. Mark (14:51) fled to his own home, where the Last Supper had been held so short a time before.

From this time to His final sentence of death, Jesus went through six trials, none of them legal. There were the three before the Temple authorities and three before the Roman tribunal. Even if the trials had been lawful, it is clear that the false witnesses brought against Him disagreed in their evidence to such an extent that their accusations should have been waived aside. Jesus' enemies now had less than twenty-four hours in which to bring Him forward, try Him, sentence, and kill Him. No one raised any objection to this unseemly haste. By Jewish law it was necessary for a day to elapse between the sentence and carrying it out; by Roman law two days were necessary. But the six examinations were put through in a matter of hours. Jesus was not given a fair chance even by the judges' own reckoning, although Nicodemus at least had protested in the Sanhedrin that any man had the right to lawful treatment. But at last the Sanhedrin had Jesus in their hands; they had no intention of letting Him go, except to a cross.

GOOD FRIDAY

By now it was the early hours of the morning, before cockcrow. Annas, we recall, was still a powerful man in the Sanhedrin and it was to him that Jesus was first brought (John 18:13). The question Annas asked was one that Jesus knew would cause Him to accuse Himself if He answered it—and that was contrary to legal procedure. Annas sent Him bound to his son-in-law, Caiaphas, who in the meantime had called together a small committee of the Sanhedrin. To call such a meeting before dawn was unlawful, even by their own regulations. At sunrise (Luke 22:66–71) the full Sanhedrin considered the verdict of "Guilty" already decided upon by the committee. Any prisoner was entitled to bring forward witnesses, but Jesus was not given this opportunity. No prisoner could be made to convict himself, but Jesus was asked questions that could lead only to that result. He kept silent, and this infuriated Caiaphas. He knew perfectly well that Jesus could rightly demand fair treatment; but he also knew that time was passing too quickly for his liking. This led him to use the information given him by Judas. Under the most sacred Jewish oath, he knew that Jesus must answer him—"Are you the Christ?" he asked. "I am," said Jesus fearlessly. (Cf. Ps. 110:1; Dan. 7:13.) That was enough. It was blasphemy; Caiaphas rent his robe from top to bottom in dramatic horror. The penalty for this was death by stoning (Lev. 24:16). But the High Priest knew that Pilate would not be impressed by this charge; that was a Jewish matter. What he needed was a charge of sedition or treason against the Roman emperor.

Meanwhile, the beastliness of the onlookers was unleashed and they spat on Jesus, blindfolded and struck Him, taunted Him. Then, still bound, He was sent to Pilate.

PONTIUS PILATE

Pontius Pilate was the fifth Procurator or Governor sent by Rome to take charge of Judaea; he was appointed A.D. 26. He is said to have been "inflexible, merciless and obstinate." He was cruel (Luke 13:1). He was in Jerusalem at this time, having come from his headquarters in Caesarea with the additional troops necessary to maintain law and order, and to control possible rioting at this excitable time of the year, when Jewish feelings ran high. Besides, since the sacred vestments of the High Priests were in the keeping of the Romans in the Castle of Antonia, he had to see that they were handed over to the High Priests for use during Passover and returned to lock and key afterward.

The Jews hated him, of course, not only because he was a Roman but also because on his arrival he had marched into the city with the Roman eagles and

"The place in which Pilate arrested and scourged Jesus."

the Emperor's image displayed for all to see. This had upset the Jews so much that they offered themselves for massacre rather than agree to allow the "graven images" to stay in their holy city. Pilate had had to give way. To this day there is a pathetic memorial to this man. On the road to Bethlehem lie pieces of the aqueduct laid by him with the money he took from the Temple treasury. When the Jews rioted, Pilate's men murdered them. Among them were Galileans, and Herod Antipas had resented the governor's ruthless treatment of his people. During the trial of Jesus this breach between them was healed.

The fear of being sent back to Rome, disgraced, was always with Pilate. It would not do to be called an enemy of Caesar, and life was reasonably pleasant in this land of Palestine. Strange as it may seem, it was an attack against the Samaritans on their sacred Mount Gerizim that eventually led Tiberius to call him back to Rome to answer for his cruelties.

THE ROMAN TRIBUNAL

Receiving a message from Caiaphas that an immediate decision regarding a criminal was needed, Pilate now went from the palace where he stayed when in Jerusalem to the Castle of Antonia. He was well aware that he would be expected to give a death sentence, for that power had been withheld from the Jews and could be granted only by a Roman court. But he had the Roman's sense of justice and was prepared to give this man a fair trial. Below the Judgment Hall, the Practorium, Jesus was brought in. There He stood, lonely and bound, on the pavement Gabbatha, whose large stone block flooring was pitted with the scratches and marks of gaming Romans. The chief priests would not come any farther; Passover was near and contact with Gentiles would make them ceremonially unclean. But they expected Pilate to agree to their decisions straightway (John 18:30).

Pilate called Jesus up to him and found "no crime in him." He saw through the plans of the priests, who were forced to admit that they were lying in an attempt to get rid of Jesus by death. To their surprise and annoyance, Pilate acquitted Him; legally, Jesus was free to go.

But Caiaphas was too determined. He persisted with his charges. This man had come from Galilee, stirring up strife. . . . Galilee? Pilate saw a way out. Herod Antipas was also in Jerusalem for the Passover; he could settle the dispute. But Herod was merely interested in Jesus as the man who did miracles; his spies had told him there was no danger from Jesus as a leader. Herod put on Jesus one of his old robes and sent Him back to Pilate. (From this time Herod and Pilate were friends once more.)

"CRUCIFY HIM!"

In the meantime, Pilate's wife had sent him a message that he should "have nothing to do with that just man." Dreams were always regarded as divine ways of warning people and she believed hers to be a warning. Pilate again found no cause for the death penalty and declared Him innocent; he would scourge Jesus and let Him go. There was an immediate outcry. Caiaphas had laid his plans well. This Jesus had set Himself against Rome (Luke 23:2). As a self-confessed Messiah He was King of the Jews, and an enemy of Caesar. If Pilate ignored that he was a traitor to Caesar! A charge of treason was too much for Pilate, and he yielded to the shouting mob. In a last effort to save Jesus he offered them a choice. But by now the spies of the chief priests had done their work; they set up a cry of "Barabbas! Release Barabbas!" as for Jesus, the cry was, "Crucify him!"—the cry of animals for a wounded quarry. Pilate did not dare risk a riot: it might lead to dismissal from his post. So, washing his hands of the whole affair (this was a Jewish custom,

not Roman), he handed Jesus over to the guard to be crucified.

It is a little difficult to realize that even now it was but 6:30 on the morning of Good Friday. The sabbath began at sundown and the Chief Priest had had to work fast to accomplish his intention. Now he had to move quickly to get Jesus out of the way before sabbath began. Delay might mean the thwarting of his plans. Jesus was scourged by Syrian soldiers of the Roman army; this meant a beating with whips of thongs carrying pieces of lead or iron that cut into the flesh—whips like scorpions (Part II, Chapter 1). Also they twisted a crown out of twigs from a thorn bush, and put it on His head; and they flung an old purple robe about him, in mockery of what they thought was his pretended kingship.

And the people shouted their mad cries. We are often told that the very people who had sung their Hosannas on Palm Sunday were now crying, "Crucify him," but this is not true. Those who welcomed Jesus on His way to Jerusalem were the loyal Galileans and Judaean followers. On Good Friday the cry for His death was begun by His enemies, spies, and paid accusers, urged on by Caiaphas and the scribes. It is, of course, possible that some of His half-hearted followers, finding their Leader defeated and disgraced, and being bitterly disappointed joined in the cries for His death.

PETER'S DENIAL

During the time that Jesus was being questioned by Caiaphas, Peter went into the quadrangle below the High Priest's room in the courtyard gallery. Attracted by the warmth and glow of the charcoal fire, he moved to the brazier. There he was recognized by the servants. Peter's denials followed one another—first in hasty contradiction, then in despair and disgust at his failure; then the cock crowed. It is an interesting point that his "north-country" Galilean accent betrayed him.

JUDAS

In great bitterness and sorrow, Judas took his thirty pieces of silver to the chief priests, but he was too late. Tradition says that when Judas attempted to hang himself, the rope broke, and, falling, he hurt himself so badly that he died. The money was now "unclean" (Acts 1:18; Deut. 23:18) and could not be returned to the Treasury. It was used to buy the Potter's Field, where foreigners, strangers and outcasts could be buried. By a strange irony, Judas may well have been the first to be buried there. The field was also called Aceldama or the Field of Blood (Acts 1:19; Zech. 11:12 ff). In his account, Matthew refers to Jeremiah, but this is evidently an error for Zechariah (11:13), either by him or the translators (Matt. 27:9).

13

The Crucifixion and Resurrection

(MARK 15:21-16:20. LUKE 23:26-24:53. MATT. 27:32-28:20. JOHN 19:17-21:23. ACTS 1:1-12)

Follow the Via Dolorosa—the Way of Sorrows—of Jerusalem. Though not between those actual buildings, is the way Jesus went to the Hill of Calvary, a hill without (outside) the city wall (Luke 23:28). The route today is marked with fourteen "stations" of the Cross at each of which some incident on the journey is remembered.

At His arrest, the thoughts of Jesus had turned to His disciples; on His way to Calvary they went to the weeping women and the city whose destruction He foresaw; on the Cross He remembered the soldiers at their cruel duty and the thieves crucified with Him, and His mother at the foot, lonely and grief-stricken.

Crucifixion was the usual form of punishment meted out to criminals; it had been brought to Palestine by the Romans, who had themselves learned it from the Phoenicians. They had used it to strike terror into the hearts of rebels. In Part II, Chapter 11 we read of the mass crucifixion of eight hundred victims—mostly Pharisees, by a Sadducean High-Priest king; and after the fall of Jerusalem A.D. 70, we learn, there were so many executions in this way that every olive tree in the district was cut down to provide wood for the crosses. All too often Jesus had seen these grim crosses bearing thieves and robbers as He journeyed through the land. Now He was on His way to the same cruel death. Most pictures of His last journey show Him bearing the weight of the whole cross. This may have been so, but it is more likely that, like other victims, He carried only the beam of the cross.

Beaten with sticks, bleeding from the thorny crown, weak with pain and loss of sleep, exhausted from the scourging,

A Roman soldier bearing the eagle standard of the legion.

Jesus was forced by the Roman soldiers and jeering onlookers through the narrow shaded streets, at whose latticed windows peered women and even children, then out of the city gates and so into the hot glare of the morning sunshine. Before Him lay the green hill He must yet climb. But the weight of the beam became too much for Him and the soldiers ordered one of the watchers to carry it for Him. This was Simeon of Cyrene, (North Africa). (See Mark 15:21.) He was evidently one of the Jews of the Dispersion, in Jerusalem for the Passover. One of his two sons may be the Rufus mentioned in Rom. 16:13 as a member of the early Christian Church.

"THEY CRUCIFIED HIM"

Kindly women gave criminals a drug to deaden their pain, but Jesus refused the myrrh and gall (Ps. 69:21) so that He might face death with a clear mind. It was now the third hour—9 a.m. He was stripped of His seamless cloak, then nailed callously to the cross by Roman soldiers, to whom this was but part of their duties. He hung between two bandits, a King. Above his head, in Greek, Hebrew, and Latin, were the words that signified His crime—"King of the Jews." At the foot of the Cross the soldiers cast dice for His cloak, for it was too good to split into pieces (Ps. 22:18). A guard was left on duty to prevent any attempt at rescue, but the women and one or two harmless looking men (including John) were allowed to remain near by. These few had come with the Galileans for Passover. And at that very time the Paschal lambs were being slain in the Temple for the feast.

We have seen how in moments of stress Jesus spoke in the Aramaic speech at Jesus' courage, were convinced they had killed an innocent man. And the Chief Priest saw the veil between the Holy Place and the Holy of Holies ripped before his very eyes.

The words of Jesus in His last moments

Lambs under a year old were sacrificed at Passover.

of His boyhood. Vinegar (sour wine) and hyssop, a mixture called by the Romans *posca,* was offered to Him on the end of a long pole that once swayed in the reeds of the Jordan.

Then, at the sixth hour, noon, came darkness: the earth quivered and shook in a thunderous earthquake.

Even the Roman soldiers were panic-stricken at the earthquake, and, amazed recorded in the narratives are clear in their meaning and message. Mark gives only one; Luke and John give the others. Some doubt may be caused by the cry, "It is finished." Jesus did not mean that His physical life was over. It was a cry of triumph. He meant that His work of living and dying for His people had ended and the purpose of the Suffering Servant had been fulfilled. His last prayer was the one that probably He had said every night all His life (Luke 23:46; Ps. 31:5).

One thing we should remember in these studies and readings of Jesus—that this day was called GOOD Friday. Our first reaction to its brutality makes us feel it was a bad day; or perhaps we have never thought much about it at all. But this was not a day of tragedy; it was a day of TRIUMPH. Good had overcome evil when Jesus, perfect man, went to the Cross for all men.

LAID IN THE TOMB

Anxious to speed the end of Jesus, Caiaphas now sent to Pilate for permission to break His legs, a common method of hastening death. He wanted to get the bodies out of the way before sunset (Deut. 21:22 ff.), and the utmost haste was necessary. Pilate was glad enough to have the affair settled without rioting. Normally, crucified criminals were thrown into the Valley of Hinnom where the vultures fed on their bodies. But when Joseph of Arimathea, a member of the Sanhedrin and a secret follower of Jesus (Luke 23:50; John 19:38), boldly asked to be allowed to bury Jesus he quickly obtained permission. His friend was that other member of the Council who had gone to see Jesus by night—Nicodemus. Together they took Jesus from the Cross, and wrapped His body in linen burial sheets and bandages. They added their spices—myrrh and aloes for embalming; Nicodemus had bought enough for a king's burial. Near Calvary (in Aramaic, Golgotha, Place of a Skull) was a garden in which Joseph had had cut a new rock tomb. In it, on a ledge, they laid Jesus, and rolled the heavy stone in its groove across the opening. Jesus was laid in His tomb in the presence of two strangers and two women, in secret; it was not even a normal burial; there were no hired mourners, there was no wailing. And there was not even time for complete embalming.

It was nearing sunset; the women had to leave their preparations of spices and anointing, for they must not work on the sabbath. Still fearing failure, Caiaphas asked Pilate to strengthen the guard at the tomb to prevent the disciples from stealing away the body of Jesus (Matt. 27:62–66). They remembered that He had said He would rise again in three days—and they would prevent it!

EASTER SUNDAY

Very early on the morning after the sabbath, the women came again with their embalming spices, prepared to wait until someone came to move the heavy stone from the cave mouth. But the tomb was open! The third day had come and Jesus had risen! Only His burial clothes lay there, undisturbed, untouched; even the linen head bandage lay there like an empty shell.

There are differences and inconsistencies in the narratives. This wonderful event bewildered them and it is not surprising that afterward the facts would not be very clear to them. Note that Peter, true to his character, goes into the tomb, while John stands outside. (Ancient manuscripts show that Mark's gospel ends in the middle of verse 8 of Chapter 16, and has been finished by another writer.) The doubts and misgivings of the followers are clearly shown. In John 20:8 it would appear that the word "not" has been left out, for as it stands it contradicts verse 9; both verses should mean that the disciples did *not* as yet believe.

"SEEN OF THEM"

For forty days Jesus visited His disciples. Nine appearances are recorded, and in every case it is evident that He came when they were downcast and frightened. He was anxious that they should learn that He was with them even though they could not see Him; He had to strengthen their faith before He left them to continue His work.

On one occasion He joined two disciples returning home to Emmaus by a footpath over the hills from Jerusalem, seven miles away. Cleopas, the husband of one of the Marys at the Cross, was one, and it is possible that the other was in fact his wife. They did not recognize Jesus and told him of the events of the week, and invited Him to sup with them; but when He took bread and blessed it they knew it was He. Quickly they retraced their steps to the city to tell everybody in the Upper Room. Note that verse 21 of this chapter shows that they were still looking for a national leader.

Meanwhile, the chief priests were in consternation. The Sanhedrin decided that reports of Jesus' resurrection must be stopped at all costs, and even bribed the Roman guard to "admit" the crime of sleeping on duty and to say that the body had been stolen while they did so.

THE MASTER RETURNS

Jesus had told His disciples that He would go before them into Galilee (Mark 16:7; Matt. 26:31 ff.). They returned home (Luke 24:13) and to their work (John 21:2–4). By the Lake (this is the second time John calls it the Sea of Tiberias—John 6:1) they were restless. Peter said, "I am going fishing," and the others agreed. Unsuccessful, perhaps because they were out of practice, or not really caring whether they caught anything or not, they found their nets still empty in the morning light. Jesus from the beach told them where to drop their nets; He had done this many times before. John knew Him to be no casual watcher who would be able to spot shoals from the shore; He knew it was the Master. But it was Peter who acted; he jumped into the water and waded ashore (John 21:1–14). Note the clear memory of

Peter in telling Mark what to write; there were 153 fish, and the net was not broken!

For his three denials, Jesus gave Peter three tests and three charges; and Peter knew he was forgiven. He knew, too, that he would follow his Master to the bitter end, even to a cross.

Jesus appeared to James, His brother, now a believer in Him; He had a special message for Thomas, too. On this last occasion He reminded His disciples of prophecies about Himself and of the reason He had chosen them. They were to go into all the world preaching the Good News. They would receive power from God—the gift of the Holy Spirit, and bear witness of Him among the Gentiles.

"ASCENDED TO HIS FATHER"

For the last time they crossed the ravine of Kedron together, and went along the familiar road to the Mount of Olives. Near Bethany Jesus blessed them, and was seen no more. He had gone to His Father. This is known as the *Ascension* of Jesus. The disciples went back to their Upper Room at the house of John Mark's mother, "in joy and gladness." Their sorrow and despair had gone, their unbelief had vanished, and they were ready for their new work.

THE END—AND THE BEGINNING

Ten days later they were gathered in the Upper Room; it was Pentecost, Whitsunday. The spirit of God came to them and gave them courage to continue the work of their Master.

In I Corinthians 15 we have the words of Paul written A.D. 54, just twenty-five years after the Resurrection and within the living memory of many disciples; they speak vividly of these things.

The Cross of Calvary was to many

people of that time the end of Christ's life and teaching. To Christians it is the beginning (Acts 2:24; John 16:33), for, as we shall see in our next chapters, the Church of Christ had begun, and nothing could stop its work in that land or anywhere else in the whole world.

Part IV

SPREADING the GOSPEL

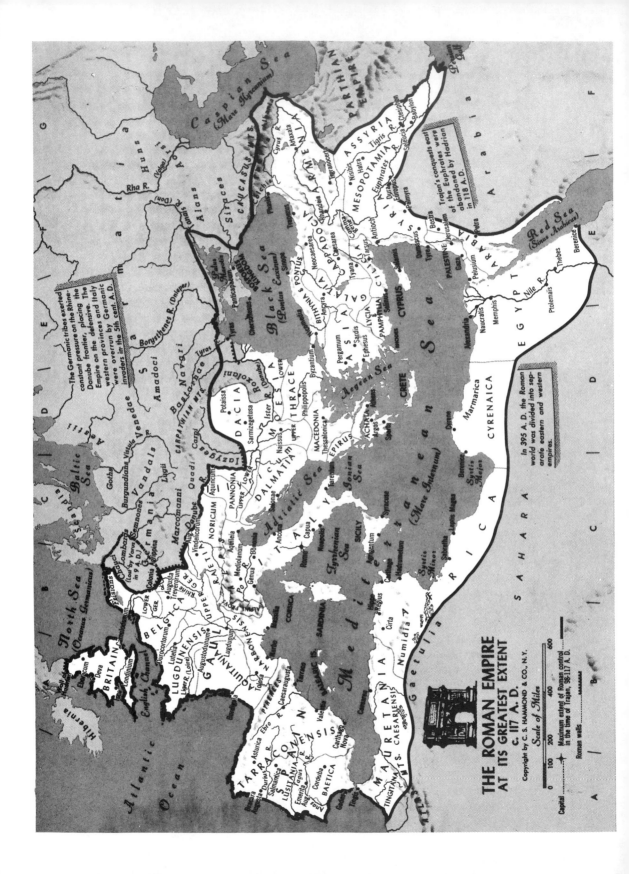

THE ROMAN EMPIRE
AT ITS GREATEST EXTENT
c. 117 A.D.

Copyright by C. S. HAMMOND & CO., N.Y.

Scale of Miles

0   100   200   300   400   500   600

Capital .... ⚔ ....
Maximum extent of Roman control
in the time of Trajan, 98-117 A.D. ....
Roman walls ....

The Germanic tribes exerted
constant pressure on the Rhine-
Danube frontier, placing the
Empire on the defensive. The
Rhine and Italy
western provinces and Germanic
were overrun by Germanic
invaders in the 5th cent. A.D.

Trajan's conquests east
of the Euphrates were
abandoned by Hadrian
in 118 A.D.

In 395 A.D. the Roman
world was divided into separate eastern and western
empires.

Introduction to Part IV

The Roman Empire

THE BOOK OF THE ACTS is sometimes called "the Gospel of the Holy Spirit." What this means we shall find in the chapters following. The narrative falls into two almost equal parts. The first fifteen chapters tell the story of the Christian Church during its earliest years, how it began and how Jews and Gentiles (non-Jews) were united in the new Christian faith. The remaining twelve chapters tell the story of Paul, whose missionary tours spread the newly begun Christian Church throughout the Roman Empire.

The *Acts* is a history book, an adventure story, a book of plots and intrigues; it is a biography, a book to stir, to challenge and to study. Its hero is Christ, but the chief character is Paul, working in the power of the Holy Spirit.

The last paragraph of Part III told how the disciples, happy in the knowledge that their Lord had gone "to prepare a place for them" and was ever present with them, went to the Upper Room to await the gift of the Holy Spirit that had been promised by Jesus. At Pentecost the Christian Church was born. *Acts* continues this story. It appears to have been written about A.D. 82.

Who wrote the Book of the *Acts?* There seems little doubt in the minds of men who make it their life work to study such matters—we call them New Testament scholars—that the author was Luke. Remember that Luke was *not* a disciple of Jesus, although he wrote the Gospel bearing his name and telling about the life and work of the Master. Luke was, in fact, a Greek doctor, probably from Philippi, and a Christian. He may have met Paul first at Troas; wherever it was, he became Paul's loyal friend and great admirer. Both men were well educated and cultured, and must have found much pleasure in each other's company, for conversation and exchange of ideas; they spent a great deal of time together, for Luke went with Paul on his travels, looking after him not only as a friend but also as a doctor, for Paul was often in need of treatment for illnesses and severe pain. There are references to Luke in Colossians 4:14; II Timothy 4:11; Philemon 24. *Acts* contains first-hand, or what we call "eyewitness" accounts of certain incidents at which we know Luke was present. These are the "we" passages. You can find them in 16:10–17; 20: 5–15; 21:1–17; 27:1; 28:16.

Knowing that Luke was so close a friend to Paul, we expect something of Paul's tremendous enthusiasm, zeal, and sense of adventure to become real and clear in the narrative. This is exactly what happens and no one can deny that Paul as a man "comes alive" in the story in such a way that the writer must have been someone who knew him better than anyone else.

Those who have made a study of such matters tell us that Luke wrote the *Acts* as well as the Gospel that bears his name. They have found that:

i. Both the *Acts* and the *Gospel of St. Luke* are dedicated to the same person, a Greek friend of noble birth named Theophilus (Luke 1: 1–4; Acts1:1).
ii. The style in *Luke* and the *Acts* is much the same. This is easier to tell by scholars who can read the original Greek in which the two books were written.
iii. There are medical words and phrases which fit in with the idea that Luke was a doctor (3:7; 8:7; 9:18).

The *Acts* reveals Paul's desire that the Christian Church should be a united body of people, in which there was joyous friendship and brotherhood and a tremendous urge to share love and happiness with one another in the belief that Jesus, their Lord and Master, was living with them, united to them by the wonderful power of the Holy Spirit.

And what about Luke himself? From his writings he seems to have been a kindly, sympathetic man, gentle and patient, modest and quietly critical—just the kind of person who makes a good doctor. He was a careful writer, too, and made it his business to be exact in his descriptions. A great archaeologist, Sir William Ramsay, has said that Luke's information is historically correct and trustworthy. Many of the references once misunderstood or contradicted by earlier scholars in translating his writings have now been found to be accurate. Much of what he wrote was based on his own experience of what Paul was doing. Paul's friends also told him about the growing Church and sent reports to Luke; and it is probable that here and there Luke collected some written information about the early beginnings of the Christian faith of which he had no first-hand knowledge himself.

Luke set himself a difficult task when he wrote the *Acts*. He chose incidents that covered the work of the apostles and Paul, and told them in a wonderfully vivid way. Some people think that he planned yet a third book, for this one ends rather abruptly. But we are grateful to him for this story that tells how the Church began and how Paul continued it. That story is only the beginning of Christianity, for it has gone on right up to this very moment.

Background to the Acts

In order to understand the story of the growth and spread of Christianity we need to be clear about its background. The then known world was the Roman Empire (see map), encircling the Great (Mediterranean) Sea, reaching "from the Tyne to the Euphrates," with Italy at its center and Rome at its heart. Palestine was but a very small part. Look at the map and see just how small it was. As we saw in Part III, Chapter 1, there were three main peoples of the world—the Greeks, the Romans, and the Jews, each of whom in different ways had important influences upon the empire, its divisions, its religions, and its cultures.

THE GREEKS

The Greeks, under Alexander the Great, had swept through Asia Minor, Palestine, and the East, taking with them wherever they had gone the culture, art, and beauty of their own land. Long after the fall of their empire (to the Romans) their architecture, poetry, philosophy, and art in many forms had left their mark, and it is for these that today we remember the Greeks. Of even greater importance, however, was their language. Conquered nations found it easy to read, learn, and speak, and it became the chief language of the whole empire and the nations within it. This enabled peoples of countries far apart to understand one another, to trade, and to exchange ideas; it became the means of spreading by word of mouth and by written letters the Good News of the Christian Faith. The New Testament was written in Greek, and the Septuagint (LXX) translation of the Old Testament (Part II, Chapter 11) was read in all synagogues throughout the empire.

When this empire was taken over by the Romans they could not conquer the wonderful influence of Greek culture. They could not make the peoples speak the Roman tongue—Latin. All over the empire there remained Greek colonies; some of them included Jews who had accepted the Greek or Hellenist ways of living and were known as Hellenist Jews. In Decapolis (ten cities) to the east of the Jordan there were Greek towns in the time of Jesus. You will recall that He healed the madman in Decapolis. Paul was to find many of these Greek communities in his travels westward.

THE ROMANS

But when the Romans conquered nations they allowed them to a great extent to continue their religions, language, and normal ways of living, so long as there were no rebellions and disorders. Thus the Herods were allowed to rule in Palestine under the power of Rome, and the High Priest had religious and civil control over the Jews in Jerusalem. The only reason Pilate was there as Governor (Procurator) was that the Jews of Judaea had rebelled against their own ruler Archelaus and had asked for Roman control.

Rome brought peace—the *Pax Romana* —and enabled the empire to settle and progress. Roman forms of government were introduced, with courts of law and justice, and captive peoples ruled themselves by these. In the chief cities were "planted" colonies of Romans, who usually were ex-service men, whose presence tended to prevent uprisings and riots, for they could quickly band together to check disorders. Remember that at this time England and much of western Europe was part of the Roman Empire, and here, too, the Roman settlers were colonies of ex-service men. Of course, the conquering Roman armies took back to Rome thousands of slaves, who were bought and sold like cattle and put to work building huge arenas and amphitheaters. Jesus was but a lad when the Galileans rebelled; many were crucified

and thousands were sent from their homes in lovely Galilee to pagan Rome. Rome taxed the people, too. In Part III we found what a great burden on the Jews this taxation really was.

Roman rule was powerful and firm. Roman armies were well trained and well equipped and were stationed in camps and garrisons throughout the empire. One important garrison was even in Jerusalem. The Castle of Antonia (named in honor of the Roman Antony) was a stronghold overlooking the Temple itself. It was necessary, especially during festivals, to keep an eye on possible uprisings and anti-Rome demonstrations. This garrison saved Paul from the angry Jews, as we shall see.

Through her armies Rome became absolute mistress of her vast empire. Yet there was great pride in being a Roman citizen. Freedom, even from slavery, could be bought or earned by some valuable service.

But the Romans were often brutal and pagan. Their gods and goddesses—Venus, Jupiter, Diana, Mars, Bacchus, Mithras, to name some—were worshiped in fear and superstition, satisfied only with sacrifices and evil rituals. These gods were thought to rule everything, and it is not surprising that the people found their lives empty and meaningless and themselves lonely and afraid. Such an empire, without love and goodness and a religion of noble worship, could not last—and as history shows, it did not. Yet it was at the height of its cruel power when the Christian Church was just beginning and spreading.

THE JEWS

It is important to remember that the Jews had spread throughout the Mediterranean lands long before the persecutions of the early Church. Indeed, we have to go back as far as the time of the Babylonian conquest (Part II, Chapter 9), and

Jerusalem today. A mosque occupies the Temple site.

no doubt there were scattered groups even before that. These were the Jews of the Dispersion (Diaspora). Some of the places in which they had settled are given in Acts 2:9–11. They had settled in the main cities as traders, fugitives, even as slaves. There they had lived their Jewish lives but obviously not without some influence from the people among whom they lived. They spoke Greek as well as their own Aramaic or Hebrew tongue, used the Greek Septuagint as well as their precious Hebrew scrolls, and wore Greek dress and clothes. They even changed their Jewish names to Greek and Roman forms, and had their meals in Greek or Roman fashion.

But wherever they happened to be, usually in colonies of the great cities, they managed to keep their own faith amidst the wickedness and cruelty of false idol worship, superstition, witchcraft, and sorcery. They kept their belief in Yahweh, the One True God. Wherever there were ten males they could form a synagogue, which they did. They maintained their rites and ceremonies and kept themselves as free from the "unclean" Gentiles as they possibly could.

The Temple in Jerusalem was their

"home," to which every year thousands of Jews made their way as a sacred duty. The most devout Jews, as we should expect, lived in Jerusalem. At a time when many Greeks and Romans were growing tired of their gods and the uselessness of their worship, weary of the vice and wickedness of the emperor's court and anxious at the low standards of behavior of the people, some found in the Jewish religion what they were seeking—a belief in a single God whose power enabled men and women to be true to their faith and so live clean lives. It seemed to be a satisfying religion when compared with their own. These non-Jews joined the synagogue and obeyed enough of the Jewish Law to be accepted in worship. They were called "proselytes" or God-fearers. They paid their synagogue dues and religious taxes but did not become full Jews.

Of course, in their blind, narrow following of the Law of Moses and the many rites and regulations springing from it called "the Tradition," the strict Jews often made their religion a burdensome keeping of rules. Jesus had had many a controversy with them over such matters (Part III). They denied and rejected Jesus and crucified their Messiah, and then refused to believe that it was He for whom they had waited. These strict Jews were enemies of the Christian belief in the Risen Christ. Some of the Palestinian Jews who did accept Him were also anxious to keep their Jewish ways; they were to find that they could not serve both faiths at once. It was left to the Hellenist Jews, with their freer and wider beliefs, to welcome the Good News and to give the first preachers and missionaries the help and encouragement needed to spread the new faith.

THE JEWS AND CHRISTIANITY

When the split came in the main Jewish religion, these Hellenist Jews were ready to pass over the old strict Laws and Judaism in order to accept the new universal faith of Christianity. The Palestinian Jews were rather more nervous about it. But the Hellenists argued that Judaism was for the Jews only, whereas Christianity was for everybody. The Gospel broke down all barriers. Jerusalem had always been "off the map," away from the important trade and caravan routes linking Egypt through Palestine with Asia Minor and the countries to the northeast. It was therefore little touched by the great movement of Christianity which would appeal to the non-Jews elsewhere. That is why—despite the first believers under Peter—Christianity did not center in Jerusalem. It really developed in Syria, among the non-Jews and proselytes of Antioch. Here were laid the foundations of the Christian world church whose members included Jews, Gentiles, Samaritans, free citizens and slaves, rich and poor, learned and ignorant, scholars, philosophers, sorcerers, soldiers. Through Christ had come a man who was neither Jew nor Gentile; he was a Christian. It was Paul who brought Christianity to the Gentiles and enabled them to see that all divisions were broken down, for there were no barriers between Christians (Gal. 3:28). He shook off the shackles of Jewish ceremonies and rituals that Jesus had so firmly denounced throughout His Ministry (Part III).

Thus it was that each of these three great nations had much to give — the Greeks, their language and culture so that everyone could hear and understand the Good News; the Romans, their strong control of different peoples, their discipline, their fine roads whereby the News could travel, the peace which enabled the Christian missionaries to continue their work without the interference of wars; the Jews, with their strong belief in the One True God, their longing for their Messiah and their desire to be His chosen people. To these three great nations came

Christianity, free from the chains of Judaism, challenging the pagan worship of Greece and Rome, bringing people of all nations into a brotherhood that mere empires have never before or since believed possible.

2

Pentecost

(LUKE 24:50-53. ACTS 1)

THE ASCENSION

Read again the wonderful account of the Resurrection in John 20:1–8, and Luke 24:1–11.

During the Forty Days from His Resurrection, as His rising from the dead on Easter Sunday is called, Jesus had appeared nine times to His disciples when they were feeling sad and uncertain about their belief in Him. Because of His appearance they had come to see that He was still alive and that, although in future they could not see Him as they had done when He was living with them, He would be near them all the time. It was this certainty of His being near to them that made such a great difference to them. Gradually they changed from being frightened, doubting, and anxious followers to brave, confident, and outspoken preachers of His Gospel—the Good News about their Master. This Good News was that Jesus, the promised Messiah, had risen from the dead and was alive and would come again soon to take charge of their lives. As Jews, they had always believed that the Messiah had chosen them as His own people, and this thought was still very much in their minds. God had proved that He was powerful over everything, even death itself, which, with sin and wickedness, was now conquered.

They expected Jesus to return quickly, and stories of the early days of their meetings and lives show that they were in readiness. It was only as time went on that they realized that God, as Jesus had said, would choose His own time. Meanwhile, they were to preach His Kingdom in Jerusalem, Judaea, Samaria, and so throughout the world (Acts 1:6–8).

Jesus had promised His disciples the gift of the Holy Spirit—the Comforter. This word really means "strengthener"—one who gives power to overcome weakness. The Holy Spirit would come upon them, but now that they were sure of Him He must return to His Father. We call this return, it will be remembered, the *Ascension.*

MATTHIAS IS ELECTED

Still in the hope that Jesus would come soon, the disciples made their way back from the Mount of Olives, a sabbath day's journey of two thousand cubits (a cubit=18–20″). They went to the Upper Room or Chamber in Mark's mother's house in Jerusalem (12:12). This was where they had met on many occasions since the Last Supper and where they held their prayer meetings. As there were eleven of them as well as friends and followers of Jesus—including the brothers of Jesus and Mary herself—it is possible that they held services very much like those followed in the synagogue (6:4; 16:13). They joined "in gladness" (2:46), in the "breaking of bread and drinking of the cup," which reminded them of the Last Supper and fellowship with their Master (Luke 24:43; Acts 10:41).

The twelfth disciple—the only Judaean, for all the others were from Galilee —had killed himself for having cruelly betrayed his Master. The story of his death in 1:16–20, is probably more accurate than that in Matthew 27:3–10, but both should be read. It was now necessary to fill the place of Judas. Peter deliberately made the scriptures fit the facts—Psalms 69:25; 109:8—as he explained the position to the others. They believed that the casting of lots would be guided by the decision of God. This was a common method of choosing; it was done for Temple duties amongst the priests.

Matthias, who had known Jesus and had seen His work, crucifixion, and resurrection, was chosen. We do not hear of him again, but that is also true of several of the original disciples. *Acts* is only a partial account of the growth of the Church, and much is left unrecorded. It would be wrong to argue that because he is not mentioned again Matthias was a failure. No doubt all the disciples in their various ways did important work in building up the new faith, for they had been "eye-witnesses" and knew what was meant by His Kingdom. We see that already the Twelve are a distinct set or group within the larger community; they may even have felt that twelve was a desirable number to correspond with the original twelve called by Jesus and possibly with the twelve tribes of Israel.

PENTECOST

It was now May, A.D. 29, ten days after the last appearance of Jesus and fifty since Passover. The time was therefore *Pentecost*, which means "fiftieth" or "week of weeks" (Lev. 23:15–21). This was the ancient festival of the giving of the Law on Sinai (Ex. 19:16–19). In time the festival had become linked with the early harvest of Syria (May and June) and was recognized as a Harvest Festival of First Fruits or Feast of Weeks (Ex. 34:22; 23:16; Num. 28:26). At this time worshipers brought to the Temple two loaves of bread (rather like pancakes, it will be remembered) made from the new corn, and the priests "waved" them before the altar. It was a time of rejoicing and thanks to God and was, of course, one of the great festivals of the year. Jerusalem would be crowded with pilgrims, for they were commanded to attend the Temple for this celebration (Ex. 23:17; Deut. 16:16). They came from as far away as Rome, Athens, Alexandria, Baghdad; in fact, if they lived within ninety days' journey of Jerusalem they were expected to attend.

So, on this "old" Day of Pentecost, the disciples were waiting, gathered in prayer. There was in each one of them a growing sense of certainty and a feeling of excited joy that overflowed in a surge of emotion and fervor which we call ecstasy (I Sam. 10:10; I Chron. 12:18). They suddenly felt that God's Holy Spirit had indeed come and that the power and energy of Jesus had entered into each one of them. They *knew* that He was with them; this was the proof of the risen and living Christ.

Luke speaks of the sound *like* a mighty rushing wind and refers to the appearance *as of c*loven tongues of fire (see also Matt. 3:11; Ezek. 37:9. In I Kings 19:11–13, there is a note of surprise that God was *not* "in the wind or the fire").

"SPEAKING WITH TONGUES"

Filled with this new power and thrilled with a great sense of purpose, the disciples seem to have broken into "babblings." These were possibly repeated cries of praise. Even today at meetings in which people are stirred deeply, like some prayer meetings, there are such out-

The modern shepherd leads his sheep to pasture.

This is picture language, which probably means that the disciples sensed a strange movement as of wind and felt their spirits burn with something rich and strange. What is more important for us to remember is that they passed through a wonderful experience that made them changed men.

bursts of emotion. Unable to express themselves in other ways, people overflowing with excitement and emotion cry out single words and phrases like "Praise to God" and "Hallelujah" (which means the same thing) or "Amen," until very often they are the only words that can be clearly heard at all. The charge made

The donkey is still a common means of transport.

against the disciples was that they were drunk, and this shows that much of what they were saying was quite unintelligible to those who listened outside. But those who stood near and felt the same thrill of praise would recognize many of the exclamations and cries. It is hardly likely that the disciples were suddenly given the power to speak foreign languages; what is more likely is that they spoke in Aramaic, the local dialect, or in Greek, which would be understood by everybody, including the pilgrim Jews of the Dispersion.

With the gift of the Spirit came the power and confidence so to speak that men of all nations, creeds, and classes might be told the Good News.

By now, the disciples seem to have left the Upper Room, for they are in the midst of a "multitude." The countries listed in 2:9–11 are really languages and give some idea of the wide sweep of the Greek-speaking Jews (Hellenists) and Jews throughout the Roman Empire. Judaea probably means here Palestine and Syria, where Aramaic was spoken. Whatever the actual events, we now see the disciples as inspired and uplifted and thoroughly convinced of their mission to establish Christ's Kingdom. They felt freed from fear, from sin, from the power of evil and death. They were filled with a joy and an exuberance that were infectious and exciting.

PETER'S SPEECH

Peter had already established himself as the leader of the company who formed the beginnings of the Christian faith. We cannot imagine any other disciple taking his place, although, as he and others of the Twelve moved from Jerusalem into the "uttermost parts," we find James the brother of Jesus taking charge of the early Church in Jerusalem. But with his usual bluntness and impetuosity, Peter takes up the challenge of the watchers. The first thing he has to deny is that they are drunk. It is but the third hour of the day, nine a.m. Morning prayers have not yet been said and wine is never taken before then. What they have seen, says Peter, is prophecy being fulfilled—the sign of the day of Yahweh, promised by Joel (2:28–32). God's people were to be inspired and the heavens would show forth wondrous things. The first of these two signs is clear to see. It is the gift of the Holy Spirit, once seen in the prophets of old and now returned to all believers in the Messiah who had descended from

David. The second part—"the great and terrible day of the Lord"—is to come. This is to be the Messiah's Kingdom, already begun by Jesus. He was the Man who had suffered, whom the Jews had crucified and whom they—the disciples—not only knew to be alive but would preach as Lord.

Note that Peter concentrates on the resurrection of Jesus as he addresses the people of Judaea, who certainly knew of the ministry of Jesus. Some of the pilgrims knew, too. The whole Jewish nation had sinned and must repent. John the Baptist and other prophets had used baptism as the sign of acceptance of a new belief, of conversion. Now Peter says those who repented and believed must be baptized. It would be the outward sign of change from disbelief and doubt and evil living to a happy belief in Jesus as the risen Messiah and Lord of the new Kingdom (John 1:25). Sins would be forgiven, and the gift of the inspiration of the Holy Spirit (sometimes called the Holy Ghost) would be theirs. In other words, there would now be the inner baptism of the Holy Spirit as well as the outer baptism of water.

THE NAZARENES

Many of Peter's hearers had known Jesus well and were ready for this call; this is why the first converts, as they are called, were in such large numbers. At present they were called people "of the Way" (of the Way of Christ, that is) or "Nazarenes." It was not until later, as we shall see, that they were called Christians, although we use the word even as early as this. Pentecost was the birthday of the Christian Church. The word "church," of course, does not mean a building; it means a group or company of people. Acts 2:42, shows that its members shared their goods and possessions, lived joyfully, and were "ridiculously happy" in the belief that Jesus would suddenly return

and set up His Kingdom. Worldly possessions were now useless for the heavenly Kingdom was theirs. It has been said that "Christian belief and Christian practice were two sides of the same coin" (Gal. 5:22) and that these people certainly "practiced what they preached." They still kept to their ordinary Jewish worship in the synagogues and at the Temple. Their main difference was their belief that the Messiah *had* come; other Jews were still expecting Him. They observed the Jewish sabbath (our Saturday) as a day of rest. But they also observed the first day of the week (our Sunday) with an early Communion or service of prayer and remembrance of the Lord's Resurrection. When, under Emperor Constantine, the Christians finally broke away from the Jewish faith, they also gave up the Jewish sabbath and kept Sunday as the Christian day of rest.

The larger the number of converts, the more difficult became the problems of sharing (Gal. 2:10; Acts 24:17). Yet there was a wonderful sense of brotherhood among them, and they joined "in prayer and breaking of bread." As yet, there were no Gentiles in the Church; upon these watchers "fear came." The word "fear" means "amazement and awe" rather than "being afraid." These watchers, the proselytes, were more than interested in the new strange religion which asserted that, in fact, the Messiah had come, and had been killed by these very Jews, but was alive again. This was a remarkable teaching. These Gentiles had not been fully accepted by the Jews for full membership of their faith unless they also accepted all the rites and ceremonies demanded by the Jews for full membership. Now the proselytes wanted to be accepted by the Nazarenes—and what would be their answer? We shall see how this problem developed and how it was solved; for it led to the making of a tremendous decision—whether the new faith should remain Jewish or become universal.

During the spread of Christianity the rite of baptism continued and, years later, this Jewish festival was marked by all English Christians as a time of purity. They wore white and the day was known as White-Sunday-Tide or Whitsuntide, which is the name used to this day.

PHARISEES AND SADDUCEES

These two groups of Jews have been mentioned many times in Parts II and III. The Pharisees were strict Jews who believed that all that was necessary for good living was the keeping of the Law and hundreds of petty rules and regulations connected with it. The Sadducees, mostly of high-priestly families, wealthy and arrogant, were, in the main, the leaders of the Jewish Council, the Sanhedrin. They hated and despised the Pharisees; they had no belief in life after death. But both sects were anxious about the spread of the new teaching of the disciples—the Pharisees because it was being said that they were responsible for the death of Jesus, and the Sadducees because they did not accept the resurrection. In any case, to preach Christ as Messiah or King was to offend Rome, which would inevitably bring trouble. Both groups had thought that the crucifying of Jesus had put a stop to His work; but here were His disciples openly and boldly defying them and claiming that this "criminal" was alive. What was more serious was their claim that the Sanhedrin had murdered their own promised Messiah. If such a belief spread it would mean that the power the Pharisees and Sadducees held over the "common people" would be gone. It was this fear that had urged them to get rid of Jesus; now they had to deal with His disciples.

3

Peter and John

(ACTS 3; 4; 5; 6:1-7)

THE LAME MAN HEALED

Peter and John kept their hours of worship as Jews, and went into the Temple Courts at the ninth hour—three p.m., the hour of the evening sacrifice. They were on the eastern side, at the Beautiful Gate (Nicanor), so called because it was cased in layers of gold and silver (Part II). Here the disciples saw the lame man who had his begging place at the gate. He expected "alms"—money—but Peter gave him his bodily health and strength. Note that the miracle was done "in the name of Jesus." We shall find this phrase much on the lips of Peter.

In Parts II and III are descriptive references to the Temple. It was not a single large church as we know such a building, but rather a series of walled courts open to the sky and entered by special gates or from steps. Around the courts were cloisters or porches formed by pillars. In these cloisters Jesus had talked with the learned doctors of the Law and from the outer Court of the Gentiles, beyond which no Gentile could go on pain of death, He had driven out the money-changers and traders and animals. In the innermost court stood the Temple itself, a small building with its Holy Place and Holy of Holies entered only by the High Priest. Sacrifices were offered on the rock altar and choirs of musicians (Levites) kept up their chants and praise while the sacrifices were made.

In Solomon's Porch or Cloister, outside the Temple itself, Peter spoke to the crowd that had gathered, and immediately connected the miracle with Jesus—whom the Jews had crucified, despite the willingness of the Gentile Pontius Pilate to release Him. But Jesus had risen from the dead and was their Messiah, who gave them the power to heal.

Needless to say, the Sadducees, especially the High Priest Caiaphas, were "sore troubled," angry, and anxious.

Once again they were being faced with the challenge of the resurrection, in which they did not believe. On their orders, the captain of the Temple Guard arrested Peter and John on a charge of preaching the resurrection of the dead and especially of Jesus. The disciples were put into a cell until the next day, when they would be questioned.

Meanwhile, almost five thousand Jews, having seen or heard of the miracle of healing, accepted Peter's challenge and were baptized into the Church. Among them must have been many who a few weeks before had cried "Hosanna" on Palm Sunday; and there were others who had screamed, "Crucify him!" They were now united as friends and brothers in their belief that Jesus was the risen Lord of them all.

BEFORE THE SANHEDRIN

Peter and John faced the Sanhedrin, the Council of seventy, and the High Priest who, under Rome, had the power to judge religious and civil matters among the Jews. The only thing they could not do was to carry out a death sentence, although they could recommend it to Rome. Annas had been deposed by Rome in favor of Caiaphas, his son-in-law; but he still held considerable power among the Jews. So far as Peter and John were concerned, these priests had put their Master to death. The healed man was there, too, ready, if need be, to speak on their behalf. But Peter needed no help; he could speak for himself at any time. Urged by the Spirit, he could speak for His Master, too. By what power and by what name had this man been healed? The Greek word for "power" contained a trap; it meant "magic" — which was against the law. Peter saw this and answered that his healing had been in the power of Jesus—whom they had crucified and who had risen from the dead. Jesus was the "head of the corner," said Peter.

He was referring to the piece of stone that often lay hidden or neglected until the builders and masons wanted it, when it became the very piece—the key piece—needed to complete the building (Acts 4:11; Ps. 118:22).

The Sanhedrin were furious. They could not deny the miracle, for the healed man—whom they must have seen themselves very often—was there before them. But this talk of Jesus must stop. They realized that Peter and John, uneducated fishermen though they were, had a strange power of speech; they remembered, too, that these same men "had been with Jesus," whose influence — if they dared to admit it—seemed to have given these men a quality that more than made up for any lack of learning.

All the Sanhedrin could now do was to release the two disciples with a warning not to continue their preaching. Perhaps they hoped that an order from the chief Council would be sufficient. But they did not expect Peter's reply—Do we obey God—or you? And, for the time being, the Sanhedrin was defeated.

ORGANIZING THE CHURCH

The disciples returned to their friends and their work, organizing the pooling of goods and money brought by the new converts. One of the first of the wealthy people to join was Joses Barnabas. His name means "Son of Consolation." He was a Greek Jew from Cyprus, and was to play an important part, as we shall see, in the growth of the early church.

In contrast is the story of Ananias and Sapphira. These two took advantage of the fact that Christians were sharing their goods, and by pretending to bring all their possessions were cheating their friends and at the same time receiving praise for what appeared to be a noble act on their part. In this way they were mean and insincere toward God as well as toward their friends. Luke's account of what happened to them makes it appear that they were struck dead because they tried to deceive God. Some people accept this explanation. Others say that the shock of discovery of their cheating caused the death of Ananias, then the double shock of discovery and the death of her husband killed Sapphira. Such things have been known to happen. Whatever the case, the two died as the result of this sin.

BEFORE THE SANHEDRIN AGAIN

It could not be long before the Sanhedrin again took action. Peter and John were flouting their warning and this time were thrown into prison. Next morning an amazed guard found the cell empty and reported to the alarmed Sanhedrin. Then came another report—the men were still preaching in the Temple Courts! This was incredible news to the pompous Council. Brought once more to the Chamber—without force or fuss, so as not to attract the people's attention—Peter and John heard Caiaphas accuse them of stirring up strife and plotting revenge against the priests for the death of Jesus. The disciples gave their same answer, that they would "obey God rather than men." The Sanhedrin had crucified Jesus, who had risen again, and of whose life and work they, the disciples, had been witnesses and through whom they had received the power of the Holy Spirit.

"Cut to the heart," but afraid that the people would seek revenge upon them for the death of Jesus, the Sanhedrin determined to kill Peter and John, to prevent further preaching. But one of their number was a respected rabbi, a Doctor of the Law and a Pharisee; his name was Gamaliel. After Peter and John had been removed, Gamaliel warned the Council not to be overhasty in their actions. Other false prophets had arisen and had failed. If these disciples were false, said Gamaliel, they, too, would fail. But if they were genuinely of God the Sanhedrin could

do nothing to stop them; they could not fight "against God."

Peter and John were therefore beaten and warned again not to preach about Jesus. But, as we should guess, they went straight to the Temple and continued their work fearlessly (Matt. 5:10). The Sadducees were anxious that nothing should create riots and disorders, either from their own actions or from the preachings of the disciples. If Rome disapproved, it would mean harsh interference and a possible end to their wealth and luxurious ways of living. They knew, too, that only a political charge such as treason could result in Rome's approval of the death sentence. The Pharisees and scribes were not so anxious. They did believe in the resurrection but were less concerned with the displeasure of Rome. Their main interest was in the Law and its Tradition, which Jesus Himself had attacked but which so far had not been challenged by the disciples. They and the disciples believed in a Messiah; the only difference at the moment was that they did not believe in the same Messiah—Jesus.

THE SEVEN DEACONS

Meanwhile, there was trouble in the new community. The Greek-speaking Jewish Christians complained that the Palestinian members were not being fair in their distributions of the goods and that the Hellenist widows were being neglected. Peter and John made it clear that they must preach, not "serve tables"; it was decided that all the administrative duties should be done by a group or committee of seven helpers, all of them Hellenists. They had to be men of high ideals and great tact; they must have received the Holy Spirit and, should the need arise, be capable of preaching and teaching (Deut. 34:9). Stephen and Philip (not to be confused with the disciple Philip) were two of the seven. Seven was the

Jewish sacred number (for example the menorah or seven-branched candlestick).

So, for a while at least, the church ran itself smoothly while Peter and John continued to preach successfully, even winning over many of the priests (Acts 6:7; John 12:42, 43).

4

Stephen, Saul and Philip

(ACTS 6:8-15; 7; 8)

Stephen evidently attended the synagogues of the Hellenist Jews from Cilicia and of the Jews from North Africa. (The word Libertines may mean "freedom" (cf. liberty) but is more probably Libyans, of the same district as the other members.)

The members of the synagogues argued with Stephen, who spoke with great wisdom and power. Obviously well-educated, and of great faith in Jesus, he even had the gift of healing. The Jews of his group and the Pharisees of the Jewish Law disputed with him about Jesus and found him a strong speaker. He was much more broadminded than they and we shall see that the Hellenist Jews had a tendency to be readier in their beliefs about the new faith than had the stricter Jews of Jerusalem and Judaea.

His enemies became jealous as well as angry, for Stephen's arguments were beginning the rift between the new religion and Judaism that was to widen through the years and end in a complete break from the Jewish faith. As so often in Jewish history, jealousy gave way to direct plotting, and false witnesses were bribed to accuse Stephen of speaking against God, that is, they laid a charge of blasphemy. The penalty for blasphemy was death by stoning (Lev. 24:16). The Pharisees were now in league with the Sadducees against the new religion. They had banded together once before—to take action against Jesus.

STEPHEN'S DEFENSE

Stephen was brought before the Sanhedrin and made to stand in the same spot Peter had occupied a short time before. The Council sat in a wide semicircle, the High Priest in the center; at each end was a scribe noting evidence—one for, the other against, the prisoner. There were younger scribes and students of the Law seated on benches in front;

perhaps Saul was among these. Most prisoners would have been overawed and frightened. Not so Peter; not so Stephen. Stephen's judges saw that his face was "as it had been the face of an angel." Despite their disbelief in angels, even the Sadducees were impressed by what they saw.

Stephen's speech made it clear that he believed that the new Law of Jesus was about to take the place of the old Law of Moses. He traced the history of the Jews from its beginnings to the time of Solomon, who had built the first Temple. Up to this point his hearers listened intently. But Stephen went on to weave into that history the idea that the Law, the land, and the Temple were not all-important but that other things came first. God had no need of a Temple made with hands; He could be anywhere. This, to the Sanhedrin, was blasphemy, an attack on their sacred Temple. They grew restless and angry. Stephen then went on to trace the Jewish persecutions of their own prophets, the very men who had prophesied the coming of the Messiah—the Just One. The Messiah had come and they—the Sanhedrin — had done exactly as their forefathers. They had rejected and killed Him and resisted the Holy Spirit. They had failed in their high duties and responsibilities. Now, Old Israel — Judaism — was passing; the New Israel—Christianity —had come in.

With his powerful words Stephen hammered in the wedge, deepening and widening the rift he had already made by his preaching. The Council seethed. They were again "cut to the heart" and "gnashed their teeth upon him." Regardless, Stephen raised his eyes and seemed to see Jesus—not sitting at the right hand of God, but standing as though waiting to welcome him. As he told them of his vision the angry judges rose at him, thrust him outside the city walls (I Kings 21:13) to the ravine called the Place of Stoning, and there killed him. The false witnesses threw, as was their right, the first and sharpest jagged stones on which they could lay their hands. This was mob law. The Roman garrison for once was too slow to act.

Stephen's dying words were those of his Master—"Lay not this sin to their charge" (Luke 23:34). So, A.D. 32, "fell asleep" Stephen, the first Christian martyr.

Among those who watched, while protecting the clothes of those throwing the stones and therefore every bit as guilty of murder as they, was Saul of Tarsus, who was satisfied that this man was receiving the kind of death he deserved. Little did he know that, a few years later, he would tell the whole world that this was something he would never forget. And as little did he dream that one day he, Saul, would continue the work of Stephen and widen this first rift with Judaism into a complete break from the old faith. For, as St. Augustine said, "We owe Paul to the prayer of Stephen."

SAUL OF TARSUS

Now that we have met the man who is to become the hero of this part of our book it would be as well to know something more about him. Then we shall understand better why and how he felt about some things and acted as he did. Luke says that Saul was a young man. This would mean that he was about thirty years of age. He was born at Tarsus, "no mean city," of Cilicia (see map). The city stood a few miles from the coast on the river Cydnus, up which many years before, in 41 B.C. the famous Egyptian Queen Cleopatra had sailed in her golden barge to meet Mark Antony. Perhaps Saul had heard of this from his father. The city itself had been established as a Greek capital by Antiochus Epiphanes (Part II) in 175–164 B.C. and many Jews lived there, too. In 64 B.C. Pompey, the Roman conqueror, had occupied it and made it a Roman colony, introducing Roman citizenship, which Saul's father in some unknown way had managed to obtain; he may have bought it or earned it by some special service to Rome.

TARSUS

Tarsus was renowned for its learning, and its "University" was equal to those of Athens, Alexandria, and Antioch. The university was not a building or group of colleges; it was rather a center of education where great and learned men, scholars, philosophers and teachers, gathered to discuss and teach and train their students. The Stoic philosophers, especially, with whom Paul was to talk in Athens years later, were well known in Tarsus.

Around the city on the foothills of the northern mountains stretched great pine forests, and Tarsus became a famous timber city, supplying wood for Roman galleys and buildings. To the north of the city rose the Taurus mountains, slashed through by the Cilician Gates, a narrow pass between mighty cliffs and frightening precipices. Here lurked panthers, bears, and wolves, and here waited brigands and robbers. Famous in history, the pass was threaded by Cyrus and his Immortals on their way to Babylon in 401 B.C. and by Alexander the Great in 333 B.C. It was the way for the trading camel caravans from the north, where lay the plateau of Asia Minor; so came silks from China, ivory from India, carpets and spices from Persia, pottery from Syria, fish from Galilee, fruits from Damascus. These would be eagerly bartered in the Tarsus market place for goods arriving by sea—corn from Egypt, marble from Italy, glass from Sidon, copper from Cyprus, cedar from Joppa, pottery from Tuscany. In the market, too, would be the signs of the local industry. Goats were raised on the hills for their

coarse black hair, which was woven into tents, sails, sacks and baling cloths, as well as into tough tunics and jackets and cloaks for protection against wind and weather (II Tim. 4:13).

SAUL'S UPBRINGING

Saul (his Jewish name) must have spent hours of his boyhood, as Jesus had done, watching and learning about people in the market place and busy streets. By the quayside, docks, and warehouses he talked with the weather-beaten fishermen and sun-tanned lumbermen, the brown sailors from Egypt, the hook-nosed Phoenicians, sallow Italians and dark Span-

Paul as he was shown in the Catacombs.

iards. He heard tales of the sea and the forests, sailed in and around the harbor, and climbed in the pine woods. He listened to the gossip and rumors of traders, picking up their signs and accents and trading slang—a mixture of their own tongues and Greek. Like Amos and Jesus, though with no idea why, he noticed the cheating and dishonesty, and learned to distinguish between the honest man and the rogue.

In the city was a Greek gymnasium where Saul watched athletes run and wrestle and play games (Eph. 6:12; I Cor. 9:24–27). Years later, when he wanted to indicate what he had done with his life, he spoke of having "fought the good fight" and "run his course" (II Tim. 4:7, 8; Phil. 3:12–16). Although he was a Jew, he was familiar with Greek customs, habits, forms of worship, and was able to recognize the statues and images of their gods and goddesses.

Saul's parents were apparently well-to-do. Their home was in the Jewish quarter of Tarsus. Although a strict Pharisee of the tribe of Benjamin, the smallest of the tribes, Saul was a Roman citizen. This he regarded as something of which to be very proud (Acts 22:27, 28; Phil. 3:5; II Cor. 11:22; Rom. 9:3). It was to serve him in good stead, as we shall see. He went to the synagogue school and, as a "Hebrew of the Hebrews," from the time he could begin to learn he was trained in the sacred scriptures, the stories of his nation learned by Jesus and all Jewish boys. Saul wore his praying "talith" when at thirteen, as a "son in the Law," he strapped on his phylacteries and worshiped in the synagogue. He learned his many texts and learned them well (Acts 9:22). In his recorded speeches he referred to nearly every book in the Old Testament and in his epistles (letters) there are 198 quotations from the scriptures.

However wealthy the parents of a Jewish boy, he still had to learn a trade, and what better craft than the local one of weaving tent cloth (Acts 18:3)? This woven cloth was called "cilicium" after Cilicia; note that the French word for haircloth is *cilice*.

We know nothing of Saul's mother, but in one of his letters (Rom. 16:13) there is a reference to someone "who was also a mother to me," which perhaps indicates that he appreciated a mother's love and care at a time when his own had died. His sister was married into a high-priestly family (Acts 23:16)

of high social standing; Saul probably stayed with her while training as a student. As one of the many devout pilgrims of the Jewish Dispersion, he must have gone many times to Jerusalem for Passover and other festivals, and to worship at the Temple; but we do not know whether he ever saw or heard Jesus.

"AT THE FEET OF GAMALIEL"

Although Tarsus was a center of education, the University would probably not have admitted him, a Jew, to its learning. In any case, since Saul was being trained for the priesthood, it was necessary for him to complete his education in Jerusalem. Therefore, at the age of about seventeen or eighteen, he left the synagogue school and traveled with great excitement and anxiety to the great city into whose Temple courts he would go, no longer a mere pilgrim but a student. It was his fortune to be under the most famous rabbi in Jerusalem, perhaps in all Palestine, the Pharisee Gamaliel (Acts 5:34). To be accepted by so great a man Saul must have been a most promising pupil—quick, intelligent, eager, "more exceedingly zealous for the Law," determined, with a deep sense of his Jewish faith and its effect upon his life as a "Pharisee of the Pharisees" (Acts 23:6; 26:5). He says of himself, "I advanced beyond many of my age in learning the Jews' religion" (Gal 1:14; Phil. 3:6). Gamaliel, as we have seen, was at least tolerant and just, and probably found his young pupil over-impetuous and hasty. Under him Saul learned to argue and discuss and prove his points of the Jewish Law, and eventually qualify as a rabbi to speak with authority in any synagogue in the Roman Empire. Note that he "sat at the feet of Gamaliel"; that was literally true, for students sat on the ground, often on thin mats, to listen to their teachers.

It has been said that Saul was a member of the Sanhedrin, but there is no proof of this. He may have attended some of their meetings as a student in the Law. He may have been present at the trials of Peter and Stephen. If he were absent from Jerusalem at the time Jesus was crucified it is more than likely that what he learned about it was from someone connected with the priests. It is easy to see that this information would have been twisted to make out that Jesus was an impostor and had no right to claim to be the Jews' Messiah. Such wrong ideas about Jesus would make Saul even more anxious to destroy those connected with Jesus, for Saul's whole life was now given over to his Jewish religion—the Law and the Tradition.

SAUL BEGINS THE PERSECUTIONS

From this background it can be seen that Saul, although Roman by birth, Greek by contact and culture, was trained in the strict faith of the Pharisees; his every move in life was controlled by the Law of Moses and the interpretations put upon that Law by the scribes. It is clear, too, why he would be so furious with Stephen, who, in his own synagogue of the Cilicians, had said that the Law of Moses was no longer powerful and that the crucified Jesus was Messiah. How could the Jews accept a crucified criminal? The Law itself said, "Cursed is everyone who is hanged on a tree" (Deut. 21:22–23; Gal. 3:13). Saul himself had probably joined in the arguments but had found Stephen too strong for him, for Stephen was "filled with the Holy Ghost" against whom no man could stand. Saul's anger at what Stephen had said was fanned by his own feelings of annoyance and inferiority at being worsted in the arguments.

Such beliefs as were held by this Stephen were blasphemous nonsense; he deserved death by stoning (Deut. 13: 6–10). The whole sect to which he belonged should be killed or cleared out, and he, Saul, "exceeding mad against

them," would do it. Only so would the Jewish faith of his fathers be preserved in Jerusalem and Palestine. Thus he began the first Jewish persecution, and, in so doing, deepened and broadened, without knowing it, the rift begun by Stephen. For Saul set out to destroy, not the immediate Jerusalem group of the Apostles still worshiping in the Jewish fashion, but the wider group of Jews and Gentiles beginning to embrace the new beliefs about Jesus—the people of "the Way," the Nazarenes.

With a band of roughs and probably a few armed men, Saul set about his self-appointed task, throwing many of the Nazarenes into prison, possibly killing some, whipping and scourging many. The Hellenists fled to other parts of Judaea, to Samaria, and beyond. Many of them, of course, returned home (Acts 11: 19, 20). Wherever they went they took with them their Good News (opening the Church to believers in other lands throughout the Roman Empire), even to Antioch, the third city of the empire, and as far north as Damascus. In his efforts to destroy the new faith Saul was spreading it!

PHILIP THE EVANGELIST

Philip, one of the seven who formed the committee to deal with the administration of the church affairs, was one of those who fled before the fury of Saul. He went to Samaria. In Parts II and III we learned how the Samaritans and Jews had hated each other from the time that the Samaritans had offered to help in the rebuilding of the Temple but had been snubbed for their mixed blood by Haggai. Jesus had always made it clear that He thought well of the Samaritans, and now Philip, with the same healing powers of His Master, had come to the capital city to preach about the Man already known by some of the inhabitants. They recalled that this Jesus had met a woman at the well of Sychar and had often passed through the province on His way to Jerusalem; they may have remembered His words about Himself as the promised Messiah (John 4:25, 26).

In Samaria (Part II) Omri and Ahab had built their magnificent palace. The prophets had foretold the fall of the city in 722 B.C. Years later Herod the Great had rebuilt it in honor of Augustus Caesar, renaming it Sebaste (the Greek name for Augustus). Ruins of the palace, temple, and Roman fortifications may still be seen, the columns and colonnades reminding us of the grandeur of such cities of long ago. But the Samaritan Jews were ready to listen to Philip. Perhaps they too, were aware of the uselessness of their ceremonies. They found in Philip's message something more positive and real. Those who believed in Jesus were baptised into the new Church, the

evidently was well-known for his evil magic arts. Many papyrus fragments and one famous collection of charms, magical formulae, spells and so on, have been found in recent years. These show the kind of gibberish and nonsense chanted by magicians and sorcerers of the day. Simon Magus, Elymas (13:6–11), and the magicians of Ephesus (19:13–20), may all have used them in their incantations over the superstitious and frightened people. Here is a cure for people possessed by evil spirits. "Take oil made from unripe olives, with herb mastic and lotus pith, and boil it with marjoram, saying Joel, Ossarthiomi, Emori, Theochipsoith, Sithemeoch, Sothe, Joe, Mimipsothiooph, Phersothi, A.E.I.O.U., come out of him!"

We hear of several occasions when the disciples were hindered by such men whose witchcraft held the superstitious

first newcomers to what had been until now a purely Jewish community.

THE SORCERER'S MAGIC

Among the converts was a sorcerer, a Samaritan, one Simon Magus. He is mentioned in other documents of the time and

Not far from Gaza was Ascalon, another Philistine city. These are excavated ruins of a Christian meeting place in that area.

people in great fear. Although he claimed special powers from God, Simon Magus felt that Philip was a greater magician than himself. But as yet there were no signs that the Holy Spirit had come to the new converts; they were not filled with the same ecstasy and understanding of their new faith. This could be given only by Peter and John who now came to see what Philip was doing and to help him. The two apostles saw that deeper prayer and blessing were needed, and when the converts were gathered together in this way the full power of the Holy Spirit came upon them. The change in them was so marked that Simon Magus put it down entirely to the "laying on of hands," which in his sorcerer's mind was a form of magic he would like to possess. It was a perfectly natural idea to him that he could buy this power; Simon Peter made it extremely clear to him that he could not. Legend tells us that Simon Magus became at this time the enemy of Peter, and was so, even in Rome, many years later. He was there in the reign of Claudius A.D. 41–54. Our word "simony" comes from Simon Magus; it means trying to buy or sell a position or privilege in the Church or getting spiritual power or favor in church matters by the use of money.

On their way back to Jerusalem Peter and John preached in the Samaritan villages and in this way approved of Philip's "opening of the door" to the Samaritans. Already we see that the faith was being extended beyond Judaea, although we should bear in mind that the Samaritans were themselves Jews who also expected their Messiah (Part II, Chapter 10). The faith had not yet accepted the Gentiles.

PHILIP AND THE ETHIOPIAN

Meanwhile, Philip had moved southward along the road to Gaza (see map). The old Philistine city had been razed to the ground in 96 B.C. and was "desert," although the main road to Egypt still ran through it following the "Way of the Philistines" (see Part I, p. 101). The newer city was much nearer the coast. On the way, Philip saw a caravan of pack animals journeying southward. In an open chariot sat a dark-skinned man, an African. This was the treasurer of the Queen Candace of Ethiopia, which country then extended over many lands south of Egypt. Candace was the title of the dynasty or "house," like Pharaoh or Caesar, rather than the personal name of the queen (Part I, p. 34). The treasurer was a "God-fearer," perhaps a proselyte who had been to Jerusalem for the Feast of Tabernacles. He was reading from the papyrus roll of the Septuagint (LXX), and the passage was the "lesson" for the Feast—Isaiah 53:7, 8. This was one of the four poems about the Suffering Servant (Part II, p. 164). He had not understood it while at the feast and was evidently trying to grasp what it meant by reading it out loud—quite a common habit in the East—as he journeyed. Philip, drawing near, heard him and offered to explain. Philip told him that the prophecy referred to the crucified and risen Messiah. The Ethiopian believed what Philip told him, and, pausing at an oasis to water the animals and rest, suggested that Philip baptize him. This Philip did and the Ethiopian went on his way, "rejoicing." We do not know what happened to him when he arrived at his Queen's palace. We can only guess at his conversations. It is possible that he found a Jewish colony and worshiped at their synagogue, and perhaps even there the envious Jews contradicted his belief in a crucified Messiah. Or, perhaps, as Jews of the Dispersion, with their freer beliefs, they welcomed him and all he had to tell of his meeting with Philip. Whatever happened, it must have been for much good.

Philip was led on to Azotus (Ashdod), another city of fame under the Philistines (Part I), and thence to Joppa. Here he preached and then went on to Caesarea.

5

The Road to Damascus

(ACTS 9:1-30)

The story of the *Acts* now picks up the threads of the persecution begun by Saul, told in 8:1–3. Thrilled with his first success, Saul offered to go to far-away Damascus in Syria, a journey of 150 miles. He had heard of a strong movement there of the people of "the Way" (8:1). The letters obtained from the High Priest could not have been permission to persecute the followers of Jesus, for even the High Priest had no power over foreign synagogues. They were more likely to have been letters of introduction to the rulers of those synagogues containing recommendations that this young Pharisee be given all possible help to seek out such people, and then to bring them back to Jerusalem for examination by the Sanhedrin (cf. 22:5).

When Luke refers to these members of the new church as "any that were of the Way" (9:2) he means "of the Way of Life or Salvation." You will remember that Jesus once said, "I am the Way."

TO DAMASCUS

"Breathing threatenings and slaughter," Saul set off on his destroying mission along the road through Samaria. He was full of excitement and bitter joy. He had tasted success and craved for more; he was zealous for the Jewish faith and would do everything he could to stamp out this new Nazarene religion that was based on the crazy idea that Jesus was the crucified Messiah. His thoughts dwelt upon what he would do in Damascus and how rapidly his fame would spread throughout the land. Damascus he knew as a great caravan city, crowded with travelers and traders. It was there that Eliezer had stayed on his way to Haran to find a wife for Isaac (Part I); Naaman had obeyed Elisha there and had been cured of his leprosy (Part II). The city was surrounded by hills and edged by desert, with miles of gardens intersected with streams and canals alive with pleasure and trading boats. In its booths, bazaars, and market squares were silks, gems, ivory, carpets, swords; thirsty travelers quenched their thirst with the juice of lemons cooled with snow from the Hills of Lebanon. Its walls and towers were pierced with massive arches and gates, and through one of these, the Eastern Gate—although he did not dream it —Saul himself was to be led, not as a fearful persecutor, but blind, stricken, and confused.

HIS THOUGHTS

But Saul's mind was not upon Damascus as a city; it was on the arrests he would make and the punishments he would mete to those who were as foolish as Stephen. Stephen—with his talk about Jesus! Jesus? Surely it was in Galilee that He did His preaching? That was where Saul was now riding, along the shore, through Capernaum, across the hills of Galilee. So this was where Jesus had walked and talked. "A Man of Sorrows . . . smitten . . . afflicted. . . ." Saul's mind roamed over the scriptures he knew so well. That was how, in his Servant Songs, the prophet Isaiah had spoken of the promised Messiah. And Stephen had claimed that this man Jesus was He who had been smitten . . . who had been afflicted . . . who had suffered. Stephen had died in his amazing belief; he had died with great courage, too. Saul had to admit that to himself; it was tremendous courage. He remembered standing by the clothes of those who threw the stones; he saw once more the cut and bleeding face and heard the words of Stephen. It was a prayer he had uttered. Saul remembered exactly the words that struggled from the bloodstained lips of the dying man— "Lord, lay not this sin to their charge." An amazing prayer . . . for his enemies. Who was this Lord, too? Was it the Jesus of whom Stephen had spoken? Could Stephen get so much faith from his

belief in Him? Suppose he, Saul, was wrong . . . and that Stephen was right? Even Gamaliel had bidden the Council beware of fighting against God . . . and Stephen had said that Jesus was the Son of God!

We do not really know what thoughts came to Saul as he made his way to Damascus, but in his mind there must have been a turmoil of questions and growing realization that what he was doing was wrong. It came to him just before Jesus spoke to him in that strange, hot, lonely, place, somewhere on the road, at the parting of the ways. . . . Saul experienced a blinding light, brighter than the sun, that struck him to the ground. He heard a voice that could be no one's but that of Jesus, asking questions that had arisen in his own mind, questions which he knew at last he must answer. "Why are you persecuting me? Why do you kick like an untamed horse or an obstinate ox against the pricking goad that forces you on? Against the prickings of your own conscience?" Note that Saul answered his own question—"Who art thou, LORD?" He knew it must be Jesus—Jesus of Nazareth, of Galilee, whose power he had seen in Stephen and in the followers he had already persecuted in Jerusalem. He was later to claim that he had seen Jesus (II Cor. 12:1-4; Acts 23:11; II Tim. 1: 12).

IN THE CITY

Blinded by the great light, Saul, a broken figure, was taken to the house of Judas, where for three days and nights he brooded upon his strange experience. Judas lived in Straight Street. We are told that this street ran right through the city and was a mile long. It was a hundred feet wide. Down the center ran chariots and horsemen and along each side were paths for pedestrians. Ananias (not to be confused with the man of the same name mentioned earlier) was a strict Jew (22:

12). But, like James, the brother of Jesus, in Jerusalem, he was a member of "the Way." Traders in the city market place had already brought news of Saul's intentions and all believers knew about him by now. It was natural for Ananias to be anxious for he would have been one of the first to be arrested by Saul.

But, told by Jesus that Saul was to be a "chosen vessel" (the Greek really means "vessel of election") or special servant and missionary and His witness to all nations, Ananias did as he was told. Saul received his sight and was baptized into the Church, receiving the power of the Holy Spirit.

It may be useful at this point to read all three accounts of Saul's conversion; each of Saul's own accounts adds to the one given by Luke (9:1-18; 22:3-16; 26:9-18).

FAILURE IN DAMASCUS

Saul lost no time in going to the synagogue, where he had every right to be, not only as a Jew but also as a rabbi trained under Gamaliel to preach and to explain the Law. But, of course, the Christians were suspicious of him. Was he not there to find out who they were and so trap them? The strict Jews were "confounded" and angry. Saul realized that there was something amiss. He could hardly expect these people to accept him after the rumors they had heard about him. Besides, he himself lacked the deeper experience of his new mission; he needed time to think about his work and to find out what he should do to prepare a plan of action. You will recall that this was precisely the decision made by Moses, Elijah, John the Baptist, and Jesus Himself. So it was that Saul went into Arabia for three years, during which time he could quietly think and pray and plan (Gal. 1:17, 18).

On his return to Damascus, Saul found that many of the Christian Jews were still afraid of him. He preached much on the lines of what Stephen had said, that Jesus was indeed the Messiah. Even after three years he recalled the words of Stephen, so it is not surprising that he copied, perhaps unconsciously, perhaps deliberately, Stephen's methods and words. Those who heard him were amazed, but believed he was merely pretending so that he could find out who were the leaders and have them arrested. They decided to get rid of him, to kill him if the need arose. Even the Governor of Damascus, then under the rule of King Aretas IV, "the King who loves his people" as an inscription says, had the gates guarded night and day so that Saul could not escape through them (II Cor. 11:32).

In fact, the only way of escape was over the walls. Built along the tops of the walls that circled great cities were houses and watchtowers. From one of these houses some of Saul's friends lowered him in a basket. The basket was a tall strong hamper. Saul described it, later, as a net, so it was probably very loosely woven or slung in a net for additional safety (Acts 9:25; II Cor. 11:32, 33).

FAILURE IN JERUSALEM

Saul made for Jerusalem, journeying most of the way on foot and probably recalling his northward trek when he had planned to destroy the very people he now wanted to help. He had failed in Damascus. Now he was entering a veritable lions' den, for he would be meeting the Sanhedrin, who had approved of his mission to persecute the Nazarenes.

As we would expect, the Christian Jews in Jerusalem were also suspicious and afraid that Saul might be spying on them. Three years had passed since he had left the city as Saul the Pharisee; now he had returned as a convert—so he said—to the faith he had gone to destroy. Against him, too, the fury of the High Priests and the Council and the antagonism of his own

Hellenist friends from Cilicia and Asia Minor. He was, therefore, welcomed by no one. At last, he found in Barnabas a friend who would listen to him and who believed in his story of what had happened on the Damascus Road. Barnabas told Peter and James and they accepted him also. Saul stayed with Peter for fifteen days. It is a pity that we have no account of what they talked about, but we may be sure that Peter admitted his denials of His Master and told Saul a great deal about His Lord.

But when the Hellenists met Saul they regarded him as a traitor to their own faith, for they had accepted Judaism to the extent of circumcision. They refused to listen to him as he preached in the very Cilician synagogue in which Stephen had taught; they even plotted to kill him. Saul had failed in Jerusalem.

RETURN TO TARSUS

The "brethren" took him to the port of Caesarea, from where he sailed to Tarsus, his home. We may perhaps wonder how Saul and his father met and how he explained to his father the remarkable change in his life. From later references it is believed that Saul then preached for some ten years in Cilicia and Syria (Acts 11:25; Gal. 1:11–2:10) during which time some of the experiences narrated in II Corinthians 11:23–30, may have occurred, since not all of them are accounted for in *Acts*.

Saul's return home was in about A.D. 34. Were the thoughts that filled his mind then such as these?

If Jesus Christ is a Man—
And only a man—I say
That of all mankind I cleave to him,
And to him will I cleave alway.

If Jesus Christ is a God—
And the only God—I swear
I will follow Him through heaven
    and hell,
The earth, the sea, the air!
        —Richard Watson Gilder

6

Accepting the Gentiles

(ACTS 9:31-12:23)

From this time there was peace. We can appreciate the wry smile on Luke's face as he wrote, "Then had the churches rest . . ." Saul had given them a great deal of anxiety as a persecutor and not much less as a preacher! Now that he had left them altogether, the churches might settle to quiet progress and organization.

PETER'S PREACHING TOUR

Peter now moved freely amongst the people, on a preaching tour. He came to Lydda, a village in the fertile plain below the foothills of Judaea. Here he healed Aeneas, a paralyzed man. Note that he said, "Jesus Christ healeth thee," not, "I." To make one's bed means to roll it up. It was, of course, a thin mattress or woven mat. This incident is an echo of two miracles performed by Jesus; even Peter's words recall those of Jesus (Mark 2:11; John 5:8).

Eight miles away, among its orange groves and on the Mediterranean coast, was Joppa (Jaffa), famed in the days of Solomon when cedars from Lebanon were floated down the coast from Tyre and then sent overland to Jerusalem to be used for the Temple building. Here had lived Dorcas (the Greek name for the Aramaic Tabitha). She had been a loved member of "the Way" and was much mourned when she died. Peter was sent for and when he arrived he found, as had His Master when He had gone to see Jairus' daughter, that the mourners were already there, mourning and wailing as was their custom. Like Jesus, Peter sent them away. Like Jesus, he prayed, and then said "Tabitha, arise." She awoke from her sleep of death. The news spread quickly and more believers joined the fast-growing church.

Peter stayed in Joppa, living at the house of another Simon, a tanner of skins. Simon's chief work would be the preparation of whole skins for wine and water.

He would see that the ends of the sheep or goatskins once covering the feet and neck were securely closed and then hang each skin in the smoke of a slow-burning fire. In this way the hide was roughly tanned. As the swaying skins hung and twisted over the fire they often appeared like bottles (see Ps. 119:83).

Normally, of course, a Jew would not dream of staying with a person of this occupation. For one thing, he was a non-Jew, a Gentile; for another, his work meant handling the skins of dead animals, and this in itself was an "unclean" occupation. But Peter, a Galilean and a disciple of Jesus, was beginning to see that a man's work did not make him any the less acceptable to His Master. He was beginning to change his mind about the people in His Master's Kingdom. He was already seeing that Gentiles themselves might be brought into the Church, and that the keeping of rites and ceremonies of the Jewish Law were not really necessary. As Stephen had said, the Law of Jesus was stronger than the Law of Moses.

PETER AND CORNELIUS

He was to learn this lesson once and for all. Thirty miles along the coast was the Roman garrison city of Caesarea, where was stationed a centurion named Cornelius. He was one of the six centurions whose men made up the Roman cohort of 600 soldiers on garrison duty at headquarters. Like the centurion of Capernaum, who had given to the Jews there a very fine synagogue (Part III), Cornelius believed in the Jewish faith and worshiped at the synagogue in Caesarea. But, unlike the other centurion, he did not know Jesus. He was a "God-fearer," one of those who formed the bridge between the two faiths. The Jews probably hoped that he would eventually accept the full rites of Judaism, be circumcized and be a converted Jew. But, like other proselytes, he was now interested in this new faith by means of which he could become a follower of the Jews' Messiah, and a member of this new church, without first becoming a Jew.

He must have heard about Peter, his preaching and his miracles. Inspired in a vision, he sent to Joppa to ask Peter to come and see him. Two of his reliable slaves and a trusted soldier of his band went on their master's errand.

Meanwhile, possibly thinking over Philip's work in Samaria and his baptizing of the Ethiopian, Peter must have pondered on what these events meant for the Kingdom of Jesus. He had gone to the roof-top to meditate. It was the sixth hour of the day—noon—and time for the midday meal. He was hungry and it is not surprising that his thoughts went to food. From the housetop he could see the white sails of ships in the harbor. In his vision, those sails became sheets filled with animals; and a Voice told him to "kill and eat." Peter saw that the animals were those that a Jew was forbidden to touch; they were "unclean" and "common" (Lev. 11:1–32, 46, 47). Strict Jews today refuse similar food for the same reasons; they eat only "kosher" or "clean" meat. When Peter refused to eat, the Voice said, "What God hath cleansed, call thou not unclean." This happened three times.

Still wondering what such a vision could mean, Peter descended the outer stone stairs to the courtyard, where he found three visitors—non-Jews. They had come to see him, on the order of their master, but by the guidance of God. Peter then knew that what he had been told by God was that ceremonial law could be waived or ignored. The Gentiles he had been taught to regard as "unclean" were, in fact, as good as he was. Made, too, by God, they were acceptable to Him. This was a tremendous discovery for Peter to make. Even Caiaphas the High Priest had once refused to go near to a Roman— Pontius Pilate — for fear he would be made "unclean" for the Passover. Now

Peter was to go right into the home of a Roman and actually to preach to him. Up till now the Gospel had been only for the Jews; now it was to be given without question to the Gentiles.

AT CAESAREA

Next day he and some friends started for Caesarea, where Cornelius had gathered his household and friends. The apostle arrived the next day. Cornelius greeted him as one sent from God and in kneeling gave Peter the homage he would have given to any of his Roman gods. Peter bade him remember that he was but a man, adding that as a Jew he really ought not to enter the house. He looked around the room with its marble and mosaic floor, furnished with Roman tables and divans, hung with silk curtains. He saw men and women in their Roman togas and gowns, soldiers resplendent in their various uniforms, slaves peeping from doorways. Peter was far from overawed. Nor did he feel "unclean" in this Gentile house. There was something in the atmosphere that made him feel the presence of God and His Master. He asked, "Why have you sent for me?" Cornelius told him of his vision and Peter knew that he was to break down the last barrier of the new faith and accept these Gentiles into "the Way."

So he preached to them the Risen Christ, and as he did so the power of the Holy Spirit came upon them all. Thrilled with their new experience, they "spoke with tongues" and burst into praise. Even Peter and his friends were amazed at what could be but a miracle—that Gentiles should receive the Holy Spirit. Peter, now convinced and, as always, a man of action, ordered baptism with water as the formal sign that the Roman household had been admitted into the Church.

PETER IN JERUSALEM

We are not surprised to find that on his return to Jerusalem Peter was sent for by the Jewish section of the church for questioning. They charged him with having broken the Jewish law—as he had, of course — by mixing with uncircumcised Gentiles always regarded as "unclean." One of the Jews' ceremonies was to wash up to the elbows before touching food, not because it was hygienic to do so but in order to cleanse themselves of contagion they might have caught from contact with Gentiles while in the street or market place or Temple Court.

Peter did not "explain"; he merely recounted his vision and what followed it, pointing out that the Romans had received the Lord's unmistakable baptism of the Holy Spirit—and who was he "to withstand God"? The Jewish disciples accepted this as the sign that God had opened the Church to the Gentiles also, but, as we shall see, many of them had misgivings and were not fully satisfied. In any case, these occasions were reasonably near to Jerusalem and there was no sign, as yet, that it would spread.

ANTIOCH IN SYRIA

Meanwhile, persecuted Jews of the Dispersion had done great work in cities throughout Phoenicia, Cyprus, and Syria, whose capital city Antioch—known for its idolatry and superstitious beliefs—became, amazingly, the new center of the Christian faith in that area. The city—"Queen of the East," "Antioch the Beautiful," the third city of the Roman Empire—was a Greek city named after Antiochus I in 300 B.C. (See Part II, Chapter 11). It was now much larger, having been captured in 64 B.C. and developed by the Romans. Many of its people were pleasure-loving with little thought for anything but wealth, luxury, and selfish enjoyment: some, as we shall see, had higher thoughts of life and worship.

Antioch was sixteen miles up the river from the Great Sea, standing on the bank of the Orontes River, with Seleucia as its seaport. A huge statue of Charon, who ferried the dead across the Styx in Hades, had been cut out of the mountainside on the orders of the hated Antiochus Epiphanes. It overlooked the colonnaded white marble avenue that ran straight and true for nearly five miles from east to west of the city. The city walls must have been tremendous, for remains today show parts eleven feet wide and forty feet high with look-out towers every fifty yards. The ruins of Trajan's huge amphitheater for gladiatorial displays and chariot racing remind us of the Roman feats of building and engineering. All the luxury of Rome and the magnificence of Greece was in Antioch — public baths, central heating, street lighting, drainage systems, fountains, arenas, temples, gardens, and statues. The well-to-do lived in well-de-

signed villas; the less wealthy occupied blocks of several stories like our modern blocks of flats.

The whole world seemed to meet in the streets of Antioch — Syrians, Jews, Greeks, Romans, Phoenicians, Phrygians, Egyptians. The Imperial Legate, Caesar's chief governor, was stationed there. Traders from faraway lands, with their enormous caravans, moved to and from its markets, thronging the bazaars and booths, bartering with metalworkers, leatherworkers, dyers, dealing in silks, cloths, spices, and pottery. Yet to its busy streets had come a group of Nazarenes, some from Cyprus—the island off the coast—many from Jerusalem. By their preaching these Nazarenes had brought the Good News of the Kingdom of Jesus. And people had listened and believed.

Peter saw his vision on the flat house top.

They had thrown away their gods and charms, and had accepted the happiness and joy offered by the new teaching.

"CALLED CHRISTIANS IN ANTIOCH"

Someone in Antioch must have referred to the Nazarenes' belief in Christ —perhaps in scorn and contempt, perhaps only in jest—for he called them "Christ-ians"—Christians. It was only a nickname, but from that time it was a name borne by all followers of Jesus; to this day they are called by the same name (Acts 26:28; I Peter 4:16).

This sudden extension of the Church annoyed the Jews in Jerusalem. They still did not accept the claim that the crucified Jesus was the Christ, the promised Messiah; they preferred to call these people the Nazarenes. But the name "Christian" had come to stay.

It was not long before the apostles in Jerusalem became anxious about this branch of the Nazarene church for a very different reason. Here was a serious challenge to the main sect in Jerusalem, for it was seen that races other than Jews were joining the Christians and the longed-for dream that Israel had of being God's ·chosen nation seemed to be shattered. These Gentiles were uncircumcised and therefore "unclean"; surely it was necessary for them to be "made obedient unto the law"—to be made full Jews—before being accepted. If not, they could even pass beyond the barrier in the Temple Court, and this would break forever the covenant between Moses and God (Acts 21:27–30).

Of course, Peter had accepted Cornelius, and the heads of the Church in Jerusalem had seen the reason and felt that this was an isolated occasion. But this movement in Antioch was much more serious. They must find out more about it. They did not go themselves, but sent someone on their behalf. This was Barnabas, friend of Saul, "a good man and full of the Holy Ghost." He was a Cypriot, too, and would therefore be able to speak more easily with people of his own land who had begun the movement by their preaching in Syria. Barnabas went to the meeting place of the Christians in Antioch; tradition says it was in Singon Street. After a while he may have felt it was necessary to have someone with greater powers of speech and leadership than he possessed, someone who had a wide and deep knowledge of the scriptures, too, a Jew who believed in Jesus as his Risen Lord, someone who knew the city and its people. There was only one such man—Saul of Tarsus.

So Barnabas went to Tarsus and found Saul; this was about A.D. 45. Over ten years had passed since Saul had gone home and he was now ready for whatever work was given him. He was His Master's "chosen vessel" to bear the Good News throughout the world. He and Barnabas returned to Antioch and joined the Christians, preaching and working there for a year.

FAMINE IN JUDAEA

At this time a Christian prophet, Agabus, foretold a famine for Jerusalem and Judaea. History tells us that there was in fact a famine during the early years of Claudius, one of the Roman emperors of this period (A.D. 41–54). Gifts of money and food were made by the Church in Antioch and these were given to Barnabas and Saul and Titus to take to the Apostles in Jerusalem. It is possible that Barnabas and Saul told the leaders of the Jerusalem Church that they planned to visit the cities of Asia Minor in a preaching tour (Gal. 2:1–10; Acts 11:30). On their return to Antioch they took with them John Mark (Acts 12:25; 13:5; Col. 4:10), who was related to Barnabas; he was but a youth, but anxious to be with two great men on a mission that promised excitement and adventure. You will remember that his mother's house was the meeting

Coins of Emperor Claudius, A.D. *41–54.*

place of the Apostles and where Jesus had held His Last Supper. Thus John Mark may have known Jesus, and may have seen Him arrested (Mark 14:51, 52). He looked forward to telling other people about His Master.

PERSECUTION IN JERUSALEM

Since the stoning of Stephen and the consequent fleeing of persecuted Hellenist Jews, things had been reasonably peaceful and quiet. The Apostles, trying desperately to fit their new teaching about Jesus into the framework of their own Jewish religion, had been left alone. They had continued within Judaism their own meetings and services and forms of worship.

In place of Herod Antipas—murderer of John the Baptist—had come (A.D. 39) Herod Agrippa I, grandson of Herod the Great, nephew of Herod Antipas (Parts II and III). Agrippa had been given Perea and Galilee, the tetrarchies of Philip and Antipas, by the Emperor Caligula, who had favored him in Rome. Claudius then gave him Judaea and Samaria, together with the title of King. As a Jew he opposed the idea that the crucified Christ could possibly be the Messiah; as a favorite of the Emperor he could not tolerate any suggestion of another king. He therefore decided to crush out any believers still left in the land. He knew that at least he would have the Pharisees and Sadducees on his side.

He chose Passover as his best time to strike. Just before the feast he sent his soldiers to arrest James, the brother of

John, the "beloved disciple." You will recall that James and John, the sons of Zebedee, together with Peter, were the three disciples closest to Jesus. Because it was so near Passover, James' trial—if he had one—was short and, like that of His Master, entirely unlawful. James was executed with the sword, the first Apostle to die for Jesus.

Agrippa's next arrest was swift. Peter was thrown into prison, below the dungeon of Antonia. When Passover was ended he would have Peter killed also. Perhaps Agrippa had heard of Peter's previous escape, so he had him securely chained between two soldiers, with two more on duty outside the cell. Each four were a quaternion.

PETER'S ESCAPE

In some miraculous way—a story vividly told in Acts 12:3–19—Peter was once again freed. Luke seems to intend the story to be taken as it stands, but some people prefer to think it is a description of Peter's release by some mysterious friend, arguing that the word "angel" means "messenger" and that Peter's rescuer could have been a man. Even so, Peter's rescue was remarkable. He hastened to the Upper Room, where he knew his friends would be gathered in prayer and anxiety for his safety. Rhoda's first peep through the grating in the door was in fear and trembling lest the knock was that of a soldier come with a guard to arrest the other Apostles. In her excited joy she returned to tell the others without letting Peter in! "It is his angel," they said. Already there was a belief in a kind of guardian angel (Matt. 18:10). We remember that the influence of such a belief came from Persia (Parts II and III). (See also in the Apocrypha, Tobit 5:21, where the angel actually travels with Tobias.) At first unbelieving, then silently, they admitted Peter, who told them how he had escaped.

He bade them tell the other James, the brother of Jesus, now chief or president of the church in Jerusalem. Next morning the Roman guards had an amazing escape to "explain," but Agrippa did not believe them and had them executed, the penalty for failing in their duty.

DEATH OF AGRIPPA

Agrippa then went to Caesarea, where a quarrel with Tyre and Sidon was settled. He had a hold over these two towns because they obtained their corn from his province of Galilee and could not afford to be his enemies. In great majesty and extravagance, the king held special shows of pomp and power. There were displays in the huge amphitheater — gladiators, athletes, conjurors, chariot racing and the like. He dressed himself in beautiful robes and jewels, and the people called out that he was a god. Thousands took up the cry

and Herod Agrippa accepted their flattery and fawning praise. Josephus, a writer of the times, says that Agrippa saw an owl on a rope over his head—an evil omen. Luke tells us simply that the king was struck with dreadful pains and was dead in three days. The people saw in it a deserved punishment for his wickedness in claiming to be a god. What is of real importance is that the first great enemy of the Christian Church had gone. Had he lived to pursue his persecution of the church in Jerusalem, the story of Christianity might perhaps not have been written. This was A.D. 44, after which the lands under Agrippa were put under the complete control of Rome. History tells us that there were outbreaks of rioting and revolts. We already know that the famine in Judaea had been foretold and this happened about A.D. 46, leading to further suffering and bloodshed.

7

The First Missionary Journey

(ACTS 13; 14)

CHOSEN FOR THE WORK

Since there were no Apostles in Antioch, the church there was organized under a small committee of five members. It is interesting to note that three of them were white, two black, and that one of them at least was a wealthy man, the half-brother of Herod the tetrarch. They discussed the work to be done and decided that the Good News should be sent farther afield. Who should take it? God's guidance (the Holy Spirit) was asked. Barnabas and Saul were chosen. This was somewhat strange, for neither of them was an original member of the group in Antioch. They had come, one as a delegate and the other as a preacher. But the Christians accepted the decision, not only because the choice had fallen to them and was believed to be God's will, but also because they recognized in Barnabas and Saul the two men who could best do the work.

IGNATIUS

It may well have been that at this very meeting in Singon Street was a lad of fifteen. Thirty years later he became the first Bishop of Antioch, Bishop Ignatius. At the age of seventy-five Ignatius was martyred for his faith. Sent to Rome A.D. 108, on the orders of Trajan, he was flung to the lions in the amphitheater. His last words were, "Let me be given to the wild beasts, for through them I can attain unto God. I am God's wheat and I am ground by the wild beasts that I may be found pure bread of Christ."

BARNABAS AND SAUL

Perhaps we wonder what these two men were like. It is difficult to say, of course, with any certainty, but some indication of their appearance may be gleaned from the narratives and letters of Paul.

Barnabas, trained as a Levite and a strict Jew, seems to have been the elder of the two, well-built and good-looking, with honest eyes and a firm mouth and chin. In Lystra the people called him Jupiter, noblest of the Roman gods, and this makes it certain that he was of fine physique. We know from the fact that he was one of the first to sell his lands and give the money to the poorer members of the early church that his religion really meant something to him. He was mild and generous, sympathetic and approachable, the "Son of Consolation." That he was a shrewd judge of character is evident, for he recognized in Saul a promising preacher and servant of God. Barnabas brought Saul from obscurity to Christian service such as the world has never since seen (Acts 9:27; 11:25, 26).

Saul — later called *Paul* — was now about forty-five years of age. He seems to have differed considerably from Barnabas in build and appearance. A second century document describes him in most uncompromising terms as "a man small in size, with meeting eyebrows, with a rather large nose, baldheaded, bow-legged. Strongly built, full of grace, for at times he looked like a man, and at times he had the face of an angel." Whatever his body, often racked with pain and fever, his face and voice had strange powers of attraction. At Lystra the people hailed him as Mercury, the messenger of the gods, small, swift, eloquent of speech; his physical courage is indicated in II Cor. 11:24. Some people believe that his eyesight was probably affected by the blinding light of his conversion (Acts 26:13) or by painful headaches. He may have had a tendency to attacks of malaria or of some other ailment. Whatever this "stake [thorn] in the flesh" (II Cor. 12:7–10) was, it was a great trial to him; you will be able to assess his courage, judgment, and devotion to his duty as you study his missionary work and read his letters.

PAUL'S METHODS

Not the least of the indications of Paul's clear mind is the way he set about his task. There was never anything haphazard about his methods. As we study the journeys we recognize his amazing ability to organize. A first glance at his travels may give the impression that his work was casual, but in actual fact he was systematic. Province by province, he moved into the chief cities for his main centers; he set up Christian groups — churches — and appointed elders whose work it was to unite the community into a kind of "mother church." When this was secure it spread its activities into the surrounding districts and smaller towns. A good example of this is seen in the church at Ephesus with its smaller church at Colossae. Paul then revisited these churches, or sent trained helpers, or wrote to explain, encourage, guide, reprove or praise.

We shall find that Paul was a wise and deep thinker. Like Jesus, he spent much time in prayer and quiet meditation. His language was practical. In Athens he spoke as a philosopher to philosophers, in Lystra, in simple Greek about the Creator; in Pisidian Antioch, as a Jew to the Jews. Once he had won his argument at the Council of Jerusalem he set out to create a world church (Gal. 3:28), and was able to adapt his words to the various peoples of that church.

Merely memorizing a list of the journeys Paul took is not the best way to come to know him. Rather, one should think of him as a man of tireless energy, a hero, a lover of adventure, and afraid of no one. He attracted men and women to his cause and inspired them to work for and with him. He was a missionary and a saint; no one did more to help the growth and development of the Christian Church. All the incidents of which we shall read illustrate various aspects of a

The harbor scene at Seleucia as it may have appeared when Paul, Barnabas and John Mark left for Cyprus.

very wonderful man who explained his secret in his letter to the Philippians—"I can do all things through Christ who strengtheneth me."

THE JOURNEY BEGINS

About A.D. 47, then, we find Barnabas and Saul and John Mark setting off on their first new adventure. The most obvious direction was toward Cyprus, partly because it was the nearest "new land" and also because it was the homeland of Barnabas, who wanted to preach first to his own people. The name Cyprus comes from a word meaning "copper"; there

were copper mines in the interior of the island.

The three men sailed the sixteen miles down the Orontes river to the port of *Seleucia,* where they boarded a small boat (large ones could not get into the harbor) to cross the eastern part of the Great Sea to the island. They landed at *Salamis,* the commercial center of the island. Here there was trading in copper, olive oil, wine, and fruits. There was a great temple to Zeus, and in the city were three forums or market places, public baths, and huge colonnaded buildings. Granite columns, called "St. Paul's Pillars" and remains of a temple still stand as they did in that

Here, the ship is off the coast and making for Cyprus.

time, but sand covers the rest, which years later was leveled to the ground by severe earthquakes. Legend says that eventually Barnabas was stoned to death in Salamis, and his body recovered by Mark and buried outside the city.

As was his custom—for Saul always preached first to his own people, the Jews — he went to the synagogue and explained his mission, preaching that the crucified Jesus was the Messiah of the new faith. Barnabas probably took the lead here, and John Mark assisted as a young helper.

They traveled through the island to the western tip, where stood *Paphos*. This was the capital city and the residence of the Roman proconsul Sergius Paulus. Valuable inscriptions have been unearthed at Paphos, giving much interesting detail about the family of the governor. Among other information, we learn that his wife and one of his sons became Christians and that another son followed his father as a Roman official in the island.

A marble forum, excavated at Salamis.

ELYMAS

Elymas (Bar-Jesus=Son of Salvation) was a sorcerer or magician—like Simon Magus—with considerable power and po-

sition. It was natural that he should regard Saul with some jealousy, and as a rival. He saw that his own position was

The Roman bath is surrounded by marble statues.

precarious if the proconsul accepted what Saul had to say. Saul, being a Roman citizen, well-educated and cultured, was the equal socially of Sergius Paulus, and they enjoyed each other's company. Like most Romans, the governor was interested in this new religion. Barnabas, too, was probably well-known as a landowner in the island. So Elymas began to feel a little disturbed. His own power seems to have been due to hypnotism. Luke, a doctor, makes it clear that Saul treated him, as we say, with "his own medicine." Paul "fixed his eyes upon him." Elymas could not withstand the strength of Saul's eyes; his blindness and consequent defeat ruined him in the eyes of the islanders. From this time, Paul uses his Roman name and becomes the chief speaker, and Barnabas tends to drop into the background. Even Luke reverses the order in which he speaks of them, and says . . . "Paul and Barnabas. . . ." The events described brought many to accept the Christian faith, for they and Sergius Paulus were "astounded at what Paul taught about the Lord Jesus."

In Paphos—a Greek church on the site of a Roman temple. Legend says that Paul was tied to one of these pillars and beaten.

JOHN MARK RETURNS

There was probably a trading ship bearing copper, fruits (lemons and olives), olive oil, and wine, on its way from Paphos to the coast of Asia Minor. The friends boarded the ship, which sailed due north, putting in at *Perga,* about eight miles up river. Paul may have suffered from the effects of malaria while staying here, in this low-lying area of marshland and swamps, so he decided to press forward into the higher, healthier mountain range that loomed in the distance. But he was to be much disappointed before he did so, for John Mark now made up his mind to return home. We do not know why, but there may have been many reasons. He was but a lad and was probably homesick; perhaps he was afraid of the perils of the mountain journey. The nearest town of any size was a hundred miles away, through dangerous mountain paths and by lonely roads. In the pine woods that fringed the foothills lurked bandit murderers and wild beasts; the thought of what these might do must have made him fearful.

Perhaps, too, John Mark was a little jealous of Paul's success. He was disappointed at seeing his cousin Barnabas take second place; it meant that he, John, was a little less important, too. Barnabas did not blame Mark and was perhaps more sympathetic toward him than was Paul; but that Paul was really angry at what he regarded as weakness and cowardice is seen later, when he planned the second journey and refused to take Mark with him (Acts 15:36–40; but see also II Tim. 4:11). Mark joined another ship bound for Caesarea or Joppa, and so returned to Jerusalem.

TO ANTIOCH IN PISIDIA

Meanwhile, Paul and Barnabas and his friends—"the company"—continued their dangerous way over the forbidding Taurus mountains, "in perils often" from man and beast, until they at last reached the city of *Antioch.* This city was called Pisidian Antioch to distinguish it from two other Antiochs, one of these being Paul's starting point in Syria. Actually, it was in Phrygia, but lay very near the border of the neighboring province of Pisidia. Once a Greek city, it was now a Roman colony, fortified and garrisoned, of course, with Roman legionaries to assist the ex-service men already settled there as part of the Roman plan for law and order. It was the chief city of the Roman province of Galatia, which included the smaller lands already mentioned. A fine Roman aqueduct brought water from the hills; now the city is gone and the aqueduct a mass of rubble and stones.

It was a prosperous city, and, as was usual in the larger towns, there was a Jewish quarter, made up of the many Jews who had come to Antioch to trade and make money. They had their own synagogue, of course. The Romans worshiped their own goddess Cybele—sometimes called Diana or Artemis, the Great Mother of All—in a magnificent temple.

As usual, when Paul was sufficiently recovered from his illness and the tiring journey, they entered the synagogue. We remember that synagogue services were exactly the same throughout the Jewish settlements, and wherever a Jew went he could follow and understand them. Among the congregation were the usual proselytes, the "God-fearers." Paul and Barnabas probably took with them on their journeys their precious fringed "taliths" or praying tunics. (Nowadays in Jewish synagogues men wear praying shawls as taliths.) The ruler or chief rabbi, called the *chazzan,* noticing the two authoritative strangers, invited them to speak. Paul and Barnabas knew their Jewish law thoroughly and Paul, at least, was a fully qualified rabbi. He took the lead, as we might expect.

PAUL'S SPEECH

We have here the first recorded speech of Paul. It is significant in its form, for it follows very nearly the speeches of both Peter and Stephen. In places it is strongly reminiscent of Stephen and we cannot help but think that Paul had him in mind as he spoke. He preached to the Jews first, to the proselytes afterward—to the "men of Israel and you who heed God." He traced the history of the Jews and won his hearers by the sheer power of his words and obvious knowledge, his quotations from the scriptures strengthening each point he made. He told them that the Messiah had come (Acts 13:23, 24). He had been crucified—that must have horrified them. God had raised Him from the dead. . . . What were they to make of that? This, said Paul, was proof of the Messiahship of Jesus and that obedience to Him was of greater importance than obedience to the Law. This was indeed a new teaching for these Jews. By keeping the Law they were endeavoring to "keep on the right side" of God. They found this hard to do and therefore felt that they could never obtain the full goodness of God. But Paul said that Christianity made it possible for them to come to God in their weakness and He would make them strong. It was Christ who had brought forgiveness for the sins they committed in not reaching the standard of living set by their own Law, and people had only to believe in Christ to be "saved." The Christian did not serve God to keep on the right side of Him, but because he was glad Jesus had lived, died, and risen again for him. The Jews were interested and the proselytes were most impressed. Here was a religion they could follow without accepting those tiresome rites and ceremonies of the Jews. What was more important, it was a religion they could understand and believe in. We need to remember that at such a distance from Jerusalem these Jews—Hellenist Jews of the Dispersion—were out of touch with the real facts of the Crucifixion and certainly of the Resurrection, although some of them had been there for the festivals. So Paul's preaching was astonishing in every way and they needed time to think about what he had said. They asked him to speak to them on the following sabbath.

"LO, WE TURN TO THE GENTILES"

During the week, however, some of the stricter Jews realized that Paul was offering his message to the Gentiles as well. They were jealous, for the Messiah was theirs alone. His chosen people were the Jews and only the Jews. So we are not surprised to find that immediately Paul began his sermon on the following sabbath, the Jews interrupted him and tried to stop him. Paul was at first perplexed, then hurt, then furious. His next words were not a hasty decision. For many years he must have given careful thought to what he was now about to say; and he must have talked it over with Barnabas. Though himself a strict Jew he had known all along that Jesus had died for *all* His people. On the guidance of the Apostles in Jerusalem he had come to preach to the Jews only, though the Gentiles might also listen and believe, too. But now, the Jews were the very ones who were preventing him from spreading his Good News. They were denying him and defying him—even blaspheming the holy name of Jesus. Let it be so, said Paul. Seeing that they were unworthy of everlasting life—"lo, we turn to the Gentiles!"

The Jews could hardly believe their ears, but the Gentiles heard him with great joy. This tremendous decision was the turning point of the Christian Church, a complete revolution. For it meant that now all Gentiles who believed in the risen Christ could accept Him and be accepted by the Church without the rules, regulations and ceremonies of the Jews. This was a religion of love—love for and obedience to a *Person,* and this could replace obedience to laws and rules.

A month or so passed, but the Jews had been plotting. Urged on by the influential "honorable women" of the synagogue — the wives and daughters of wealthy Roman proselytes — the angry Jews planned to drive Paul and Barnabas from the city. In the interests of law and order, the city magistrates instructed the two to leave. They did so. On the outskirts of the city they took off their sandals and shook them to show that they regarded the Jews as having hindered their work (see Matt. 10:14 and Luke 9:5).

TOWARD THE EAST

The missionaries made their way along the fine new road for some ninety miles, when they came to *Iconium* (Konieh), a Greek city of Phrygia on the borders of Lycaonia. It was high on the plateau of Asia Minor, the mountains rising to the northwest (see map). This journey was considerably less difficult because there was easier means of transport, perhaps by mule, even in a wagon of some kind. There were marching soldiers on the route, travelers, traders, long strings of camels laden with merchandise, pilgrims, and, occasionally, Roman processions of wealthy people returning to or from the far coast. Wayside khans and inns offered rest and food and conversation by the brazier, and Paul and Barnabas would learn much from traders and pilgrims; they, in turn, would speak of Jesus and so spread their work farther afield than they would ever know.

Acts 14:1, tells us that many of the Jews accepted what Paul had to say, but the rulers of the synagogues were jealous of the Greeks, who showed great interest. Arguments led to violence and the two decided it would be safer to leave the town and proceed to *Lystra.*

IN LYSTRA

This city, some twenty miles further southwest, was mainly a Roman colony, with its Jewish and Greek quarters. Here

The ruined Temple of Jupiter in Baalbek, 35 miles from Damascus. Perhaps the temple at Lystra was similar to this one.

they were welcomed and stayed four or five months. During this time it is more than likely that Paul saw the altar dedicated to Augustus Caesar as a god and realized more vividly that here was something he would have to contend with in the future—the worship of the Roman Emperor. For to preach against such a thing would be treason—and that would mean death. This altar still stands on the hill outside Lystra—or Lustra, as the Romans called it.

Paul's first recorded miracle was performed here. The healing of the lame man was done "in the name of Jesus." There was a legend in Lystra that the gods Zeus (Roman Jupiter) chief of the gods, and Hermes (Roman Mercury) messenger of the gods, had once appeared and had been rejected by all the people except Philemon and Baucis who had been the only survivors of the flood sent by the gods as punishment. Now, seeing the miracle, the people immediately imagined that the gods had come again. They shouted and argued excitedly in their Lycaonian tongue, which was unfamiliar to Paul who did not at first realize what they were about to do. But when he saw them preparing a sacrifice at the gates of the temple of Jupiter outside the city, he knew at once. He and Barnabas had to rush from the market place to stop the priests, tearing their cloaks as they did so as a sign of grief and distress.

Paul spoke to them in Greek, a tongue they would all understand. He spoke of God as the Creator of all nature and urged them to change their ways. The mob was gradually restrained from its first intentions, and slowly realized that the two were merely men. In this mood of disappointment they were easily encouraged into anger, and it needed very little cunning on the part of jealous Jews, who had by now come from Iconium and Antioch, to arouse them against Paul and Barnabas. It needed only one stone to begin the attack and, like the first martyr Stephen, whose death he had watched, Paul was struck to the ground. Bruised and bleeding from sharp-edged rocks, his maimed body was left for dead and for the vultures to swoop down on and devour. But, unlike Stephen, Paul recovered; he still had great work to do for His Master.

In the crowd, jostled and frightened and anxious for Paul, was a young lad named Timothy (16:1) who was to remember this dreadful incident for many years (II Tim. 3:11, 14, 15). It may have been his mother Eunice and his grandmother Lois who attended to Paul and nursed him in secret. We shall hear of Timothy again.

THE RETURN TO ANTIOCH

They made a short visit to *Derbe,* where Gaius was converted. Near Derbe —even to this day—are found Roman milestones marking the route at every one thousand paces, and Greek altars among fragments of pottery, granite, and marble. Paul and Barnabas decided not to go farther eastward. Perhaps Paul wanted to do his work in Roman territory. The Jews had not come to Derbe, probably because they believed that Paul was now dead. But the two friends returned fearlessly through *Lystra* and *Iconium.* It seems that they were allowed there because they did not speak openly. Their work was to organize the groups of believers into churches whose "elders" could then control the work to be done. They continued to Pisidian *Antioch.*

We now find that Luke's narrative moves swiftly and with very little detail. The Apostles, as the two are now called, preach in Pisidia and Pamphylia and then set sail from *Attalia* southeast to *Seleucia* and thence to *Antioch* in Syria—home, after an absence of two years and a journey of fourteen hundred miles!

JEWS AND GENTILES

Paul and Barnabas went at once to Singon Street, where they recounted their adventures and success. The church listened with joy to all they had to say, but were especially impressed when Paul told them how God had "opened the door of faith unto the Gentiles." This door of faith was the acceptance of Gentiles into the church without their having to take upon themselves the full burden of the Jewish Law and Tradition. It was, of course, not the Jewish faith but the new Christian faith based on belief in Jesus the crucified as the risen Messiah. This was certain to be questioned by the Christian Jews in Jerusalem. These insisted that all Gentiles wishing to enter the church must first be circumcised according to the Law of Moses and become Jews. Circumcision was the outward sign of the Covenant between God and His chosen people. All Jewish baby boys were circumcised when only eight days old; it was a definite Law of Moses (Gen. 17:10–13; Lev. 12:3; Luke 2:21). The Jews therefore argued that if the Gentiles were also to be accepted as chosen people, it was only right that they should first become Jews by circumcision. Delegates were sent from Jerusalem to Antioch to make this plain to the church there. Among them may have been Peter, for Paul tells us in Galatians 2:11–14, that he argued with Peter over this question, pointing out that Peter himself had accepted Gentiles (Cornelius, especially) and had eaten with them. But Peter had shown some fear of what the other Jews of Jerusalem thought, until Paul chided him for trying to make the Gentiles do what he was not doing himself. Perhaps this is why we find Peter on the side of Paul at the meeting in Jerusalem, when the whole subject was discussed.

EPISTLE TO GALATIANS

It was necessary for Paul and Barnabas to report to Jerusalem on their tour; in any case, Paul was determined to settle once and for all the position of the Gentiles. It is believed by some scholars that it was on his way to Jerusalem that Paul wrote his letter to the churches he had visited in Galatia. This would now be about A.D. 48–49 (Acts 11:1–18; 15: 1–29; Gal. 1:15–2:14). Other scholars prefer to date it somewhat later, A.D. 52. It was written to the pagan people who had become members of the churches Paul and Barnabas had set up. It is an angry letter. Some Jewish Christians from Jerusalem had sent preachers to these churches to say that Paul's teaching was false and that the people should accept circumcision like the Apostles in Jerusalem and become full Jews. Paul was furious, yet astonished that such lies should not only be spoken but actually believed. To him the survival of the Christian Church was at stake (Gal. 6: 15). He is angry and tender by turns; sometimes he is bitter and affectionate. He emphasizes his own authorship by signing his name. He does this in large letters, perhaps because of his bad eyesight. Read his letter in a modern version.

Jupiter, the chief Roman God.

8

The Council at Jerusalem

(ACTS 15)

THE DISPUTE

It is clear that Paul does not agree with the demands of the Apostles in Jerusalem and that a meeting between them is likely to be one of arguments and bitterness unless they can come to a solution to which they can all agree. We do not know where they met, but it is possible that they gathered at the house of John Mark, in the familiar Upper Room.

James, the brother of Jesus, was now Bishop of Jerusalem. The word "bishop" here does not mean quite the same as it does today; James was the president or chief apostle of the Christian Church of the believing Jews. He was, of course, a strict Jew and kept the usual Jewish ceremonies as well as the services and meetings of the Christians. He was the leader of the Judaistic party. Opposing him was Paul, also a strict Jew (in up-bringing, at least) and leader of the Christian party in Antioch. Because of his wider experience and education, Paul had greater sympathy with the Gentile groups than had any of the Jerusalem Jews. Each opponent was certain that he was right and each were sure that God's authority was on his side. Argument might lead to a serious split in the Church, but James and Paul both hoped it might be checked.

Perhaps we feel strongly that Paul was right. If so, we must not overlook the fact there was good reason for the Jerusalem Jews to feel anxious. They did not wish to be outnumbered by Gentile converts, for they knew how strong was the idolatry and heathen worship of the non-Jews and how quickly these same Gentiles might forget their new beliefs and even bring into their worship the evil heathen forms of worship they had once practiced. The Christian Jews remembered, too, that Jesus and they (His disciples) were Jews, that their beliefs were governed by the Law of Moses,

338

First century catacomb paintings of Peter and Paul. Peter has thick gray hair and beard; Paul's is receding and dark and his beard is pointed.

obedience to which was to bring in the Kingdom of God.

DISCUSSION OF THE PROBLEM

The real question they had to answer seemed to be this—was the new Christian Church part of the old Judaism, tied to the Law of Moses, or was it something entirely new, offering to believers everywhere—Jews and non-Jews—the opportunity of being Christ-followers? In other words—which was important, the baptism of the Holy Spirit or the rite of circumcision? Both sides realized that underlying the question was the fact that if the Law was all-important Christ had lived and died for no real purpose at all.

In the actual debate Paul has very little to say. After preliminary "disputing" it is Peter who takes charge. It is possible that his meeting with Paul had made clear in his own mind what decision he should take and for whom he should speak. He recounts his own experience with Cornelius, and argues that forcing the Law on the Gentiles would be to make a burden that even they as born Jews could not carry. It was not God's wish that this should be done. The grace of the Lord Jesus was sufficient and the Gospel was universal — for everybody (Gal. 2:21; Col. 3:11). Barnabas and Paul then tell of their travels and newly-formed churches. They make it abundantly clear that they did these things under the influence of the Holy Spirit and the power of God. We note here the reversed order of their names; in Jerusalem Barnabas—as their delegate—is still the more important; Paul, even now, is not fully accepted by the Apostles. James and Peter—and perhaps others—appear to be impartial, but there is obviously a small but powerful group against Paul.

THE CHURCH DECIDES

If you have read the verses telling of this debate and have pictured this solemn meeting of serious men, you will have felt something of the atmosphere of challenge between them. You will also experience the great sense of relief when James announces his decision. To everybody's surprise, perhaps, he accepts the arguments and proofs of the experiences of Peter and Paul. One cannot help feeling that he ignores the missionaries, turning rather to the scriptures (Amos 9:11) to strengthen his points. The Gentiles need *not* accept circumcision. We can imagine the sigh of agreement from all sides. But —there were heathen practices that the Gentiles must give up so that their lives would become clean and pure and fit to offer to Jesus Christ. They must keep three rules:

1. No sharing in any form of heathen worship and sacrifices.
2. No wrong living, especially of the kind found in such heathen worship.
3. No bloodshed of any kind, even the eating of meat from which the blood has not been removed or which has been offered to idols (Lev. 7:26; 17:10).

The missionaries returned to Antioch carrying this decision in a letter from the "Apostles and elders unto the brethren of the Gentiles." They were happy at the success of their meeting in Jerusalem. Judas, Barsabas and Silas accompanied them in order to explain further—from the Jerusalem point of view—any matter not clear in the letter. Silas stayed in Antioch.

Closer study of Paul's letters shows that there was still strong feeling on the part of the Jews in Jerusalem. The decision was really a compromise, that is, it was not finally a satisfactory answer for both sides. It made clear that there were still two groups—the Jews and the Gentiles. It was many years before the Jews will-

ingly joined with the Gentiles in worship, for the belief that it was "unclean" for a Jew to mix with—certainly to eat and drink with—a Gentile, was ingrained from their earliest training and could not lightly be thrown on one side. Even in Antioch the separate groups are seen (Gal. 2:11). In Jerusalem the Christian Church tended to remain strongly Jewish and even anti-Paul (Acts 21:20, 21; Rom. 15:31). Most of the group fled A.D. 65, when under persecution they found safety in Pella on the east of the Jordan. Pella was a Greek city, where they would meet Hellenist Jews. We wonder how they met and if they joined together under the fear of persecution. Five years later than this, A.D. 70, as Jesus had foretold, Jerusalem itself was laid waste. But by then the Christian faith had spread far and wide and was something that Roman oppression could not stamp out.

WHAT HAPPENED TO PETER?

This is the last time we hear of Peter. Legend has it that he went to Rome. It is believed that about A.D. 64 he gave to Mark the stories of Jesus that he had been preaching for the past thirty years; Mark's Gospel certainly reflects Peter's blunt, impetuous character. Imprisoned under Nero's persecutions, he is said to have escaped, but, meeting His Master, asked *Quo vadis?* ("Where are you going?") Jesus said He was going to Rome to be crucified afresh. Peter returned, and was imprisoned with Paul. Led out together to die, Peter bade Paul goodbye and was crucified—as he had asked —head downward, unworthy to die as His Master had died. Over his supposed tomb in Vatican Fields now stands the great Cathedral of St. Peter.

9

The Second Missionary Journey

(ACTS 15:36-18:22)

It was now A.D. 49. Paul and Barnabas planned to revisit the churches they had set up in Galatia during their previous preaching tour. But there was an unhappy disagreement between them over John Mark. Barnabas wished to take him, as before, but—still angry at John's leaving them at Perga—Paul refused to let him join them on this second journey (but see II Tim. 4:11). Barnabas therefore took Mark with him and sailed to Cyprus. Paul chose Silas, of whom we have already heard. Silas was also a Roman citizen, his Roman name being Silvanus (I Thess. 1:1; II Thess. 1:1). They traveled in the opposite direction, northward through Syria and Cilicia (I Pet. 5:12).

TIMOTHY

Passing *Derbe* they now reached *Lystra,* where, you will recall, lived Timothy. Paul had a great affection for the lad and saw in him a promising preacher and worker for Jesus. Timothy's mother was a Jewess, but his father was a Greek, a Gentile. But Paul wanted to train him as a missionary and decided it would be better to make Timothy technically a full Jew by having him circumcised. This would make it easier for Timothy to lodge and mingle with the stricter Jews without question; he could eat with them and take part in the synagogue services (I Tim. 1:18; 4:14; II Tim. 1:6; cf. Gal. 5:11).

THROUGH ASIA MINOR

Paul, Silas, and Timothy took copies of the letter made at the Council of Jerusalem to each Christian community, but there is no record that they continued to do so with all the new churches. They moved through *Iconium* and *Antioch* in the provinces of Phrygia and Galatia (South Galatia), westward toward Mysia, intending to enter Bithynia (see map). They reached *Troas,* an important seaport on the western coast of Asia Minor. Here they must have seen the enormous Greek theater, in which actors of comedy and tragedy attracted vast crowds to watch and cheer the Greek plays. Sometimes the same crowds went to see racing and fighting and even murder in gladiatorial shows. Overlooking the sea was the gymnasium where young Greeks raced naked for the honour of winning the race, their only reward a crown of olive or laurel leaves. Even today we speak of "winning our laurels." There was wrestling and javelin-throwing and discus-throwing. Troas was once called Troy, famed in Greek stories.

PAUL MEETS LUKE

The really important fact for us is that at Troas Paul met the man who was to write his life story. This was Luke, a Greek doctor. The narrative says that Paul saw a man in a vision who asked him to go over to Macedonia—to Greece —and so to Europe. Had Paul never obeyed his urge to by-pass Mysia and come down to Troas, despite his intentions of going to Bithynia, the story of his life work—indeed of Christianity— might never have been written; it would certainly have been a different story. Some scholars believe that Paul was inspired by his new friend and thought deeply about him and of what he told him. He then decided to cross the Aegean Sea to Greece. Luke appears to have been from the city of Philippi and was probably about to return home. The friendship begun between the two men encouraged Luke to persuade Paul to go with him.

One of the interesting points about Luke's narrative is that every so often there is a passage containing the pronoun "we"; such passages are called "we" sections. They indicate that Luke was actually present at the time of the events he describes (see Introduction). The first of these appears now, immediately after Paul's vision, told in Acts 16:10-17.

Being a doctor, Luke was able to look after Paul and treat him for his painful

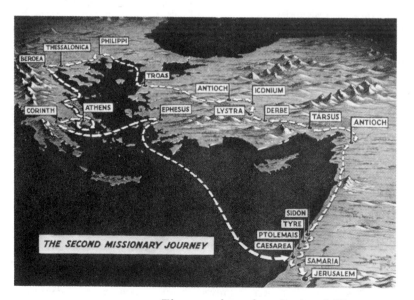

The map shows how Paul and Silas traveled to Europe.

complaint—his "thorn in the flesh." One of the most pathetic phrases in Paul's second letter to Timothy is proof of Luke's love and care for him. It is the sentence, "Only Luke is with me." Paul was in prison in Rome, and his other friends had fled.

Paul's decision to go with Luke brought Christianity to Europe. Boarding a small trading ship, they sailed swiftly across the Hellespont, taking only two days because of the favorable winds; the return journey later on (20:6) took five days. *Samothracia* was an island half-way across. They landed at *Neapolis* (Kavalla), a seaport nestling below a hill on which stood a temple to Venus. Eight miles farther on, they reached the Greek city of *Philippi*.

IN PHILIPPI

This was now a Roman colony, proudly described by Luke as "the first of the district." It had been begun by Augustus Caesar to mark the beginning of the Roman Empire. It was here that Octavius and Antony had defeated Brutus and Cassius. Today its ruins lie beneath many feet of rubble from which have been unearthed tesselated pavements, part of the forum, and stretches of the famous Via Egnatia, one of the great Roman highways.

Finding no synagogue—there being very few Jews in the locality and not enough to form one—Paul and his companions set out to find a group of Jews. About a mile north of the city, by the riverside, they came across a group—all women. It was a favorable spot for such meetings, for there was water for baptism and ceremonial washing. The leader was Lydia. She was a "God-fearer." As a "seller of purple" she was a wealthy woman and had probably come from Thyatira, a town famous for its dyes. The purple dye was most likely obtained by trading with Phoenicia for its sea shells,

which, crushed and boiled, gave the dye. Lydia therefore dealt with royalty and well-to-do people, who bought robes of silk and fine linen from her (see Luke 16:19; 23:53; Mark 15:17). She offered hospitality to Paul, accepting his message about Jesus and being baptized with all her household.

IMPRISONED

The Apostles continued their work for some days but soon became aware of a tiresome girl who pestered them with her cries. She possessed "powers of divination" which enabled her to tell fortunes and "look into the future." She was a medium or kind of crystal-gazer; she may even have been a ventriloquist. Whatever her powers, she made money for her masters by performing for them. Something in her crazy mind told her that Paul and his friends had greater power and were men of God. Tired of her shouts, Paul turned to her. It was still believed that mad people were possessed of an evil spirit, and, like Jesus years before, Paul ordered the spirit to come out, doing it "in the name of Jesus." The poor creature, probably feeling that this same Jesus was giving her a clear mind and freedom, felt her madness go and became a healthy-minded girl once more. Naturally, the men who employed her and made money out of her gifts were furious, for they saw at once that she had lost her magical powers and was normal. They forced Paul and Silas to appear before the chiefs of police. The city, like all Roman cities, was governed by a *senate* and two magistrates who were called *praetors*. There were also *lictors* who carried a bundle of rods called *fasces* which were used for punishing culprits and offenders against the law. (The sign of the Italian Fascists in the Second World War was a bundle of such rods.)

The angry men made their charge, but note that it had nothing to do with their own loss; they were too cunning for that. They accused Paul of causing trouble in the city, that he was a Jew trying to win proselytes by teaching beliefs that Romans could not accept. Knowing how the Romans had little thought for anything but law and order, however it was obtained, the men would be making a charge that would readily be accepted. The Jews were evidently unpopular—which was probably why there were so few of them in the city—and the Romans were proud of their Roman citizenship (16:21). Paul and Silas were given summary—instant—punishment. They were stripped and beaten by the *lictors* with their rods. Paul may have wanted to use his rights as a Roman, but if he had cried, *Civis Romanus sum!* his voice would have been drowned by the shouts of the crowd. The two were thrown into an underground cell and their feet put into stocks. But, undaunted, they sang the Psalms they had learned as boys and had sung so often in the synagogue.

It was then that the earthquake happened. The account of their escape as the shaking earth loosened the stocks and their chains and broke open the heavy cell door is vivid and exciting (16:25–end). The jailer's life was forfeit if his prisoners escaped; that is why he wanted to kill himself and die honorably. Paul prevented the act. Convinced that these were men of God, the jailer and his family believed what Paul had told them and were baptized. The power of the Holy Spirit came upon them and Paul realized that God had accepted them. Note that the jailer's first acts were those of a Christian—to heal and bathe their new found friends' wounds and then give them food.

There is a "twist" to this story that gives us some amusement. The overbearing magistrates were frightened when they discovered that they had had two Roman citizens beaten—worse still, without a trial (22:25; 25:11). Paul decided to make an example of them. Very much on his dignity he demanded that the magistrates should "eat humble pie" and come themselves to the cell and publicly request them to leave! We can picture this scene and imagine that many of the watchers laughed heartily at the discomfiture of the cowed magistrates.

CONTINUING THEIR JOURNEY

Anxious not to cause further unnecessary trouble, and having bidden farewell to Lydia, the Apostles left the city. Luke stayed behind, probably to carry on his work as a doctor; with Timothy he also helped to organize the new church. Paul, Silas, and the others went by the fine Via Egnatia to the next cities. On their way they fell in with other travelers—traders, pilgrims, athletes, Roman bodyguards; sometimes wealthy citizens were on their way to Rome itself, riding in their richly draped litters or wagons, attended by slaves with pack mules carrying personal property and gifts for their friends. The Apostles passed through *Amphipolis* some thirty miles along the road, and another thirty brought them to *Apollonia*. Eventually they arrived at *Thessalonica* (Salonica). This was the capital of Macedonia; it stood on the rising hill overlooking the blue Aegean. It was a "free city," having been honored by Antony for its help in the battle of Philippi. It had its own magistrates, called "politarchs"; this unusual name has been found in ancient manuscripts, and confirms Luke's use of it in his account. Paul immediately went to the synagogue and, as was his custom, preached to the Jews, then to the Greeks. He stayed in the city, probably for a longer period than the three weeks mentioned in the *Acts*. Meanwhile, Timothy had joined them. Money was sent from the church in Philippi (Phil. 4:16) to assist them in their work. But Paul also had to put to good use his trade of tent-making

(I Thess. 2:9) and earn enough to pay for his food and lodging.

Paul taught that it was necessary for the Messiah to have suffered, died, and risen again. This, Jesus had done; their Messiah had come and was this Jesus in whom they should believe. But the Jews grew jealous. They incited a gang of toughs to attack the home of Jason, who had given hospitality to Paul and Silas (Rom. 16:21). They dragged Jason and some of his friends before the city governors, accusing them of encouraging traitors to Caesar, for, they said, the Apostles claimed Jesus as King—and there was "no king but Caesar." Note that their charge is a political one, so as to win the favor of the Roman magistrates. To worship Christ was contrary to the worship of Caesar (cf. the dedication at Lystra) and was treason. Jason was released on his promise not to commit treason and on payment of security —"on bail," as we say. It is indicated in I Thessalonians 2:18 that Paul, who had had to leave so as not to make the situation more difficult for his friends, could not easily return without bringing them again into danger or trouble. Persecution and serious rioting followed this incident (I Thess. 2:14–16; 3:1–5; II Thess. 1:6). But the church he had begun grew fast (I Thess. 1:8). Timothy was left behind to organize it.

ON TO ATHENS

Paul and Silas left in secret and by night. They traveled some forty miles to *Beroea* (Verria), lying six hundred feet above the plain. As usual, they went straight into the synagogue, where they were better received by both honest, open-minded Jews and Greeks of culture and nobility (Acts 17:11, 12), who even searched the scriptures to check and prove what Paul was preaching about Jesus. One of Paul's converts was Sopater. But, as we can almost guess by now, it

was not long before jealous Jews of Thessalonica came to the town and made accusations against the Apostles and stirred up trouble. Some of the kindly Beroeans helped the two to the harbor, where a trading ship took Paul and some of these friends toward Athens, of ancient fame. Silas and Timothy, who had come to Beroea to warn Paul, stayed behind to help the elders of the new church in their duties.

For three days the ship coasted along the serried harbors and inlets, passing Olympus—the home of the Greek gods, Ossa and Pelion—giant mountains, Marathon, Thermopylae—renowned in Greek legend and history. Paul must have recalled his learning and the great deeds of the heroes of a past age. In the sunshine and sea air he regained physical strength.

IN ATHENS

Athens was the home of heroes, philosophers, orators, poets, teachers, students. No longer powerful, it still retained some of its past glory. Already Paul could see the magnificent buildings looming on the sky line. There were temples to Zeus, Apollo, Minerva, Dionysus and lesser gods and goddesses; theaters, arenas, amphitheaters, the Tower of the Winds were raised in colonnaded wonder. And crowning them all, white and gold on its Acropolis hill, stood the Parthenon, built in 480 B.C., the temple of Athena, goddess of Wisdom. Many of its beautiful carvings and friezes are today in the British Museum, preserved from further destruction and ruin. They are now called the Elgin Marbles.

Once in the city, Paul lost no time in wandering about its streets and squares. Wherever he went there were statues of gods and goddesses, lifelike in size, but gaudy and unreal in their shrines. He felt that the people must be as powerless as their own gods whom they worshiped

The amphora shows Athene as a warrior.

in sheer superstition and fear. When it thundered, Zeus was angry; when harvest failed, Demeter was annoyed. The gods had to be appeased. Worship was pagan and false (17:16). The people were blindly obedient and lost to their idols; they bowed down to graven images (Ex. 20:3–5).

In the great heat of the Mediterranean summer Paul watched the heathen festivals and processions, sacrifices and reli-gious celebrations full of the same superstitious fear of evil spirits. One day, probably still depressed and sad at having had to leave Thessalonica so hurriedly, he was walking through a street when he saw an altar. This was not unusual, except that it was "to an Un-known God" which had been erected at the time of some calamity when no one knew which of the gods had been offended. A similar altar has been unearthed at Pergamum. It set Paul thinking. He had already spoken in the market place, the civic center, with its senate house, law courts, town hall, and porches.

An altar "To the Unknown God" found at Pergamum.

There, as in the Roman forums men gathered to talk and discuss philosophies and ideals of life, wisdom, and goodness. They worshiped Athena, whose forty-feet-high statue, adorned with gold, jewels, and ivory, stood in the Parthenon. They were interested in the perfect life, the after life, the power of the gods and the power of men, government, and so on. Paul had argued with the Stoics and the Epicureans, philosophers who were searching for answers to the riddles of the universe—"What is man?" "Why is he here?" They tried to explain their beliefs and to provide patterns for living the perfect life.

PAUL AND THE PHILOSOPHERS

The *Epicureans* were followers of Epicurus, 300 B.C. They believed that the answers to life's problems lay in happiness at whatever cost. "Eat, drink and be merry, for tomorrow we die." (I Cor. 15:32). The *Stoics* were followers of Zeno, also about 300 B.C. Their name came from *stoa,* the Greek word for porch, where they used to meet. They had a finer attitude toward life than had the Epicureans. They said gods and men were part of God, therefore they must obey the laws of God, bear their pains and difficulties bravely and well, listen to the voice of conscience and take life calmly. The names of these philosophies remain with us. An "epicure" is one who enjoys extravagance in food and living; a "stoic" is one who is indifferent to pain.

These two sects or "schools of thought," as we call them today, were widely different, as can be seen. Both of them listened to Paul courteously, as he spoke to them in the *agora,* the Greek word for market place. They realized that he was a fluent, educated speaker; they also saw that he was putting forward theories and ideas about life that were new. They were not by any means ready to accept his philosophy; they were too proud, and regarded Paul with contempt. Indeed, after hearing him they called him a "babbler," using a Greek slang word which meant "seed-picker"—someone who picks up things fallen from a laden cart. They meant that Paul's knowledge was second-hand and not genuinely his own. Yet they had to admit that when he talked about a "strange god" named Jesus he seemed to have some authority. Of course, neither sect believed in an after life; that was quite impossible to accept.

"TO AN UNKNOWN GOD"

But it was the custom to give a new speaker every opportunity to say in public what his philosophy was. So Paul, standing on a platform of rough rock, faced the famous Areopagus, the court or senate responsible for education and religion; its members were scholars and cultured men of high position. The stone benches on which they sat are still to be seen. Gathered around, too, were the ordinary, curious citizens of Athens. Read 17:22 ff. These verses give the impression that this was on Ares (Greek) or Mars (Roman) hill, but it is more likely that it took place in the court of the senate.

Paul adopts the style of the market place and refers to the known philosophy, which inclined toward idolatry. The word "superstitious" in verse 22 is misleading, and even sounds rude. What Paul said was really a compliment— "Men of Athens, I see you are rather *religious.*" He was thinking of the many altars, statues, shrines, and temples he had seen. One of these, he said, was to

Paul, quoting from one of their own Stoic philosophers, Aratus, of whom he had learned while at school in Tarsus. But this God should not be thought of as an idol of gold or silver or carved stone, as—in their ignorance—their ancestors had done. He did not live in temples made with hands, as did Athena in the Parthenon. He was the Creator and had made all nations; He was now revealed, and Paul had seen the One this God had sent to be His judge on earth. His people, the Jews, had crucified Him, but God had raised Him from the dead. . . . Paul got no further than this. He was met with roars of scornful laughter and shouts of derision. The crowd dispersed and the senate, perhaps impressed at

On the walls of the Parthenon were carved wonderful friezes of Greek life and activities.

an Unknown God—of whom he would tell and so give them new knowledge. Some of his hearers would perhaps recall that four hundred years before, the great philosopher Socrates had spoken to the men of Athens in much the same way. This, said Paul, was the One True God who created the universe and everything in it. "We also are His offspring," added

Paul's obvious sincerity, asked to hear him again.

Paul had failed—not for the first time in his career, and probably not for the last. He had not moved the philosophers of Athens (I Cor. 1:23, 24). He did not dream that one day the Parthenon itself would be a Christian church! Of the few converts, two named were Damaris, a woman, and Dionysius, one of the senate. Legend says that Dionysius was later sent by Clement of Rome to preach Christianity in Gaul, where he became known as St. Denys, the patron saint of France.

TO CORINTH

So far as we know, no church was founded in Athens then, though later we read of those who "clave to Paul." About A.D. 50, Paul left and made his way to *Corinth,* fifty miles away. Corinth was a busy commercial seaport. Even in those days the canal across the narrow isthmus had been begun. Long before, Alexander the Great, then Julius Caesar had attempted it. Later, Nero—with thousands of captives from Galilee—tried to dig the canal. But it was never finished, and Paul must have seen ships moving overland on rollers, making a land journey of four miles to save the long sea route of two hundred miles from gulf to gulf. Corinth was a flourishing Roman center, where Paul was reminded of his boyhood days in Tarsus among the Egyptians and Phoenician seamen and boats, traders and caravans, Roman soldiers and Greek athletes. Here he might have a greater chance of success than in Athens. Many of the Jews of the Dispersion lived here, too, and might prove the nucleus of a new group of believers. The lintel of their synagogue has been discovered (Acts 18:4).

But here were Greeks, Romans, Egyptians, Jews, lost in their search for new pleasures, money and luxuries, sunk in evil living and selfishness (I Cor. 9: 24–27). They were superstitious and worshiped gods like Pan and the Nereids. When not feasting and drinking they were in the theater "at the games"—the Isthmian Games—in which naked athletes raced and wrestled for a laurel wreath and brief fame, and chariots hurtled around the arena and gladiators slew one another.

The ancient city of Corinth is now in ruins. The rocky Acro-Corinth, of course, still rises, a tawny yellow, two thousand feet behind excavated sites of temples, baths, squares, wide streets, fountains, and triumphal archways. In the center once stood the temple of Athena; there was another to Aphrodite, goddess of love. Seven huge columns of a temple to Apollo, god of light and power, still stand.

PAUL'S WORK IN CORINTH

Although he had planned not to stay long (I Thess. 2:17, 18) Paul had to find employment to pay for food and lodging. Making his way to the working quarter of the town, by the dockside and quays, he found a tent-maker, one of his own trade. This was Aquila, a Jew of Pontus who had been sent away from Rome by Emperor Claudius, who had become tired of the rioting over "Chrestus" between the Christians and the stricter Jews. Aquila and his wife Priscilla, probably a Roman lady and called Prisca— the family Roman name—in Romans 16:3, allowed Paul to stay with them and listened to his Good News. Aquila, in his turn, told Paul about Rome and— if tradition is true—about Peter and his work in the great city. Paul decided there and then that one day he, too, would go to Rome and from there speed his message to Spain. Paul must have heard of Britain by now. Claudius himself had been at the taking of Colchester and Roman soldiers had returned from overseas "posting" with their reports of this new land across the sea from Gaul. But for the time being Paul thought only of Rome; he did not know that he would be there in chains as a prisoner. He was not very anxious to begin his preaching in Corinth after his failure in Athens (I Cor. 2:3). But in the workshop and at the weaver's loom he did good work among his new friends and their customers.

Of course, on the sabbath, he attended the synagogue, but the Jews would not believe that the crucified Christ was their promised Messiah. Some of them probably had been in Jerusalem for the Passover in A.D. 29 and vaguely remembered the crucifixion of the "King of the Jews," now twenty years ago. How could that criminal be the Son of God? In their defiance they cursed Jesus—as had the Jews of Pisidian Antioch.

Paul stood as much as he could of their hostility and disbelief, but in the end his patience vanished. He shook his cloak at them (18:6; cf. Neh. 5:13). He would preach from now on to the Gentiles only. They, at least, would listen to what he had to say. This would anger the Jews, too, for they always hoped that eventually all the God-fearers would become circumcised and accept the Jewish faith; the Jews wanted their membership. Now they were likely to lose them to Paul and his new teaching. Paul, however, struck another blow at them by converting no less a person than their own ruler

of the synagogue—Crispus (I Cor. 1: 14). It was natural that the new ruler, Sosthenes, should be his enemy. Then Paul moved into a near-by house, the home of a Roman believer, one Titus (probably Titius) Justus.

One night he had a dream—always accepted in those days as God's way of talking to people—and learned that he was to preach and continue working in Corinth without fear, for the Master was with him. Paul lost no time. Perhaps remembering his failure at Athens, Paul changed his style and method: the Corinthians were a very different kind of people, too. Instead of following a philosophical theme, he went straight to the point of his message about the crucified Christ (I Cor. 2:2). His hearers were by no means scholarly and cultured; they were neither wise nor noble (I Cor. 1:26); many were of the most wicked

The "chorus" of a Greek play.

and degraded people to be found in the city (I Cor. 6:9–11). Paul evidently needed money for his work and was happy to receive from Macedonia gifts that helped tremendously (II Cor. 11:8, 9). Silas also rejoined him at this time, having perhaps gone back to Philippi for a short time (Phil. 4:15). Perhaps it was Silas who brought the gifts. It was necessary that someone should visit the churches as frequently as possible so that they could make sure everything was going well.

EPISTLE TO THE THESSALONIANS

At the time of his successes Paul had a visitor—his beloved Timothy—with good news from Thessalonica. Unable to do so, but wishing to go there to see for himself and speak once more to his friends, Paul decided to write a letter instead (I Thess.). This denied the lies of jealous Jews and encouraged the church to live in united friendship. One important point among many is Paul's insistence that since Jesus died and rose again "so shall we all rise again"; there was no sorrow in death (I Thess. 3:6; 4:13, 14; 5:14–22).

This letter is regarded by some scholars as being earlier than the one to the Galatians, that is, his first letter to any church at all. The contents certainly seem to show that he looked for an early return of Jesus—the Second Coming—which was expected by all the first Christians. Later, as we see in *Colossians*—and there is some sign in *Galatians*—he regards the Second Coming of Christ as a coming into the heart of a new believer who has entered into Christ's Kingdom on earth. The letter to the *Thessalonians* and the one to the *Galatians* form the beginnings of the New Testament, for as yet none of the Gospels had been written (Part III, Introduction). Silas was present when Paul wrote this letter and probably penned it on the papyrus sheets as Paul dictated it, for Paul's eyes, as we believe, were too weak for him to write long letters (I Thess. 1:1). Later, Paul sent another letter to this church, encouraging it to continue in its work, not to worry about the Second Coming of Jesus, but to carry on with its duties. He reminded the members to be busy bodies but not busybodies! (II Thess. 1:3, 4; 2:2; 3:7–12).

THE CHURCH AT CORINTH

Paul stayed at Corinth, where he formed a church among the poorest Gentiles, and trained leaders to carry on with the duties involved so that the church would run smoothly. He also introduced to them the service of the Lord's Supper (Part III). It was not a united church; there was considerable disagreement and disorder and even opposition to Paul himself. But it was large and there was evidence of "speaking with tongues," so Paul felt that the Holy Spirit was working for him. He stayed for some eighteen months and then early in A.D. 52 decided that he must return to Antioch and thence to Jerusalem.

Before he could do so, however, he was brought by a mass gathering of jealous Jews before the new Roman proconsul of Achaia, Gallio. An inscription about Gallio, dated A.D. 52, has been found at Delphi, and this has helped to date this period with accuracy. Gallio was brother to Seneca, the Roman philosopher and tutor to Nero. Seneca once said, "So live with men as if God saw; so speak with God as if men were listening." This ideal of life is strangely like Paul's.

Seated at the judgment seat in the Basilica or Judgment Hall, Gallio sensed the jealousy of the Jews and saw through their vague charges that Paul was preaching a new religion which by Roman law he was not allowed to do. He told them that it was not his business to judge mat-

Weaving on a vertical loom as Aquila might have done.

ters of their own law and religion; they must deal with such things themselves. So far as he could see, Paul was not preaching treason against Rome. Christianity could continue if it would. Seeing that Gallio had snubbed the Jews (18: 14–16), the Greeks turned on the new synagogue ruler Sosthenes and beat him; Gallio ignored this, too.

PAUL LEAVES CORINTH

With Aquila and Priscilla, Paul sailed for Syria, pausing at *Cenchraea,* the eastern port of Corinth lying between two horns of land on the ends of which stood temples—one to Aphrodite, the other to Iris. Here Paul had his head shaved to indicate that he had taken a vow (Num. 6). The ship sailed across the bay, passing a rock on which stood a huge statue of Poseidon (Roman Neptune), god of the sea, bearing his dolphin and trident. Arriving at *Ephesus,* Aquila and Priscilla stayed, for they had planned to live there. Paul had time to speak but once in the synagogue, for, having found another ship and anxious to complete his journey, he sailed across the eastern Mediterranean to the Roman seaport of *Caesarea*. He promised to revisit Ephesus at some future opportunity (18:21). From Caesarea he traveled southward to *Jerusalem*. Scholars tell us that the "church" in verse 22 was at Jerusalem, where, as he had taken the vow at Cenchraea, Paul could redeem (buy back) his vow by offering on the Temple altar the hair that had grown during the previous month. He may have had a cold reception from the Jews in Jerusalem, but in *Antioch* was certainly received joyfully.

His arrival in Antioch ended his second missionary journey in Greece. The rest of Acts 18 begins the third journey—this time into Asia.

10

The Third Missionary Journey

(ACTS 18:23-21:17)

After a few months, Paul prepared to set out once again. The roads were hard once more after the winter rains had softened them into muddy tracks. He passed through Galatia and Phrygia, revisiting the churches established on his first mission. He had promised to return to *Ephesus* and hastened on to do so. In the meantime, a new leader, "eloquent and learned," had arisen at Ephesus. This was Apollos. He had already been in Corinth when Paul was there (I Cor. 1:12). Coming originally from Alexandria, he knew something of the message of John the Baptist but little of Jesus; his preaching therefore lacked the conviction that came from the acceptance of Christ as the Messiah. He did not possess the power of the Holy Spirit and knew nothing of Christian baptism. Apollos was advised to go to Ephesus so that he could receive instruction and guidance from Paul. Aquila and Priscilla, who had by now settled in Ephesus, carrying on with their craft of tentmaking, gave Apollos considerable help; they probably told Luke about him, too. Apollos returned to Corinth where he had many followers, some of them preferring his preaching to that of Paul.

Traveling with Paul at this time were Timothy and Titus, young preachers in training. The city was a great commercial and governing center. With six other fine cities not far from it, it made the "seven churches" of Revelation 1:9–3:22. But it was also a pagan city, given over to the worship of the goddess Artemis (Diana), whose huge temple was the glory of Ephesus and once one of the seven wonders of the world. It was built in 330 B.C. Fragments of its ruins are now in the British Museum; the rest lie beneath mosquito-infested, stagnant swamps. It was shown on the coins of the Greeks, with the beautiful Diana represented with her deer or with lions crouching to spring. But the actual image was not that of a

354

Paul's third journey enabled him to revisit his earlier churches where he praised, reproved and encouraged the members to continue in their faith.

beautiful goddess familiar to us in pictures of the moon-goddess or huntress of Greek stories. It was originally a rough black lump of rock (a meteorite) that had fallen from the skies and which the superstitious Ephesians believed had come from heaven itself, sent by Jupiter. Some sources tell us that it was a roughly carved piece of wood resembling a woman. Its shrine was curtained and surrounded by a hundred columns of shining jasper, each on a marble base. The roof of the temple was painted in red and gold. Priests, priestesses, and musicians served in the temple, while dancers and even acrobats performed and magicians and sorcerers practiced their arts. The people themselves were filled with fear of these servants of the goddess, and were in greater fear of Artemis herself (Eph. 6:12).

PAUL AND THE EPHESIANS

But Paul found many Ephesians who were looking for something better in life than fear and superstition. They, too, had a faith, but only that of John the Baptist; they were still hoping for the promised Messiah and had never heard of the power of the Holy Spirit (Acts 19:2 ff.). So Paul taught them about Jesus and Pentecost, and the power of the Spirit came upon them even as he blessed them.

Naturally, he went to the Jewish synagogue. The Jews simply would not accept the crucified Messiah. So, with the help of a teacher named Tyrannus, Paul took over a kind of lecture room, probably in the local gymnasium. Normal school hours were from sunrise until 11 a.m., after which it was too hot for work. So Paul had to use the hall from the fifth to the tenth hour, the hottest period of the day, from 11 a.m. until just before sunset, after which it would be required again by the owners for educational work in the cool evening. For two years Paul preached in this hall (I Cor. 16:6, 8; II Cor. 1:15, 16). His Good News was

The theater at Ephesus was like this.

simple and direct—"repentance towards God and faith towards our Lord Jesus Christ." He seems at this period to have worked several miracles through the great faith the people had in Jesus. Because of this power the seven sons of Sceva, a Jew and a chief priest, tried to copy Paul, believing that they had only to use the words "Jesus" and "Paul" for this strange magic to be theirs. But they did not succeed. Those who heard of their failure believed all the more firmly in what Paul was preaching, for they saw for themselves that he had a power no others could possess—a power that came from Jesus Christ.

"GREAT IS DIANA OF THE EPHESIANS!"

Paul's teaching was clear and the Ephesians had long wanted such a religion. They were tired and disgusted at the heathen rites and witchcraft of the false gods, and gave up their idolatry in order to accept the new teaching. Even the sorcerers, seeing the wrong they were doing and realizing the foolishness of their so-called magic, brought their scrolls of spells, magical formulae and charms into the market place. There they had an enormous bonfire, the value of the "books" (they were really papyrus rolls) being fifty thousand pieces of silver; it is difficult to assess this in present-day money, but it would not be less than $14,000. One inscription they did not destroy, for on a block of marble found at Ephesus we read one of their superstitions—"If the bird is flying from right to left, then, whether it rises or settles out of sight, it is unlucky." But Paul's success was not complete. It was now May, A.D. 55, and the pagan spring festivals were being held. May 24 was the day of Artemis. Diana was her Roman name. In Part II is told how the god Marduk was brought

through the city of Babylon in processions of rejoicing. It was a common celebration in Eastern countries. Now the Greek goddess Artemis, goddess of fertility, the "Great Mother," was to be honored. Her statue was to be drawn by deer through the city streets, the people singing and chanting hymns of praise and falling down in worship. The city was packed with visitors and pilgrims, all bent on the search for good luck and blessing on their crops and journeys and homes. Usually, the silversmiths and other craftsmen did an enormous trade in their little figurines and statuettes of Diana done in silver, terra cotta and wood; the people bought these as souvenirs and charms. Demetrius was one of these craftsmen. Since Paul came with his new religion, Demetrius had seen his trade diminish; people who believed in this Jesus had no further use for charms and images. He was losing trade; and Diana was being despised. Roused to anger, the smiths and their workmen forced two friends of Paul—Gaius and Aristarchus (Col. 4:10; Phile. 24)—into the auditorium or amphitheater, which held over 20,000 people. They had tried to find Paul, but by now Aquila had persuaded him to leave (Rom. 16:3, 4).

Paul had wanted to face the crowd, but the presiding governors, or Asiarchs, as they were called, advised him not to do so. They were the rulers of the Roman provinces in Asia Minor. They may have favored Paul as an educated preacher and a Roman, but they also wanted to prevent trouble. The mob—which for the most part did not know for what or why it was shouting—chanted its slogans unintelligently for two whole hours. The people would not listen to Alexander, a Jew (II Tim 4:14), but drowned his voice in their cry of "Great is Artemis [Diana] of the Ephesians." It was not until the "town clerk" or mayor—a city official—spoke sternly to them that they calmed down, no doubt quite exhausted and glad of the opportunity to be quiet and go home. The official reminded them that Ephesus was "sacristan" or keeper of the temple of Diana; this was a title of honor given to those who worshiped Caesar. Paul and his friends had done nothing against the city and had not robbed the temple (Rom. 2:22). Their rioting might be questioned by Rome and as a result Ephesus might lose its privilege of being a "free city" (Acts 19:38). If Demetrius wished to make a charge he could do so in the usual courts of law.

The Jews were probably glad that the riot had not turned against them, as it might easily have done once the rioters had realized that Paul was a Jew. The fact that he was a Christian Jew would have escaped them.

THE EPISTLE TO THE CORINTHIANS

At this time Apollos returned from Corinth (I Cor. 12, 17) with disquieting news that there was disunity and backsliding in the church there. Many of the members had returned to their former heathen beliefs and ways of living; others were anxious because their new beliefs were not being fulfilled. They had looked for an early Second Coming of Jesus and were getting tired of waiting. Paul decided to write to them. "I hear sad things of you," he said, "and you are not ashamed." He told them he now knew of their wickedness, drunkenness, even feasting at the Lord's Supper; he was perplexed at their return to idolatry. He knew there were divisions among them. Some followed him; others, Apollos. What did it matter? He had planted the seed, Apollos had watered it, but God had made it grow—and this meant that they had to work together for full success of the church. His letter is forceful and to the point throughout. The well-known thirteenth chapter of I Corinthians sums up his teaching of the power of Jesus' love.

Titus took Paul's letter to Corinth and Paul went on to *Troas* (II Cor. 2:12; 7:5-7) accompanied by Luke. Paul was too ill to preach (II Cor. 1:8; 4:7), so the two traveled through *Macedonia* and other parts of Greece. It is probable that Paul visited *Corinth* during this time (II Cor. 2:1; 13:1 ff.). He was anxious at further news of the church and depressed at his "thorn in the flesh" (II Cor. 1:8; 4:7 ff.; 12:7, 9). Titus returned to *Philippi* to tell him more of the quarrels (II Cor. 7:6). The majority were loyal to Paul and this gave him great joy. But those who were not loyal to him were being urged on by Jews from Jerusalem and were plotting against him, his requests for money, and his teaching. They even said he was a coward, a charge no one could justifiably make against a man who had dared and suffered as had Paul. He rose to the occasion and promptly wrote another letter—the latter part of II Corinthians—in language that was bold, almost threatening and full of sensitive anger. Begin reading it at Chapter 10. In Chapter 11:24-28, he lists more than sufficient evidence that he was no coward.

Timothy now arrived and Titus took this letter to Corinth. Later, Paul and Timothy themselves went (Acts 20:2) to refute the mean charges made against him. Scholars tell us that the two epistles as we have them are really made up of fragments of four.

EPISTLE TO THE ROMANS

While he was at *Corinth,* Paul sent a letter to the church in Rome. It was written down for him by Tertius (Acts 20:1 ff.; Rom. 15:25). In Rome was a group of Christians, the beginnings of a Christian church. A good introduction to the letter is to read Chapters 7, 3, 12, in that order; these chapters tell of Paul's guidance in "getting right with God" (cf. Luke 18:9–14). He underlines and explains the difference between the power of faith in Jesus and the acceptance of the Jewish Law and Tradition, and partly echoes his letter to the Galatians. The following references will help you to see that he showed them how their faith in Jesus would enable them to lead the right kind of life, however difficult they found it—Romans 8:38, 39; 7:21; 5:3, 4. Read also 3:24–27; 8:35. He told them that he hoped to visit them in person, to preach what he was then writing—1:14, 15; 15:24, 25, 30, 33. Chapter 16 reveals Paul's wonderful capacity for friendship.

CONTINUING THE WORK

Despite criticisms, he continued to collect money to send to the church in Jerusalem (I Cor. 16:1–4; II Cor. 8; Rom. 15:26). After three months he seems to have decided to return, perhaps in one of the pilgrim ships bearing hundreds of Jews of the Dispersion to Caesarea on their way to Jerusalem to keep Passover. But he was warned of a plot by the jealous Jews to kill him, so he changed his plans and went overland through Macedonia, spending Passover in *Philippi.*

In *Troas* once more—about A.D. 56— he met the members of his party. There were Sopater from Beroea, Aristarchus from Thessalonica, Luke from Philippi, Gaius from Derbe, Timothy from Lystra, Tychicus and Trophimus from Ephesus. These were all bringing gifts and money for Jerusalem. Note that the "we" passages begin again at 20:5–15, indicating that Luke is once again with Paul. Of course, he may have been there before, but is certainly with Paul on these occasions. In 20:7, we read that the company met to "break bread" in remembrance of the Lord's death (Part III). This would be in a private house on the evening before the sabbath day. The meeting followed an order of service not unlike that of the synagogue—Prayer (cf. I Cor. 14: 16) and Praise (Eph. 5:19; Rom. 12:11, 12), then a Reading—from the Greek Septuagint, LXX—followed by an explanation of how its teachings bore out the life and work of Jesus. On this occasion Paul spoke well into the early hours of the morning. It is not surprising that Eutychus should fall drowsily from his perch at the window of the upper room. Paul revived him.

HOMEWARD BOUND

We next find Paul walking alone the twelve miles to *Assos,* probably to think and prepare for his immediate return to Jerusalem. There had already been a definite plot against his life and he knew perfectly well that the nearer he moved toward the city, the greater his danger. He rejoined the company who had gone by sea. Assos stood high on a hill overlooking the blue Aegean Sea. Ruins show that in Paul's day there was a temple to Athena and a fine agora or market place and also a Roman bath. The whole company then sailed on to *Mitylene,* taking advantage of the strong breezes that blew by day and dropped by night. Then to *Chios, Sàmos,* probably "tarrying at *Trogyllium*"; then they arrived at *Miletus.* Paul had planned to by-pass *Ephesus* because of his wish to hurry to *Jerusalem* for Pentecost; it is possible, too, that he did not want to create fresh trouble in the city by showing himself so soon after his hasty exit. But not wishing the loyal Ephesians to feel he was neglecting them,

The ruins of the Temple of Apollo at Miletus, where Paul bade good-bye to his Ephesian friends.

he sent for the elders of the church. Their journey of twenty-five miles across the coastal mountains and probably a sea crossing caused a delay of three or four days. While the sailors prepared the boat for the next run, the Ephesians talked with Paul on the sandy shore.

In his farewell speech to them Paul used his personal experiences as an example and begged them to be likewise diligent and conscientious in their work against all opposition from within the church (Acts 20:30; I Tim. 1:3–7). In Acts 20:35, is a saying not recorded in the Gospels—which, we must remember, were not yet written—though to most people so familiar that they would say it was. Paul's use of it shows that the sayings of Jesus were already being used in the churches. So it was, in the shadow of the temple to Apollo and within a short distance of the huge Roman theater, with its special seats "Reserved for Jews and God-fearers," that Paul bade a sad good-bye to his Ephesian friends. Among these were surely Aquila and Priscilla. They "sorrowed most of all for the words which he spake, that they should see his face no

more." Sad at heart, the elders escorted Paul down the Sacred Way to the seashore and watched the ship bear away their beloved preacher. No doubt Paul raised his hand high in blessing on them as the boat sped on and away from the shore and they could see him no more.

SWIFT RETURN

The ship made a fast run by *Coos* and *Rhodes*—where the 112-feet-high bronze Colossus (Apollo), once one of the Seven Wonders of the World, now lay in pieces across the harbor entrance. It had been overthrown by an earthquake as early as 224 B.C. Nine hundred years later it was sold to the Saracens for scrap metal!

Following the course taken for this return journey you will see that it kept closely to the coast, which indicates that the boat was a coasting vessel. At *Patara* they boarded a larger trading ship and made across the eastern Mediterranean, passing the southwestern tip of Cyprus, toward Phoenicia, finally landing at *Tyre*. Here the cargo took seven days to unload and Paul's friends of the seaport begged

*A Corinthian wine jug dug up at Rhodes.
Paul saw and used many like it when he
stayed in Corinth.*

him not to continue to Jerusalem, for
they felt it would be dangerous for him
to do so. Despite their prayers and pleadings, Paul, Luke and the others boarded
the ship again and it sailed down the
coast to *Ptolemais* (Acre). Here they
landed and next day walked the thirty
miles to *Caesarea*. This was the Roman
political capital of Palestine and the residence of the Roman procurators. It had
been built by Herod the Great in honor
of Augustus Caesar; it had a magnificent
harbor, and fine streets threaded the city.
Temples of marble and lofty palaces indicated the wealth and luxury to be found
there. Cut in the hillside was a hippodrome called an "odeon." It held twenty
thousand people. Seawater could be

flooded into the theater arena so that sea battles, races, and displays could be shown.

Here, however, was a Christian community. We remember it was here that Peter had baptized Cornelius and that Philip the Evangelist had his home. It was with Philip that Paul now stayed. While in Caesarea they met Agabus, a prophet of Judaea, who foretold danger to Paul if he went to Jerusalem. Note that Agabus revived the tradition of the Old Testament prophets, who illustrated their prophecies by something the people could see. He used Paul's girdle to signify that Paul would be bound hand and foot in Jerusalem (cf. Jer. 13:1–11). But Paul was "willing to die at Jerusalem." His Master had once "set his face steadfastly to go to Jerusalem" and so would he (Rom. 15:25–32). So his friends prepared the pack mules and donkeys—to carry them and the heavy chest of coins and jewels collected for the relief fund in Jerusalem—and started for the city. They had only two days if they were to arrive in time for Pentecost, and there was no time to walk. Accompanying them was an "early disciple" of the first persecutions, a Greek Jew named Mnason. He probably gave Paul hospitality while he was in Jerusalem. Paul may also have stayed with his sister (23:16).

Paul in Jerusalem

(ACTS 21:17; 22; 23)

As always at times of great feasts, Jerusalem was thronged with pilgrims. Thousands of them had come for Pentecost from all parts of the Roman Empire. Some of them were from far-away cities in which Paul had preached and where he had been hindered and even badly treated by the jealous Jews. They came from Pisidian Antioch, Iconium, Athens, Corinth . . . Some of them had even followed Paul for the very purpose of stirring up trouble in those cities. They hated Paul for opening the door of the Christian faith to the Gentiles and they hated him because—in their eyes—he was a traitor to his own Jewish faith.

IN THE TEMPLE COURT

At first welcomed — "they glorified God"—Paul faced the Jews of the Jerusalem church now under James. We do not know what happened to the original disciples; they must have been scattered throughout the empire and beyond, tak-

ing the story of Jesus with them. It is believed, for instance, that Thomas went to India, Peter to Rome, and, later, Mark went to Alexandria. Paul presented the money and gifts he had brought and recounted his adventures and experiences. But instead of real joy at the vast growth of the church there was some coldness and even antagonism toward him. Paul was made to feel that he had gone too far; the Christian Jews of Jerusalem obviously did not approve of his methods. Now that he was in Jerusalem he must behave like a good Jew and join in the Temple rites and sacrifices. In fact, it would be a good idea to do this publicly by paying the expenses into the Temple treasury of four men then under a vow. (It appears from this that Paul was now wealthy; we do not know where he obtained his money, but he was able later to rent a house, whereas we have seen that he had to work at tentmaking for his living.)

Paul agreed to this public act and had

his own head shaved, joining in the vow. On the last of the twelve days' attendance at the Temple he was recognized by some of his Asian (Ephesian) enemies. He and a Gentile friend, Trophimus, were in the Court of the Gentiles, which was the only part of the Temple precincts in which a Gentile was allowed. A barrier wall of marble stretched across the entrance to the next court. On it were the words, "No foreigner may enter within the screen and enclosure round the Holy Place. Whosoever is caught so trespassing will himself be the cause of death overtaking him" (Part II, p. 88). The angry Ephesians jumped to the conclusion that Paul had so far defied the ban on Gentiles as to take Trophimus beyond the warning inscription. They shouted that he had already preached against Moses and the Law and the Temple, and now he had deliberately desecrated the Temple itself (cf. 24:6).

Paul was dragged beyond the Beautiful Gate and out of the Temple courts. His enemies were bent on stoning him to death outside the city walls for breaking their Jewish law. He was dramatically rescued by the Roman garrison of the Castle of Antonia which overlooked the Temple. The legionaries were always on the lookout for disturbances during feast times. From time to time there were rebellions and uprisings. One was under Judas, in Galilee, A.D. 7. Another, led by his two sons, followed. A Messianic uprising took place under Theudas, who led his followers toward Jordan to cross as Moses had done at the Red Sea; this was A.D. 44, wrongly dated in Acts 5:36. There were wars between the Samaritans and the Zealots. The members of one section of the Zealots were called the "Sicarii" or "dagger-men" or the "Assassins." They were anxious to overthrow Roman rule at any cost. Not long before this incident involving Paul, an Egyptian had gathered his followers on the Mount of Olives, promising that the walls of Jerusalem would fall like those of Jericho; they would then enter the city and pillage it. They were, however, scattered by the Roman soldiers; four hundred were killed and two hundred captured. The Egyptian leader escaped. When Paul was taken, Claudias Lysias believed that he had at last captured the Egyptian! (21: 38). Lysias was a *chiliarch,* commander of a *cohort* of 600 men (ten cohorts made a *legion*). His duties were those of a magistrate and commander combined, so he was really a *tribune* or military governor. He was surprised to hear Paul speak to him in Greek.

Protected but bound in chains, Paul offered to speak to the mob. Lysias welcomed any effort to stop rioting and recognized Paul as obviously a brave and educated man. Paul held the crowd for a time in their own Hebrew tongue—he may even have spoken Aramaic—and told them of his conversion on the Damascus road when actually on his way as a zealous Jew to persecute the Nazarenes. They listened until he reached the point that he was sent by Jesus "far hence unto the Gentiles." Again furious that he should make the Gentiles equal to themselves, the Jews rose up against him. "Away with him! It is not fit that he should live!" Some of their fathers had cried, "Crucify him!" against their Lord. Lysias had to thrust Paul up the steps into the stronghold for safety.

But Lysias was still worried at the possible consequence of Paul's speech. Without further questioning, he gave the customary orders to strip and scourge the prisoner to make sure that he would confess. It was then that Paul claimed his rights as a Roman citizen; there was no point in undergoing punishment that was then unnecessary. Note the difference between their "freedoms." Lysias had bought his—hence the "Claudius," his Emperor's name; Paul was "freeborn." Lysias was, of course, most anxious over his personal responsibility and was greatly

A bronze statuette of Nero in armor.

relieved that, in the nick of time, he had avoided the dreadful crime of punishing a Roman citizen! Paul's chains were removed.

PAUL AND THE SANHEDRIN

Next day Paul met the Sanhedrin, or Council of the Jews, Lysias being hopeful that such a meeting would solve his problem. The Council had seen Paul before; he had been a student under Gamaliel, who himself may have gazed in perplexity on his wilful ex-pupil. They were all set against him; they were like the Council that had condemned Jesus thirty years before. Even Ananias the High Priest so far forgot himself as to order Paul to be struck; he was to meet his death soon after, at the hands of the Zealots. Paul had called him a "whited wall"—strongly reminiscent of the words of Jesus (Matt. 23:27). Note how cleverly Paul divided

the seventy among themselves and diverted attention from himself. He asserted his loyal Jewish beliefs as a Pharisee and said he had been called before them because of his belief in the resurrection of the dead. This created an uproar as the Sadducees and Pharisees shouted and argued over the resurrection and existence of angels. The Pharisees supported Paul, agreeing that if an angel had spoken to him they could not fight against God; the Sadducees denied such things. Paul was then taken to the Roman cells. That night he dreamed that His Master told him to be of good cheer, for, as in Jerusalem, so was he to bear witness for Him—in Rome!

ESCAPE FROM JERUSALEM

You will recall that Paul had a sister who had married into a high-priestly family and lived in Jerusalem. Her son, Paul's nephew, now came to the prison to warn Paul not to attend the Sanhedrin again, for a group of forty men had plotted to kill him. The Jews knew they could not get at Paul in the Castle, therefore they would murder him with the full knowledge—and consent—of the priests in the Council. Lysias was told. He was not very happy about it, for he had not only to protect Paul as a Roman citizen but also to maintain law and order. He therefore decided to send Paul to headquarters in Caesarea, where Felix the Governor (procurator) would take him in charge.

So Paul was put in the charge of two centurions and two hundred foot soldiers, two hundred spearmen and "beasts" (mules) to bear him. This seems an unusually large escort, but there was danger of an ambush from Paul's enemies and also from brigands and robbers on the way. Lysias was taking no chances. They traveled by night, leaving at nine o'clock, and journeyed the thirty-five miles to Antipatris. Here, on the edge of the plain and beyond the mountainous hideouts of possible murderers, the foot soldiers and spearmen left to return to Jerusalem. Paul was taken the remaining thirty miles to the coast in the care of the horsemen. He was put into yet another prison to await trial. Read the covering letter sent by Lysias and compare its contents with what actually happened; you can see how he distorts the facts to his own advantage (cf. 22:23–29, and 23:26–30).

Paul was to stay for two whole years in his prison in the palace of Herod the Great, then the residence of the Governor. Cilicia, his home province, was—with Syria—under the Legate, who was Felix's superior military governor. As the Legate's deputy, Felix could, therefore, try Paul. Felix, we are told, was a cruel, wicked procurator; he had enforced his control of Judaea by crucifixion and murder. But Paul escaped torture and scourging because, although a Jew, he could claim Roman rights.

The footsoldiers included slingers.

12

Paul and the Roman Governors

(ACTS 24-26)

Five days after his arrival in Caesarea, Paul was brought before the Governor's tribunal or court. Paul's accusers, furious that he had slipped through their fingers, came from Jerusalem to make their charges. Ananias the High Priest, still smarting at Paul's remark, was there, and Tertullus, the lawyer, put the case against Paul. It is easy to see how he tries to curry favor with Felix (24:2) and puts the blame on Lysias but for whom the Sanhedrin might have dealt with Paul. The accusation is that Paul is a rebel, a troublemaker and a ringleader of the Nazarenes; further, he is a profaner of the Temple. It would be better to get rid of him before further rioting took place because of him.

PAUL AND FELIX

Felix has the level-headed sense of justice we saw in Pontius Pilate (Part III) and does not allow himself to be persuaded against Lysias by Tertullus. He gives Paul the opportunity of defending himself. Paul denies the charges and adds that there is no proof of them even if he had done the things of which he is accused. He asks where are his false accusers, the Ephesians, and explains why he was in the Temple and how Lysias had protected him. His "crime" is his belief in his Master and in the resurrection, which, he says, is what the Sadducees regard as "wrong-doing."

Felix is impressed and feels that there is no case against Paul. But he adjourns the trial for further evidence from Claudius Lysias. (This was only an excuse, for Lysias was never sent for.) He grants Paul reasonable freedom—imprisonment but with the right to have frequent visitors, Luke, Timothy, Aristarchus, Philip, and others. It is believed that during this time Luke collected material for his Gospel and, no doubt, for the *Acts*.

What Paul had said made Felix think

a good deal. So far as their religion was concerned, the Romans had few if any rites and rules to keep—as had the strict Jews—but they were interested in the gods and anxious to keep on the right side of them. Paul had spoken of his God and a criminal that one of Felix's predecessors had crucified—a certain Jesus. Felix was perplexed. His wife was Drusilla, a young Jewess and daughter of Herod Agrippa I, who had murdered James and had himself died a dreadful death at the moment of his vainglory. Paul was sent for and, upon being asked, told Felix and Drusilla about his beliefs. Drusilla—who had wrongfully married Felix—saw him as a second John the Baptist, who had once accused Herod and his wife Herodias of wickedness. Felix remembered the cruelties of his own rule and his conscience troubled him as he heard Paul speak of his being judged. Paul was dismissed sharply; but note that Felix said he would send for him "at a more convenient season"—or some other time.

Meanwhile, Felix hoped for a bribe, and sent for Paul several times for that reason, believing him to be wealthy enough to produce it. But by his failure to make a decision he missed his real opportunity of believing in Paul's preaching. A short while later Felix was recalled to Rome by Nero to answer for his cruelties to the Jews. He left Paul in prison to appease the more influential Jews.

PAUL AND FESTUS

A year later Paul is still in chains and in prison. There is a new Governor, Festus, whose duty it now is to decide what is to be done with Paul. The Jews of Jerusalem cunningly demand a new trial, to be held in Jerusalem, believing they can hoodwink the new Governor into doing what they want. But Festus is by no means slow to see through this deception and says that if they want a new trial they must come to Caesarea. Reluctantly, they do so. Their charges are, of course, false and angry assertions —without proof—that Paul has spoken against the Law (25:8) and against the Temple (28:19), and against Caesar. Festus, probably bored with the whole affair, but wishing to satisfy the Jews, asks Paul if he is willing to go to Jerusalem for trial. Paul knows perfectly well that this would mean his own death, probably on the journey to the city before he ever got there. He was entitled to justice. He therefore makes his amazing demand. He had long thought about it; it was no decision on the spur of the moment. Despite his chains he would go to Rome where Jesus had said he would one day "bear witness" for Him. He makes his claim as a freeborn citizen —"I APPEAL UNTO CAESAR." He would be tried by Nero, in Rome.

Felix consults his legal advisers and then replies, "Unto Caesar, then, thou shalt go." He is concerned that the business has so far got out of hand and is probably already wondering what kind of report he is going to make to Rome. We may be sure that the Jews were furiously angry. Paul had now slipped from their grasp and they could do nothing about it.

AGRIPPA II

Before sending Paul to Rome, Festus had visitors. King Agrippa II and his sister Bernice came to visit the new Governor now living in the palace where previously their sister Drusilla had held court. Agrippa II was a Jew, ruling under Rome. He had the right to choose the High Priest and had already deposed Ananias. We are told that the priests hated him and had even built a wall in the Temple area to block the view of the king from his palace windows! He came of a line of murderers. His father Agrippa I had murdered James and had

367

A familiar scene in Roman times. A centurion leads in his foot soldiers and their prisoners.

sought the life of Peter, too; his great-uncle Herod Antipas had murdered John the Baptist and had taunted Jesus with kingship. His great-grandfather Herod the Great had murdered the babes of Bethlehem. Note that all these evils had been connected in some way with Jesus, and now Festus was to tell Agrippa about Paul, who actually believed that this crucified Jesus was still alive! Festus was probably anxious that Agrippa should hear Paul speak, and then advise the Governor how best to make out his charge sheet and report to Rome. Agrippa was probably curious, since as a Jew he partly sympathized with the Sanhedrin. But he would now be able to listen to Paul, of whom he had heard, and the man's preaching would be a relief from the dullness of a state visit to Caesarea.

PAUL AND AGRIPPA

Paul's meeting with Agrippa is sometimes interpreted as another trial. It was not. It was merely an occasion to satisfy Agrippa's interest. Paul did not by any means treat it as a trial. He knew that he could have no further inquiry now that he had demanded to go to Rome.

But it was a great opportunity for him to tell his story once more, this time to a king and to a Jew. Try to picture the scene. The gaily cloaked Romans, the soldiers in their glittering mail and plumed helmets, trumpeters announcing the king and his sister—who came exquisitely robed and wearing jewels in her hair and on her wrist—"with great

Coins of Emperor Nero, A.D. 54–68.

pomp." And before them stands a little, dark man, his hair greying, his eyes fiercely bright, burning with zeal that not even the chains on his wrists can withhold.

Paul spoke in cultured, careful Greek. He reminded Agrippa of their common Jewish belief in a Messiah, who, said Paul, had indeed come, had been crucified under Pontius Pilate and had risen from the dead. That was over twenty years ago, but he knew that it was true. Jesus had appeared to him on the Damascus road and had sent him to "proclaim light to the people and to the Gentiles."

This he had done, first to the Jews, then to the Gentiles, witnessing only what Moses and the prophets had said about the Messiah. For that he had been ill-treated by the Jews. Perhaps anxious that his royal visitors should not be offended, Festus interrupted Paul, who, in turn, appealed to Agrippa as to the king's belief in the Messiah. Agrippa did not commit himself. He was probably annoyed at being pressed in front of the gathered courtiers and officials. Many people accept his reply, "Almost thou persuadest me to be a Christian," as a cry of willingness to believe. But scholars tell us that the Greek version indicates that it was an answer made in jest. Agrippa, like the Jews of Jerusalem, was

Bronze head of the Emperor Augustus, 27 B.C. to A.D. 14.

The kind of ship in which Paul left Caesarea on his voyage to Rome.

too proud and scornful to believe. In Moffatt's translation his words read like a sneer—"At this rate it won't be long before you believe you have made a Christian of me."

Paul's reply was an outburst of sincerity; would that Agrippa and all who heard him might be believers as he, Paul, was—*without the chains!* Paul must have impressed Agrippa, vaguely irritated though the king may have been. He remarked to Festus that had Paul not appealed to Nero he might have been released forthwith. But the appeal to Rome had to be carried out. Festus was still far from clear on what Paul's "crimes" really were, but his report to Rome must have been a favorable one, for Paul was probably freed by Nero on his first trial. The report would have made interesting reading had it been preserved with that of Lysias written three years before.

The Journey to Rome

(ACTS 27-28:16)

It is now August, A.D. 58. You will see by his use of "we" that Luke is with Paul. His eyewitness account is extraordinarily vivid and accurate. Paul is put in the care of Julius, the centurion in charge of one of the corps of soldiers whose special work it was to carry out duties connected with Rome and the armies scattered throughout the Empire. Possibly part of the Praetorian Guard, they acted as couriers and escorts to the more important prisoners; they also had to visit towns and areas and report on the efficiency of the existing forces. This body of men was called the Augustan Band, probably because Augustus Caesar had made it a permanent corps for these purposes.

THE JOURNEY BEGINS

Sailing in the eastern Mediterranean was dangerous after mid-September and the season ended for the winter in No-

vember. No ship would be going across the sea direct to Rome, but there was no time for delay if the company were to get there by winter. They embarked at *Caesarea* in an Adramyttium coaster whose captain touched at harbors along the coast in order to reach safety from sudden storms and high seas. The ship put in at *Sidon,* and Paul was released "on parole" to visit his friends. Then the boat continued westward around the coast of Cilicia. No doubt Paul longed to land and make a brief visit to Tarsus. The prevailing westerly winds drove the boat under the shelter, and to the east, of Cyprus, the normal route for the time of the year (despite 27:5). Ships of those days carried a mainsail and foresail; they could not tack against a strong wind and had therefore to move under the force of these prevailing winds. Most ships from Alexandria found it easier to sail northward to Asia Minor and thence in the lee of the coast, rather than precious cargo of grain was thrown overboard, then the rest of the ship's movable gear, including the heavy mainyard. In the darkness those on board gave themselves up for lost. Without sun or stars, they could not have steered even if the storm had abated, for in those days there were no other means of navigation. Like Jesus, Paul found strength in prayer, and his confidence gave the others great courage. After two weeks' drifting in the Sea of Adria, the sailors' name for the eastern Mediterranean, experienced ears caught the sound of breakers dashing on some shore (28). Soundings proved that land was near. Four anchors were dropped from the stern to prevent the ship from swinging on to the rocks; then all "wished for day." What a world of despair and lost hope those words hold.

SHIPWRECKED

Pretending to attend to the anchors, some of the sailors lowered the ship's boat in order to escape. But Paul—and we see here his forcefulness of character and practical nature—advised Julius to stop them. He pointed out the need for food, then "took bread," gave thanks, and broke the bread and they all ate. The rest of the cargo serving as ballast was put overboard, and, driven by its mainsail, the ship struck a sandbank stretching between two seas. This is the neck of land still showing across St. Paul's Bay, on the northern tip of Melita, the island now known as Malta.

Julius, in order to save Paul, ordered the soldiers not to kill their prisoners, although it was their duty to do so to prevent escape. They all reached "safe to land." The inhabitants of Malta were non-Greeks of Phoenician origin; Luke calls them "barbarians," but they were kindly people, and they prepared a fire and food for the shipwrecked company. They regarded Paul as a criminal when a snake clung to him there, when he shook the snakes off, they thought he must be a god. Publius, the chief man of the island, gave Paul and the chief officers hospitality for three days, during which time Paul and Luke healed and tended many sick people, including the father of Publius.

AND SO TO ROME

It was now about February, A.D. 59, and although it was much before the safe sailing period began, Julius decided to take advantage of the presence of another ship from Alexandria which had wintered in the island. This was the "Twin Brothers," named after Castor and Pollux. These were the gods of sailors and a ship with their name would appeal to the superstitious; the Roman soldiers felt that such a good sign meant a safe voyage. They touched at Syracuse in Sicily, perhaps unloading grain or taking on extra cargo or more passengers; this made three days' delay. Then, on to Rhegium, along the "toe" of Italy; Vesuvius, belching smoke over the unsuspecting city of Pompeii at its foot, came into view as a favorable wind drove them along the west coast of Italy to Puteoli (Pozzuoli). This was a large trading port, 140 miles from Rome. The grain ship proudly entered with her topsails set— an honor to which she was entitled. There was a Christian community here, which is not surprising at such a trading center. Tradition says that Peter had already been in Rome and that he had founded a church at Puteoli. Paul and Luke stayed here with friends for seven days.

Forty miles from Rome, along the Appian Way, was Appii Forum (market of Appius). All roads led to Rome; and, like all of them, this one from Brindisi was measured from the Golden Milestone in the center of the Imperial City. It was but one of the many Paul had traversed. His Good News had passed along many of them and would go out northwest to Sicily and Italy. At *Myra*, they changed to a larger government ship making for *Puteol*. Here is a fine description of such a ship by Lucian, a Greek writer:

"What a big ship she is, a hundred and twenty cubits long the shipwright said, and more than a quarter of this in breadth; from deck to bottom there are nine and twenty cubits. And then how huge the mast is, and what a great yard, and what forestays! To see the stern curving up gently like a goose's neck, and the prow stretching out so far, with the image on both sides of Isis after whom the ship is named! Then the decorations, the paintings and the bright-colored topsail, the anchors and capstans and windlasses and the cabins aft—all this seemed to me completely wonderful. Why, you might compare the number aboard to an army, and enough corn was there, I am told, to feed the whole of Attica for a year."

Julius had the power to take command of the ship. There may have been the full 276 persons mentioned in the narrative, but some manuscripts omit the two and give the number as seventy-six. The winds drove the ship from *Cnidus* southward toward *Crete,* and for securer control it was steered around the northeast point and along the south of the island. This gave the ship the benefit of shelter in the lee of the mountain range that lay across the island edging the sea in great jagged cliffs. *Salmone* was a promontory jutting eastward into the sea. They arrived at *Fair Havens* (the present-day name of the harbor) halfway along the coast, and there decided to shelter. During the delay it is possible that Paul visited *Lasea* (27:7, 8).

A DANGEROUS VOYAGE

It was now realized that the rest of the journey would be extremely dangerous, since the ship would soon be at the mercy of the winds at a bad time of the year. The reference (27:9) to the Fast —the Day of Atonement (Part III)— which was held at the end of the Feast of Tabernacles, indicates that it was then early October. It was, therefore, now past the safety period, and Paul, at a meeting of the chief officers of the ship and soldiers, warned them of the possible hazards. He knew only too well of the perils of shipwreck (II Cor. 11:25). You may wonder why he, a prisoner, was present at such a meeting; perhaps it was because in his conversations with Julius and the ship's captain, Paul had spoken of his travels and knowledge of the sea. In any case, he was an unusual prisoner on his way to see Nero, the Emperor.

Julius wanted to get to Rome, and the ship's officers—probably a little jealous of Paul, and also anxious to be with their wives and families—supported the centurion in his decision to continue the journey. They planned to reach *Phenice* (Phoenix), forty miles farther on. Rounding the promontory in a favorable breeze, the ship now lost the shelter of the island and was exposed to the full fury of the storm. The powerful and stormy Euraquilo (Euroclydon) blew across Crete and down the frozen slopes of Mount Ida, and caught them unprepared. For twenty miles the ship sped helplessly before the wind until it gained the lee of a tiny island of *Clauda* (Cauda), where the crew hauled in the water-logged ship's long boat, which had been in tow during the calmer weather a few days before.

DESPERATE MEASURES

Passengers, crew and soldiers cleared the deck of gear and tackle. Then they undergirded the ship to ease the strain on the timbers.

There was a new danger to the south —the quicksands of Syrtis, off the North African coast. The ship, with a small storm sail, was allowed to drift. The

The last stages of Paul's journey to Rome.

uplifted and strengthened. In this great joy and greater relief he arrived at the gates of *Rome.*

ROME

It was A.D. 59. This was Rome, the Imperial City, "Mistress of the World," wicked, wealthy, godless. From the hilltop Paul could see the aqueduct of Claudia and the pyramid of Caius Cestius, the capitol, the palace and the senate house. There were triumphal arches commemorating past victories and campaigns. There were hundreds of shrines and temples to dozens of gods and goddesses—to Romulus, Vesta, Serapis, Isis, Mithras. Luke would note a temple to the god of medicine, Aesculapius. There lay the Forum and the huge Circus Maximus, where thousands of slaves and, later, Christians, were killed by wild animals. Some of Paul's companions would be sacrificed in that very arena to amuse the watching crowds. That was where the great fire was to begin in A.D. 64, of which Nero would make his excuse to persecute the Christians. The Colosseum, in which Ignatius of Antioch was to die was yet to be built—five years after Paul's own death—by twelve thousand Jews sent in chains to Rome after the sack of Jerusalem by Titus, son of the Emperor Vespasian, A.D. 70.

Paul had said he would see Rome; and now he was there. Julius handed him—

and along them to the whole world. Christians now came as far as this to greet Paul with a great welcome. They traveled another ten miles to *The Three Taverns,* where for years men had found a forge, a store, and refreshment. Here more Christians joined them.

Thus welcomed, Paul "took courage." The strain of the voyage had taken toll of his energy and spirit; the malarial effect of the Pontine Marshes made him weak and listless. But now he was with friends and in sight of his goal. He was

This is how Paul may have entered Rome, chained and a prisoner.

chained by his right hand to his Roman guard's left—to the officer in charge of the camp on the Coelian Hill just outside the city walls. This guard was part of the special corps of which Julius was centurion—the Imperial Couriers.

PAUL MEETS THE JEWS

For two years Paul was to live a shackled prisoner "on bail" in a house rented at his own expense. Three days after arriving, unable to attend the synagogue, he called a meeting of the elders of the Jewish synagogue. He gave them a brief summary of his experiences and why he had come to Rome. The Jews appeared to be somewhat unfriendly. To them, he was a strict Jew who had denied his upbringing to preach belief in a crucified Messiah. They had no knowledge of his appeal to Caesar, and their idea of Christianity was that it was not a very highly thought of religion but one which they had heard of as everywhere "spoken against." They accepted the fact that Paul was the leader of the new sect and asked to hear more about it. He promised to explain his Good News. They came again and he did so, but they were divided in their opinions. Paul remembered his scriptures. The quotation he made (28:26, 27) is from Isaiah 6:9, 10 —from the LXX. His decisive point was that "salvation of God is sent unto the Gentiles." The Jews of Rome could not accept this—"they agreed not among themselves"—and Paul knew that the old opposition of the Jews was once more against him. But he continued to preach to all who wanted to listen to him.

Luke's story ends here, and the rest of our information is obtained from Paul's epistles and traditional legends. There may have been a third book by Luke, but we have no trace of it. But this was not the end of Paul, nor was it the end of his work. The message of Christianity had at last reached the heart of the Empire from which it must spread throughout the whole world.

The Colosseum is now in ruins. Once it echoed to the screams of victims, the roars of lions, the shouts and cheers of onlookers.

375

14

"Throughout all the World"

During the two years that Paul was held, he preached freely. Philippians 1:12 and 4:22, indicate that much good work was done with his guards. This is not surprising, for to be chained to a man like Paul was indeed the first step to being converted to his faith.

PAUL'S LETTERS

Luke was still with him and, for a time, so was Timothy. There was John Mark, too, now forgiven by Paul, and a likely young preacher. While a prisoner, Paul wrote several letters to friends and churches. One of these, sent to a Christian friend in Colossae, is the only private letter of Paul's we have. It is about a slave. In many cities four out of every five people were slaves. Rome had twice as many slaves as free citizens. Life for a slave was short and held cheap; no one cared for him. But a runaway slave, Onesimus by name, comes to

Rome. He has probably robbed his master and seeks in Rome adventure and fortune. Probably having heard his master speak of Paul, Onesimus goes to him, and after a while admits what he has done. Paul has grown to love the lad but knows it is his duty to send him back to his master. As a slave, Onesimus could be brutally but lawfully beaten, even to death. Paul therefore writes to *Philemon,* telling him that Onesimus is to be "redeemed," that is, given his freedom, and is to be adopted as his "brother in Christ." Philemon owes this to Paul (verse 19. Cf. Col. 3:22,–4:1). Greatly trusting, Paul hands the letter to Onesimus to deliver by hand to his master. We can only guess at what happened, but, knowing Paul and remembering that the name of Onesimus means "worth," we may feel that the slave found in his master a Christian brother. There is a tradition that Onesimus became a bishop. It is worth noting that some scholars

In the huge arena chariots hurtled in furiously fought races to thrill the spectators packed on either side.

think Paul wrote this letter when imprisoned at Ephesus, not far from Colossae. If so, Onesimus sought adventure in Ephesus, not Rome.

THE "PLAN" OF PAUL'S LETTERS

Like most Eastern writers, Paul usually followed a set plan in his letters, which were written, of course, on papyrus (Part I). In the letter to Philemon it will be seen that verses 1–3 form the greeting; 4–7 contain thanksgiving and prayer; 8–22 are the main contents of the letter; 23–25 convey a greeting and benediction or blessing. This was the form or style of the time and is to be found in letters by writers other than Paul. The scribe often adds his own message, for example, Romans 16:22, and Paul occasionally "autographs" his letter —I Corinthians 16:21; Galatians 6:11; II Thessalonians 3:17. This signature was appreciated by those who received the letter, as it was a special mark of favor to write a letter in one's own hand.

Greek scholars tell us that Paul wrote in the same colloquial speech that he used in his preaching. This meant that, wherever they came from, people could understand his message. Translated into the beautiful Elizabethan English of the King James Version of our Bible, Paul's letters are often difficult to follow, not only because they often deal with problems of which we know nothing but also because not always the best and most exact words were used in this version. It is important to use a modern translation in studying Paul's letters, so that one can appreciate how straightforward and "modern" his letters really are. One thing is certain: Paul could never have dreamed that his letters would be read nineteen hundred years later by people all over the world in hundreds of languages.

TO THE COLOSSIANS AND EPHESIANS

Another visitor at this time was Epaphras, one of the chief members of the church at Colossae, a hundred miles east of Ephesus. His problem was that a new preacher was bringing strange ideas into the Christian Church. Although he had never been there, Paul was asked to help. He wrote a letter, and his friend Tychicus took it. Paul advised the Colossians on what the Christian faith really was and asked them to practice the Christian virtues, to be kind, forgiving and forbearing. Tychicus accompanied Onesimus on his way home to Philemon (Col. 4:7-9).

In this letter Paul refers to a similar one written to the church in Laodicea (Col. 4:16; cf. Rev. 1:11; 3:14). He tells them to exchange their letters. It seems that this particular one was more of a "circular" letter outlining Christian life and behavior. It is possible that this is the letter today called the Epistle to the *Ephesians,* because it is the only copy of the letter existing. It lacks the friendly touches one would expect from Paul to friends in the city (cf. Eph. 3:2) who had journeyed to Miletus to bid him a last farewell. Yet this letter has been regarded as among the finest of all Paul's epistles. It is inspired and noble. Paul says that even before the coming of Jesus, God's plan was to rid mankind of evil, and that Jesus was sent to do this and to bring all men everywhere back to God. This was to be done through the Church of Christ, His Kingdom on earth (Eph. 2:12-22; 3:11; 4:1-6, 17, 22-32; 5:1, 2, 8, 11, 21-25; 6:5, 6, 9). Therefore, says Paul, they should behave worthily of this great calling and form a united church.

With an eye on the burly Roman guard to whom he was chained, Paul wrote words that have become memorable to us all; you can read them in Ephesians 6:10-18.

EPISTLE TO THE PHILIPPIANS

On one occasion Paul was visited by Epaphroditus, who brought gifts from Philippi. Epaphroditus became ill and when he had recovered Paul decided to send by him a letter to his friends in the city—the jailer, Lydia, and others. It was a happy letter, full of joy, written in the desire to cheer the Christians who had been anxious about him and to urge fellowship and sharing (Phil. 4:1, 4, 10). In 4:8, we have some of the most beautiful words in the whole Bible. His many friends included the servants of Caesar's household, who sent their greetings.

Paul speaks of several imprisonments, but nothing is certain about the "captivity epistles," as they are called— *Ephesians, Colossians, Philemon,* and *Philippians.* They may have come from Caesarea, or Ephesus, but it is generally accepted that they were written from Rome.

ROMAN SUSPICION

Meanwhile, in Rome there was already unrest in the Emperor's Court. The emperors held highest place in the people's worship, for emperors had been accepted as gods since the days of Octavius. There were "mystery" religions with magical rites and strange forms that attracted the common people; there were religions based on philosophy that tried to "explain" life; there were different beliefs in gods from other lands—Cybele from Phrygia, Isis from Egypt, and Mithras from Persia. The worship of Mithras was the strongest of all, and for years, even in England, was a rival to Christianity. It offered belief in an after life and drew soldiers especially to its temples.

But Christianity offered all the good things that the other religions had—freedom, life hereafter, and a *real* God and Saviour.

378

Until now, the Christians had been regarded indifferently, so long as their beliefs did not challenge law and order or the power of Caesar. Now these Christians were now refusing to burn incense at the statue of Nero or to join in pagan festivals and processions. They held "secret meetings" and shared a secret meal. They were beginning to talk of their Messiah Christ as a great God and Saviour—words previously used by the Romans to describe their own emperors. Julius Caesar had been hailed as "God made manifest . . . the Saviour of human life." Augustus Caesar was called "God of God" . . . and "Son of God." He and Claudius were even called "God and Lord." Nero was now being called "Lord" (Acts 25:26) and "Emperor-God." The emperors' royal decrees were described as "Holy Scriptures."

It was natural that in their worship of the emperor-god the Romans should view with suspicion anyone who not only refused to acknowledge the emperor as God —which Christians could not do without denying the one and only God—but who also described their own God with the

On the base of an early Christian drinking-cup found in the Catacombs is this etching. Peter and Paul receive "crowns of righteousness" from their Master.

very words—Lord, Saviour, Divine God —used for the Roman Caesars.

Rome became antagonistic and resolved to take a firmer hold on these obstinate Christians. There is no doubt, of course, that, pagan as they were, the Romans did realize that the new way of life of these people offered rest and joy and a better life. But they deliberately rejected it and became not only suspicious but also hostile. It needed but one incident to begin open persecution, which,

One of the chief attractions in a gladiatorial show was the duel between man and beast. One or the other had to die before the crowd was satisfied.

once started in the capital city, would flare up through the whole Roman Empire in an effort to stamp out this Christian religion. It was becoming unsafe even then to admit publicly that one was a Christian.

The one incident came in A.D. 64—the great fire of Rome. Eager to find a scapegoat, Nero put the blame on the Christians, and so began the dreadful persecutions the awful stories of which have come down to us through history. Christians were tortured, crucified, sewn into the skins of animals and put before wild beasts in the arenas; some were even covered in tar and burnt alive as human torches to light up the emperor's gardens while he and his friends feasted and drank.

WHAT HAPPENED TO PAUL?

Where was Paul at this time? It is generally believed that at the end of two years he had been released by Nero, probably because of the favorable reports of Festus and Julius and possibly Agrippa. We are told that according to Roman law no prisoner could be kept beyond eighteen months if no charge was made against him. The Jews in Jerusalem seem not to have followed up their original charges and the Romans had none to make, so Paul was probably freed after the eighteen months, that is, "about" two years.

About A.D. 61, therefore, Paul was free to travel once again, preaching the "Lord Jesus Christ" and establishing more firmly the Christian faith. He may have visited Philemon in Colossae, as he had promised in his letter he would do. Tradition says he went as far as Spain. At the time of the persecutions he was far from Rome, somewhere in Asia Minor, and possibly at Ephesus. He would be watched, and any one of his enemies would betray him. In II Timothy 4:14, he refers to the accusations of "Alexander the coppersmith"; it may have been he

who gave away his whereabouts, somewhere near Troas, for at last Paul was arrested. Because of his right of appeal to Caesar he was brought back to Rome, his only companion the faithful Luke. Legend says that he was thrown into prison with Peter. He was closely guarded, no longer able to see his friends. Most of them had fled. "They have all turned away from me," he wrote.

THE "PASTORAL LETTERS"

It was while he was in prison at this time that Paul may have written his three letters to encourage Timothy and Titus. They are full of wise advice on Christian conduct and encouragement in their work as church leaders. A minister today is called a "pastor," hence these letters are called "pastoral letters." Scholars tell us that only fragments of the letters are really by Paul, but we can sense the words that only Paul could have written.

Titus had been put in charge of the church in Crete. Later, Paul visited him but not for a stay long enough to do all he wished. As Titus was very young, some of the older members did not want to obey him. Paul therefore wrote to instruct him in church matters and gave him advice similar to that he gave to Timothy.

Timothy was now Bishop of the Church at Ephesus; the word "bishop" really means "president" or even "overseer." Timothy was well qualified for this honor, for he was "well grounded in the scriptures" and had been trained by Paul himself. For his personal guidance see I Timothy 6:11–16. Throughout these letters Paul breathes his great love for his "beloved son in the faith," whom he warns to beware of false teachers and false doctrines. If the first letter was written when Paul was in Macedonia—as is sometimes believed—the second certainly was sent from prison in Rome. Paul is now an old man, doomed to die for his

In London is St. Paul's Cathedral, like St. Peter's in Rome, it is world famous, a reminder to us of the faith and work of the early followers of Christ.

faith and longing to see Timothy once more before the end (II Timothy 1:4; 4:9, 21). This letter, too, is full of wise counsel, just in case Timothy does not arrive in time. Paul asks him to bring his tough Cilician cloak to keep him warm in the cold cell—and the books, his scrolls, and parchments—"especially the parchments." In 4:6–8, are written Paul's unforgettable words of triumph and certainty in his faith in Jesus.

PAUL IS EXECUTED

Paul's trial, like that of any Christian of that time, was without hope. He was the chief of the Christians and must certainly die. Many of them had been massacred by fire, sword, torture, thrown to the lions, or crucified in the Circus. To the end, Paul found his Roman citizenship served him, for he was spared all these things. He was to die a Roman's death—by the sword. Tradition says that he and Peter went out to die together, Peter to the Circus, Paul to the Salvian Springs, a pine wood three miles outside the city. This spot was by the same Pyramid of Cestius that he had seen when he first arrived; it was near the long Roman road that ran to the harbor of Ostia. Perhaps Julius and some of Paul's personal Roman guards watched sadly as the old man, then nearly seventy, knelt for the last time—at the executioner's block. We do not know the exact date, but it was about A.D. 64.

CHRISTIANITY IS BROUGHT TO ENGLAND

All through the story of Paul England was being invaded and settled by Roman soldiers at this time. Roman armies had landed in the south and from London (Londinium) had moved across England westward, eastward, and to the north. Wherever they went they defeated the Britons and set up their own villages and towns—Verulamium, Caerleon, Camalodunum, Eboracum and dozens of others remembered in British history. The Roman soldiers who had worshiped Mithras brought with them their statues of him and set up their shrines. He was an ancient god even in the days of the Persians. Even today there are excavations at Erech in Mesopotamia (Gen. 10:8–10) revealing his temple dated 3,000 B.C. Mithras had been taken over by the Romans (Part II, p. 84) and was one of the few Roman gods that offered any kind of immortality and after life. But amongst these same soldiers were many who had heard of the new Christian faith and had been converted to it. Some of them remained faithful to Mithras but also worshiped Jesus. They knew of Paul and at some time may even have been his guards. They knew of the wonderful bravery of the Christians who had died for their faith in the belief that with Jesus they would "rise again." This certainly had made a deep impression on them and they felt that here was a religion they could accept. It was finer even than that of Mithras.

So it was that Romans and Britons alike grew in the Christian faith, so that when missionaries at last came to England to preach they found many Christians already serving Jesus as Paul had taught that they should.

Some lived their lives around the hill north of the marshy Thames. There they built a temple to Mithras. But they met, too, to worship the Lord of all, and years later, on that hill, was built the most famous cathedral in the land—the Cathedral of Saint Paul. The Mithras temple has been discovered and will be preserved as a relic of past centuries, its religion dead. St. Paul's stands today as a reminder of the great missionary Paul and his work in carrying to the "uttermost parts" of the world Christianity—the faith by which men live!

This Roman temple to Mithras—the soldiers' god—has been found in London. It dates from the second century A.D.